THE RENTAL OF HOUSES IN THE NEO-BABYLONIAN PERIOD

(VI-V CENTURIES BC)

STEFAN ZAWADZKI

THE RENTAL OF HOUSES IN THE NEO-BABYLONIAN PERIOD

(VI-V CENTURIES BC)

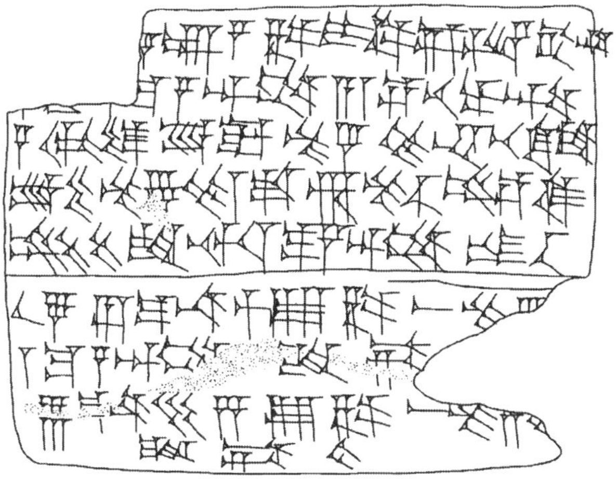

Wydawnictwo AGADE

WARSZAWA 2018

The study was made possible thanks to a grant from the National Science Centre (Narodowe Centrum Nauki) under the number UMO/2014/13/B/ HS3/04870.
On the cover: the BM 61244 by Stefan Zawadzki. Published with the kind permission of the Trustees of the British Museum.

Printed in Poland
ISBN 978-83-87111-75-5

www.ksiegarniaorientalna.pl

To Maria, my beloved, beautiful and brave wife.

Contents

Preface

The scope of the final version of the book differs substantially from my original intention. I thought at the outset that the book would be devoted exclusively to the lease of temple houses belonging to the Ebabbar temple in Sippar. Such was the plan when I started to work on the unpublished tablets in the British Museum. I found a fairly large number of administrative documents comprising the names of tenants of the houses of the Ebabbar and the amount of rent (*idi bīti*) paid by each person. While going through these documents I recognised that they present important data leading to revision of the idea of free housing allocation for personnel of the Ebabbar temple. The research perspective had to be further widened when I identified a contractual agreement between the Ebabbar temple and the temple rent collector (*ša muḫḫi idi bītāti*). No such document had been known before. Additionally, another document came to light containing an assessment of the amount of the income due from the contractor.

A further widening of the scope of the planned study followed when I identified a few texts from Sippar and Uruk, in which the temple (or its representative) rented houses to individuals who did not belong to the temple personnel. At that point it was necessary to compare these contracts with contracts in which both partners acted on their own behalf, all the more so that the structure of all those documents showed obvious similarities. I believed that the best way of making a comparison was to look more closely at the main elements of such contracts, especially since the last scholar to have undertaken such research was A. Leo Oppenheim in a book published 80 years ago (1936).[1] At that point it became quite evident that my research project could not be limited to the rental of temple houses (as originally planned), and the subject of the study had to be broadened, as clear in the title of this book.

As I am writing these words I am aware that two eminent scholars have announced forthcoming books on the subject of Neo-Babylonian houses. But it seems to me that the present study only incidentally, if at all, pertains to their research. The book by Cornelia Wunch is intended to study the houses of the Egibi family as part of their commercial activity and family relations. The

[1] See also Ries 1993, 174-178; Jursa 2005, 30-31.

book by Heather Baker, judging from her studies published so far, will focus on houses within the urban space, on topography and the structure of houses and their functions.

I need not say that I planned to study all the British Museum texts concerning the rental of houses available through the published catalogues and preliminary version of the catalogue of texts from Babylon prepared by Christopher Walker. Some texts were copied by Bertin and are accessible in the Arched Room of the British Museum Middle East Department. Sadly, life circumstances have forced me to revise my intentions and to cancel two intended visits to the British Museum. As a result, several dozen tablets have not been included in this study. This is unfortunate, although historians are only seldom able to use all texts relevant for a given subject. It is now difficult to say whether and to what extent the results presented here might require revision after the omitted tablets are interpreted.

This book could not have been written without the *Catalogue of the Babylonian Tablets in the British Museum vol. VI-VIII* prepared mostly by the late Professor E. Leichty with participation of A. K. Grayson, J. J. Finkelstein and C. B. F. Walker. I have received access to the unpublished catalogue prepared by C. B. F. Walker but the texts dealt with there are not included in this study owing to insufficient time to study them. For additional information I am indebted to John MacGinnis (BM 64481 and BM 64852), Małgorzata Sandowicz (BM 40044 and 67707), and Radosław Tarasewicz (BM 114446). A few texts from Borsippa I know from the dissertation of Joanna Wojciechowska (née Paszkowiak) on the Bēliyā'u family prepared under my supervision and supported by my personal grant. I have made extensive use of the catalogue of Borsippa tablets prepared by Ran Zadok, in which a majority of sources needed for my study are included. I wish to thank Christopher Walker for reading a part of the study and making important comments on the issue of intercalary dates. Małgorzata Sandowicz kindly discussed with me some detailed problems, read the manuscript and added valuable suggestions. Special thanks are addressed to Radosław Tarasewicz, who carefully read the translation of the texts, collated some texts (noted in the appropriate places), copied three tablets (BM 33980, BM 42393 and BM 114446) and helped me to prepare my copies for edition and to resolve some technical problems. I am thankful to Grant Frame for his collation of FLP 1421. Last but not least I wish to thank warmly Irving Finkel who read carefully the whole text, offered important suggestions and improved my English. I am deeply obliged for his generosity. Needless to say that any misreading and misinterpretation are own my responsibility.

My warm thanks go to Aleksandra and Zygmunt Podhorodecki, my London friends, for many months I have spent in their home in the friendly atmosphere.

Unpublished texts from the British Museum are published or quoted with the kind permission of the Trustees of the British Museum. I wish to thank the staff of the British Museum for their friendly assistance during my study in the Reading Room.

The study was made possible thanks to a grant from the National Science Centre (Narodowe Centrum Nauki) under the number UMO-2014/13/B/HS3/04870.

Abbreviations

A.	Siglum of the tablets housed in the Bodleian Library.
AHw	W. von Soden, *Akkadisches Handwörterbuch*, Wiesbaden 1959-1981.
ArOr	Archiv Orientální.
AMI	Archäologische Mitteilungen aus Iran.
AoF	Altorientalische Forschungen.
Bard	S. Graziani, *Testi editi ed inediti datati al regno di Bardiya (522 a.C.). Supplemento n. 67 agli ANNALI – vol. 51 (1991)*, fasc. 2, Napoli 1991.
Barton 1900	G. A. Barton, "Some Contracts of the Persian Period from the KH[2] Collection of the University of Pennsylvania," AJSL 16 (1900), 65-82.
BE	The Babylonian Expedition of the University of Pennsylvania, Series A: Cuneiform Texts.
BE 8/1	A. T. Clay, *Legal and Commercial Transactions, dated in the Assyrian, Neo-Babylonian and Persian Periods, chiefly from Nippur*, Philadelphia 1908.
BE 9	H. V. Hilprecht and A. T. Clay, *Business Documents of Murashû Sons of Nippur dated in the Reign of Artaxerxes I (464-424 B.C.)*, Philadelphia 1898.
BE 10	A. T. Clay, *Business Documents of Murashû Sons of Nippur dated in the Reign of Darius II (424-404 B.C.)*, Philadelphia 1904.
Bēliya'u	see Wojciechowska.
Bertin	unpublished copies of BM tablets by G. Bertin.
BIN 1	C. E. Keiser, *Letters and Contracts from Erech written in the Neo-Babylonian Period* (Babylonian Inscriptions in the Collection of James B. Nies, vol. 1), New Haven – London – Oxford 1918.
BM	British Museum, London.

BR 6	M. San Nicolò – H. Petschow, *Babylonische Rechtsurkunden aus dem 6. Jahrhundert v. Chr.*, München 1960.
BR 8/7	M. San Nicolò, *Babylonische Rechtsurkunden des ausgehenden 8. und 7. Jahrhundert v. Chr.*, München 1951.
BRM 1	A.T. Clay, *Babylonian Business Transactions of the First Millennium B.C. in the Library of J. Pierpont Morgan*, New York 1912.
BRM 2	A.T. Clay, *Legal Documents from Erech Dated in the Seleucid Era (312-65 B.C.)*, New York 1913.
BSA	Bulletin of Sumerian Agriculture.
CAD	The Assyrian Dictionary of the University of Chicago.
Cam	J. N. Strassmaier, *Inschriften von Cambyses, König von Babylon*, Leipzig 1890.
CDA	A Concise Dictionary of Akkadian, edited by J. Black, A. George, N. Postgate, 2nd (corrected) printing, Wiesbaden 2000.
CM	Cuneiform Monographs.
CT	Cuneiform Texts from Babylonian Tablets in the British Museum.
CT 51	C. B. Walker, *Cuneiform Texts from Babylonian Tablets in the British Museum. Miscellaneous Texts*, Part 51, London 1972.
CT 55	T. G. Pinches, *Cuneiform Texts from the Babylonian Tablet in the British Museum*, Part 55: *Neo-Babylonian and Achaemenid Economic Texts*, London 1982.
CT 56	T. G. Pinches, *Cuneiform Texts from the Babylonian Tablet in the British Museum*, Part 56: *Neo-Babylonian and Achaemenid Economic Texts*, London 1982.
CT 57	T. G. Pinches, *Cuneiform Texts from the Babylonian Tablet in the British Museum. Miscellaneous Texts*, Part 57: *Neo-Babylonian and Achaemenid Economic Texts*, London 1982.
CTMMA	Cuneiform Texts in the Metropolitan Museum of Art.
CTMMA 3	I. Spar – E. von Dassow, *Private Archive Tetxs from the First Millennium B.C.*, New York 2000.
CUSAS	Cornell University Studies in Assyriology.
CUSAS 28	L. E. Pierce – C. Wunsch, *Documents from Judean Exiles and West Semites in Babylonia in the Collection of David Sofer*, Bethesda 2014.
Cyr	J. N. Strassmaier, *Inschriften von Cyrus, König von Babylon*, Leipzig 1890.

Dar	J. N. Strassmaier, *Inschriften von Darius, König von Babylon*, Leipzig 1892-97.
GC 1	R. P. Dougherty, *Archives from Erech, Time of Nebuchadrezzar and Nabonidus*, New Haven 1923.
GC 2	R. P. Dougherty, *Archives from Erech, Neo-Babylonian and Persian Periods*, New Haven 1933.
GMTR	Guides to the Mesopotamian Textual Record.
JANEH	Journal of Ancient Near Eastern History.
JEOL	Jaarbericht Ex Oriente Lux.
JEOL 40	see MacGinnis 2007.
JCS	Journal of Cuneiform Studies.
KAR	E. Ebeling, *Keilschrifttexte aus Assur religiösen Inhalts*, Bd. I, Leipzig 1915-1919.
L.	Siglum of tablets housed in the Oriental Museum in Istanbul.
Liv.	J. N. Strassmaier, *Die babylonischen Inschriften im Museum zu Liverpool*, Leiden 1885.
MDOG	Mitteilungen der Deutschen Orient-Gesellschaft.
MR	See Waerzeggers 2014.
NABU	Nouvelles Assyriologiques Brèves et Utilitaires.
Mich	E. Moore, *Neo-Babylonian Documents in the University of Michigan Collection*, Ann Arbor 1939.
NAPR	Northern Akkad Project Reports.
NBC	Siglum of the tablets housed in the Nies Babylonian Collection in Yale.
Nbk	J. N. Strassmaier, *Inschriften von Nabuchodonosor, König von Babylon*, Leipzig 1889.
NBN	K. L. Tallqvist, *Neubabylonisches Namenbuch zu den Geschäftsurkunden aus der Zeit des Šamaššumukîn bis Xerxes*, Helsingfors 1905.
Nbn	J. N. Strassmaier, *Inschriften von Nabonidus, König von Babylon*, Leipzig 1889.
NISABA	Nisaba. Studi Assiriologici Messinesi.
NRV	M. San Nicolò – A. Ungnad, *Neubabylonische Rechts- und Verwaltungsurkunden*, Leipzig 1935.
OBO	Orbis Biblicus et Orientalis.
OIP	Oriental Institute Publications.

OIP 122	D. B. Weisberg, *Neo-Babylonian Texts in the Oriental Institute Collection*, Chicago 2003.
OLA	Orientalia Lovaniensia Analecta.
Peek	T. G. Pinches, *Inscribed Babylonian Tablets in the Possession of Sir Henry Peek, Bart.*, London 1888.
PIHANS	Publications de l'Institut historique-archéologique néerlandais de Stamboul.
PNAE	The Prosopography of the Neo-Assyrian Empire, Helsinki.
RA	Revue d'assyriologie et d'archéologie orientale.
RLA	Reallexicon der Assyriologie und Vorderasiatischen Archäologie.
RGTC	*Répertoire Géographique des Textes Cunéiformes.*
SANER	Studies in Ancient Near Eastern Records.
Str.	unpublished copies of BM tablets by J. N. Strassmaier.
TCL 13	G. Contenau, *Contracts néo-babyloniens II. Achéménide et Séleucide*, Paris 1929.
TuM 2-3	O. Krückmann, *Neubabylonische Rechts- und Verwaltungstexte*, Leipzig 1933.
WdO	Welt des Orients.
WZKM	Wiener Zeitschrift für die Kunde des Morgenlandes.
VS	Vorderasiatische Schriftdenkmäler der (Königlichen) Museen zu Berlin.
YOS	Yale Oriental Series.
YOS 3	A. T. Clay, *Neo-Babylonian Letters from Erech*, New Haven 1919.
YOS 6	R. P. Dougherty, *Records from Erech, Time of Nabonidus (555-538 B.C.)*, New Haven 1920.
YOS 7	A. Tremayne, *Records from Erech, Time of Cyrus and Cambyses (538-521 B.C.)*, New Haven 1925.
YOS 17	D. B. Weisberg, *Texts from the Time of Nebuchadnezzar*, New Haven – London 1980.
YOS 19	P.-A. Beaulieu, *Legal and Administrative Texts from the Reign of Nabonidus,* New Haven 2000.
YOS 21	E. Frahm – M. Jursa, *Neo-Babylonian Letters and Contracts from the Eanna Archive,* New Haven – London 2011.
ZA	Zeitschrift für Assyriologie und Vorderasiatische Archäologie.

ZA 3, no. 14 and no. 16, see Strassmaier 1888.

Abbreviations of dating of the texts

Kings

Ach.	Unidentified king from Achaemenid dynasty	
Kand	Kandalānu	648-627 BC
Sši	Sîn-šar-iškun	627-620 BC
Nbp	Nabopolassar	626-605 BC
Nbk	Nebuchadnezzar	605-562 BC
Am-M	Amēl-Marduk	562-560 BC
Nrg	Neriglissar	560-556 BC
Lb-M	Lābāši-Marduk	556 BC
Nbn	Nabonidus	556-539 BC
Cyr	Cyrus	539-530 BC
Camb	Cambyses	530-522 BC
Nbk IV	Nebuchadnezzar IV	522 BC
Dar	Darius I	522-486 BC
Xer	Xerxes	486-465 BC
Š-e	Šamaš-erība	484 BC
Art	Artaxerxes	

Months

I	iti.bár	Nisannu
II	iti.gu$_4$	Ayāru
III	iti.sig$_4$	Simānu
IV	iti.šu	Du'ūzu
V	iti.ab	Abu
VI	iti.kin	Ulūlu
VIa	iti.kin u$_4$.1.kam	month Ulūlu preceding intercalary Ulūlu
VII	iti.du$_6$	Tašrītu
VIII	iti.apin	Araḫsamna
IX	iti.gan	Kislīmu
X	iti.ab	Ṭebētu
XI	iti.zíz	Šabāṭu
XII	iti.še	Addaru
XIIb	iti.še.kin.kud	intercalary Addaru

Notes to the edited (or cited) texts

The edition of each text is preceded by a dating: day, month, name of the king and year. A dating in half brackets (...) means that the date is reconstructed on the basis of internal information, not on the basis of a dating formula.

⸢...⸣	sign(s) damaged
x	sign illegible or reading uncertain
[ ]	broken and restored sign(s)
[.]	dots following the restored sign(s) suggest that a sign or signs are expected
⸢ ⸣	partially preserved sign or signs
< >	sign or signs omitted by the scribe
{ }	redundant sign or signs written by the scribe
*	reading established as result of collation
!	suggested emendation followed by (T: x), where x denotes the sign actually written by the scribe
b.	brother
coll.	text collated
DN	divine name
[KN]	king's name
L.e.	lower edge
L.h.e.	left hand edge
Obv.	obverse
PN	personal name
Rev.	reverse
s.	son
U.e.	upper edge

Filiation

In the three-tier genealogy PN1/PN2//AN: / indicates "son" and // indicates "descendant of."

Additional remark

If number is repeated, e.g. JEOL 40, no. 1, no. 16, the latter indicates the edition in this volume. In translation the numbers of verses are given only in the tabulated texts and tablets of similar content.

1. Introduction

Houses in ancient Mesopotamia were, as in our times, the subject of various transactions as evidenced by a large number of documents applying to the sale and purchase of houses, antichretic contracts,[2] rental of houses, and receipts confirming payment of rent for the house and novation. Without doubt, just as today, one of the important sources of income was widespread rental of houses in the large cities,[3] which, except in periods of crisis, gave a fairly stable income. This observation is supported by the fact that in the extant documents no known example refers to a legal dispute about unpaid rent, although cases of novation are known.[4] Despite the importance of the rental of private houses the question has never been the subject of a comprehensive study. Only occasionally has it been discussed by editors of documents, in a synthesis,[5] or in a chapter (or part of it) on family archives.[6]

Even less interest has been shown by scholars to the issue of rental of temple houses. Rich temples, such as Esagila – that of Marduk in Babylon, Eanna – of Ištar of Uruk, Ezida – of Nabû in Borsippa, and Ebabbar – of Šamaš at Sippar, to mention only the most important, had many employees performing a variety of tasks in and outside the city. A majority of them who belonged to *širkus*, temple servants, "donated," or *nīšē bīti*, "domestic servants," received rations (*kurummatu*), including barley and dates, wool for the manufacture of clothes, sometimes oil, seldom meat, and some also beer.[7] The texts do not state that the temple provided free accommodation for these people, but it had seemed to be obvious. However, as we shall see below, this assumption is wrong. Important observations on the rental of houses owned by temples in the Neo-Babylonian

---

[2] For discussion of houses taken in an antichretic pledge, see Petschow 1956, 106-108. Such documents are not the subject of the present study.

[3] Renting of houses in the countryside was in Mesopotamia rare, because clay – main building material – was commonly available and building a small house was cheap and easy.

[4] I.e. CTMMA 3, 97.

[5] For general overview San Nicolò and Ungnad 1935, 49-52 and 154f.; Jursa 2005, 27-30.

[6] See Wunsch 1993, 58-61; Waerzeggers 2000-2001, 76-79 and the most comprehensive study by Baker 2004, 47-62. Many other aspects of urban space are discussed in a number of articles by Baker 2005, 2010a, 2014.

[7] The detailed study of remuneration in the first millennium BC, see Jursa 2008.

period has been made by A. C. V. M. Bongenaar. In his fundamental work devoted to the prosopography of Neo-Babylonian Sippar he pointed out the existence of a specific official charged with the collection of rental fees, the *ša muḫḫi bītāti*, which we might translate as "house rent collector".[8] In an article on the role of money in the temple economy, Bongenaar stressed that the income from the lease of the houses constituted an important position in the economy of the Ebabbar temple.[9] However, at the same time he emphasized that the rent was low and that some houses were in ruins.[10] One document (and now two further examples), the basis for Bongenaar's statement, is also relevant for the question of the sublease of houses.[11]

While a detailed study of all aspects of the building and trading of houses is still missing, the present study is limited mostly to the rental of houses, especially those owned by the Ebabbar temple at Sippar. The lack of a broader interest of researchers in the lease of temple houses is mainly due to the nature of the documents known up till now. Almost all data about the rental of the houses (*idi bīti*) come from administrative documents, which reveal how the money raised from the lease of the houses was used. The majority of texts only give the amount of silver used but without information on the tenant or tenants.[12]

My study is based on a fairly large number of texts discovered during my own research in the British Museum enlarged by several colleagues, as mentioned above. The basis for the study has been significantly enlarged not only because we have many new texts, but also because they relate to diverse aspects of the rental of temple houses. This gives better insight into the organisation of the rental system as well as the social and to some degree legal position of the holders of temple houses.

As indicated my initial intention was to study only the documents which threw light on rental of temple houses to individual persons, mostly its subjects. Although contracts between the temple and the members of the temple personnel are unknown, and it is doubtful if any such contracts had a written form, administrative documents of the Ebabbar temple do give us insight into the lease system of the temple houses and allow comparison with the leasing clause known from private contracts. This makes it possible to grasp all the

[8] For this title, see below p. 109.

[9] Bongenaar 1999, 164 and Jursa 2010, 170.

[10] Bongenaar 1999, 164f.

[11] Discussed below, p. 126-128.

[12] Two exceptions in this respect are Nbn 201, no. 29 and BM 75208, no. 28, the main basis of Bongenaar's observation. Both texts contain long lists of tenants and the amounts of rent paid by them. BM 75208 points out additionally the material condition of the houses. They are discussed in detail below, p. 122-123.

similarities and differences in the organisation of the collection of the rent due.

The first part of the study (Chapter 2) begins with the presentation of the structure of private house rental contracts and receipts. Several problems concerning such contracts are discussed in detail, especially where my observations differ from the opinions of other scholars. This part of my research does not pretend to be a comprehensive study of the lease of private houses.

Chapter 3 and 4 deal with the rental of temple houses. First, a typology of accessible texts is presented, and then the discussion is focused on the organisation of the collection of the fees, and on social positions of the tenants and the rent collectors.

The second part includes transliterations, translations of the documents and indices.

2. Rental of private houses

2.1 Contracts and receipts

Two types of documents concern the rental of private houses, i.e. contracts and receipts of house rent. The following main elements are present in such documents:

	Contracts	Receipts
1.	The object of the contract	The object of the receipt
2.	Location of the house	-
3.	The owner	The name of the owner or his agent receiving the rent
4.	The tenant	The name of the tenant paying the rent
5.	The rent fee and rental period	The rental period and (rarely) the rent fee
6.	Deadline for payment of the rent and means of payment	Means of payment
7.	Obligations of the tenant	Obligations of the tenant (rarely)[13]
8.	Beginning of the rental period	
9.	Witnesses	Witnesses
10.	Place and date	Place and date

As the structure of the second type of document is rather simple, this group is discussed first, but since contracts and receipts are closely related, attention will focus here on some general observations.

[13] I.e. the payment of the *nūptu/šugarrû* or *ūm Enlil* and *kīnajātu* by the tenant: VS 4, 146 = Baker 2004, no. 121; an oath sworn by the tenant that he will care for a house: VS 4, 129 = Baker 2004, no. 117; VS 4, 110 = Baker 2004, no. 119.

The receipts either indicate the whole period for which the rent was paid ("from month x to month y") or only the deadline ("till the month y"). The sum paid is sometimes quoted,[14] sometimes is omitted.[15]

Because the majority of contracts operated for several years with rent to be paid twice a year, the number of the preserved receipts should theoretically be much higher than the contracts, while in fact the number of known receipts is much smaller than the number of contracts. The small number of extant receipts might be explained on analogy with loan documents: after the debt has been paid the promissory note was destroyed. It is possible that in a case of rental of a house after the obligation of the tenant was fully settled, the receipt(s) might have been destroyed. The small number of receipts might also be explained by the fact that the first installment was sometimes paid on the day or before the day of writing the contract (see below, p. 62) and this fact was noted in this contract. Obviously, in such a case a separate receipt for the first installment was unnecessary. Only when the tenant paid the rent after the issue of contract was a receipt needed including the period for which the rent was paid. Such situation occured quite often as demonstrated by the receipts discussed in ensuing chapters:

2.1.1 *Praenumerando* and *postnumerando* rent payment

Receipts with payment of rent before the tenant moved into the rented house (i.e. *praenumerando*) are unknown, presumably because if such situation took place, the payment was noted in the contract. Extremely rare are receipts of rent for a whole year paid in advance a few days after the tenant moved into the house.[16]

[14] *Bēliya'u*, no. 276; BM 25690 (Zadok 2008, 76*); BM 31355 = Bertin 2775; BM 82620 (Baker 2010, 132f.); BM 109876 = no. 136; CTMMA 3, 37 and 58; Cyr 274; Cam 253; Dar 210; Mich 56; MR 138; VS 4, 99 = NRV 117; VS 4, 129 = Baker 2004, no. 117 (only one monthly installment is paid, for interpretation of the text, see below, p. 85); VS 4, 137 = NRV 125; VS 4, 138 = Baker 2004, no. 120; VS 4, 154 = NRV 134 and probably VS 4, 182 = Baker 2004, no. 123.

[15] Dar 482, no. 121; Dar 554, no. 124; L. 1636 (Joannès 1989, 238); MR 93; Nrg 52 (sum paid *postnumerando* is not mentioned, but sum paid *praenumerando* is given); VS 4, 106 = Baker 2004, no. 118; VS 4, 110 = Baker 2004, no. 119; VS 4, 129 = Baker 2004, no. 117; VS 4, 146 = Baker 2004, no. 121; VS 4, 151 = Baker 2004, no. 122.

[16] CUSAS 28, no. 98/99 written on 8 Abu (V), while the rent was paid for the period from Abu until next Abu (in fact to the end of Du'uzu (IV)), and CUSAS 28, no. 100, written on 9 Ulūlu (VI) while the rent was paid for the period from period Ulūlu until next Ulūlu (in fact to the end of Abu (V)). For payment in advance for the whole year, see Cyr 231 and MR 95. All these texts are discussed below, p. 69. Maybe here belongs also BM 31355 = Bertin 2775, to be published by M. Sandowicz. 10 shekels of silver, the house rent has been paid for the period from the month Ayaru (II) 33rd year to the end of the month Nisannu 34th year, however, as the date of writing the tablet is not preserved, it is difficult to say whether the rent was paid *praenumerando* or *postnumernado*.

Except for the above-mentioned cases (n. 16), all other receipts concern *postnumerando* payment:[17]

L. 1636 = Joannès 1989, 238, written on 15.IX.Nbk 41: the rent was paid to the end of month Kislīmu (IX), the same year. Comparison with other texts suggests that it was *postnumerando* payment in the last month or six moths rental period.

Nbn 224 written on 22.II.Nbn 6. In the signed agreement the tenant promises to regulate his debt of 15⅔ shekels of silver till the end of the month Ayaru (II) and to pay regularly 2 shekels of silver monthly from the month Simānu (III).

Nrg 52 written on 25.II.Nrg 3. The tenant has paid the outstanding rent for the period of one year beginning from 1.IV.Nrg 2 till 1.IV.Nrg 3 (in fact to the end of month III), i.e. he delayed about 10 months, and additionally paid 10⅗ shekels for the period beginning from 1.IV.Nrg 3. It seems that he regulated arrears and paid the first installment for next rental year (*ina rēš šattišu*) in advance fearing that otherwise the owner might remove him from the house. Both conditions were fulfilled and the contract was prolonged.

Cyr 274, written on 25.IX.Cyr 7. The tenant has paid 19½ shekels of silver "to the end of the year". Such a large sum suggests that it was rent for half a year, paid in the middle of the first or second instalment, i.e. the payment was delayed.

CTMMA 3, 37, written on 18.I.Camb 2.[18] The tenant has paid at least 3 shekels of silver for the period of half a year, from Ṭebētu (X) till the end of month Simānu (III), i.e. a month before the end of the first half of the rental year.

VS 4, 110 = Baker 2004, no. 119, written on 24.II.Dar 6[?] (or rather Dar 5). The payment concerns the period of one and half a years, from Nisannu (I), the fourth year till Ulūlu (VI) of the fifth year. If we accept the possibility that the text was written in Ayāru (II) of the sixth year,[19] this means that the tenant did not pay the rent for the following half a year.[20] This might explain the attitude of the owner, who forced the tenant to swear an oath that he will repair the cracks of the wall footing.[21] It means also that the tenant neglected his obligation to maintain the house in good condition, but despite this the contract was prolonged.

VS 4, 129 = Baker 2004, no. 117, a receipt written on 28.V.Dar 10. In this month the tenant has paid the rent for half a year lasting from Simānu (III)

---

[17] The texts are discussed in the chronological order.

[18] In CTMMA 3, no. 42 the situation is unclear as according to it the tenant has paid the rent for one year, but because of damage of the tablet it is impossible to recognise if it was delayed payment or also the payment for a few months in advance.

[19] See the comments to l. 18 by Baker 2004, 194.

[20] See, however, below.

[21] Ll. 10-11 *ki-i a-di/[bat]-qa šá a-sur-ru-ú a-ṣa-ba-ta*, "I will repair (the cracks) of the footing."

until the end in Araḫsamna (VIII), i.e. with a delay of about three months, and additionally 1½ shekels of silver, i.e. a rent for one month in advance (for such interpretation, see below, p. 85). The oath sworn by the tenant suggests that the owner was dissatisfied not only because of a delay in payment of the rent but also that – like the tenant in VS 4, 110 – he neglected his obligation to repair damages to the house.[22] Despite this trouble, the owner did not decide to terminate the contract.

VS 4, 138 = Baker 2004, no. 120 (30.[x].Dar 13+[x]): the tenant paid house rent amounting to 29¾ shekels of silver, but the period is not mentioned. We may assume that by this receipt the obligations of both parties were definitely settled, i.e. the rent was paid *postnumerando.*

MR 93, written on 6.II.Dar 15: the tenant paid the rent for the period beginning from the 1st Nisannu (I) till the end of Ulūlu (VI), i.e. with a delay of about 35 days.

VS 4, 146 = Baker 2004, no. 121, a receipt written on 6.XII.Dar 17: the tenant paid rent till the end of Abu (V), the 18th year, i.e. for a half a year, from the very beginning of the month Addaru. It means that the receipt concerns house rent for the first half of the rental year, but the installment was paid and the receipt written shortly after the contract was signed.[23]

BM 109876, no. 136, written on 15.XII.Dar 18. The tenant paid the outstanding rent for the last three months from Ṭebētu (X) to Addaru (XII). The sum paid is omitted; however, it is stressed that the payment does not apply to 'the previous debt.'

Dar 482, written on <x>.II.Dar 19. As the tenant paid the rent till the end of Nisannu, the same year, it is clear that the rent was paid *postnumerando.*

VS 4, 154 = NRV 134 (2.XI.Dar 20). The tenant paid 7½ shekels of silver for the half a year (VI-XI), again in the last month of the period, i.e. *postnumerando.*

BM 82620 (quoted partly and discussed by Baker 2010, 132f.), a receipt for house rent written on 25.VI.Dar 22. The payment concerns the period from Abu (V) 21st year to the end of Du'uzu (IV) 22nd year of Darius. It means that the tenant paid the outstanding rent for the past rental year, but not for the next rental year which began in the month Abu (V) Dar 22.

Dar 554, no. 124, a receipt for house rent for the period from Ulūlu (V) 22nd year to the end of Ṭebētu (X) of 26th year. The sum is not given, but the document clearly states that the problem is definitely settled (arrears paid) and the house will return to the owner in the very beginning of the month

22 Ll. 18-19: *ki-i a-di-i bat-qa šá é/a-ṣab-ba-ta*, "I shall care for repairs to the house."

23 An additional note stating that the owner has received (*maḫir*) the *šugarrû ina mišil šatti* makes certain that the expression *ina mišil šatti* applies to the first half of the rental year, i.e. the proper translation is "half a year", not "Mitte des Jahres" (San Nicolò), or "middle of the year" (Baker).

Šabāṭu. There is, however, a serious problem with the interpretation of this text because according to the copies of both Strassmaier and Bertin, it was written on the 14th day of month Ṭebētu (X), but the year is missing in both copies. Since there are no differences between the copies of the two scholars, it is certain that the year was omitted by the ancient scribe.[24] If we accept the possibility that the text was drafted in the 22nd year (as suggested by Strassmaier in the heading of his copy) it would be *praenumerando* payment for over four years, a highly unusual case. It is more than improbable that the tenant paid the rent five months after he moved into the house but for four years in advance. More probable is that the text was written in the 26th year and that the tenant settled the unpaid rent for the whole four years and five months in Ṭebētu (X), i.e. in the month mentioned at the beginning of the text as the final date of the period. This is supported by the note that the house will return to the owner from the month Šabāṭu (XI), i.e. after the month the debt was paid.

MR 138 written on [x x].Dar 28. The tenant paid 1 mina and [18 shekels], a debt for rental of a store (*kuruppu*) for three years and three months (from VIII.Dar 25 till X.Dar 28) and promised that when the house owner gave him back a tablet (presumably the promissory note) he will pay 2 shekels of white silver for each month of his use of the house over three years and three months.[25]

Bēliya'u, no. 276[26] written on 12.XI.Dar [x]. Šaddinnu paid the rent of 6 shekels of silver, but another debt was still on him. The lack of mention of the period for which the rent was paid suggests that it was last installment so that with this payment the relation between them were settled.

VS 4, 191 = NRV 138, written on 3.III.Xer 1. The tenant paid the rent for the past period till the end of the month Ayāru (II) Xer 1, i.e. presumably for the past half a year.[27]

The situation in a few other receipts seems more complicated:

CTMMA 3, 58 (Moldenke I, 28), a receipt written on 14.I.Nbn 14. Itti-Marduk-balāṭu//Egibi paid 9 shekels of silver to three co-owners of a house, presumably a debt due from his deceased father, Nabû-aḫḫē-iddin.[28] This

---

[24] This is now supported by collation made on my request by Radosław Tarasewicz.

[25] My translation of ll. 11-14 differs from Waerzeggers' translation: "When Marduk-rēmanni will bring the tablet, Bēl-zēri will pay to Marduk-rēmanni 2 shekels of white silver for (each) month which passed beyond three years and three month."

[26] BM 29231.

[27] A similar situation might well be observed in VS 4, 106 = Baker 2004, no. 118, but this is uncertain as the term until which the rent is paid (*adi* iti.[x]) is not preserved.

[28] Nabû-aḫḫē-iddin, the father of Itti-Marduk-balāṭu died in the 13th year of Nabonidus, see Wunsch 2000, 16.

is suggested by a note revealing that the partners differed in their estimation of works made by Nabû-aḫḫē-iddin "in bricks, reeds, and beams" because it is stressed that the accounts concerning those works have not been settled. Eventually they agreed as Itti-Marduk-balāṭu dwelled this house later (Nbn 845). One may assume that Itti-Marduk-balāṭu paid off the debt because he wanted to stay in the rented house.

Cam 253, written on 7.VIII.Camb 4. It is said there that 8 shekels is the house rent *ša rēš šatti*, i.e. according to our interpretations for the first half of the (rental) year, but the tenant is owed also 4 shekels. As the silver is described later as *rīḫit idi bītišu* (l. 10) it is uncertain what is meant: only 8 shekels, total 12 shekels, or only 4 shekels.

VS 4, 137 = NRV 125 written on 12.X.Dar 13. According to this the owner Šaddinnu/Balāssu//Bēliya'u received 9 shekels of silver as house rent as well as *nūptu* and *kīnajātu* for the 13th year of Darius from the tenant Balāssu/Šulā// Ea-ibni. Because according to the contract VS 5, 67, no. 119 Balāssu/Šulā// Ea-ibni rented this house already in the 5th year of Darius, it was probably in his possession during all the years until the 13th year. However, as the rent paid for the 13th year is lower (only 9 shekels instead of 13 shekels paid earlier) it is difficult to say whether the rent was lowered or was payment for the part of the year.

VS 4, 99 = NRV 117 (15.I.Dar 14) is a highly interesting receipt explaining the relation between the house owner and the tenant. It follows from it that the tenant could not pay the rent on time and issued the promissory note. Now he has paid the rent and interest for the past period and for one month in advance. It means that the contract was still valid and the tenant occupied the house.

A few general observations result from the above documents:

- When a tenant paid the outstanding house rent but owed another debt, to avoid ambiguity the receipt precisely explained the title of payment and stressed that another debt still existed. The aim of such receipt was to secure another creditor's claim.
- When the receipt omitted the sum paid we may assume that all obligations for the given period are settled and the mention of sum paid was unnecessary. However, when the sum paid is given, it is unclear whether it is full installment or only the unpaid part of the installment.
- Payment of the outstanding rent in the last month of the half-year period (or sometimes a shorter time), as happened quite often, suggests that the tenant feared that the owner will remove him from the house, while he wished to continue dwelling in it.
- Delayed payment of rent is relatively frequent and occurs in the north as

well as south of the country. A drastic case is known from Uruk (AnOr 8, 70)[29]. While the value of two houses rented out for commercial activities was estimated in the seventh year of Nabonidus at 11 minas 6 shekels, i.e. 5 minas for a house located in the district of the Meslamtaea Gate and 6 minas 6 shekels for a house in the Egahalanki district, their value had decreased after 22 years respectively to 2 minas, i.e. 40% of the previous value and to 4½ minas, i.e. ca. 70% of previous value; moreover, the temple had not made any profit. Eventually, the descendants of the tenants were obliged to pay the difference in the value of the houses, but the situation shows that the owner's supervision was in fact ineffective and the temple suffered serious loss.

- A common feature of the discussed receipts is tenants' trouble paying rent on time. Almost complete absence of other receipts suggests that when the rent was paid so that the mutual obligations of the owners and tenants were settled, the receipts were destroyed.

2.2 Contracts

Ten main elements of rent house contracts can be recognised (see above, p. 25), but their order within a document does not follow a strict pattern.

2.2.1 The object of the contract

The document usually begins with the word é = *bītu*, "house". If it is followed by the particle *ša*, it is almost certain that the object of the contract is a residential house. If, however, é = *bītu* is followed by another word (usually in status constructus) it almost certainly deals with a non-residential object, an annex or the like, destined for some economic activity. A rare exception from this rule concerns the naming of parts of the house by location:[30] *bīt iltāni*, "the north (facing) wing,"[31] *bīt sūti*, "the south (facing) wing,"[32] *bīt šadî'* "the east (facing) wing,"[33] *bīt amurri*, "west (facing) wing."[34]

[29] For edition, see Janković 2013, 387f.

[30] See Oppenheim 1936, 61.

[31] For examples, see CAD I/J 270. For the suggestion that "north wing" meant in fact "north-facing wing," i.e. "south wing," etc., see Baker 2008, 27.

[32] GC 1, 35:1 (BR 6, 29).

[33] For examples, see CAD Š I 61 and GC 1, 35: 2 (BR 6, 29).

[34] *Bēliya'u*, no. 168a (BM 25653).

The following examples of structures or buildings can be identified:[35]

bīt asuppu	"outbuilding, annexe" (TuM 2-3, 30)[36]
bīt babtu	"penthouse" (BM 21999)[37]
bīt kāri	"storehouse (in the harbour district?)"[38]
bīt kuruppu	"reed building," (MR 99: 1), "the store" (MR 138: 8); "shop" (Baker 2010a)
bīt qāti	"*handhouse*" (Nrg 29: 3; TuM 2-3, 30)[39]
bīt pāni	"front house" (Nrg 29: 3; Nbn 48, no. 1)
bīt tenû	"annex"(?)[40] (BIN 1, 118: 1 = BR 6, 33)
bīt ṭīpi	"building addition, annex" (MR 109: 1)
taṣlīlu	"attic or porch" (TuM 2-3, 26: 4-5; 27: 5-6)[41]

The object of the lease might also be a fenced yard: ***tarbaṣu***, "enclosure, courtyard," (Nbn 48, no. 1, TuM 2-3, 27) adjacent to the house. A number of texts concern the rental of reed huts (***bīt ḫuṣṣu***),[42] however, it is not certain if they were rented as storehouses, workshops, or as dwellings, or a combination.

2.2.2 Location of the houses

The location of houses was described in different ways:

a. by indicating the street where the house is located:[43]

bītu ša mālaku ša bābi sāmu, "the house (situated) by the passage to the Red Gate" (BRM 1, 85: 1)

bītu ša ina mālaki ša Mār-bīti, "the house, which is in the passage to the temple of Mār-bīti" (Dar 378: 1; Dar 428: 2)

35 Only examples are given here, see also Oppenheim 1936, 59; cf. Baker 2004, 57-59.

36 For discussion of the meaning of the term and other structures built upon or next to *asuppu*, see Oppenheim 1936, 60-61. Note that é im.ḫi.a (in é im.ḫi.a *i-šak-kan*) in Nbn 845: 7 and similar in TuM 2-3, 26: 6; 27: 7, for which Oppenheim suggested an Akkadian reading *bīt šâri* and transalted "Haus der Wind(richtungen)" (Oppenheim 1936, 61) applies to covering of a house with clay , i.e. é im.ḫi.a. means there *bīt ṭīdu* (see CAD Ṭ 106).

37 Zadok 2009, 94, no. 104.

38 Dar 60, no. 118: 1; Nbn 499, no. 111: 1, 19.

39 Cf. Oppenheim 1936, 63; CAD Q 198-200.

40 CAD T 345.

41 BE 8/1, 112: 1 concerns é *ta-bi*, but it cannot be excluded that the rental of the whole house (*bīt gab'-bi)* is meant there.

42 For the detailed discussion of the meaning of the term, see Joannès 2016.

43 Only single examples are cited here.

mūtaq ili u šarri, "passage of the god and the king,"[44] or
mūtaq Nabû u Nanāya lā aṣû, "one-way passage of Nabû and Nanāya" (VS 5, 131 = Baker 2004, no. 104)
sūqu rapšu mūtaq Nabû u Nanāya, "broad street, the passage of Nabû and Nanāya" (VS 5, 82 = Baker 2004, no. 102)
sūqu rapšu mūtaq Nergal, "broad street, the passage of Nergal" (UET 4, 38)
sūqu lā aṣû mūtaq Nabû u Nanāya, "one-way street, the passage of Nabû and Nanāya" (VS 5, 64 = Baker 2004, no. 99)
sūqu qatnu, "narrow street," (BM 30782: 2)[45]
sūqu qatnu aṣû, "narrow through-street," (VS 5, 38 = Baker 2004, no. 79)
sūqu qatnu lā aṣû, "narrow one-way street" (BM 77513 = Baker 2004, no. 80, purchase of house)
pānāt bābi adi mūṣî, "in front of the gate as far as the exit" (Nbn 845: 6)

b. by indicating the near-by gate or the temple:

abulli ša bīt Šarrat Sippar, "near the great gate of the temple of Šarrat Sippar," (Nbn 48, no. 1: 1-2)
abul Zababa, "the gate of Zababa" (BM 92796 = Baker 2004, no. 92, purchase of house)
[***ina***] ***abulli Enlil***, "in the gate of Enlil" (*Bēliya'u*, no. 12: 1[46])
ṭāḫ bīt Mār-bīti, "adjacent to the temple of Mār-bīti" (Cyr 231: 1, Cam 147: 1)

c. by indicating the institutional owner:

bītu makkūr Šamaš, "house, property of Šamaš" (Nbn 48, no. 1: 1)
makkūr Eanna, "property of the Eanna temple" (AnOr 8, 70: 3)

d. by indicating the adjacent house or houses and its/their owner(s), the most commonly:

bītu ša* PN1**, ***itâ (***da***) ***bīt ša* PN2**, "the house of PN1, adjacent to the house of PN2." Sometimes the location of the house is described in general terms only: usually only one neighbour,[47] or two neighbours are mentioned by name.[48]

---

44 See CAD M I 207.

45 Bertin 2709.

46 BM 28995.

47 Baker 2004, no. 84; VS 5, 61 = Baker 2004, no. 85; VS 5, 81 = Baker 2004, no. 86, where it is stated that the leased house (the same in all these texts) located in Babylon is adjacent to the house of Ṭāb-ṣilli-Marduk, son of Balāṭu, descendant of Rab-banê.

48 See for example CTMMA 3, 97, a house located in Babylon adjacent to the house of Nabû-ittannu, son of Marduk-zēr-ibni, descendant of Esagilaya and to the house of Nanāya-iddin (without filiation).

e. other locating:

bītu ša muhhi arammu ša Bēl, "the house near the causeway of Bēl" (TuM 2-3, 29)

bītu ina qaqqad gišri, "the house at the head of the bridge" (Nbn 500, no. 112: 1; cf. Dar 64: 1, Dar 379: 12)

bītu ša muḫḫi nāri, "the house by the river" (BM 26689, quoted by Baker 2010, 140)

ina erṣēti kaṣīri ša qēreb Bābili, "in the Kaṣīr district in Babylon" (Dar 275)[49]

***bītu ša ina eqli kīri ḫallat* Bēl**, "the house in the field, the *ḫallatu*-garden of Bēl" (BM 31781: 1;[50] BM 36432: 1).[51]

The location of one house was sometimes described in different ways. Such is the case of a group of texts from Babylon, where the same house is located adjacent to "a one-way street, the thoroughfare of Nabû and Nanāya" (***mūtaq Nabû u Nanāya lā aṣû***),[52] while in VS 5, 82 = Baker 2004, no. 102 it is adjacent to "a broad street, the thoroughfare of Nabû and Nanāya" (***sūqu rapšu mūtaq Nabû u Nanāya***).

It is worth noting a sharp contrast in the description of house location in purchase contracts and in lease contracts. When a house was purchased the measure of each side and the names of all neighbours were precisely given. In case of lease of a house there are contracts in which only one neighbour is indicated (i.e. Dar 60, no. 118 in this book, VS 5, 61 and 81= Baker 2004, no. 85 and 86), or street (i.e. VS 5, 64 and 78 = Baker 2004, no. 99 and no. 101), bridge (i.e. Nbn 500 = no. 112 in this book), etc.; two neighbours (i.e. CTMMA 3, 97) or street and one neighbour (i.e. VS 5, 67, no. 119). However, it happens that the location of a house is omitted (i.e. Nbn 499, no. 111 in this book, VS 5, 23, no. 109 in this book, VS 5, 59 and 68 = Baker 2004, no. 115 and 116). Such location elements as street, bridge, etc. make it possible to say that the reference points are not the co-tenants of the house but the adjacent houses or other external factors like streets, etc. A more accurate description was recognised as unnecessary as there was no danger that the tenant might try to appropriate the house. In general all houses located near the main

[49] For a possibility that TE-E, the district of Babylon, might be read Kaṣīri, see George 1992, 377, where the relevant texts are quoted. Add also BM 30782: 1 = Bertin 2709 (4.I.Dar 32), BM 66159: 1 (frg., time of Nbk).

[50] Wunsch 1993, no. 311.

[51] Wunsch 1993, no. 326.

[52] VS 5, 64 = Baker 2004, no. 99; VS 5, 84+151 = Baker 2004, no. 103; VS 5, 131 = Baker 2004, no. 104 and VS 6, 201 = Baker 2004, no. 100 (the leased house is adjacent to the one-way street, the thoroughfare of Nabû and Nanāya).

streets of the city, the place for great religious festivals with the participation of gods and kings' belonged to the most prestigious quarter of the city. It is not surprising that houses located there were in the hands of the wealthy, belonging to the élite of the city, sometimes related to the state or royal circles or the temple administration.

It should be stressed that the size of the leased houses is never given in contracts.[53] The only information which is sometimes found concerns part of the house (e.g. northern, southern, etc. wing) which was let.[54] However, it is not only the outside dimensions, but also the number of rooms in a rented house is not given. It can be assumed that a higher rent indicates a larger area in a rented house, but other factors might also have affected the amount of the rent, for example location in a district more prestigious, closer to the center ("the city"), or close to a prestigious street, etc.[55]

2.2.3 The owner and tenant

The owner of a rented house and tenant is sometimes identified by short filiation: PN1, son of PN2, but more often by full filiation: PN1, son of PN2, descendant of family x" (derived from the name of person or profession).

The material or social status of owners of rented houses and tenants is an interesting issue. We will look at it briefly using the data from three centres with a relative abundance of records, i.e. Babylon, Borsippa and Sippar.[56]

---

[53] An estimation of the house size is possible on the basis of sale and exchange contracts or contracts for division of houses between relatives, where appropriate data are given (Baker 2004, 478, 57-61), or on the basis of archaeological evidence (Baker 2004, 61-62, with previous literature). See also Baker 2005, 16-29 and Baker 2014.

[54] See above, p. 31.

[55] Undoubtedly, the owner's authority increased if he had a house in the street through which religious processions passed with the participation of gods (in their statues) and the king, described as *mūtaq ili u šarri*, "passage of the god and the king," or *mūtaq Nabû u Nanāya*, "passage of Nabû and Nanāya" (see above, p. 33), or when a house was located close to the residential part of the city with the royal palace(s) and temples and where senior officials of the temple or state administration lived.

[56] The findings are based on the study of the archives of the following families conducted thus far: Nappāḫu from Babylon (Baker 2004), Šaddinnu of the Bēliya'u family from Borsippa (Wojciechowska 2005), Ea-ilūta-bāni from Borsippa (Joannès 1989), Ṣāḫit-ginê from Sippar (Waerzeggers 2014). C. Wunsch (as mentioned) announces a book about the houses of the Egibis in Babylon. My intention is not to replace those detailed studies but to make a more general interpretation of the data on rental of houses.

2.2.3.1 Families of owners of rented houses in Babylon

Family / Owner	Texts
1. Balāṭu:	
^{f}Inṣabtu/Nabû-šum-līšir	Dar 554, no. 124 (Dar <26>)
2. Bēl-ēṭir:	
Iqīša-Marduk/Aplā	CTMMA 3, 39 ([x.x].Camb 7); CTMMA 3, 42 (16.VII.Dar [x])
3. Dābibī:	
Bēl-erība/Marduk-zēr-ibni	BM 31355 = Bertin 2775 ([Dar 34])
4. Dannêa:	
Nabû-zēr-līšir/Bēl-aḫḫē-erība	CTMMA 3, 37 (18.I.Camb 2)
5. (Ea)-Eppēš-ilī:	
Marduk-šum-ibni/Šulā	BM 77625+, no. 120 (10+[x].XII.Dar 12)
6. Ea-ilūta-bāni:	
Nabû-šum-iškun/Paḫḫuru	YOS 17, 5 (17.V.Nbk 13); TuM 2-3, 25 (13.I.Nbk 22)
7. Egibi:	
Nabû-aḫḫē-iddin/Šulā	Nbn 224 (22.II.Nbn 6)
Itti-Marduk-balāṭu/ /Nabû-aḫḫē-iddin	Nbn 299 (14.V.Nbn 8);[57] Nbn 500, no. 112 (2.II.Nbn 11); Cyr 228 (9.VI.Cyr 6); Peek 16 (5.IX Cyr 6); Cyr 274 (25.9.Cyr 7); Cam 97 (7.[x] Camb 1); Cam 117 (16.V.Camb 2); Cam 184 (4.VII.Camb 3); Cam 187 (15.VII.Camb 3); TEBR 85 (Camb [x]);[58] Dar 275 (18.VI.Dar 1)[59]
Marduk-nāṣir-apli (or Širku)/ /Itti-Marduk-balāṭu (or Idinna)	Dar 60, no. 118 (9.I.Dar 3); Dar 256 (26. VI. Dar 9)[60]; BRM 1, 74 (13.XII.Dar 9); Dar 330 (6.VI.Dar 12);[61] Dar 378 (22.V.Dar 14); Dar 499 (2.III.Dar 20); BM 30782[62] (4. I.Dar 32)
Nidinti-Bēl/Marduk-nāṣir-apli (or Širku)	BM 42393, no. 128 (15.IV.Dar 36); BM 33966, no. 129 (5.V.Dar 36);[63] CT 51, 54, no. 130

[57] His slave acted instead of the owner.

[58] The name of the father of Itti-Marduk-balāṭu is written Šar-aḫḫēšu. According to Joannès, TEBR 320, n. 1 this is the diminutive from Nabû-šar-aḫḫēšu. However, in all other texts the name of Itti-Marduk-balāṭu's father is Nabû-aḫḫē-iddin, in TEBR 85 it is presumably a scribal mistake.

[59] His slave acted instead of the owner.

[60] Together with his brothers.

[61] Together with his brothers.

[62] Bertin 2709.

[63] Nidinti-Bēl, the husband of Šušannu, the daughter of Rēmūt-Bēl, acted in her name.

	(7.V.Dar 36); BM 31363[64] (Dar [x]); BM 33980, no. 133 (13.IV.Xer 1); BM 33979, no. 134 (21.IV.Xer 2*); ZA 3, no. 16, no. 135 (22.VII.Š-e. 0)
8. Ēṭiru:	
Bēl-nādin-apli/Bēl-ikṣur	cf. Wunsch 2005, 371 (active Camb 7 – Xer 1)
Ea-aḫḫē-uṣur/Ea-aḫḫē-iddin	cf. Wunsch 2005, 370 (active Ner – Nbn)
9. Gaḫal:	
[x]ea/Kalbā	BM 31824, no. 126 (26.[III].Dar 35)
10. Nappāhu:	
Iddin-Nabû/Nabû-zēr-ibni	VS 5, 61 (15.VII.Dar 2); CTMMA 3, 97 (28.II.Dar 8); VS 5, 64 (21?.IV.Dar 4); VS 4, 106 ([x].VIII.Dar 5); VS 5, 68 (9.[VIII].Dar 5); VS 4, 110 (24.II.Dar 6?); VS 4, 129 (28.V.Dar 10); VS 5, 131 (3.[x].Dar 10+[x?]; VS 6, 201 ([x.x].Dar 11); VS 5, 82 (13.III.Dar 16); VS 4, 146 (6.XII.Dar 17); VS 5, 84+151 ([x].V.Dar 18)
Šellibi/Iddin-Nabû	VS 4, 151 (29.VIII.Dar 19)
11. Nûr-Sîn:	
Iddin-Marduk/Iqīšā	Cyr 231 ([x].VI.Cyr 6);[65] Cam 147 (5.[V].Camb 2)[66]
12. Pappaya:	
Nabû-ēṭir/Bēl-iddin	CTMMA 3, 120 (24.X.Dar 25)[67]
13. Rab-banê:	
Bēl-iddin/Nabû-ēṭir	BM 31781 (13.VII.Cyr [x]);[68] BM 36432 (16.VI.Camb 2)[69]
Erība-Marduk/Nabû-aplu-iddin	VS 5, 99 (27.X.Dar 1)[70]
14. Saggilaya:	
Marduk-šāpik-zēri/	Dar 482 (<x>.II.Dar 19)[71]

[64] Bertin 2772.

[65] Wunsch 1993, no. 303. Cf. Jursa 1995/96, 261.

[66] Wunsch 1993, no. 330. Cf. Jursa 1995/96, 261.

[67] On relation between the lessor and tenant, see commentary to the edition of the text. It would by the only case of rental of a house by lessor to his brother.

[68] Wunsch 1993, no. 311.

[69] Wunsch 1993, no. 326.

[70] Baker 2004, no. 112.

[71] The house was located in Bīt-Ḫaḫḫuru, near Babylon.

/Mušēzib-Marduk	
Marduk-šum-iddin/Šāpik-zēri	Nbn 261 (13.VII.Nbn 7)
Idinnya/Itti-Marduk-balāṭu[72]	Dar 485, no. 123 ([22].VIa.Dar 19)
Iddinaya/Mušēzib-Marduk	JCS 28, no. 46 (22.VIa.Dar 19)
15. Sîn-ili:	
Marduk-šum-ibni/Ṭābiya	VS 5, 32 (13.VI.Nbn 13)
16. Ṣāḫit-ginê:	
Bēl-uballiṭ/Iqīša	Nbn 996 (7.IX.Nbn 16)[73]
Nabû-ēreš/Bēl-ilē'i	
and fBānītu-ēṭirtu and fAmat-Nanāya, the daughters of Marduk-šum-uṣur	Nbn 597 (22.II.Nbn 12); CTMMA 3, 58 (14.I.Nbn 14) Nbn 845 (25.II.Nbn 15)
17. Šangû-Ninurta:	
Presumably Nabû-ēṭir/Iqīšā[74]	
18. Šumu-libši:	
Arad-Bēl/Kalbā	BM 30594 (22.X.Dar [x])[75]

2.2.3.2 The families of tenants of houses in Babylon

1. Atkuppu:	
Bēl-uballiṭ/Nabû-ēṭir-napšāti	Dar 60, no. 118 (9.I.Dar 3)
2. Andaḫar:	
Nabû-uṣuršu/Nabû-kēšir	VS 4, 146 (6.XII. Dar 17)[76]
3. Arad-Marduk:	
Ina-ṣilli-Bēl/Bēlšunu	Dar 330 (6.VI.Dar 12)
4. Ašgandu:	
Gūzānu/Mušallim-Marduk	Cyr 274 (25.IX.Cyr 7)
5. Bā'iru:	
Gimillu/Šāpik-zēri	Cam 117 (16.V.Camb 2)
6. Ea-pattanu:	
Ubār/Bēl-iddin	Dar 554, no. 124 (Dar <26>)

[72] See the comments, p. 51, n. 160.

[73] MR 5.

[74] The involvement of the family in renting of houses is suggested by the preliminary Babylonian catalogue prepared by C. Walker. Comparison of dated documents, BM 44002 (Nbk 34), BM 45448 (Nbk 42), and BM 46694 (AmM) shows that in these documents Nabû-ēṭir/Iqīšā was active in the period Nbk 33 – Nbn 13, cf. Wunsch 2005, 370; Jursa 2005, 71.

[75] Bertin 2798.

[76] Baker 2004, no. 121.

7. Egibi:	
Iddin-Nabû/Bēl-kēšir	BM 120099, no. 132 (10.[IV].Xer 1);
Nabû-aḫḫē-iddin/Šulā	Nbn 597 (22.II.Nbn 12)
Itti-Marduk-balāṭu (Iddinaya)/ /Nabû-aḫḫē-iddin	CTMMA 3, 58 (14.I.Nbn 14);[77] Nbn 845 (25.II.Nbn 15);[78]
Marduk-nāṣir-apli (or Širku) //Itti-Marduk-balāṭu (Iddinaya)	JCS 28, no. 46 (22.VI.Dar 19); Dar 485, no. 123 (22].VIa.Dar 19) BM 31273 (28.X.Dar 33+[x])[79] and, probably BM 30594 (22.X.Dar [x])[80]
Nidinti-Bēl/Marduk-nāṣir-apli (or Širku)	BM 31355 = Bertin 2775 ([Dar 34]); BM 31824, no. 126 (26.[III].Dar 35)
8. Eppēš-ilī:	
Arad-Marduk/Marduk-šum-ibni	BM 77421, no. 125 (4.VII.Dar 2⌜9⌝)
Itti-Šamaš-balāṭu/Šadûnu	BM 42393, no. 128 (15.IV.Dar 36); CT 51, 54, no. 130 (7.V.Dar 36)
Silim-Bēl/Iddina (or Šumā)	TuM 2-3, no 25 (13.II.Nbk 22)
9. Esagilaya:	
Lābāši/Balāṭu	CTMMA 3, 39 ([x.x] Camb 7); CTMMA 3, 42 (16.VII.Dar [x])
10. Ina-ṣilli-[x]:	
[PN]/Sîn-ili	BM 77625+, no. 120 (10+[x].VIII.Dar 12)
11. Ir'anni:	
Nabû-mukīn-apli/Ibnāya)	Cyr 228 (9.VI.Cyr 3)
Nabû-nāṣir-apli/ /Ina-Esagila-zēr-ibni	Cam 97 (7.[x].Camb 1)
Murašû/Aplā	Cam 187 (15.VII.Camb 3)
Bēl-uballiṭ/Aplā	Cam 184 (4.VII.Camb 3)
12. Miṣiraya:	
Erība/Balāssu	Dar 256 (26.VI.Dar 19)
Nabû-mušētiq-uddê/Šāpik-zēri	CTMMA 3, 97 (28.II.Dar 8); VS 4, 129 (28.V.Dar 10)[81]
13. Murašû:	
Enlil-šum-iddin	TuM 2-3, no. 29 (4.I.Dar I, 4)

[77] The same house was rented in Nbn 597 and Nbn 845; cf. Waerzeggers 2014, 32, n. 21 and the commentary to CTMMA 3, 58.

[78] Rented by the slave of Itti-Marduk-balāṭu.

[79] Bertin 2749.

[80] Bertin 2798.

[81] Baker 2004, no. 117.

14 Nabû-iddin:	
Bēl-aplu-iddin	VS 5, 119 (Art. I, 7)
15. Naggāru:	
Bēl-iddin/Mār-bīti-ikṣur	Dar 378 (22.V.Dar 14)
16. Nannûtu:	
Iddin-Nabû/Pir'u	VS 4, 106 ([x].VIII.Dar 5)[82]
17. Nazua:	
Iddin-Bēl/Šamaš-šum-līšir	BE 8/1, 112 (12.VIII.Dar 16)
18. Nūr-Sîn:	
Nrgal-ruṣûa, slave of Iddin-Marduk	BM 31781 (2.II.Dar 9)[83]
19. Paḫāru:	
Ḫaddaya/Nabû-mušēṭiq-uddê (or: Niqūdu)	Cyr 231 ([x].VI.Cyr 6)[84]; Cam 147 (5.[V].Camb 2)[85]
20. Pappaya:	
Ubār/Bēl-iddin	CTMMA 3, 120 (24.X.Dar 25)
21. Rab-banê:	
Marduk-šum-uṣur/Nabû-zēr-uṣur /Nabû-zēr-uṣur	Nbn 996 (7.IX.Nbn 16)[86]
22. Rē'û:	
Nergal-bān-aḫi/Bēl ušallim	VS 5, 32 (13.VI.Nbn 13)
Nabû-ēreš/Ana-Bēl-upāqu	ZA 3, no. 16, no. 135 (22.VII.Š-e 0)[87]
23. Suhaya:	
Nabû-aḫḫê-iddin/ /Nabû-aplu-iddin	Peek 16 (5.IX.Cyr 6)
24. Šamaš-abāri:	
Šamaš-ina-tēši-ēṭir/Šamaš-iddin	Dar 482 (<x>.II.Dar 19)[88] JCS 28, no. 46 and Dar 485, no. 123[89]

[82] Baker 2004, no. 118.

[83] Wunsch 1993, no. 311.

[84] Wunsch 1993, no. 303.

[85] Wunsch 1993, no. 330.

[86] MR 5.

[87] Maybe the member of the same family occurs as house tenant in VS 5, 32: 7 = NRV 114 (Nergal-bān-aḫi/Bēl-ušallim), but the family name is badly preserved.

[88] The house was located in Bīt-Ḫaḫḫuru, near Babylon.

[89] The last two were written presumably on the same day of 22.VIa.Dar 19. For discussion, see below, p. 51.

25. Šangû-Gula:
Dīna/Ilu-danānu-Gula Nbn 500, no. 112 (2.II.Nbn 11)
26. Šangû-parakki:
Bēl-supê-muḫur/Bēl-ibni VS 5, 68 (9.[VIII].Dar 5)[90]
27. Šumu-libši:
Marduk-ēṭir/Nabû-šum-iškun Dar 499 (2.III.Dar 20)
28. Ṭābiḫ-kāri:
Nabû-ēṭir-napšāti/Bēl-aḫ-iddin VS 4, 110 (24.II.Dar 6?)[91]

2.2.3.3 Families of owners of rented houses in Borsippa

1. Aqar-Nabû:
fIsḫunnu/Bāniya BM 82668 (10.V.[Ach x])[92]
2. Arad-Ea:
fṬabluṭu/Nabû-ušallim BM 21999 (5.XII.Dar 22)[93]
3. Bēliya'u:
Nabû-mukīn-apli/Balāssu VS 5, 23, no. 109 (9.II.Nbn 4)
Šaddinnu/Balāssu VS 5, 67, no. 119 (7.X.Dar 5); *Bēliya'u*, no. 103 (29.II.Dar 11);[94] VS 4, 137 (13.X. Dar 13); *Bēliya'u*, no. 136 (15.[x].Dar 14);[95] *Bēliya'u*, no. 187 (11.II.Dar 20);[96] BM 29433 (20.IX.Dar 24);[97] *Bēliya'u*, no. 242 (3.3.Dar 26[+x?]);[98] *Bēliya'u*, no. 279 (24.VI.Dar [x]);[99] VS 5, 117 (12.VIII.Xer 0)
4. (Ea)-ilūta-bani:
Bēl-iddin/Rēmūt VS 4, 99 (15.I.Dar 4)[100]
fLurindu/Mušēzib-Bēl L. 1652 (29.XII.Dar 30)

90 Baker 2004, no. 116.

91 Baker 2004, no. 119.

92 Zadok 2009, 250, no. 14.

93 Zadok 2009, 94, no. 84.

94 BM 96323.

95 BM 29053.

96 BM 96243.

97 Zadok 2009, 220, no. 66.

98 BM 29036. The reading of year is uncertain: 25 (Still 2016, 167); 26 [+] (*Bēliya'u*, no. 242) and 26[+3?] (Zadok 2009, 192, no. 212).

99 BM 96137.

100 Baker 2004, no. 112.

Mūšēzib-Bēl/Zēr-Bābili	NBC 8345 (28.IV.Nbn 11);[101] A 105[102] (6.XII.Nbn 11)[103]
Nabû-aplu-iddin	TuM 2-3, 24 (21.XII.Nbk 4)
Nādin/Lūṣi-ana-nūri	BRM 1, 58 (6.3.Nbn 5)
Širiktu/Lūṣi-ana-nūri-Marduk	BRM 1 68 (29.VII.Camb 2); TuM 2-3, 30 (16.[x.KN] 3)
Zēr-Bābili/Nabû-šum-ukīn	NBC 8378 (1.VII.Nrg 2)[104]
Zēr-Bābili/Šumā	HSM 1899.2.141 (16.VII.Nbn 1)[105]
5. Ēda-ēṭir (or: Aššur):	
Nabû-ušabši/Nabû-ēṭir-napšāti	BM 28689 (20.VI.Nbk IV 1)[106]
6. Egibi:	
Marduk-nāṣir-apli/ /Itti-Marduk-balāṭu:	Dar 64 (9.II.Dar 3); Dar 210 (3.IX.Dar 6); Dar 259 (7.VIII.Dar 9); Dar 428 (28.VI. Dar 16)
7. Ibnāya:	
Nādin/Šūzubu	BM 29748 (9.12?Nbk 41)[107]
8. Ilīya:	
Marduk-šum-ibni/Šulā	BM 82744, no. 116 (15.X.Cyr 7); BM 25832 (4.[x].Camb 0);[108] BM 26757 (1.IX. Camb 2);[109]
9. Ir'anni:	
Bulluṭu/Iddin-Nabû	BM 46955 (12.I.Dar 25)[110]
10. Kidin-Nanāya:	
Kunā/Šum-iddin	BM 29523 (4.VIII.Dar 4)[111]
11. Kidin-Sîn:	
Marduk-šum-ibni/Rēmūt	*Bēliya'u*, no. 12 (26.XII.Camb 1)[112]

101 Joannès 1989, 341 (H = YOS 13,10).

102 Joannès 1989, 273-274.

103 Joannès 1989, 273-274.

104 Joannès 1989, 349 and 93.

105 Zadok 2008, 88*-89*. Presumably Zēr-Bābili/Nabû-šum-ukīn and Zēr-Bābili/Šumā is the same person, as Šumā is probably a hypocoristicon of Nabû-šum-ukīn.

106 Zadok 2009, 155, no. 507.

107 Zadok 2009, 233, no. 134. According to Baker 2010, 138, the reading of the month is certain.

108 Zadok 2009, 117, no. 886.

109 A house is located in Tīl-burri near Borsippa.

110 Zadok 2009, 238, no. 421.

111 Zadok 2009, 228, no. 156.

112 BM 28995.

12. Ilūta-bāni:	
^{f}Lurindu/Mušēzib-Bēl	L. 1652 (29.XII. Dar 30)[113]
13. Rab-asû:	
^{f}Amti-Sutīti/Iddinaya	BRM 1, 43 (11.VI.Nbk IV, 1); L. 1667 (19. VI.Nbk IV, 1)[114]
14. Sikkûa:	
Nabû-rē'ûšunu/Šamaš-iddin and his mother ^{f}Karibtu	VS 5, 50 (20.III.Camb 4)
15. Šangû-Ninurta:	
Nabû-šum-uṣur/ /Nabû-mukīn-apli	BM 109876, no. 136 (15.XII.Dar 18)
^{f}Dirutu/Nidintu	BRM 1, 85 (6.IV.Xer 2)
16. Šēpē-iliya:	
Nabû-uṣuršu/Nabû-aḫḫē-iddin	BM 26653 (18.3.Xer 0)[115]
17. Šigûa:	
Bēl-ēṭir/Gūzānu	BM 26566 (20.IX.Dar [x]+3)[116]
18. Šumu-libši:	
Nabû-aplu-iddin/Arad-Nabû	BM 85611 (2.V.Cyr 6)[117]

2.2.3.4 The family of tenants of houses in Borsippa

1. Amēl-Ea:	
Bēlšunu/Bulṭaya together with Sîn-šadûnu family	VS 5, 23, no. 109 (9.II.Nbn 4)
2. Arkāt-ilī-damqā:	
Mūrānu/Mukkea	BM 25628 (10.XI.Dar 35)[118]
3. Bēliya'u:	
Šaddinnu/Balāssu	*Beliya'u*, no. 276 (12.XI.Dar [x]);[119] BM 82668 (10.V.[Ach x])[120]
4. Bēl-usātu:	
Iddinaya/Šulā	*Bēliya'u*, no. 136 (15.[x].Dar 14)[121]

[113] Joannès 1968, 246.

[114] Joannès 1968, 252f.

[115] Zadok 2009, 150f., no. 471.

[116] Zadok 2009, 141, no. 384.

[117] Zadok 2009, 273, no. 418.

[118] Zadok 2009, 105, no. 682.

[119] BM 29231.

[120] Zadok 2009, 250, no. 14.

[121] BM 29053. Note that Zadok 2009, 193, no. 229 reads Ardiya instead of Iddinaya.

5. Ea-ibni:
Balāssu/Šulā — VS 5, 67, no. 119 (7.X.Dar 5); VS 4, 137 (12.XI.Dar 13)

6. Eppēš-ilī:
Nāṣir/Bunanu — Dar 64 (9.II.Dar 3)

7. Gallabu:
Nabû-zēr-ukīn/Nabû-šum-ukīn — BM 85611 (2.V.Cyr 6)[122]

8. Giššapakam:
Iddin-Nabû/Nabû-šum-ukīn — Dar 428 (28.VI.Dar 16)

9. Ibnāya:
Nabû-šum-ukīn/Nādin — BM 29523 (4.VIII.Dar 4)[123]

10. Iddin-Papsukkal:
Nabû-mušētiq-uddê/ /Nabû-aḫ-ušabši — VS 5, 50 (20.III.Camb 4)

11. Ilūšu-abušu:
Basia/Nabû-itannu — L. 1652 (29.XII.Dar 30)[124]

12. Itinnu[!]:
Nabû-uṣuršu/Rēmūt — BM 25690 (21.VI.Dar 21)[125]

13. Mubannû:
Aplā/Šamaš-iddin — Dar 259 (7.VIII.Dar 9)

14. Naggāru:
Bēl-iddin/Šumā — BM 109877 (10.IV.Dar 21)
Nabû-aḫḫē-ušallim/Ardiya — BRM 1, 85 (6.IV.Xer 2)

15. Nergal-ušallim:
Iddin-Nabû/Ubār — *Bēliya'u*, no. 187 (11.II.Dar 20)[126]

16. Ninurta-ušallim:
Hašdaya/Iddin-Nabû — BM 26566 (20.IX.Dar [x]+3)[127]

17. Rēšaya:
Ṣillaya/Mušēzib-Marduk — NBC 8378 (1.VII.Nrg 2)[128]

---

[122] Zadok 2009, 273, no. 418.

[123] Zadok 2009, 228, no. 156.

[124] Joannès 1989, 246.

[125] Zadok 2008, 76*. The reading of the name Itinnu (šitim[!]) instead of LAH_4, was suggested by Zadok, 76*, n. 3. Nabû-uṣuršu rented the house together with Bēl-ēṭir/Gūzānu of Šigûa family. For different interpretation of the text, see Still 2016, 166.

[126] BM 96243.

[127] Zadok 2009, 141, no. 384.

[128] Joannès 1989, 349. and 93.

Hadaqu/Ardi-Gula	BM 26653 (18.III.Xer 2)[129]
18. Ṣuḫurtu:	
Ilu-iddin/Nabû-aplu-iddin	BM 26689 (20.VI.Nbk IV, 1)[130]
19. Ṣillaya:	
Bēl-aḫḫē-iddin/Tabnēa	VS 5, 77 (12.XI.Dar 13)
20. Sîn-šadûnu:	
Rēmūt/Etellu, together with Amēl-Ea family	VS 5, 23, no. 109 (9.II.Nbn 4)
21. Šigûa:	
Bēl-ēṭir/Gūzānu	BM 25690 (2.VI.Dar 21);[131] *Bēliya'u*, no. 242 (3.III.Dar 26+x?)[132]

2.2.3.5 The family of the tenants of the houses in Sippar

1. Itinnu:	
Bēl-zēri/Šaddinnu	MR 99 (22.V.Dar 17)
2. Rē'i-sīsê:	
Bēl-ušallim/Šamaš-udammiq	Nbn 48, no. 1 (21.XI.Nbn 1)
3. Ṣāḫit-ginê:	
Bēl-bullissu/Maduk-rēmanni	MR 167 (2.III.Dar 35)
Bēl-nāṣir-apli/Bēl-uballiṭ	MR 176 (23.X.Xer 1)
Tabnēa/[x]	BM 99091, no. 4 ([Nbn])
4. Šangû-Agade:	
Isḫaya/Ša-pī-Bēl	Barton 1900, no.24 (21.IX.Dar 34)

While data referring to the renting of houses come both from several main cites and certain small towns: Babylon, Borsippa, Sippar, Nippur,[133] Uruk,[134] Ur,[135] Našar,[136] Jaḫūdu,[137] only those from the first two are sufficiently numerous to allow analysis in greater detail.

[129] Zadok 2009, 150f., no. 471.

[130] Zadok 2009, 155, no. 507f.

[131] Zadok 2008, 76*.

[132] BM 29036.

[133] Only four texts are known to me (TuM 2-3, 26-28, 31).

[134] Ten texts are known to me (AnOr 8, 57 and 58; BIN 1, 118; BM 114472; BRM 2, 1; GC 1, 35; YOS 7, 2 and 45; YOS 6, 85; W. 20010, 8 = Ph 84379).

[135] Five texts: UET 4, 36-40.

[136] CUSAS 28, no. 98 (and duplicate no. 99), no. 100.

[137] CUSAS 28, no. 46.

In Babylon at least 18 identified families were owners of rental houses.[138] Only five of these families belonged to the priestly families,[139] i.e. only 27.7% of all known house lessors. Additionally, we can only be certain with three of those families (Nappāḫu, Saggilaya and Ṣāḫit-ginê) that house rental was an important branch of their economic activities. While this finding is based on incomplete data and may be subject to revision, it is worth noting that only seven priestly and non-priestly families (Egibi, Ea-ilūta-bāni, Ēṭiru, Saggilaya, Sîn-ili, Ṣāḫit-ginê and Šangû-Ninurta) leased houses in the pre-Persian period. For two only we know of this activity from the reign of Nebuchadnezzar (Ea-ilūta-bāni, and presumably Šangû-Ninurta), but only Ea-ilūta-bāni continued this business in Persian rule. Three other families, Egibi, Ēṭiru and Saggilaya, began to lease houses (according to the currently available data) only at the time of Nabonidus and also continued into Persian times. For the majority of lessor families, making a profit from leasing houses is evidenced by the activity of just one individual (1-6, 9, 11-12, 15, 18) and it is impossible to determine in a given case whether or not the renting of the house was incidental or how long the house had been owned by the family. Only in the case of Iddin-Nabû, son of Nabû-zēr-ibni, descendant of Nappāḫu does it seem certain that he had been purchasing houses to secure for himself a stable source of income from rent.[140] Unfortunately, the fairly extensive set of records concerning the activity of Iddin-Nabû's sons, especially Šellibi, contains only one document referring to the lease of houses.[141] Thus, we do not know whether or not this aspect of business activity was continued.

Although 13 non-priestly families who lived in Babylon rented their houses (72% of all), only in the Egibi case is there strong argument that such business was a significant part of economic activity. At least three successive generations of the family leased their houses. The number of houses leased by Itti-Marduk-balāṭu (551-522 BC) cannot be established because the contemporary texts omit the exact location of the houses. This situation changes when Marduk-nāṣir-apli takes over management of the business (521-487 BC), although, in document Dar 60, no. 118 of the third year of Darius I's reign, the location of the leased house is still missing. From the ninth year on location is specified in the contracts. This allows us to determine that

[138] I know of over 80 contracts or receipts from Babylon. Note that documents in which a house is taken as pledge are excluded because the aim of such contracts was to prevent an increase of debt, not obtain a real income. In at least 18 cases the family name is omitted, and in few damaged.

[139] Ea-epeš-ili, Ea-iluta-bani, Nappaḫḫu, Saggilaya and Ṣāḫit-ginê.

[140] Baker 2004, chap. 5. As Baker says (see 55-56) Iddin-Nabû leased at least four houses. Assuming the yearly income from four houses to have been no less than 1 mina of silver (it was probably higher) this was a substantial source of income.

[141] VS 4, 151 = Baker 2004, no. 122.

in each of four successive contracts a different house is leased. In Dar 256 (26.VI.Dar 9) the rented house is common property of Marduk-nāṣir-apli and his brothers and it adjoins the house owned exclusively by Marduk-nāṣir-apli and a broad street (*sūqu rapšu*). Contract BRM 1, 74 is dated at the end of the same ninth year of Darius. Here the house leased is undoubtedly Marduk-nāṣir-apli's property, adjacent to a house owned by Bēl-uballiṭ and another jointly owned by Marduk-nāṣir-apli and his brothers. A further contract, Dar 330 (6.VI.Dar 12), refers to a house of Marduk-nāṣir-apli and his brothers that adjoins a house owned by Marduk-zēr-iddin son of Nabû-šum-uṣur, descendant of Damqā and by Marduk-nāṣir-apli. This is certainly not the house leased in Dar 256, because the rent is twice as big (15 shekels annually in Dar 256 versus 30 shekels in Dar 330). According to the last Dar 378: 1 (22.V.Dar 14), a house located "on the passage to Mār-bīti" was purchased earlier from Nabû-nāṣir. Although the document was written in Babylon, it refers to a house located in Borsippa, as is clearly demonstrated in Dar 379: 9-10, written on 24.XI.Dar 14.[142] It is evident from the latter document that this house had been received by Marduk-nāṣir-apli on division of inheritance from his father Itti-Marduk-balāṭu. Since Dar 378, half a year earlier, does not refer to the house as joint property of the brothers, we may assume that the real division of the inheritance had been made several months earlier. This means that in two cases Marduk-nāṣir-apli leased houses co-owned with his brothers, but that at that time already he also personally owned houses not part of the inheritance estate. We can assume that he leased all or most of the houses inherited by him in Babylon and Borsippa and earned substantial revenue from these transactions.

Marduk-nāṣir-apli's heir was his only son Nidinti-Bēl (490-482 BC), who continued this way of earning revenue. Incidentally, most documents known from this period refer, with one probable exception, to lease of the same house.[143]

What concerns house tenants in Babylon, if the collected material is representative, suggests that the majority of them (just like majority of the lessors) made only one contract. Out of 28 families of house tenants in Babylon only four are recognized as priestly (Eppēš-ili, Esaggilaya, Atkuppu and Šamaš-(a)bāri).[144] Among the tenants are immigrants from other cities or territories (like Suḫaya or Murašû from Nippur), descendants of deportees

[142] é *šá ina bár-sipa*^{ki}/*šá ina ma-la-ka šá* é ^{d}dumu-é *šá ina qa-at* ^{md}*ag-na-ṣir* dumu-*šú šá* ^{m}ki-^{d}en-*lum-mur* {*ina*} *ma*-[*ḫir*].

[143] About this, see below.

[144] Atkuppu and Šamaš-abāri families are recognized as priestly because they had prebends (Jursa 2005, 80 and 109, respectively). The names of some families suggest that they might belonged to the priesthood for example (Bā'iru, Šangû-Gula, Šangû-parakki), but this cannot be proved at present.

(Miṣirāya), or people of practical professions (Naggāru, Rē'û), which perfectly expresses the imperial character of the capital city. The texts, unfortunately, do not allow us to determine the circumstances that made these individuals rent a house. Perhaps running one's own business was one of the reasons. Surprisingly, only five out of 28 tenants in Babylon identified by family names rented houses in the pre-Persian period.[145] We may conjecture that for the period before Nabonidus' reign this might result from the small number of private archives texts. But house lease contracts from the reign of Nabonidus are just as few, notwithstanding the abundance of documents from private archives at that time; an overwhelming majority of contracts are dated to Persian rule or later.

A few texts suggest that tenants sometimes wished to rent a house for a longer time. This can be observed in the case of the Egibi family, as Itti-Marduk-balāṭu, after the death of his father Nabû-aḫḫē-iddin/Šulā, took over the obligations regarding the house leased by the deceased (Nbn 597 and CTMMA 3, 58; see the comments to the edition of the latter text), and lived in it later because an additional contract with the same members of the Ṣāḫit-ginê family had been signed by a slave of Itti-Marduk-balāṭu (Nbn 845).

Nabû-mušētiq-uddê of the Miṣiraya family signed the first contract for lease of a house from the Nappāḫu family for a period of two years beginning from 1st Simānu of the eighth year, i.e. his obligations ended at the end of Ayāru of the tenth year (CTMMA 3, 97). VS 4, 129 = Baker 2004, no. 117 is a receipt for the rental of a house paid by Nabû-mušētiq-uddê to the same owner for half a year beginning 1st Simānu tenth year, i.e. the previous contract was prolonged for some period.[146] However, in light of a clause in CTMMA 3, 97: 27-29 it is clear that before this contract another contract had been signed some time earlier and renegotiated.

The house rental texts suggest a close relation between Ir'anni (tenants) and Egibi (lessors) families. In the period between Cyr 3 and Camb 3 (536-527 BC) four members of the Ir'anni family, i.e. two sons of Ina-Esagila-zēr-ibni, a.k.a.Ibnāya (Nabû-mukīn-apli and Nabû-nāṣir-apli), and two sons of Aplā (Murašû and Bēl-uballiṭ) rented houses from Itti-Marduk-balāṭu (a.k.a. Iddinaya), son of Nabû-aḫḫē-iddin of Egibi family. This might suggest that the families were bound by special relations. Although a comprehensive study of the Ir'anni family is awaited, some texts support the idea. Relations between the families began – according to existing data – in the time of Nabonidus. In the eighth year of Nabonidus (548 BC), in a loan of silver by Nabû-aḫḫē-iddin, son of Šulā, one witness is Ea-iddin, son of Marduka (Nbn 316). Two

---

145 Egibi, Eppēš-ili, Rab-banê, Rē'û and Šangû-Gula.

146 For the interpretation of this document, see below, p. 85.

years later, in the tenth year of Nabonidus (546 BC) Ina-Esagila-zēr-ibni, son of Bēl-uballiṭ borrows 20? shekels of silver from Nabû-aḫḫe-iddin, who took the debtor's adjacent house as pledge (Nbn 433). In the same year Nabû-zēr-ibni, son of Bēl-aplu-iddin is witness in the document of purchase of a field by Nabû-aḫḫē-iddin, son of Šulā (Nbn 418). In the twelfth year (544 BC) Aḫḫē-ša, son of Iqīša is the scribe of a document concerning the purchase of a slave by Itti-Marduk-balāṭu (Nbn 681). In the same year Nabû-aḫḫē-iddin paid for a field which he purchased from Esagila-zēr-ibni, son of Bēl-uballiṭ of the Ir'anni family and, additionally, he regulated his earlier debt of 20 shekels of silver owed to Esagila-zēr-ibni (Nbn 633). In the thirteenth year (543 BC) Nabû-ukīn, son of Bēl-ušallim occurs as witness in a document concerning dates borrowed from Itti-Marduk-balāṭu and his brother and the members of Rabbanê family by members of the Etellu and Arad-Ea families (Nbn 715). In the fifteenth year (541 BC) another Ir'anni member, Bēl-aḫḫē-erība, son of Balāssu is first witness in document concerning the purchase of slave by Itti-Marduk-balāṭu (Nbn 837).

In total, about 50 members of Ir'anni occur in the documents of Egibi.[147] The majority acted as witness, most often first or second, sometimes as third, and seldom as fourth or fifth.[148] Although the earliest texts of Egibi in which the members of Ir'anni occur are dated to the time of Nabonidus,[149] the majority with Ir'anni are dated to the floruit of Itti-Marduk-balāṭu, son of Nabû-aḫḫē-iddin, during the time of Cyrus and mostly Cambyses, then from the time of his son Marduk-nāṣir-apli (521-487 BC), although data are less numerous. The plain fact that so many members of Ir'anni occur in the Egibi documents suggests that relations were profitable for both families. This is supported by a few texts in which Ir'anni played a more important role. In VS 4, 66 (Cyr 8) three sons of Bēl-iddin of Ir'anni borrowed 1 mina 20 shekels of silver from Ina-Esagila-ramât, the daughter of Balāṭu of Egibi, giving her as a pledge their house located adjacent to Balāṭu's house, obviously the father of Ina-Esagila-ramât. It is the second indication that both families were neighbours. According to Dar 472 = Abraham 2004, no. 128 (and its duplicate BM 31977 = Abraham 2004, no. 65), written in Dar 18 (504 BC) Nidintu, son of Kabtiya, paid in the name of Marduk-nāṣir-apli his debt of 3 minas 45 shekels to a

[147] Most texts were published by Strassmaier, chiefly from the times of Cyrus, Cambyses and Darius. New texts are published and others re-edited by Wunsch 2000b, see Index, 299-300. Additional texts are in Abraham 2004 and CTMMA 3, Wunsch 1993. and single texts in other publications.

[148] Two other members of the Ir'anni family occur as witnesses in Iddin-Marduk's archive, related by marriage to Egibi (Wunsch 1993, no. 307 and 358).

[149] Wunsch 2000, no. 50 dated to Nbn 4, cf. also Wunsch 2000, no. 40, 88 and 135 for this time.

member of Šigûa family.[150] In CTMMA 3, 68 (Dar 25, 497 BC) certifying that Širku//Egibi has paid *ilku* to certain Amurru-aḫ-iddin/Šum-iddin, the scribe is another member of Ir'anni, Nabû-itannu, son of Ea-iddin. Obviously both were recognized by Egibi as trustworthy persons.[151]

Highly intensive contact took place between Nabû-mukīn-apli (= Kīnaya), son of Nūrea of Ir'anni, who occurs as first or second witness in almost 30 documents,[152] the majority dated to the short period between the seventh year of Cyrus (532 BC) and the last year of Cambyses/first year of Bardiya (522 BC). About 20 are dated to closer period Camb 3 – Camb 8/Bardiya 1 (527-522 BC). Such intensive involvement by Nabû-mukīn-apli is the best demonstration of the close ties between him and Itti-Marduk-balāṭu, then chief of Egibi family. Itti-Marduk-balāṭu trusted Nabû-mukīn-apli not without reason, for the mother of Nabû-mukīn-apli was Ina-Esagila-bēlet, daughter of Rēmūt-Bēl of the Egibi family.[153] Although data for the later period are much poorer, it seems that close ties continued between both families.[154] It means that such vivid contacts between families were based on family ties, trust, solidarity and intimacy.[155] It is not accidental that when the member of Ir'anni needed to lease a house they went to Egibi. In general it seems that Ir'anni, and especially Nabû-mukīn-apli, were in a slightly inferior position to Egibi. It seems that at a later time, about 500 BC, relations between Ir'anni and Marduk-nāṣir-apli, a.k.a. Širku, the then chief of Egibi, changed substantially, because in a series of documents Širku is debtor of silver and dates to Bēl-uballiṭ, son of Bēl-eṭir, presumably the main person of Ir'anni.[156]

[150] Nidintu, son of Kabtiya occurs also in CTMMA 3, 122 written in Dar 27 (495 BC) as fourth witness besides his brother Bēl-iddin as the seventh witness.

[151] Close contact is suggested also by TCL 12, 103 concerning a loan of silver, first given by Nabû-aḫḫē-iddin, father of Itti-Marduk-balāṭu and in 12th year of Nabonidus by Itti-Marduk-balāṭu but the debtor house was taken as a pledge. The document was written by the scribe of Iranni family.

[152] For a list of these documents, see NBN 90, s.v. Kin-apli/Nûrea and 135, s.v. Nabû-kīn-apli/Nûrea. New texts are published (and older re-edited) in Wunsch 2000, Index, 299. Add also CTMMA 3, 68.

[153] This is confirmed by Cam 348 (Camb 6, 524/23 BC), where Nabû-mukīn-apli and his mother borrow from Itti-Marduk-balāṭu, son of Nabû-aḫḫē-idin 1 mina 10 shekels of silver for one year (*adi ṭuppi ṭuppi*) without interest, i.e. on very favourable terms.

[154] Cf. the documents published by Kathleen Abraham (2004), see Index, 491 (but delete the last entry (Ubār, S of Erībaya is the member of Itinnu family).

[155] The investigation of trust, intimacy and friendship with the help of modern sociological method was offered lately by B. Still who reached highly interesting results (Still 2016, esp. chap. 4).

[156] See Dar 507, 536, 537, 539, 545 and 560 dated to the period Dar 20-Dar 23 (502-499 BC).

Three documents concerning rental of a house, property of Saggilaya family, deserve attention because they shed new light on changes in property inside the family and their relation with Egibi and in turn between the Egibi and Šamaš-(a)bāri families. Additionally, the documents demonstrate that these individuals lived in the same geographical location, i.e. a suburb of Babylon, and that their houses were located adjacent to one other.

The earliest document is Dar 482, no. 121 written in Ayāru, nineteenth year of Darius I (503 BC). It is a receipt of rent paid by Šamaš-ina-tēši-ēṭir, son of Šamaš-iddin, descendant of Šamaš-(a)bāri to Marduk-šāpik-zēri, son of Mušēzib-Marduk, descendant of Saggilaya for the period till the end of Nisannu that year. The payment of the rent to the end of Nisannu made in Ayāru may suggest that this document terminates their mutual relations, but this is not the case. First, it is said that while paying the rent Šamaš-ina-tēši-ēṭir still lives in the house (*ašbi*) and this is clearly confirmed by second text, JCS 28, no. 46, no. 122 written on 22nd day of first month Ulūlu, nineteenth year of Darius.[157] This time, only about four months after Dar 482 was written, the same house was leased by Iddinaya, son of Mušēzib-Marduk, i.e. the brother of the previous owner, to Širku (= Marduk-nāṣir-apli) son of Iddinaya (= Itti-Marduk-balāṭu) of Egibi family for 24 shekels of *ginnu* silver yearly.[158] The tenant accepted the usual obligations, i.e. he would repair cracks in wall' footing and roof and pay *nuptu*. However, ll. 12-14 makes certain that Šamaš-ina-tēši-ēṭir still occupied part of the house and for this reason he was obliged to pay rent for the period from 1st Ayāru to 1st Tašrītu of the nineteenth year of Darius, i.e. exactly for half a year,[159] beginning from the last payment which covered the period ending in the very end of Nisannu. Highly interesting is the fact that (if I understand the text properly) Šamaš-ina-tēši-ēṭir is obliged to pay his rent to Širku and he (Širku) will pay it personally to Iddinaya, the house owner. If the presented scenario is correct it means that Šamaš-ina-tēši-ēṭir retained the right to dwell in part of the house he leased earlier, but from the day when the house was rented by Egibi, he should pay the rent not to the owner, but to the new tenant of the Egibi family. It means that Šamaš-ina-tēši-ēṭir is treated here as sub-tenant of Širku of Egibi. From a formal point of view Širku is responsible for payment of rent not only for the part of the house that is in his real possession, but also for that occupied by Šamaš-ina-tēši-ēṭir.[160]

[157] The year was miscopied by Stigers as the ninth year. The photo of the tablet makes certain that it was written in the nineteenth, not ninth year of Darius I.

[158] For extensive discussion of the meaning of *ginnu*, see Jursa 2010, 480-490.

[159] The nineteenth year of Darius was a year with an intercalary month Ulūlu as JCS 28, no. 46: 23 mentions first month of Ulūlu (iti.kin u_4.1.ka+m).

[160] The reason for composing Dar 485, no. 123 is unclear, as the content is practically identical to JCS 28, no. 46 (the same location of a house, quantity and quality of rent, the same obligations and

The situation in which a former tenant still lives in a house and pays rent to a new tenant is atypical and needs explanation. Presumably we can explain this by the close relationship of Šamaš-ina-tēši-ēṭir with Egibi in an earlier period. This is confirmed by Dar 359 written in Dar 13 (508 BC).[161] In this year Šamaš-ina-tēši-ēṭir signed a business venture (*ḫarrānu*) for three years with Marduk-nāṣir-apli, son of Itti-Marduk-balāṭu, based on the enormous amount of 51 *kurru* of dates, the tithe of Bēl (= Marduk) delivered by Marduk-nāṣir-apli. Šamaš-ina-tēši-ēṭir was responsible for running the company in such a way that the capital would not be reduced but would bring profit to be divided equally.[162] In the fourteenth year (507 BC) Šamaš-ina-tēši-ēṭir occurs as witness in documents in which Marduk-nāṣir-apli borrows barley (Dar 387), and again in the same function in the fifteenth year (506 BC) in which another member of Egibi, Nidintu, son of Marduk-erība borrows 13 shekels of silver (Dar 412). The relations of Šamaš-ina-tēši-ēṭir with Egibi were continued also after the nineteenth year, when Egibi leased a house from Saggilaya in which Šamaš-ina-tēši-ēṭir had earlier lived. In the twentieth year (502 BC) Šamaš-ina-tēši-ēṭir borrowed from Marduk-nāṣir-apli the quite large amount of 17 *kurru* 2 *pān* of dates and 2 *kurru* 2 *pān* 5 *sūtu* of barley (Dar 498).

In fact, the economic ties between the Egibi and Šamaš-(a)bāri families began much earlier. The earliest document is dated to the twenty-fifth year of Nebuchadnezzar (580 BC), where a member of the Šamaš-(a)bāri family is the last but one witness in a purchase document for a plot in the Te-e district of Babylon by Nabû-aḫḫē-iddin, son of Šulā (Nbk 164). The next document is dated the sixth year of Nabonidus (559 BC), in which certain Nabû-zēr-līšir of Šamaš-(a)bāri is the document scribe for the purchase of a date garden located in Bāb-Nār-Barsip in the province of Babylon by Nabû-aḫḫē-iddin, son of Šulā (Nbn 178). The promissory note written in the sixteenth year (540 BC) reveals that Rēmūt-Bēl, son of Balāssu of Šamaš-(a)bāri, together with the member

the same list of witnesses and scribe), with only two differences, i.e. information about Šamaš-ina-tēši-ēṭir's obligation is in JCS 28, no. 46 in lines 12-16, i.e. about middle of the text, while in Dar 485 it is added at the very end of the text (ll. 23-25). Because the content of this statement seems the same we might recognize the texts as duplicates, maybe written in the same day, one copy for each partner. The difference in place might result from scribe's absent-mindedness. The second difference is that the owner of a house in Dar 485 is not Iddinaya, son of Mušēzib-Marduk, descendant of Saggilaya, but Iddinaya, son of Itti-Marduk-balāṭu, descendant of Saggilaya. It cannot be excluded – because the full father's name of Širku of Egibi was Itti-Marduk-balāṭu – that the scribe mistakenly changed the father's name of the owner instead the father's name of tenant. The argument for this proposal is the same content of JCS 28, no. 46 and Dar 485 in high probability that they were written in the same day.

[161] Abraham 2004, no. 114.

[162] For such a contract where capital was given by one partner, while the second was responsible for the running the business and sometimes for losses of the invested capital, see Lanz 1976, 7-49.

of another family was in possession of date garden belonging to Itti-Marduk-balāṭu, son of Nabû-aḫḫe-iddin of Egibi (Nbn 973). Economic relations were probably stronger in the time of Darius. Before Šamaš-ina-tēši-ēṭir two of his brothers entered earlier in relations with Egibi. Already in the fifth year of Darius (517 BC) Iddin-Nabû, presumably the older brother of Šamaš-ina-tēši-ēṭir, leased a house located in Borsippa from Marduk-nāṣir-apli of Egibi.[163] His second brother was Nidintu, who occurs as witness in the document of purchase of slave by Širku (= Marduk-nāṣir-apli).[164]

Relations were not limited to the sons of Šamaš-iddin. Quite active was Gimil-Šamaš, son of Līšir. In the fifth year of Darius (517 BC), as the promissory note shows, he rented barley, sesame and emmer fields of Egibi from Marduk-nāṣir-apli, who acted in his own and his brothers' names (Dar 155). In the eleventh year (511 BC) Gimil-Šamaš paid rent dates from the date palm grove, with by-products to the slave of Marduk-nāṣir-apli (Dar 313). Two years later (509 BC) he is obligated to paid rent date from the palm grove to Itti-Marduk-balāṭu (Dar 353). In the sixteenth year (506 BC) a promisssory note was written obliging him to pay dates to Marduk-nāṣir-apli and his brother Nergal-ušallim (Dar 425). Already in the tenth year (596 BC) Bēl-aḫḫē-iddin, son of Gimil-Šamaš should pay 80 *kurru* of dates from date palm grove rented from Nabû-aḫḫē-bulliṭ, son of Itti-Marduk-balāṭu of Egibi (Dar 372).[165] In two Egibi documents occurs Nabû-mukīn-zēri, probably son of Šamaš-ina-tēši-ēṭir.[166] In the first, Dar 325, Marduk-nāṣir-apli purchased a plot with one side adjacent to the plot of Nabû-mukīn-zēri, i.e. they became neighbours. In the second, Abraham 2004, no. 45 he is only a witness but in an important document concerning regulation of debts owed by a third party to Marduk-nāṣir-apli. The above documents lead to the obvious conclusion: rental of Egibi's houses in Babylon and Borsippa by members of the Šamaš-(a)bāri family resulted from long relations in which more often Šamaš-(a)bāri were the clients of Egibi, but the opposite situation also occurred. Using Still's terminology one may see here a kind of intimacy or friendship.

The discussed texts also shed some light on relations between Saggilaya and Egibi, which began at least in the time of Nabonidus, as in his accession

[163] He occurs also in Dar 498 as a witness (cf. above).

[164] Dar 537 (Dar 22, 583 BC). Presumably he occurs also in Dar 560 (Dar 23, 582 BC, father's name missing) as witness in documents on debt in dates owed to Puršu (= Nergal-ušezib), son of Itti-Mraduk-balāṭu.

[165] One of witnesses was Arad-Gula, son of Itti-Marduk-balāṭu of Šamaš-(a)bāri.

[166] In both the father's name is written in abbreviated form: Tēši-eṭir (Dar 325) written in twelfth year of Darius (510 BC) and Ina-tēši-eṭir in Abraham 2004, no. 45 (BM 31360, written in Dar 26, 496 BC).

year (556 BC) Bēl-zēr-iqīša, son of Marduk-šarrāni of Saggilaya, occurs as second witness in a loan document of 24 shekels of silver by Nabû-aḫḫē-iddin, son of Šulā (Nbn 8). Usually the members of Saggilaya were witnesses in Egibi documents[167], and only seldom as a party. In the eighth year of Nabonidus, Lābāši, son of Dummuqu loaned 10 shekels of silver from Itti-Marduk-balāṭu of Egibi (Nbn 308). In the thirteenth year of Nabonidus (543 BC) three promissory notes (TCL 12, 103; CTMMA 3, 56, and Nbn 1110) reveal that Itti-Marduk-balāṭu lent silver to fNūpta, daughter of Niqūdu (= Nabû-mušētiq-uddê) of Saggilaya for which he held a house as pledge.[168] In the eighth year of Cyrus (533 BC), Itti-Marduk-balāṭu of Egibi purchased a plot adjacent on one side to a plot of Bēl-lē'i of Saggilaya, i.e. they became neighbours (Cyr 345). In general, although in the nineteenth year of Darius Egibi decided to lease a house from Saggilaya, it seems that – despite the fact that Saggilaya was priestly family, the Egibi position was stronger. As in the previous cases the decision to lease a house from Saggilaya was not accidental, as both families had enjoyed in long relations, although there is no ground to describe them as friendly.

Important observations result from comparison of owners of houses and their tenants. It turns out that Egibi rented their houses to 12 (ca. 43%) out of 28 tenant families, suggesting that the family dominated the market. The picture may be to some extent distorted by the fact that Egibi archive is the best preserved private archive of the city of Babylon. Although the percentage share in the home rental market could be misleading, undoubtedly it was significant.

In the case of Borsippa the picture differs substantially from that in Babylon. In Borsippa out of 16 families identified as the lessors of houses, 11 (68.75%)

---

[167] Cf. AmM 7 (AmM 0, 562 BC): Kidin-Marduk, son of Dummuqu is third witness in a document concerning the debt of Marduk-erība, son of Marduk-šum-ibni of Egibi; Nbn 701 (Nbn 13, 543 BC): Nabû-zēr-līšir, son of Iqīšaya (!), is first witness in a document concerning payment of a debt of 140 *kurru* of dates by Itti-Marduk-balāṭu of Egibi; Dar 166 (Dar 5, 517 BC): Itti-Marduk-balāṭu, son of Nabû-zēr-iqīša of Saggilya is third witness in a document concerning debt of 40 *kurru* of dates by Puršu (= Nergal-ušēzib), son of Itti-Marduk-balāṭu of Egibi; Dar 175 (Dar 5, 517 BC): Marduk-rēmanni, son of Nabû-zēr-iqīša of Saggilya is first witness in the promissory note according to which Marduk-nāṣir-apli of Egibi should receive 17 *kurru* of dates as *imittu* from date grove in Bāb-nār-Barsip; Dar 204 (Dar 6, 516 BC): Nabû-ušallim, son of Marduk-zēr-ibni is a witness in a document of transfer of provision for a person by Širku to an administartive official; Dar 302 (Dar 11, 511 BC): Nidintu, son of Nabû-apal-iddin is second witness in a document of payment of debt of 3 minas of silver by Marduk-nāṣir-apli of Egibi; Dar 340: (Dar 12, 510 BC): the same person is a witnees in a document of purchase of a slave and his wife, by Nabû-aḫḫē-bulliṭ, son of Itti-Marduk-balāṭu of Egibi; Dar 449 (Dar 17, 504 BC): Bulṭā, son of Ibnaya, a witness in a document of loan of 2 minas 41 shekels by Širki of Egibi.

[168] Cf. commentary to CTMMA 3, 68.

belonged to priestly families,[169] among them five (45.45%) to the highest group of the temple-enterers families,[170] three (27.27%) to the baker's,[171] two (18.2%) to the brewer's[172] and one (10.75%) tothe butcher's prebendaries.[173] Only two priestly families began this kind of business activity at the time of Nebuchadnezzar (Ibnāya and Ea-ilūta-bāni), but the former is known only from one document while members of the latter continued to lease houses during the reigns of Neriglissar, Nabonidus and the Persian period.[174] Also the Bēliya'u family leased houses since the time of Nabonidus, but the main data concern almost exclusively (with one exception) Šaddinnu, son of Balāssu, who had leased houses since the beginning of the reign of Darius to Xer 1, i.e. most likely to the end of the known archives (484 BC). The members of at least five families were the tenants of Šaddinnu: Amēl-Ea, Bēl-usātu, Ea-ibni, Nergal-ušallim and Šigûa. That the contracts were concluded with different families suggests that renting of houses might have been more significant than it can be recognized on the basis of preserved data. Quite close were the relations with Balāssu, son of Šulā, descendant of Bēl-usātu family as he rented the house of Šaddinnu for at least eight years (Dar 5-13, 517-509 BC).[175] Long relations with Bēliya'u are also attested in the case of Bēl-eṭir of Šigûa family.[176]

Out of four non-priestly families (22.25% of all) only the Egibi family owned a considerable number of houses, thus a source of significant income.[177]

---

[169] Classification to particular branches is based on Waerzegger 2000 and Still 2016.

[170] Aqar-Nabû, Arad-Ea, (Ea)-ilūta-bani, Ēda-ēṭir and Kidin-Nanaya.

[171] Bēliya'u, Kidin-Sîn and Šēpē-iliya.

[172] Ilīya and Sikkûa.

[173] Ibnāya.

[174] If, as it seems, Zēr-Bābili, son of Nabû-šum-ukīn, descendant of (Ea)-ilūta-bāni was the father of Mušēzib-Bēl, activity of the same clan of the family lasted at least two generations. Most likely each of the four known contracts concerns a different house. In two texts in which the owner was Zēr-Bābili, the house in NBC 8378 (Joannès 1989, 349. and 93) has different neighbours to the house in HSM 1899.2.141, and the rent differs substantially (10 and 3¼ shekels of silver, respectively). Two contracts in which Mušēzib-Bēl is house owner (NBC 8345 = Joannès 1989, 341) and A 105 (Joannès 1989, 273-4) were concluded in the same year with different tenants, which speaks against the idea that the same house was the subject of these contracts.

[175] As the first contract between them was concluded for two years in Dar 5 (VS 5, 67) and next is the receipt of payment of rent year for 13th year of Darius (VS 4, 137), it seems highly probable that the partners had concluded in the meantime another contract or contracts and that the house was for all the years from Dar 5 till Dar 13 in the hands of the same tenant.

[176] For detailed discussion of their relation, see Still 2016, 165-168.

[177] In light of Dar 379: 9 and 13, as the result of inheritance division after the death of Itti-Marduk-balāṭu, Marduk-nāṣir-apli received seven houses in Babylon and three in Borsippa, while his two brothers received four houses in Babylon (l. 31), and two in Borsippa (l. 34-35). This is confirmed by four documents from Borsippa (one contract and three receipts) in which Marduk-nāṣir-apli is a party.

However, it is not excluded that members of Ilīya family also derived considerable income from house rental. The published documents record four house lease contracts or receipts for Egibi at the time of Dar 3 – 16 (519-506 BC) and three for Ilīya at the time of Cyr 7 – Camb 2 (532-528 BC), i.e. within a short time span. In other years similar activity might well have occurred but corresponding documents are not preserved or have not yet been published. The known sources suggest that no family in Borsippa leased houses on a scale similar to that of the Egibi in Babylon.

21 family names of tenants are known from Borsippa, but members of only three families were active as tenants in the last years of the Neo-Babylonian period: Rēšaya (Nrg 2, 558 BC), Amēl-Ea and Sîn-Šadûnu (Nbn 4, 552 BC). All other tenants whose family names are known were active in the Persian period. There is uncertainty as to how much the collected data are indicative of common practice at that time. This is doubtful because with the exception of just four families, the others occur as tenants only once.

A peculiar situation takes place in BM 109877 (10.IV.Dar 21), where Bēl-iddin, son of Šumā, descendant of Naggāru rented from himself (*ul-tu rama-ni-šú i-bu-ku*) a small outbuilding (*bīt ṭipu qallu*) for five years for 4 shekels of silver yearly. Although the owner is not mentioned in the text, it seems that Bēl-iddin acting as proxy decided to rent the house for himself for the price determined by the owner. However, in a few texts where the tenants are oblates of Nabû,[178] they presumably concluded the contracts in their own names because they were personally responsible for the payment of rent and fulfilment of additional obligations.

The data for Sippar are poor, as I know only 21 documents of house leases, among which are five contracts between the temple and private persons, which will be discussed later (chapt. 3.2). All other rental documents from Sippar in which the family names are given are dated to the short period from Dar 15-Š-e 0 (507-482 BC). Only three families are known. There are five documents of Ṣāḫit-ginê in which the owner of the rented houses is Marduk-rēmanni, son of Bēl-uballiṭ (MR 93, 95, 99, 109 and 138), and in one his son Bēl-bullissu (MR 182); in addition one member of the Būru-zēr-iddin family (MR 167) and one of the Ea-iddin family (BM 67913, no. 108) is known.

A few texts from Uruk will also be discussed later, but one text, BIN 1, 118 (Cyr 8)[179] deserves our attention here because the house, described as "royal property" (*makkūr šarri*) was rented out for the noticeably high rent of half a mina of silver per year. This means that the Persian king recognised house rental as a good source of income for the royal treasury, especially since the

[178] TuM 2-3, 24 and 30; BRM 1, 68.

[179] Edited in BR 6, no. 33 (28.XI.Cyr 8).

new authority must have known that substantial income from the rental of houses was earned by Babylonian temples. We do not know, however, whether the Persian administration in Babylonia owned additional houses, or whether this was an exceptional case.

In general the collected material suggests that in Babylon as well as in Borsippa (less clearly so in Sippar, due to the paucity of data) there was a rise in the number of records of house rentals in the Persian period. This could be due merely to an increase in the number of the documents preserved, but these cities maintained the status of important centres – economic, religious and to some extent also political. The conquest of Babylonia by Persians did not hamper the development of the main Babylonian cities. On the other hand, this pattern might reflect an increase in the number of individuals who had insufficient means to build a house, particularly if it necessitated the purchase of a building plot. The problem, which is important, can only be solved with the publication of additional appropriate texts.

It is obvious that the initiative to a sign contract favoured the person who needed accommodation. In light of a few texts we might take it that future tenants would look for accommodation among families with whom they had more or less permanent business if not family relations. It seems that the dominant position in market in Babylon was held by the Egibi family. This is not certain in case of Borsippa as there are other families there, who could have enjoyed a similar business position. The data suggests that in Borsippa this type of market activity was determined by priestly families, but, as already remarked, this may result from the fact that the majority of Borsippaean documents comes from persons belonging to priestly families of Ezida temple.

2.2.4 The period rental and rental fee

The majority of contracts specify the period of time for which a house is rented. Usually the houses were rented from two to five years, seldom for a very long time,[180] but sometimes also for one year,[181] or just a few months.[182] In the latter case it seems that the tenant needed lodging for a temporary stay in the city. The reasons for renting a temporary residence are usually unknown but we

---

[180] "Reed houses" (*bīt ḫuṣṣi*) were rented for about 20 years quite often with an obligation to rebuild and enlarge them. The long-term house leases are known, especially in case of the antichretic loans, i.e. when the debtor did not pay interest, while the owner used the house of the debtor without paying the rent.

[181] If we accept Baker's opinion that the expression *ṭuppi adi ṭuppi* means "for one year" (Baker 2010).

[182] VS 5, 59 = NRV 115 = Baker 2004, no. 115 (for three months).

might assume some commercial activity or the need to settle family matters. A highly exceptional situation is described in TuM 2-3, no. 29 dated to the accession year of Darius II.[183] A house located on the ramp of Bēl was rented out by Aplā, son of Ḫarmaḫi to Bēl-nādin-šumi, descendant of Murašû for 1½ minas of white silver beginning from the day when the contract was signed, i.e. the fourth day of Šabāṭu. The final date is first described as *adi muḫḫi agê šarri*, "until the coronation of the king" and later *adi muḫḫi aṣê šarri*, "until the departure of the king."[184] One may assume that Bēl-nādin-šumi who was not a member of the royal administration recognized the presence of the new Persian king in the Babylonian capital as a good opportunity for establishing or strengthening his relations with influential representatives of the royal court or for asking the king for a lease of land of the state or temple.[185] By contrast, when the tenant rented the house for some years, he presumably did not own a house or intend to build one, at least not before the final term of the contract.

According to the majority of texts tenants were obliged to pay rent in two installments each year, but monthly or even daily payments are also known (see below). In some documents the annual rent is expressed together with the length of lease, i.e. "for x year(s) for x shekels of silver per year". However, many contracts do not indicate the final date of the lease agreement, meaning that each party (lessor and tenant) could terminate the contract at any time.

The contracts indicate precisely the yearly rent agreed by the owner with the tenant ranging from a few shekels to a dozen, depending presumably on the size of the house, its physical condition and location.

Sometimes the rent was very low, only one shekel yearly (TuM 2-3, 26 and 27), but in such cases the tenants were additionally obliged to rebuild the rented houses.

2.2.5 The deadline for rent payment and means of payment

In numerous contracts the date for payment of house rent by tenant is clearly defined by the use of the almost homonymous formulae:

aḫi kaspi ina rēš šatti aḫi ina mišil šatti

"half of the silver at the beginning of the year, half in the middle of the year," or

[183] Published also in BE 10, 1. Cf. transliteration and translation in BE 10, p. 22f.

[184] On this text, see Stolper 1985, 122.

[185] Jursa 2007, 83 stresses that "the loss of the king's personal protection could disrupt (...) businessmen's activities." Presumably the journey of Itti-Marduk-balāṭu in 538 BC and later had the same purpose, Jursa 2007, 85f.

aḫi kaspi ina rēš šatti (u) rēḫet ina mišil šatti[186]

"half of the silver at the beginning of the year, (and) the remainder in the middle of the year"

Occasionally a different formula occurs:

aḫi kaspi ina rēš šatti rēḫet ina qīt šatti,[187]

"half of the silver at the beginning of the year, the rest at the end of the year."

Exceptional is the case in Nbn 299:[188]

aḫi kaspi ina mišil šatti u rēḫtu ina qīt šatti

"half of the silver in the middle of the year and the rest at the end of the year."

The first statement seems clear: the tenant should pay the first installment at the beginning of the year and the second in the middle of the year. Probably on this basis, San Nicolò assumed the rent was paid in advance ("im voraus"). As the contracts were concluded in different months of the year San Nicolò properly recognised that the rent had to be paid at the beginning and in the middle of the rental year, and this interpretation is commonly accepted.[189] The purpose of this system was to prevent the occupation of a house without any payment or leaving without settlement of arrears.

The payment of the installment was expressed in contracts (more seldom in receipts) by three slightly different formulae:

1. ***kaspi* (*idi bīti*) *ina* (or: *ša*) *rēš šatti* PN1 *ina qātê* PN2 *maḫir***, "PN1 (the lessor) has received from PN2 (the tenant) the silver, (the house rent) for the beginning of the (rental) year:"

Peek 16: 13 (5.IX.Cyr 6): kù.babbar *šá re-eš* mu.an.na [m]ki-[d]amar.utu-tin *ma-ḫir*, "silver for the beginning of the (rental) year Itti-Marduk-balāṭu (the lessor) has received."

Cam 253: 1, 6-9 (7.VIII.Camb 4), a receipt: 8 gín kù.babbar *i-di é-šú šá re-eš* mu.an.na (…) [7m]ki-[d]amar.utu-tin (…) [8]*ina* šu[ii] [m]ìr-den (…) [9]*ma-ḫir*, "8 shekels of silver, the house rent for the beginning of the (rental) year (...) Itti-Marduk-balāṭu (the lessor) has received from Arad-Bēl (the tenant)."

---

[186] A slightly different sequence of words with repetition of *idi bīti* occurs in Nrg 29: 8-9: [*ina*] *rēš šatti aḫi idi bīti mišil šatti aḫi idi bīti*.

[187] YOS 17, 5 (17.V.Nbk 13, 592 BC), BRM 1, 78: 7 (23.1.Dar 20[?], 502 BC) and VS 5, 139: 3' = NRV 140. Oppenheim (1936, 16) recognised the same formula in VS 5, 78, however, it have to be shifted to the first clause, see Baker 2004, no. 101: 7 (*re-ḫi-it* kù.babbar <<U>> *ina m*[*i-šil šat-ti*].

[188] Noted already by Oppenheim 1936, 17.

[189] San Nicolò, NRV, 156. The only exception is R. Zadok interpretation of BM 82668 written in Borsippa on the tenth of Abu (V) while the house was given at disposal of the tenant on the 1st Ulūlu. In his opinion (Zadok 2009, 250) the first installment "is to be paid at the beginning of the year (1.I, i.e. within slightly less than seven months)."

Dar 210: 1-7 (3.IX.Dar 6), a receipt: 1½ *ma-na* ½ gín kù.babbar (…) ^{2}*ina i-di* é *šá re-eš* mu.an.na (…) ^{4md}amar.utu-pap-a (…) ^{5}*ina* šu^{ii} ^{m}ìr-^{d}en (…) ^{7}*ma-ḫir*, "30½ shekels of silver (…) for the house rent for the beginning of the (rental) year (…) Marduk-nāṣir-apli (the lessor) has received from Arad-Bēl (the tenant)."

CTMMA 3, 97: 13-14 (28.II.Dar 8): 10 gín kù.babbar babbar-*ú* (…)/*ina re-eš šat-ti-šú* ^{m}mu-^{d}ag *ma-ḫi-ir*, "10 shekels of white silver (…) for the beginning of his (rental) year Iddin-Nabû (the lessor) has received."

VS 5, 81: 7-9 = Baker 2004, no. 86 ([x].II.Dar 16): kù.babbar *ina re-eš*/mu.an.na-*šú* ^{m}mu-^{d}ag *ina* šu^{ii} ^{md}ag-*bul-liṭ-su*/*ma-ḫir*, "the silver for the beginning of his (rental) year Iddin-Nabû (the lessor) has received from Nabû-bulliṭsu (the tenant)."

JCS 28, no. 9: 9-10 (6.II.Dar 24): kù.babbar *šá re-eš mu-šú* ^{md}en-a-mu/*ina šu*^{ii} ^{md}utu-mu-dù *ma-ḫir*, "silver for the beginning of his (rental) year Bēl-aplu-iddin (the lessor) has received from Šamaš-šum-ibni (the tenant)."

Barton 1900, no. 24: 11-12 (21.IX.Xer 34): 4 gín kù.babbar *ina* sag mu-*šú*/ ^{md}utu-mu *ina* šu^{ii} ^{m}*iz-ḫu-ia ma-ḫir*, "4 shekels of silver for the beginning of his (rental) year Šamaš-iddin (the lessor) has received for Izhuya (the tenant)."

Mich 56: 12 (9.II.Art. <9>), a receipt: 1 gín kù.babbar babbar-*ú i-di* é/ *šá* sag mu.an.na-*ti-šú* (…) ^{5m}*lib-luṭ* (…) *ina* šu^{ii} ^{f}*bi-il-šú* (…) *maḫ-rat* (for *maḫir*), "1 shekel of white silver, the house rent for the beginning of his (rental) year (…) Libluṭ (the lessor) has received from ^{f}Bilšu (the tenant)." The rent is for the period from the <end> of Nisannu till the end of Tašrītu, i.e. for half a year.

VS 5, 78 = Baker 2004, no. 101: 12'-13' (2$^{?}$.V.Dar 15): [kù.babbar *ina re-eš šat-ti-šú*]/^{m}mu-^{d}ag *ina* šu^{ii} ^{m}*mu-*[*ra-nu ma-ḫir*], ["the silver for the beginning of his (rental)] year Iddin-Nabû (the lessor) has received from Mū[rānu] (the tenant)."

BRM 1, 85: 23-25 (6.IV.Xer 2): 2 gín kù.babbar *i-di* é/^{m}ku x-a *ina* šu^{ii}/^{md}ag-šeš.meš-gi *ma-ḫi-ir*, "2 shekels of silver, the house rent [PN (the lessor)][190] has received from Nabû-aḫḫē-šullim (the tenant)." Note that the expression *ina sag šatt*i or *ša mišil šatti* is missing, but it is clear that the payment is for the first installment.

2. ***kaspi ina* (or: *ša*) *mišil šatti* PN1 *ina qātê* PN2 *maḫir*,** "PN1 (the lessor) has received from PN2 (the tenant) the silver for the half of the (rental) year."

BM 33966, no. 129: 16-18 (5.V.Dar 36): kù.babbar *a-*<*na*> *mi-šil* mu.an.na-*šú* ^{m}*ni-din-ti-*^{d}en *ina* šu^{ii} ^{f}geme-^{d}*na-na-a maḫ-ru*, "the silver for the half of

[190] The name of the lessor is expected, but in l. 3 ^{f}*di-ri-tu*$_{4}$ is written.

his (rental) year Nidinti-Bēl (the lessor) has received from Amat-Nanaya (the tenant)."

BM 120099, no. 132: 10-12 (10.[IV].Xer 1): kù.babbar-' *šá mi-šil* mu.an.na-*šú* ^{f}*ni-din-tu*$_4$*ina* šu^{ii} ^{m}mu-^{d}ag *maḫ-rat*, "that silver for half of her year ^{f}Nidintu (the lessor) has received from Iddin-Nabû (the tenant)."

BM 33979, no. 134: 8-10 (24.IV.Xer 2*): kù.babbar *šá mi-šil* mu.an.na-*šú* ^{m}*ni-din-tu*$_4$-^{d}en *ina* šu^{ii} ^{md}en-*ši-man-ni ma-ḫi-ir*, "the silver for the half of his (rental) year Nidinti-Bēl (the lessor) has received from Bēl-šimānni (the tenant)."

BM 42393, no. 128: 13-14 (15.IV.Dar 36) kù.babbar *šá mi-šil* mu.an.na ^{m}*ni-din-ti*-^{d}en *ina* šu^{ii} ^{m}ki-^{d}utu-tin dumu *ma-ḫi-ir*, "the silver for the half of the (renting) year Nidinti-Bēl (the lessor) has received from Itti-Šamaš-balāṭu (the tenant)."

BRM 1, 74 (13.XII.Dar 9): 21-23: 5 gín kù.babbar [babbar]-*ú*/*ina* sag mu.an.na-*šú*/^{md}amar.utu-pap-a *maḫ-ḫir* (for *maḫir*), "5 shekels of [whit]e silver for the beginning of his (rental) year/Marduk-nāṣir-apli (the lessor) has received."

BE 8/1, 104: 8-9 (3.XII.Dar 28): 2 gín kù.babbar babbar-*ú i-di* [é]/^{f}*bu-'-i-tu*$_4$ *ina* šu^{ii}/^{m}*ni-din-tu4 ma-ḫi-ir-tu*$_4$, "2 shekels of white silver, the [house] rent, ^{f}Bu'itu (the lessor) has received from Nidintu (the tenant)."

Mich 2: 13-14 (4.VIII.Art 9): kù.babbar *i-di* é-*šú šá mi-šil* mu-*ti-šú*/^{f}*zer-ra-ni-ia ina* šu^{ii} ^{md}be-*bul-liṭ-su maḫ-rat* (for *maḫir*), "silver, the rent of his house for the half of his year ^{f}Zēraniya (the lessor) has received from Ea-bullissu (the tenant)."

Mich 13: 12-13 (6.III.Art 8): kù.babbar *i-di* é-*šú šá mi-šil mu-šú*/^{md}en-kam *ina* šu^{ii} ^{md}en-tin^{it} *ma-ḫir*, "silver, the rent of his house for the half of the year Bēl-ēreš (the lessor) has received from Bēl-uballiṭ (the tenant)."

Mich 14: 11-13 (5.III.Art 8, or 9): kù.babbar *i-di* é-*šú*/*šá m*[*i-šil* mu-*šú* ^{md}en]-*šú-nu ina* šu^{ii} ^{md}en-mu-*na*/*ma*-[*ḫir*], "the silver for the ha[lf of his (rental) year Bēl]-šunu (the lessor) has received from Bēl-iddin (the tenant)."

3. *kaspi ša mišil šatti* PN2 *ēṭir*, "silver for half a year was paid by PN2 (the tenant)."

BM 77421, no. 125 VII.Dar 2⌜9⌝): 11-12: kù.babb[ar-*a*$_4$ 10 gín *šá mi-šil* mu] ^{m}*še-el-li-bi* [*e-ṭir*], "the silver - that [10 shekels], Šellibi (the tenant) [has paid for the half of the year]."

BM 68440, no. 137 (date missing): 10'-11': kù.babbar *šá mi-šil* mu.an.n[a PN]/*ina* šu^{ii} ^{m}⌜*bul*⌝-[*lu*]-⌜*ṭu*⌝ *e-ṭi-ir*, "the silver for the half of the (rental) year [PN] (the lessor) was paid by Bulluṭu (the tenant)."

Atypical is the receipt BM 25690: 5-6 = Zadok 2008, 76* (2.VI.Dar 21), where it is said that the rent is paid for six month.[191]

2.2.6 Praenumerando payment of the house rent in the contracts

Because house rental contracts with a note about the *praenumerando* payment are rare we can conclude that payment in advance was not as frequent as one would expect from the repeated clause that "he will pay half the rent at the beginning of the year and half in the middle of the year" (seldom: "at the end of the year"). The clause expresses the rule that would apply throughout the period of contract. If, however, the statement that a tenant has paid the first installment is missing in the contract, it must be assumed that the first installment has not been paid until the contract was written. This is supported by a few cases where the tenants paid part of the first installment on or before the day of signing the contract:

Text	Rent in shekels for half a year	Sum paid and percentage of the installment	Date of writing of the tablet and payment of part or whole rent	Day of moving into the house	Time of payment
Barton 1900, no. 24	7½	4 (53.3%)	21.IX.	1.X	before entering a house
BE 8/1, 104	2¼	2 (88.8%)	3.XII	1.I	before entering a house
BRM 1, 74	6½	5 (ca. 77%)	13.XII	16.XII	before entering a house
BRM 1, 85	5	2 (40%)	6.IV	from the end of the month IV[192]	before entering a house
Cam 117	11½	5 (47.5%)	16.V	1.VI	before entering a house
Cam 147	35	5 (ca. 14.3%)	5.[V]	1.VI	before entering a house

[191] Ll. 5-6: 5 gín kù.babbar *šá i-di šá* 6 iti.meš ^{md}en-sur/*ina* šu^{ii} ^{md}ag-ùru-*šú ma-la* ḫa*.la-*šú ma-ḫir*, "5 shekels of silver as the house rent for six months Bēl-ēṭir (the owner) has received from Nabû-uṣuršu in accordance with his share."

[192] I.e. presumably from the very beginning of month Abu (V).

MR 99	7 yearly	Sum not given	22.V	1.VI	before entering a house[193]
CTMMA 3, 97	9	10 (111%)	28.II	1.III	before entering a house
Cyr 231	35	70	[x.V]	[1].VI	Paid for whole year in advance
Dar 378	25	25 (100%)	22.V	not given	before or on the day of entering a house
VS 5, 119 = NRV 139	50	10 (20%)		not given	before entering a house[194]
VS 5, 84+151 = Baker 2004, no. 103	15	10 (66.6%)	[x].V	[1.VI?]	before entering a house
BM 25690 = Zadok 2008, 76*	5	5 (100%)	2.VI		the tenants occupied the house on the basis of earlier contract.[195]

In the above cases – with two exceptions (CTMMA 3, 97 and Dar 378, where the tenants have paid full installment for half a year before moving into the house and Cyr 231, where he paid for one year in advance) – the tenant had to pay at least a part of the first installment in order to enter the house; the payment varied from 14.3% to 88.8% of the installment. It seems

[193] This contract needs detailed comments. According to it the tenant should pay 7 shekels of *ginnu* silver yearly. The rental period is not stated, but it is said that the house will be at the tenant's disposal from the 1st day of Ulūlu (VI) and that the rent will be paid in two installments (*aḫi kaspi ina rēš šatti u rēḫtu kaspi ina mišil šatti*). This is followed by the additional clause that *kaspu ša* 1en.kam *šatti-šu* PN1 *ina qātê* PN2 *maḫir*, translated by the editor "PN1 (the owner) has received the rent for the first year from PN2 (the tenant)," which makes the former expression senseless. It seems that the second clause concerns the payment of rent for the first half of the year, in fact the first installment for six months beginning from Ulūlu when the tenant entered the house, i.e. "the silver for the first <half > of his year PN1 has received from PN2."

[194] This is based on the information from ll. 5-6: ta u_4.1.kam *šá* iti.b[ár] mu.8.kam, "from the 1st day of month Ni[sannu]," and ll. 11-13: 10 gín kù.babbar en ⌜*qí-it*⌝ mu.8.kam [m*ar-ta*]*k-šat-su*/ [*ma-ḫir*], "10 shekels till the end of the eighth year of [Arta]xerxes [he (the tenant Bēl-apla-iddin) has received]," and the fact that the text was written in the seventh year of Artaxerxes.

[195] The two tenants already occupied the house earlier. As it is stated one of them paid the rent *mala zitti-šu*, 'in' accordance with his share," we do not know if they occupied equal parts of the house or not. Certainly one of them paid the rent for half a year, probably in advance.

that in receipts where the sum is omitted the full installment was presumably paid. It is interesting that although the expressions cited above vary, in fact the majority of them concern payment of the first installment. The scribe who used the expression *ina rēš šatti* stressed clearly that the payment is for the first part of the (rental) year, while *ina/ša mišil šatti* expresses that the payment is for half a year, usually (as established on basis of the date of writing the contract) also for the first installment.

2.2.7 Day of writing the contract and day when the tenant moved into the house

Some interesting observations can be drawn from comparison of day of issue of a contract and the day of entering the house by the tenant.[196]

Day and month of signing the contract	The day from which the tenant used the house or period for which he paid the rent	The number of days between conclusion of the contract and the day when the tenant entered the house	Means of payment declared in the text: A: *rēš šatti – mišil šatti* B: *rēš šatti* – qīt šatti* D: daily M: monthly Y: Yearly Blank: no data in the text[197]	Text
5.VII	from 1.VII	4 days earlier	A	VS 5, 61 = Baker 2004, no. 85
6.XII	paid to end of month V, i.e. for half a year	5 days earlier[198]	Rec.	VS 4, 146 = Baker 2004, no. 121
21.XI	15.XI	6 days earlier		AnOr 8, 58
9.II	1.II	8 days earlier		Dar 64
10.IV	1.IV	9 days earlier	A?[199]	BM 109877 (unp.)

[196] If one data (the yearly rent or the sum paid in advance for half a year) is missing (cf. VS 5, 139) such text is not taken into account here.

[197] As in the some receipts it is possible to establish the day when the tenant moved into the house, but the expression *rēš šatti – mišil šatti, rēš šatti – qīt šatti* is for obvious reasons not in use, such documents are marked by "Rec".

[198] Assuming that the tenant, in accordance with standard, has paid the rent for half a year.

[199] L. 9-10: *a-ḫi* kù.babbar *ina re-eš* mu/*ri-ḫi* kù.babbar *ina* ⸢x x x⸣ mu but ⸢x x x⸣ are not similar neither to *mi-šil* nor to *qí-it*.

15.IV	1.IV	14 days earlier	A	BM 42393, no. 128
18.III	1.III	17 days earlier		BM 26653[200]
20.IX	1.IX	19 days earlier	M	BE 9, 54
12.XI	1.X[201]	ca. 40 days earlier	A	AnOr 8, 57
1.VII	10.V	ca. 50 days earlier		HSM 1899.2.141[202]
24.II	from month I	ca. 53 days earlier	Rec.	VS 4, 110[203]
2.II	2.II	0	M	Nbn 500, no. 112
3.II	3.II	0	B	Nbn 1030
19.VI	19.VI	0	M	L. 1667[204]
4.VII	4.VII	0	A	BM 77421, no. 125
21.XI	21.XI	0	A	YOS 7, 2
17.V	18.V	1 day	B	YOS 17, 5
28.XI	1.XII	2 day	A	BIN 1, 118
28.II	1.III	2 days		CTMMA 3, 97
28.IV	1.V	2 days	M	NBC 8345
12.VIII	15.VIII	3 days	M	BE 8/1, 112
7.X	10.[X?]	3 days		VS 5, 67, no. 119
27.X	From month XI	ca. 3 days	M	VS 5, 59 = Baker
9.II	14.II	5 days	M	VS 5, 23, no. 109 = NRV 113
24.XII	1.I	ca. 6 days	B	BM 114446, no. 7
23.X	1.[XI?]	ca. 7 days		MR 176
22.VIII	1.IX	ca. 8 days		BM 74949 (unp.)

200 Zadok 2009, 150f., no. 471.

201 With the atypical phrase: *ul-tu* u_4.1.kam *šá* iti.ab mu.7.kam *i-di* é/ *ina* igi ᶠ*su-qa-a-a-i-tu*$_4$. As from this day she was obliged to pay rent, we assume that she already occupied the house.

202 Zadok 2008, 88*-89*.

203 Baker 2004, no. 119.

204 Joannès 1968, 252f.

22.XII	1.[I]	ca. 8 days	A	BM 30594[205]
22.V	1.VI	ca. 8 days	A	MR 99
22.VII	1.VIII	ca. 8 days	D	ZA 3, no. 16, no. 135
21$^{?}$.IV	1.[V$^{?}$]	ca. 9 days	A	VS 5, 64 = Baker 2004, no. 99
11.VI	20.<VI>	9 days		BRM 1, 43
21.IX	1.X	ca. 9 days	A	Barton 1900, no. 24
20.VI	[1$^{?}$].VII	ca. 10 days	A?	BM 26689[206]
5.IX	15.IX	10 days	A	Peek 16
3.VI	15.[VI$^{?}$]	12 days	A?	TuM 2-3, 31
29.VII	12.<VIII$^{?}$>	ca. 12 days	A	BRM 1, 68
2.III	15.III	13 days	A	Dar 499
16.V	1.VI	ca. 14 days	A	Cam 117
13.III	1.[IV]	ca. 17 days	A	VS 5, 82[207]
13.IV	1.V$^{!}$	ca. 17 days	Y	BM 33980, no. 133
13.VII	1.VIII	ca. 17 days		Nbn 261
11.IV	1.V	ca. 18 days	yearly in advance	UCLM 9-2919[208]
11.VIII	1.IX	ca. 18 days	A	YBC 11599[209]
12.XI	1.XII	ca. 18 days	A	VS 5, 77
6.XII$^{?}$	25.XII	19 days	D	A 105
10.III	1.IV	ca. 20 days		BM 26566[210]
10.[IV]	1.V	ca. 20 days	A	BM 120099, no. 132

205 Bertin 2798.

206 Zadok 2009, 155, no. 507.

207 I follow San Nicolò, who reads iti.šu, while Baker 2004, no. 86 reads iti.kin. His reading is supported by the shorter distance between the writing of the document and entering the house by the tenant. As noted by San Nicolò the sign is heavily damaged. This suggests that the copy of sign is presumably inaccurate.

208 Stolper 2000, 668.

209 Stolper 2000, 673.

210 Zadok 2009, 141, no. 384.

10.V	1.VI	ca. 20 days	A	BM 82668[211]
10.XI	1.XII	ca. 20 days	A	BM 25628[212]
9.XII?	1.I	ca. 21 days		BM 29748[213]
9.III	1.IV	ca. 21 days	A	Cyr 228
9.[VIII]	1.IX	ca. 21 days	A	VS 5, 68 = Baker 2004, 116
7.IX	1.[X]	ca. 23 days	A	Nbn 996
6.IV	from end IV, i.e. from 1.V	ca. 24 days	A	BRM 1, 85
6.[VII!]	1.VIII	ca. 24 days		ZA 3, no. 14
5.I	1.II	ca. 25 days		VS 4, 64 = NRV 307
4.VIII	1.IX!	ca. 26 days		BM 29523[214]
3.III	from the end of III, i.e. from 1.IV	ca. 26 days		*Bēliya'u*, no. 242[215]
3.XII	1.I	ca. 27 days		BE 8/1, 104
28.12.	2.2.	ca. 30 days	[...]	Dar 191

The data allow a few important observations:

1. In a few cases the contracts (in one case VS 4, 146, a receipt) were signed a few days or even about two months after the tenant had moved into the rented house. The reason is difficult to establish, but it seems that in such cases the house was informally in the possession of the tenant before the day declared in the contract. In AnOr 8, 58 the tenant can deduct 3 shekels of silver from the the house rent as compensation for a repair made earlier. According to HSM 1899.2.141, the tenant occupied the house about 50 days before the document was written and had made some works in the previous year (*ina šatti maḫrītu*). The date of 10.V in this document might denote the beginning of the new rental year. In BM 109877 the tenant moved into the house 9 days before the contract was written. As the name of the house owner is not mentioned and

[211] Zadok 2009, 250, no. 14.

[212] Zadok 2009, 105, no. 682.

[213] Zadok 2009, 233, no. 134.

[214] Zadok 2009, 228. no. 156.

[215] BM 29036.

tenant rented the house "from himself" (*ul-tu rama-ni-šú*) he – presumably as the agent of the owner – decided first to enter the house and then to issue the document.

As already stressed, all these texts (with the exception of HSM 1899.2.141 dated to the first year of Nabonidus) date back to the Persian period. Yet, their limited number does not allow us to decide whether such conditions are typical for that period only. Although the background to such agreements is unknown, it seems that the owners of the leased houses had confidence in the tenants.

2. The majority of texts fix the term (day and month) when the tenant came into the possession of a house. In only few texts the tenant had use of the house from the date of signing the contract (five cases) or shortly after signing the contract: one day (two cases), two days (three cases), and three days (three cases). Quite often the time span was about one week, but longer periods were not infrequent, even to three or four weeks. Different circumstances influenced decisions of owners and tenants, but they are never explained in the documents.

Although the initial terms of the contracts varied, usually they have been in force since the very beginning of the month; later days are more rarely.

3. The majority of contracts with preserved data were signed in the first half of the Babylonian year. About two-thirds of the contracts known to me were signed in the first half of the calendar year and only one-third in the second half. I cannot find a good explanation for this phenomenon, although the influence of the climate cannot be ruled out. In the Babylonian calendar, the first half of the year is the warmer, facilitating moving to a new place of living.

4. In all documents where the formula *rēš-mišil* or *rēš-qīt* occurs, it denotes the first half and the second half of the rental year. The application of the formula *rēš-mišil* might be due to the lack in Akkadian of a term comprising half a year independent of the calendar year. It cannot be excluded that some scribes avoided using the formula,[216] conscious that it did not express precisely the actual state of the things.

In a few documents it may seem that the rent was paid in advance for a period a little over half a year or over one year, but this is not a case.[217] Such a situation occurs in Mich 56 "from the month Nisannu (I) of the ninth year to the end of month Tašrītu (VII) of the ninth year," (^{3}*ul-tu* iti.bár mu.9.kam ^{4}*a-di qí-it* iti.du$_6$ mu.9.kam), i.e. for seven months. However, it is possible that, as in the receipt from Sippar (discussed in the second part of the book), the scribe omitted <*qīt*> before Nisannu i.e. "from the <end> of Nisannu (*ul-tu*

[216] See the table above with the blank space in the penultimate column.

[217] I left out the settlement of the arrears for the longer period discussed above.

<*qí-it*> iti.bár), i.e. in fact from Ayāru, and the tenant paid only for half a year. In CUSAS 28, no. 98 (and its near duplicate in no. 99): the rent was paid for the period "from the month of Abu (V) of the fifth year to Abu (V) of the sixth year" of Cambyses, where the final month was presumably the end of the month of Du'uzu (IV). In CUSAS 28, no. 100 the rent was paid for the period "from the month Ulūlu (VI) of the first year to Ulūlu (VI) of the second year" of Bardiya (written Barziya), where again the final date has to be, in fact, the end of Abu (V). However, since the fifth year of Cambyses and the first year of Bardiya were intercalary years with the second Addaru month the payment comprised no less than 13 months.[218] As the period of payment was to be 12 months, to avoid future complications, the intercalary month was counted as part of the year and did not affect rent increase.

Note that in CUSAS 28, no. 98/99 the rent was not paid directly by the tenant to the owner of the house but to two persons acting in the name of the owner, while in CUSAS 28, no. 100 the rent was received directly by the owner. Both documents indicate that the rent was paid once a year in a cycle beginning about the middle of the year, the standard known from the Ebabbar temple. We do not know why the owners in CUSAS 28, no. 98/99 did not collect the rent personally; we might suspect that they did not live in Našar, where the documents were written and for this reason they decided to use an agent whose role was similar to that of *ša muḫḫi idi bītāte* in Sippar. Given that such a system was first in use in the Ebabbar temple, its influence on the relations between private contractors seems probable. Importantly, these documents testify that not only the temple, but sometimes also private house owners used the services of an agent who collected house rent from tenants.

2.2.8 Means of payment and frequency of payment

The rent was rarely paid in installments shorter than half a year. In a few texts the rent was paid on a monthly or even daily basis. When the payment was on a monthly basis, the rent was paid, like in the half-year system, in silver, while in all other cases where the rent was paid in some products (mostly bread,[219] exceptionally barley or even bricks) the daily payment was used.

It seems that the documents with an unusual form and period of payment might be divided into two groups. The first group includes these documents

[218] But sometimes the period of rental was in fact longer, see CUSAS 28, no. 5, where the slave was rented for the period from the 1st day of the month Abu (V) until the first day of the month Ulūlu (VI) of the ninth year of Nabonidus, i.e. for 13 months.

[219] Four such texts are mentioned in Jursa 2005, 31, n. 166 (BM 29291, BM 82744, no. 116, BM 96243 and VS 5, 145). More such texts are discussed below.

in which the decision to rent a house with an unusual form of payment was presumably caused by the personal situation of the owner. To the second group belong texts where the form of payment was presumably caused by an unusual political situation, or other reasons, such as climate changes (see below).

2.2.9 Monthly or daily payment and personal situation of the house owner

Only two such texts are known from Uruk, the first dated on the 28th of Šabāṭu, 22nd year of Nebuchadnezzar.[220] The south and east wing of a house with an upper storey or loft[221] of a house belonging to Bēl-iddin, son of Nabû-ēṭir was rented out by the lady fAmata. Her relation to the owner is not described, but since she rented the house without an order, or permission from the owner, it is likely he was no longer alive. This is also suggested by the presence of fKullâ, his or her daughter (written dumu.mi-*šú*) and the kind of payment. This means that the tenant wished to know that the agreement had been made with the acceptance of fAmata's daughter. The tenant of the house was Kī-Nabû, slave of Arad-Nabû, who rented the house for four years promising to pay 12 loaves of bread daily, i.e. about 4,320 annually, and half a shekel of silver annually, i.e. in total two shekels for four years. It is interesting that all persons mentioned in the document (apart from fKullâ and Ibni-Ištar, the second witness) bear the names atypical for traditional Urukaean families, but known for people from the north of the country. It is probable that both families came from the north and lived among northern migrants, carrying on commercial transactions among themselves.

Similar conditions occur in BM 29291 from Borsippa dated to the seventh or eighth year of Cyrus where the tenant Nabû-šum-ukīn, son of Nādinu, descendant of Ibnāyu, was to pay to the slave of the owner 4.5 shekels of silver annually and 20 loaves daily, i.e. ca. 7,200 loaves annually. Additionally, he was obliged to seal the roof and repair the footing of a wall.[222] BM 96243 dated to 11.II.Dar 20 (502 BC), also from Borsippa, belongs to the archive of the prebendary baker Šaddinnu, son of Balāssu, descendant of Bēliya'u.[223] The house described as *bīt kāri*, i.e. situated in the harbour district, was rented out to Iddin-Nabû, son of Ubār, descendant of Ninurta-ušallim for 20 loaves daily made of 1⅙ *qû* of flour. The size and weight of each of 20 loaves is unknown, however the total of about one litre of flour used suggests that each loaf was

---

220 GC 1, 35, cf. p. 22 in that volume and BR 6, no. 29.

221 It is not clear if the scribe had in mind a loft above two wings or only in the eastern wing.

222 Mentioned in Jursa 2005, 31, n. 166; see also Zadok 2009, 208, no. 467.

223 *Bēliya'u*, no. 187.

small. A similar text is VS 5, 145 = NRV 143 (undated). The house, like that mentioned above, is also described as *bīt kāri* and as *bīt qāti,* the latter term presumably denoting kind of storeroom. Similarly as in the text from Uruk, ᶠBaba-šarrat,[224] rented part of her house to Gûzu-Bēl-ṣabat, a slave of Šumā, son Ṣillaya of ⸢Šamaš?⸣-lūmur family, "for 3 *qû* of bread daily", i.e. for bread produced from 3 litres of flour. As no relatives of ᶠBaba-šarrat are mentioned and she act in her own name, we may suppose that also she was a widow, renting out part of the building to secure bread for herself, presumably the basis of her and her children's daily diet. The lack of witnesses and atypical stipulation that *baṭlu ul iššaknu*, "no interruption will occur" (without any real warranty), suggest that her relation with the owner of the slave must be close, probably her or her husband's relative. This suggests that the decision to rent part of the house was caused in stressing situation after the death of ᶠBaba-šarrat's husband, although her and her sons material position was certainly good.[225]

[224] She was wife of Ṭāb-ṣill-Marduk = Tābiya, son of Nabû-apla-iddin, descendant of Sîn-ili, attested in the period Nbk 35-Camb 7, see Jursa 2005, 69ff. with earlier literature.

[225] The couple had two daughters, who were adult and married before their father's death: ᶠAmat-Ninlil in or before Nbn 10 (VS 4, 46) while ᶠṬabluṭūtu in Nbn 8 or erlier as she occurs in DCS 130 (Joannès 1980, no. 1) as daughter-in-law of Marduk-zēr-ibni, son of Bēl-upaḫḫir, descendant of (Ea)-Eppēš-ilī, dated to this year. They had also four sons, the oldest Marduk-šumu-ibni and three younger: Nabû-ēṭir-napšāti, Nabû-balāssu-iqbi and Bēl-iddin, all mentioned with their names in VS 3, 115 = NRV 436, written in the 14th year of Darius. Cf. also VS 3, 166 = NRV 437 (Dar [x]), mentioning Marduk-šumu-ibni, Nabû-ēṭir-napšāti, Basia and Bēl-iddin, i.e. Basia is presumably a hypocoristicon of Nabû-balāssu-iqbi. Begininng from the 12th year of Nabonidus, i.e. after the death of Ṭabiya, husband of Baba-šarrat, their oldest son Marduk-šum-ibni began his activity acting also in the names of his brothers (but their names are not given until the 14th year of Darius): VS 6, 84 (cf. Sandowicz 2012, O. 50), VS 3, 54 = NRV 413 (Nbn 13); VS 4, 49 = NRV 540; VS 3, 62 = NRV 417 (Cyr 3); VS 3, 93 = NRV 425 (Dar 2); VS 3, 96 = NRV 426 (Dar 4); VS 3, 97 = NRV 427 (Dar 6); VS 3, 106 = NRV 433 (Dar 10) and VS 3, 116 = NRV 438 (Dar 15). All this documents makes sure that the material situation of Ṭabiya's sons was good. At the same time their mother ᶠBaba-šarrat acted independently, renting mentioned building for bread (VS 5, 145). In VS 6, 290 = NRV 627 she ordered repairing the house promising to pay 1 shekel for each 370 bricks to be laid. The contractor is obliged to perform any necessary work with bricks that appear in one year (*adi ṭuppi ṭuppi*). Also this document (undated) was certainly composed after the death of ᶠBaba-šarrat's husband. In VS 4, 199 = NRV 220 ᶠBaba-šarrat (here with her nickname ᶠBabunu) leased 3½ shekels of silver to a man and his wife, (she was the slave-women of Ṭabiya). Important is also VS 3, 56 = NRV 414 (Nbn 15) as according to which Baba-šarrat rented a cornfield obliging the tenant to pay rent according to her measurer (*ina mašīḫu ša ᶠBaba-šarrat*), clear proof of her independence. The last document is VS 3, 70 = NRV 251 (written in Camb 1, "King of Babylon", but presumably the second part of titulary "King of Lands" was omitted), a receipt of some amount of figs due to ᶠBaba-šarrat from part of an orchard. The documents suggests that Ṭabiya secured material independence of his wife, but nothing indicate that mutual relations of mother and sons were tense.

The next document is BM 82744, no. 116, written in the town of Bīt-Zēriya, which must have been located in the vicinity of Borsippa.[226] Although written on 15.X.Camb 7, the agreement was concluded earlier as *idi kāri* (denoting a rent for a house located presumably in the harbour district or *kāru*-storehouse) amounting to 1 *qû*[227] of bread daily comprised the period from the tenth of Kislīmu (IX) till an unknown day in the month of Šabāṭu (XI). The house was rented by Marduk-šum-ibni son of [Šu]lā, descendant of Ilīya to Šum-iddin,[228] son of <Ina>-tēšê-ēṭir, who should deliver 1 *qû* of bread (maybe only a part of the rent) to ᶠBaba-ilat, the daughter of Lābāši, presumably related in some way to the owner of a house.[229] Such a condition might be caused by the general situation in the country. While the data are poor, we know that the revolt of Bardiya began already at the end of the seventh year of Cambyses (Behistun §11) and that the rebel king was recognised in Babylonia no later than in the second month, the eighth year of Cambyses (April 522 BC). BM 82744, no. 116 dated to the 15th Ṭebētu, seventh year of Cambyses (i.e. mid-January 522 BC) might suggest that fear of the future was felt in Babylonia a few months earlier, already at the end of the seventh year of Cambyses.

GC 1 35 and VS 5, 145 suggest that the material situation of the women who rented out the houses was highly difficult and the only opportunity available to them was renting part of the house to secure a regular supply of bread. In both documents the agreements were concluded not with a free man, but with slaves, whom, as one might suppose, the owner ordered to bake the bread, or who might have acted on their own account.

It seems that the type of bread might be identified on the basis of the number of loaves to be delivered by the tenants on daily basis. The daily norm varied from 12 to 30 loaves. Such amount of bread can be linked with *kusāpu* bread. In the texts published by Zadok,[230] the following numbers of *kusīptu* loaves were issued each day:

2 *kusīptu*	once
10 *kusīptu*	18 times
15 *kusīptu*	once
20 *kusīptu*	17 times[231]

[226] Zadok 2009, 258, no. 62. The assumption is based on the fact that the family Ilīya and protagonist of the document Marduk-šum-ibni, son of [Šul]ā, his brothers and sister are well known from the Borsippa archive, see Waerzeggers 2010, 375, and 735, esp. 736f.

[227] Not 9 *qû* as in Zadok 2009, 258, no. 62.

[228] Not Šamaš-iddin as in Zadok, 258, no. 62.

[229] ⁶ᶠᵈ*ba-ba*$_6$*-i-lat* dumu.mí-*su šá* ᵐ*la-ba-ši* ⁷*là*-igi ᵐmu-mu a-*šú šá* ᵐsùḫ-sur ⁸*ta-ka-al*.

[230] Zadok 2005/2006.

[231] One time (BM 96519 = no. 99) a payment of 20 *kusīpt*u per month is not taken into account here.

21 *kusīptu*	2 times
30 *kusīptu*	7 times[232]
40 *kusīptu*	2 times?[233]
50 *kusīptu*	2 times[234]
60 *kusīptu*	2 times[235]
70 *kusīptu*	once
84 *kusīptu*	once
100 *kusīptu*	once

As we can see, a norm of 10 *kusīptu* (16 cases) and 20 *kusīptu* daily (17 cases) was most common, i.e. similar to the amount known from the above discussed contracts. We may imagine that a smaller amount of bread daily was destined for a single person with a larger number for a family. Much larger numbers: 40, 50, 60, 70 or even 84 and 100 *kusīptu* which occur in the texts edited by Zadok are rare, usually accuring only once. There is reason to think that such large amounts were destined for large groups of workers, as in BM 94889 = Zadok 2005/2006, no. 194 where 84 *kusīptu* of bread was destined for the house of specialised craftsmen (*bīt ummanī*).

There are a few texts in which the payment of rent is in another commodity, most often in barley. According to ZA 3, no. 16, no. 135: 4 dated to Šamaš-erība 0 (484 BC),[236] a reed hut (*bīt ḫuṣṣu*) located in Babylon was rented by Nidinti-Bēl, son of Marduk-nāṣir-apli, descendant of Egibi to Nabû-balāṭu-ēreš, son of Ana-Bēl-upāqu, descendant of Rē'û for 3 *qû* of barley daily, i.e. 3 *kurru* annually. Payment of 2 *kurru* of barley annually as rent for the house occurs in a badly preserved document from Borsippa dated to the accession year of Cambyses (530 BC).[237] The same amount occurs in BE 9, 54: 3 written in Nippur on 20.IX.Art 37. This concerns the rental of a house or the storeroom (*bīt kāri*) located at the Sailor Gate (*bāb malāḫu*) by the Persian Tirikam,[238]

[232] Or maybe one or two less as in BM 96516 = no. 175 the word *kusīptu* is almost completely destroyed, although taking into account the number the reconstructions seems probable and in BM 22361 = no. 162 the number is read by Zadok 30+[10].

[233] Cf. commentary to BM 22217 = no. 15.

[234] In BM 96548 = no. 35, the number is reconstructed.

[235] Or maybe only one time as in BM 29607 = no. 101 the reading is uncertain.

[236] For the dating the revolt of Bēl-šimānni and Šamaš-erība to the second year of Xerxes (484 BC), see Waerzeggers 2003/2004.

[237] BM 25832 (Zadok 2009, 117, no. 886).

[238] For etymology of this name, see Tavernier 2007, 325, 4.2.1704, and Zadok 2009a, 302, no. 525a, both with full bibliography.

son of Bagapanu,[239] to Mannu-lū-šulum, the slave of the priest (lúkid.bar) for 2 *kurru* of barley per year but paid 5 *sūtu* or 30 *qû* per month.

In Nbn 261, written in Babylon on 13.VII.Nbn 7 (549 BC) the tenant Nabû-ušallim, son of Īnēya,[240] who rented a house from Marduk-šum-iddin, son of Šāpik-zēri, descendant of Saggilaya for five years for five shekels annually is obligated to deliver additionally to the owner one hundred strings of onions and one hundred strings of garlic. According to CUSAS 28, no. 46 (Dar [x]) the tenant should pay 10 shekels annually and maybe 3 baskets of herbs, but the last data is reconstructed and uncertain. In all the above texts it is difficult to detect a general reason for such type of payment; the term resulted presumably from the personal situation of the owner.

2.2.10 Impact of political (economic) crisis on means of payment and frequency of payment of house rent

In her commentary to VS 5, 59 = NRV 115 = Baker 2004, no. 115, Heather Baker suggested that monthly payment of rent in silver might be explained by the short duration of only three months of the contract,[241] but it seems that the reason should be sought elsewhere. An alternative explanation may be found when we look at the dates of the conclusion of the contracts:[242]

Text	Date	Year BC	Form of payment	Frequency	City
Nrg 72	[x].XIIb.Nrg [3]	557	silver + [x]	monthly, daily	Sippar
VS 5, 23, no. 109 = NRV 113	9.II.Nbn 4	552	silver	monthly	Borsippa
YOS 6, 85 = BR 6, 30	[x].X.Nbn 4	552	silver	monthly	Uruk
Nbn 499, no. 111	1.II.Nbn 11	545	bread	daily	Babylon
Nbn 500, no. 112	2.II.Nbn 11	545	silver	monthly	Babylon

[239] For Bagapanu, see Tavernier 2007, 137, 4.2.274 and Zadok 2009a, 143, no. 196, both with full bibliography.

[240] miginé-ya, a hypocoristicon from Itti-DN-īnēya, or Itti-šarri-īnēya, see NBN, 79. Cf. the name Itti-Nabû-ēnāya known from the Neo-Assyrian period (see PNAE 2/I, 589).

[241] Baker 2004, 191.

[242] Undated documents, such as VS 5, 134 and VS 5, 145 are omitted in this list.

NBC 8345 = YOS 19, 10 = Joannès 1989, p. 341	28.IV.Nbn 11	545	silver	monthly	Borsippa
BM 65288, no. 113	27.VIII.Nbn 11	545	bread	daily	<Babylon>
A 105 = Joannès 1989, 273-4	6.XII? Nbn 11	545	bricks	daily	Borsippa
Cyr 231	[x].VI.Cyr 6	533	silver	for the whole year in advance	Babylon
Cam 213, no. 115	15.XI.Camb 3	527	bread	daily	Babylon
CUSAS 28, no. 98/99	8.V.Camb 5	525	silver	for the whole year in advance	Našar
BM 82744, no. 116	15.X.Camb 7	523	bread?	daily	Bīt-Zēriya[243]
CUSAS 28, no. 100	9.VI.Bar 1	522	silver	for the whole year in advance	Našar
BRM 1, 43	11.VI.Nbk IV, 1	521	silver	monthly	Borsippa
L. 1667 = Joannès 1989, pp. 252-3	19.VI.Nbk IV, 1	521	silver	monthly	Borsippa
VS 5, 59 = Baker 2004, no. 115	27.X.Dar 1	521	silver	monthly	Babylon
Dar 60, no. 118	9.I.Dar 3	519	bread	daily	Babylon
VS 5, 67, no. 119	7.X.Dar 5	517	silver	monthly	Borsippa
VS 4, 129 = Baker 2004, no. 117	28.V.Dar 10	512	silver	monthly[244]	Babylon

[243] In the vicinity of Borsippa.

[244] For the interpretation, see below.

Dar 275	18.VI.Dar 10	512	bread	daily	Babylon
TCL 13, 187	5.IX.Dar 10	512	bread	daily	Babylon
MR 95	5.III.Dar 16	506	<silver?>	for the whole year in advance	Sippar
BE 8/1, 112	12.VIII.Dar 16	506	silver	monthly	Babylon
Abraham 2004, no. 86	19.[IX].Dar [36]	486	barley?	Daily	[Babylon]
BM 74476, no. 131	17.II.Xer 1	485	silver	yearly	Sippar
BM 33980, no. 133 = Bertin 2851	13.IV.Xer 2*	484	barley	yearly	Babylon
ZA 3, no. 16, no. 135	22.VII.Š-e 0	484	barley	Daily	Babylon

The earliest text is Nrg 72,[245] from Sippar, dated to the intercalary month of the [third] year of Neriglissar. The reconstruction of year is certain, since although the Addaru intercalary month is known both from the accession and the third year of the king,[246] only the latter possibility is acceptable, because at the end of l. 12 there is enough space for mu.[3.kam] but not for mu.[sag.nam.lugal.la]. According to this text, Saggilu, son of Nādin-aḫi, descendant of Bēl-ēṭeru rented out his house to Mukkēa, son of Šamaš-rīṣūa for 1/8 shekels monthly (1.5 shekels yearly) and maybe bread, daily.[247] Since the contract was signed at the very end of the third year of Neriglissar, who lost the throne at the very beginning of the following year, in the month of Nisannu, it cannot be excluded that this kind of payment was caused by political instability.

Such an explanation seems certain in cases of texts composed in the time of Cambyses and in the following years. In CUSAS 28, no. 98/99 written on 8.V.Camb 5 the tenant has paid 2 shekels of silver in advance for the whole

[245] Evetts 1892, Nrg 72 and Sack 1994, no. 72.

[246] See Parker and Dubberstein 1956, 28-29.

[247] The same number of loaves daily occurs in the contract from Uruk, dated to the 22nd year of Nebuchadnezzar. For loaves of bread paid daily, see above, p. 70.

year beginning from V.Camb 5 till V.Camb 6.[248] It seems likely that this exceptional rent payment period occurred at the time of Cambyses' expedition against Egypt. The text from 523 BC (preceding year: death of Cambyses and the revolt of Bardiya) and texts from the following years placed against the background of political events are provided with a plausible explanation for their form. CUSAS 28, 100 written on 9.VI.Bar 1 with the payment of 2¾ shekels for the period from VI.Bar 1 until VI. Bar 2[249] comes at the time of growing turmoil in Persia and her Babylonian province. Although Babylonia recognised Bardiya as the successor of Cambyses, political instability continued: the uprisings of Nebuchadnezzar III and Nebuchadnezzar IV (at the very end of 522 or beginning of 521) and finally the intervention of Darius' army in Babylonia, the defeat of the rebels at the battle of Zazannu, and the siege and capture of Babylon.[250] The political situation migh have affected the decisions of both contracting parties. Presumably house owners insisted on payment of rent for the whole period: only three months in VS 5, 59, or – according to the standard – for half a year in advance in two other documents BRM 1, 43 and L. 1667. Such a solution would be unacceptable for the tenant, unwilling to pay for a longer period in an extremely unsettled situation, and so an intermediate solution, i.e. the payment in monthly installments was eventually adopted.

A similar reason for paying a monthly rent may have occurred in two texts VS 5, 23, no. 109 and YOS 6, 85,[251] dated to the fourth year of Nabonidus (552 BC), i.e. the year when the king left Babylonia and stayed in Teima for the next ten years. Here also settling for a monthly rent points to the atmosphere of uncertainty in the north (Borsippa), but also in the south (Uruk) of the country, and presumably in other cities, including the capital. Addtionally, in VS 5, 23, no. 109 both tenants commited themselves not to pay the rent without the presence of ^{f}Qunnabatu,[252] whose relation to the owner is unknown. As the first text is dated to the second month and the second to the tenth month, this suggests that the state of insecurity persisted for almost the whole year.

Likewise, a relationship between system of payment and political situation is suggested in the case of the document dated to 484 BC (ZA 3, no. 16, no. 135). An interpretation of this document will be preceded by the discussion

[248] Actually to the end of month Ayaru (IV).

[249] Actually to the end of month Abu (V).

[250] Zawadzki 1994a, 1995, 1995a, 1995b; Lorenz 2008, 5-35; Jursa in YOS 21, 19-21; Beaulieu 2014a.

[251] Cf. BR 6, no. 30.

[252] *šá la ^{f}qu-un-na-ba-tu$_4$(...) ul i-nam-di-nu*, "without the presence of ^{f}Qunnabātu (...) they will not pay."

of four other documents[253] concerning presumably the same reed hut. Such identification is suggested by fact that the house[254] laid adjacent to the house of Sūqaya[255] and lady Rašattu.[256]

The oldest document BM 42393, no. 128 was written on 15th Du'uzu,[257] 36th year of Darius I (486 BC). In this document the contractors are Nidinti-Bēl, son of Marduk-nāṣir-apli, descendant of Egibi and Itti-Šamaš-balāṭu, son of Šadûnu, descendant of Eppēš-ilī. Itti-Šamaš-balāṭu rented the reed hut (*bīt ḫuṣṣu*) adjacent to the houses of Sūqaya and ᶠRašattu on terms customary for a stable political situation: he was to pay 14 shekels of white silver per year, divided into two half-year periods (with the first half paid in advance); he was also responsible for renewing the roof, repairing the footing of a wall and the payment of *nūptu*. Important, however, is that the tenant paid the rent for half a year in advance.

The next document BM 33966, no. 129 was written on the fifth Abu 36th year of Darius, i.e. only 20 days later. As the house was identified as the reed hut and laid adjacent to the houses of Sūqaya and ᶠRašattu it is certain that it was the same property. According to this tablet Nidinti-Bēl, the husband of ᶠŠušannu, daughter of Rēmut-Bēl rented out the reed house at the order of

253 BM 33966, no. 129; CT 51, 54. no. 130 and 42393, no. 124 from 486 BC (36th year of Darius I) and BM 33979, no. 134 from 484 BC (2nd* year of Xerxes; for such dating of this document, see below, n. 265), i.e. from the same year as ZA 3, no. 16, no. 135 dated to the accession year of Šamaš-erība (484 BC).

254 This opinion was expressed already by Wunsch 2003/2004, 239, who adds also BM 33980, no. 133; however the location of this house (adjacent to that of Ša-Nabû-šū and the passage of *Nergal-ša-ḫadê*) makes such identification doubtful.

255 Sūqaya is also present in ZA 3, no. 16: 1, copied as kur and read Šadai in the editio princeps by Strassmaier. Although the sign resembles kur more than sila the proper reading is established by comparison with BM 42393: 1 where the name occurs in similar context as owner of the house adjacent to the same reed hut which is also adjacent to the house of lady ᶠRašattu, and where the name is written syllabically *Su-qa-a-a*. Note that in ZA 3, no. 16: 2 the scribe omitted the female determinative before the name of ᶠRašattu, which hampered the understanding of the text. No text known to me gives any information that Sūqaya and fRašattu belonged to the Egibi family or were the relatives of Nidinti-Bēl.

The reading of the month in l. 21 deserves comment. Wunsch 2003/2004, 239 reads iti.kin = Ulūlu which, in my opinion, cannot be accepted. Note that the same shape of the sign occurs in l. 8, where *nūptu* for Nisannu (I), Du'uzu (IV) and Kislīmu (IX) is mentioned and *nūptu* paid for the month after Nisannu (I) and before Kislīmu (IX) was always paid in Du'uzu (IV), Sūqaya.

256 The etymology of the name is unclear to me. The reading Ramattu cannot be excluded, although it is doubtful; for similar names, Ramateia and Ramatî, see PNAE, vol. 3, Part I, 1031f.

257 The reading of the month in l. 21 deserves comment. Wunsch 2003/2004, 239 reads iti.kin = Ulūlu which, in my opinion, cannot be accepted. Note that the same shape of the sign occurs in l. 8, where *nūptu* for Nisannu (I), Du'uzu (IV) and Kislīmu (IX) is mentioned and *nūptu* paid for the month after Nisannu (I) and before Kislīmu (IX) was always paid in Du'uzu (IV), not in Ulūlu (VI). It means the month in 8 and 21 should be read iti.šu, in accordance with the shape of the sign.

fŠušannu,[258] to the lady fAmat-Nanāya, the daughter of Abdi-Esi[259] on almost the same terms as in the previous document with only one change: the yearly rent was a little lower, exactly 13 shekels yearly, one shekel less. As in the previous document, fAmat-Nanāya paid the rent to Rēmut-Bēl for half a year in advance. The contract was signed on the fifth day of Abu but was valid "from the month Abu" (l. 8), which suggests that fAmat-Nanāya entered the house already before signing the contract. The contractors agreed that the contract would be valid *adi ṭuppi ṭuppi*, according to the interpretation of the idiom by Baker, for one year.[260] This means that the previous contract was cancelled. Even though Itti-Šamaš-balāṭu paid for half a year in advance, the reed hut was taken away from him after only about two weeks. The text does not mention if Itti-Šamaš-balāṭu received any compensation for breaking the contract.

Only two days later, on the seventh Abu a new contract CT 51, 54, no. 130 was signed by Nidinti-Bēl,[261] again with Itti-Šamaš-balāṭu, son of Šadûnu, descendant of Eppēš-ilī. Although the house is described only by the term *bītu* (é), the facts that it laid adjacent to the house of Sūqaya[262] and the rent was the same (14 shekels of white silver yearly) makes it certain that the same reed hut was the object of the new contract. This means that Nidinti-Bēl invalidated the contract concluded with fAmat-Nanāya (despite the fact that fAmat-Nanāya paid the rent for half a year in advance) and rented it again to Itti-Šamaš-balāṭu. It is interesting that the new contract did not repeat all the previous terms (to care for roof, the footing and *nūptu*), presumably because both contractors treated this document as a return to the previous agreement. The repeated formula stating that Itti-Šamaš-balāṭu paid the rent for half a year might be interpreted as a confirmation of the fact that the rent had already been paid in contract BM 42393, no. 128. More surprising is the clause that if Nidinti-Bēl returns (*ú-te-e-ri*) the silver to Itti-Šamaš-balāṭu, then Itti-Šamaš-balāṭu would release (*un-taš-šir*) the house to Nidinti-Bēl, i.e. also this contract would be invalidated! I cannot find the reason for such a stipulation, so evidently unfavourable to Itti-Šamaš-balāṭu.

The reasons for the invalidation of the first contract, and the surprising provision in CT 51, 54, no. 130 are equally unknown. The contract suggests that

---

258 Presumably with her knowledge.

259 "Servant of Isis." For other names with this element, see CUSAS 28, no. 42 (fBaḫi-Esi, "desired by Isis.") The name of her father suggests that she had an Egyptian background, while the fully Babylonian name of his daughter shows that she was at least to some degree acculturated.

260 Baker 2010.

261 In this document the name is abbreviated to Nidintu and his father is introduced with his nickname Širku.

262 Note that in this text and in BM 33979, no. 134 Sūqaya is mentioned, but fRašattu is missing, but this is accidental as she occurs in the latest text in this dossier, ZA 3, no. 16, no. 135.

there was distrust between the spouses, but it cannot be excluded that the cause might also have been the political situation at Babylon in the last year of Darius' reign (486 BC). This is suggested by Abraham 2004, no. 86, written presumably on the 19th [Kislīmu], thirty-third year of Darius I. The reconstruction of the month is suggested by l. 9 stating that the tenant should deliver bread beginning from the 20th day of the month Kislīmu (IX), to the month [x] of 36th year. Since the name of Darius I is preserved in the dating, it seems certain that the document was written in the thirty-sixth year, that of the king's death. Since we know that the gap between the day when the document was written and the day when the tenant moved into the house was usually short, in general less than one month, the document must have been written in the month of Kislīmu. The 36th year was the year of Darius' death, i.e. the document must have been signed before his death.[263] An additional argument for such interpretation is that the house was rented for quite a short time, from the 20th Kislīmu (IX) till the end of the month [x] of thirty-sixth year, i.e. if [x] means [Addaru] no longer than a little over three months. Again, payment in bread is presumably related to the upcoming change on the Persian throne, always a period of uncertainty.

The next text with atypical rent payment period is dated to the beginning of the first year of Xerxes (485 BC). According to it – BM 74476, no. 131 – written on 17.II.Xer 1 the tenant paid to the owner, Ḫandaukku, son of Zimaga' 25 shekels of white silver as the rent for a house for the period from 1.III.Xer 1 till <end> of II.Xer 2. Handaukku, evidently of non-Babylonian origin and maybe associated with Persian court, recognised the poliltical situation as unstable and demanded (and received) the rent for whole year in advance.

The text BM 33980, no. 133 dated to 13 Du'uzu Xer 1 (485 BC) presumably relates to a different house of Nidinti-Bēl as it is adjacent to the house of Ša-Nabû-šū and the walkway (*mūtaq*) *Nergal-ša-ḫadê*.[264] The house (*bītu*) is rented out to Bēl-ēṭir, son of Mušēzib for two years for 10 *kurru* of barley yearly with typical conditions and two additional provisions: a fine for breaking the contract and the responsibility of the guarantor for breaking the contract by the tenant. These conditions again might reflect instability, but it is surprising that the contract was concluded for two years and the tenant accepted an obligation to take care of the house and pay *nūptu*.

Two contracts from 484 BC present quite a different picture. The first is BM 33979, no. 134 written on 21st Du'uzu Xer 2.[265] The house adjacent to the

[263] Concerning the time of death of Darius I, see Stolper 1989, 303-305, Zawadzki 1992 and Zawadzki forthcoming note 4.

[264] Neither Sūqaya nor Rašattu is mentioned here; the previous texts did not mention *mūtaq Nergal-ša-ḫadê* to which the house is adjacent.

[265] Wunsch 2003/2004, 239 and Wunsch 2000, 11, n. 56 suggest that the text was written in Xer 1. This opinion is accepted by Waerzeggers 2003/2004, 170 and Abraham 2004, 14, n. 21. According to

house of Sūqaya was rented out by Nidinti-Bēl to Bēl-šimānni, the oblate of Marduk for 13 shekels of silver yearly, under the typical conditions discussed above.[266] Only payment for half a year in advance might be seen as a symptom of instability. More symptoms are present in the second text, ZA 3, no. 16, no. 135, which concerns the same reed house, rented out on the 27th day of Tašrītu, i.e. only three months and one week after BM 33979, no. 134 was written. It means that the contract with Bēl-šimānni, the oblate of Marduk, had been invalidated, despite the fact that he (like ᶠAmat-Nanāya earlier) paid rent for half a year in advance. The new tenant Nabû-ēreš, son of Bēl-upāqu, descendant of Rē'û pledged to pay to the owner not silver but 3 *qû* of barley daily. The instable situation is suggested by a solemn declaration of the tenant that no interruption in barley payments would occur.

Summing up: the above analysis shows that already in the last years of Darius' reign signs of instability occurred and growing fear of the future could be seen especially in concluding and invalidating contracts, occurrence of additional guaranties (payment in advance, payment in barley, a fine to be paid in case of breaking the contract (*nabalkattānu*-clause), a solemn declaration not to interrupt the payment – all this clearly corresponds to instability in the country. Especially in 484 BC the situation should be related to political events. This is the year of the uprising of Bēl-šimānni (in the months of Abu (V) and Ulūlu (VI)) and Šamaš-erība (from the beginning of the month of Abu (V) till the month of Tašrītu (VII)).[267] The last document suggests that anxiety or the fear of lack of food affected even rich people, such as Nidinti-Bēl, son of Marduk-nāṣir-apli of the Egibi, head of the last, fifth generation of this famous family. As we see, even he, the chief of a powerful and affluent family, decided to secure his basic needs by providing himself and his family with bread made from 3 *qû* of flour daily. The fear of suppression of the revolt was not unfounded: after the collapse of the revolt, the Egibi family disappeared.[268] Presumably the Egibi family actively partcipated in the uprising and after its suppression was deprived of its property; Nidinti-Bēl might even have been killed.

The data from the eleventh year of Nabonidus is the most difficult to interpret because – apart from a fragment of the *Chronicle* according to which the *akītu* festival was not performed – there are no reports about the events

Wunsch 2000, 11, n. 56 "die Jahreszahl is über eine "10" geschrieben." In fact over one vertical wedge bent slightly to the left (which is typical writing of this time) two vertical wedges are clearly seen, i.e. the text was actually composed in the 2nd year of Xerxes, the year of uprising of Šamaš-erība.

[266] Ll. 11-12 concern presumably another stipulation, which – because of the damage to the text – is not clear to me. The verb [*i*]*p-pu-uš* at the end of l. 12 suggests that something should be done there, but maybe by the owner.

[267] Waerzeggers 2003-2004, 152-156.

[268] The discussed document is the last one in which Nidinti-Bēl is present.

of that year. Assuming that the payment at short intervals and in other means than silver points to an exceptional situation in the city or country, the texts suggest that this situation lasted quite long, almost from the beginning to the end of the 11th year.

The earliest document – Nbn 499, no. 111[269] from Babylon – concerns the rental of *bīt asuppu* and *bīt kāri ša* [lú]*nuḫatimmi* (an outbuilding and the baker's storehouse).[270] The buildings belonged to a certain Šušranni-Marduk, son of Marduk-šum-uṣur of the Adad-šum-ēreš family, but the decision to lease was taken by Šaridu, his grandfather, who rented them to Bēl-ṣullê-šeme, a slave of Bēl-aḫḫē-iddin of the Egibi family. The tenant was obliged to pay him 2 *qû* of bread daily. The mere fact of the payment of rent in bread indicates an extraordinary situation in Babylon in the month of Ayāru. The contract was concluded for an indefinite period, which allowed both contractors to withdraw from it at any time. The tenant was not obliged to carry out any repairs or to pay *nūptu*, which means that the terms of the contract were very favourable for him.

In Nbn 500, no. 112, written a day later, there occurs a house of a high standard, as the annual rent was established at 35 shekels. However, the contract was signed *adi ṭuppišu*, only for one year. The tenant was obliged also to pay the owner two *sellu* baskets of herbs, each worth 1 *qû*. Additionally, the lack of any mention of *nūptu* – the additional payment – suggests that the tenant was not obliged to pay it. Although the tenant was obliged to repair the roof and wall footing, it is stressed that – unlike in other contracts – the costs were borne entirely by the house owner.

Similarly favourable terms of contract were obtained by a woman, tenant of a house in NBC 8345.[271] The rent was low, only 2½ shekels annually, and here also the costs of repairs rested with the owner; nor was the tenant obliged to pay *nūptu*.

The last text from this year – A 105 – is atypical, because it is our only record of house rent paid in bricks, 44 each day, i.e. about 1,200 bricks monthly.[272] Maybe such a form and time of payment was caused by the owner's plan to renovate an old building or build a new one; however, it might equally be that it resulted from the tenant's difficult situation, who wished to rent a house but had neither silver nor bread at his disposal. One can imagine a situation when the owner of the house had no more favourable offer and decided to accept such atypical payment rather than receive none. Such an interpretation is supported by the fact that the tenant was not obliged to care for the house

[269] Meissner and Tallqvist 1890, 117f.

[270] Ll. 18-19 record that together with *bīt kāri* the tenant received also a reed hut.

[271] YOS 19, 10 = Joannès 1989, 341.

[272] The owner of the house occurs already in NBC 8345 written a few months earlier.

or pay *nūptu*. Payment in bricks suggests that the tenant manufactured bricks, but the daily payment indicates the fear of the owner that problems with the collection of the payment might develop.

In this context it is worth quoting the highly interesting document BM 65288, no. 113, although it does not concern a house rental (among other things, it lacks witnesses list) but is a family agreement between Munaḫḫiš-Marduk, son of Itti-Marduk-balāṭu, with ᶠKabtiya, his daughter and with his slave. Under the agreement Munaḫḫiš-Marduk will receive *mandattu* and 1 *kurru* (= 180 *qû*) of bread to the amount of 1 *qû* daily beginning from the first of Kislīmu (IX), i.e. for the next 180 days, or half a year. The term *mandattu* is applied to a fee paid by a slave (temple or private) to the owner if he acted independently. Unusual is that the daughter of Munaḫḫiš-Marduk and his slave guarantee each other not only in that they will fulfil their personal duty, but also take responsibility for the other's obligation if unfulfilled. The agreement was signed in the presence of Iddin-Nabû, brother of Munaḫḫiš-Marduk, and uncle of ᶠKabtiya, which means that also he accepted the condition.[273] Evidently this document also points to an extraordinary situation and fear of difficulties about getting food.

Although in documents from Babylon and Borsippa from the eleventh year of Nabonidus there is no reason given for non-standard agreements that favour tenants while securing the owners' assets better, it seems that such information does occur in a document from Uruk, YOS 6, 154.[274] According to it, ᶠBānat-Innin, the daughter of Nergal-iddin declared to the assembly of Eanna that she was widowed, and because of the famine in the country (⁶*su-un-qa* ⁷*ina ma-a-ta šá-kin-ma*) she had marked her two small sons (*ṣaḫarūtu*) with a star (a symbol of the property of Ištar of Uruk) and given them to the Lady of Uruk as her *širku*s on condition that the temple provide them with food to survive. Based on royal inscriptions, in Beaulieu's opinion, the crisis "lasted for a long time and was prevalent all over Babylonia." It is not certain if the shortages of food affected only the south of the country, but the texts analyzed here indicate that the fear of such shortfalls (confirmed by YOS 6, 154) also occured in the north of the country. It seems that food shortages and famine resulted from poor rainfall and the lowering of water levels in the main rivers and canals, reducing the area under cultivation. This is stressed by inscriptions from Harran composed after the return of Nabonidus from Teima

[273] Munaḫḫiš-Marduk occurs only in the second year of Nabonidus in the document written in Babylon concerning the purchase of a house located in Borsippa, see Nbn 85 (Liv. 61), last edition in Wunsch 1993, no. 109.

[274] For transliteration and translation Dougherty 1923, 33; cf. Oppenheim 1955, 72, Dandamayev 1984, 484 and Beaulieu 1989, 202 (ll. 5-15).

that, "Adad, the canal keeper of heaven and the underworld" provided people with rain and Ea "opened his underground springs."[275]

Summing up: the owners of the houses under lease had great difficulty in the eleventh year of Nabonidus in concluding lease contracts on favourable terms. The tenants did not pay *nūptu* and were free from the obligation to take care of repairs, or – if they did such work – the owner paid the costs in full. The payment of rent for short periods (silver – monthly, bread and bricks – daily) points out the extreme uncertainty, and, in the case of bread, real need. It follows that some individuals feared major food shortage. The terms of contract reveal uncertainty about what might happen and fear whether the concluded contract would be adhered to, or even executed at all.

The next document with unusual conditions of rent payment is Cyr 231, written in Ulūlu, Cyr 6 (533 BC).[276] In ll. 13-14 we read that kù.babbar *i-di* é-*šú šá a-di qí-it šá* iti.ne/*šá* mu.7.kam ᵐ*ku-raš* lugal e[ki] lugal kur.kur ᵐmu-ᵈamar.utu *ina* šu[ii] ᵐ*ḫad-da-a e-ṭir*, "silver, the rent of the house to the end of month Abu Iddin-Marduk has received from Ḫaddaya," i.e. the rent was paid in advance for the whole year, including *kīnajātu* offering.[277] Since we know nothing about the political and economic situation in Babylonia as well as in Persia at that point, the reason of concluding a contract under such condition cannot be established.

Documents with unusual forms of payment are also known from the third, fifth, and tenth years of Darius. In the first, Dar 60, no. 118, written in Babylon in the third year (519 BC) Nabû-nāṣir-apli, son of Itti-Marduk-balāṭu acting also in the names of his brothers, i.e. before the division of the assets of their deceased father,[278] rented out their *kāru*-storehouse to Bēl-uballiṭ, son of Nabû-ēṭir-napšāti, descendant of Atkuppu, whose house laid adjacent to the storehouse for 4 *qû* of bread daily, without any of the additional obligations discussed above. The lack of any additional obligation for the tenants is surprising and may suggest an extraordinary situation.

VS 5, 67, no. 119 written in Borsippa in the fifth year of Darius (517 BC). Šaddinu, son of Balāssu of the Bēliya'u family, rented out his house for two years for 13 shekels annually to Balāssu, son of Šulā of the Ea-ibni family. The usual obligation to care for the house rested with the tenant, who also had to pay *nūptu* for the day of Bēl and *kīnajātu*. In general, such terms were typical,

[275] Inscriptions 13 and 14 in Beaulieu 1989, 32-33.

[276] For edition, see Wunsch 1993, no. 303; cf. Jursa 1995/96, 261 for the reading of the name of the tenant.

[277] According to the reading of Wunsch. Note, however, that 2 baskets of *tabilu*-herbs for each year should be paid (*inamdin*) later.

[278] Dar 379.

and the only deviation from the standard is the monthly payment of rent. As all other duties fell on the tenant, nothing suggests that there was any major reason underlying such a decision; it is more probable that the tenant was unable to pay the rent in advance for half a year, as was the custom, and the owner decided to meet him half way and accepted a monthly payment. Such an interpretation of this document is possible but uncertain, because we do not have the necessary knowledge of the events of that time.[279]

Three documents were written in Babylon in the tenth year of Darius (512 BC): in one the rent in silver, in two in bread. The first is VS 4, 129 (Baker 2004, no. 117), written on 28th of Abu, recognised by scholars as a receipt for a house rented out by Iddin-Nabû, son of Nabû-bān-zēri, descendant of Nappāḫu to Nabû-mušētiq-uddê, son of Šāpik-zēri, descendant of Miṣiraya.[280] Only Baker stressed the unusual clause according to which 1½ shekels of silver belonging to the tenant are at the disposal of the owner (1½ gín kù.babbar babbar-*ú* *šá* mdag-*mu*-dib-ud.da 8*ina* igi msum-*na*-dag). The comparison of this silver amount with the earlier contract CTMMA 3, 97 between the same partners, with rent equal to 18 shekels of silver per year, makes certain that 1½ shekels of silver is equal to sum due for one month, i.e. the rent did not change. This means that in VS 4, 129 the tenant paid rent for half a year, from Simānu (III) till Araḫsamna (VIII), and additionally one month in advance.[281] In such a situation we can understand why the owner forced the tenant to swear an oath obliging him to carry repairs to the house. Evidently, according to the owner, the tenant not only paid the rent with a half-year delay, but also did not carry out the needed repair at that time.

The next is Dar 275 written on the 18th of Ulūlu.[282] According to it, Šamaš-iddin, a slave of Itti-Marduk-balāṭu, son of Nabû-aḫḫē-iddin, descendant of Egibi, acting as his master's agent, rented a house to Ša-Bēl-bani, the slave of Nidintu, son of Iddiya for two years for 2 *qû* of bread daily. He (Ša-Bēl-bani) was responsible for the payment of rent(?),[283] but according to the next sentence the house was at "their disposal", i.e. presumably the slave and his master Nidintu. Two things are surprising, i.e. that the main role in the contract seems to be played by a slave, not his master, and the lack of mention of any other obligation on the tenant(s).

---

[279] Cf. Briant 2002, 141: "for the years 518-517, historians find themselves in a difficult situation. It is virtually impossible to compose a continuous narrative".

[280] See, the commentaries to editions NRV 3, 123; CTMMA 3, 97 and Baker 2004, no. 117.

[281] For similar payment of debt and for one month in advance, see VS 4, 99 = NRV 117.

[282] For transliteration and translation, see Dandamayev 1994, 706, no. 81 and 341f.

[283] Note, however, the atypical expression: *maṣṣartu ša sūti inaṣṣar*, "he will care of the *sūtu* payment," while *idu* is expected instead of *sūtu*.

The third is TCL 13, 187 written in Babylon on the fifth day of Kislīmu (IX). Lābāši, son of Bēl-uballissu rented his house to Bēl-uballiṭ, son of Bēl-ittannu for 3 *qû* of bread (for making) 6 (loaves) from (each) 1 *qû* of (flour) of the best quality.[284] The tenant promised that if he caused any interruption he would pay an indemnity.[285] Additionally the tenant should pay *nūptu*, while either partner who breaks the contract before the expiry of two years would pay a penalty of 10 shekels. After this, it is again repeated that Bēl-uballiṭ was obliged to deliver food to Lābāši.

Unfortunately, we do not know what happened in Babylonia in 519 and 512 BC, but the question is whether daily payment of rent in bread or monthly in silver do not indicate exceptional situation similar to those for 552, 545, 521 and 484 BC. At least in the case of Dar 275, it is difficult to assume that, even in an extraordinary situation, Itti-Marduka-balāṭu would be threatened by the lack of food; rather it might reflect the deep insecurity that troubled even the head of family of such wealth.

The standard way of payment (two installments yearly) was also abandoned in two documents dated to the 16th year of Darius (506 BC). According to the receipt MR 95 from Sippar written on fifth Simānu (III) Marduk-rēmanni, son Bēl-uballiṭ of the Ṣāḫit-sattukki has received house rent from the tenant, Šamaš-iddin, son of Nabû-šum-iškun until the month Simānu, the 17th year, i.e. for the whole year in advance beginning from Du'uzu, Dar 16.[286] In BE 8/1, 112, a contract from Babylon written on 12th day of Araḫsamna, Nergal-aḫḫē-iddin, son of Pattazu[287] rented his house to his father Pattazu and Iddin-Bēl, son of Šamaš-šum-līšir, descendant of Nazua for one year[288] for 3⸢6⸣ shekels of silver, but they should pay the rent monthly. Such atypical payment in both documents suggests again that the situation was unstable and that the owners tried to protect himselves against the negative impact on their income. The lack of relevant data on the situation in Babylonia makes impossible to find the

[284] Ll. 4-5: *a-na u_4-mu* 3 *qû* nínda.ḫi.a/1 *qû* 6 *bab-ba-nu-ú*. Such interpretation is suggested by Abraham 2004, no. 86: 5, where we read that the tenant promised to deliver each day 4 sìla nínda.ḫi.a 1 sìla 5 *šá* giš.bán.meš *bab*!-*ba-nu-ú*. Although the sense giš.bán.meš is unclear (maybe a specific kind of bread) on the basis of ll. 9-11 it is certain that the tenant should deliver bread made of only 4 *qû*: *ul-tu* u_4.20.kam *šá* iti.gan [*u_4*-mu**]/4 sìla nínda.ḫi.a *i-di kar-ri u ru*[*g-bu*]/*i-nam-din*, "beginning from the 20th day of Kislīmu, he will deliver 4 *qû* of bread as the rent for the *kāru*-storehouse and the loft." The above quoted line 5 should be translated: "(daily) he will deliver 4 *qû* of bread, (i.e.) 5 giš.bán.meš-bread of best quality from each 1 *qû* (of flour)."

[285] Ll. 6-7: *baṭ-la šá i-šak-kan/i-zaq-qap*.

[286] The sum and means of payments is not given, presumably silver.

[287] For this name, see Tavernier 2007, 487 and Zadok 2009a, 280, no. 415.

[288] L. 13: *a-di ṭup-pi*! *ṭup-*⸢*pi*!⸣.

reason for resigning from the standard payment of house rent twice yearly,[289] but comparison with other texts with atypical payment, as we have seen, makes the possibility of political reason at least probable.

2.3 Obligations of the house tenant

The principal duty of the house tenant was to pay the rent regularly in strictly defined terms (see above). Quite often (but not always) tenants were obliged to undertake several duties reflected in following expressions:

batqa ša asurrî ṣabātu
ūra šanû and *ṭīda šakānu*
gušūrē ina libbi ṣabātu

Additional obligations concern:
the payment of *nūptu/šugarrû* (for this expression, see below)
the penalty to be paid by the contravener breaching the terms of the agreement.

2.3.1 *batqa ša asurrî ṣabātu*

This clause imposed on the tenant an obligation to care for the *asurrû*. Sometimes instead of the expression *batqa ša asurrî iṣabbat* there is only *batqa iṣabbat,* "to repair damage". It seems that if this shorter clause is followed by the obligation to repair the roof, it is an abbreviated version of the full expression. However, in those texts in which it is the only expression, it denotes probably an obligation to repair not only the cracks in the wall footing, but also to repair the roof.

The dictionaries suggest a similar meaning for the term: "Grundmauer" (AHw 77), "foundation structure, lower (damp) course of a wall" (CAD A II 350), "lower course, footing of wall" (CDA 2000, 26). In the case of powerful structures built on strong brick foundations covered with layers of baked bricks surrounded with limestone or marble plates one can talk about the classical meaning of the term 'foundation'. However, a majority of houses were built on weak foundations or with none at all, which exposed houses to dampness, affected stability of the walls and threatened the possible collapse of the house. Systematic repair of the wall footings was supposed to preserve their good condition.

However, a new interpretation of the term has been suggested, according to which *asurrû* referred to the drain through which the water from the

[289] Maybe this is connected in some way with the travels of Babylonian businessmen to Susa this year (Waerzeggers 2010a, 781; cf. Tolini 2011, 332, 354-56).

underground part of the wall was removed.[290] I personally doubted in this interpretation because if such installations were effective it have to be built under all outer walls of the house, but such system of drainage of the walls footing of the houses, is – to my knowledge – not confirmed by archaeological excavations. Structures functioning as a drain were discovered only under some walls (for example in Babylon),[291] but another famous wall – the Median Wall – was built on a foundation made of baked brick laid in bitumen.[292] Preparing this study I accepted an older translations "to repair (the cracks) of the wall footing."[293]

Happily the comprehensive study of Andrew George has been published,[294] in which two different meanings of the term are indicated, the first denoting sewer discharging water from a toilet, and the second, used later in the first millennium, denoting the footing of the wall.

Only in VS 5, 78 the expression *batqa ša asurrî* is followed by *ina* sig$_4$.ḫi.*a* *ši*[*birra*] /*iṣabbat*,[295] which presumably describes the type of work to be done, i.e. the replacement of the damaged lowest part of the wall (*asurrû*) with new bricks.

The tenant's care for the *asurrû* was recognised as his most important obligation, present in almost all contracts of the house rental. The significance of this obligation for the maintenance of the house in good condition is demonstrated in VS 4, 110 = Baker 2004, no. 119 (Babylon, Dar 6?, cf. VS 4, 129 = Baker 2004, no. 117) where in the receipt confirming the payment of rent, the tenant swore solemnly by the name of Darius (in the first case "by the king") to repair *asurrû*. One may suspect that in both cases the tenants had not fulfilled their obligations and the owner (the same in both documents) exerted pressure on them with the threat that they would commit "the sin against the king" (*ḫīṭu ša šarri*). This procedure clearly indicates the importance of the repair the footing of a wall for the maintenance of the houses in good conditions.

In a rather small number of Neo-Babylonian contracts the obligation to care for *asurrû* is missing and the reason not mentioned. It seems that at least in some cases the owner did not impose it on the tenant as he might have lived in a part of the house and personally taken care of all ongoing repair. In other cases discussed below, the clause is missing because the tenant was in a position to refuse acceptance of this obligation due to difficult political

290 The opinion was ascribed to Andrew George, first by H. Baker in Baker 2004, 166, and later by other scholars, see George 2015, 76, n. 3.

291 George 2015, 95.

292 NAPR 1.

293 Cf. Petschow 1956, 107: "Risse der Mauern wird er (...) reparieren."

294 George 2015.

295 Baker 2004, no. 101: 8 reads *ina* sig$_4$.ḫi.a *u* x [...]/*iṣabbat*, but as the sign *ši* following sig$_4$.ḫi.a is clear, the reconstruction suggested by Oppenheim 1936, 75 *ina* sig$_4$.ḫi.a *ši*-[*bir-ra*]/*iṣabbat* is in my opinion correct.

situation, which forced the owner (or his agent) to grant the tenant more favourable conditions.

2.3.2 *ūra šanû* and *ṭīda šakānu*

The second expression, present in almost all contracts known to me, requires the tenant to care for the roofing. The general sense is clear, i.e. the tenant is responsible for sealing the roof in order to prevent water seeping to the room below. The translation of CAD Š I 408 (and similar in CAD U 261) assumes that the existing clay roof should be wetted down and then covered with new plaster sealing the leak. This is supported by expressions describing the tenant's duty, i.e. *šinīti ūri* (VS 4, 64 = NRV 307: 15) and *šinīta išanni* (TuM 2-3, 27: 9), where *šinītu* describes new plaster. Both *ūra išannu* and *šinīti ūri* have, in fact, the same meaning.

In a few texts the expression *ūra išannu* is followed by *ṭīda šakānu* (BM 114472, no. 9: 8; TuM 2-3, 26: 6; 27: 7, Nbn 845: 7 and probably in BM 67913, no. 108: 8; cf. also BM 136872: 11 (im igi *u ku-tal-la i-šak-kan-u'*),[296] and UCLM 9-2919: 11-12:[297] im *pa-ni u ku-tal-la* é *i-šak-kan*). In BM 114472, no. 9: 6-8 the obligation "to cover the whole house with clay" is separated from "to seal the roof,"[298] suggesting that it describes an obligation other than repairing the roof. This is supported by Nbn 845, a contract concerning (re)building[?] of the "reed house", where there is no mention of roof or repairing of cracks in the footing, but the tenant is obliged "to cover (the house[?]) with clay." Also in TuM 2-3, 26 the tenant is obliged "to remove the old porch or portico" (*taṣlīlu*) and to roof the dilapidated porch and cover the house with clay.[299] Either two different porches are meant here, the portico which to be removed and the rest repaired, or two different parts of one building. This is followed by the obligation to cover the house with clay. Compare TuM 2-3, 27, which concerns the same arrangement, removing the old portico and repairing of dilapidated roof, followed by the clause that the tenant will cover the buildings in the enclosure.[300] In these applying clay is not connected with roofing but rather (at least in Nbn 845, BM 136872, and UCLM 9-2919), with plastering the outer and inner side of the reed walls to protect them from rain and sand during sandstorms.

---

[296] Walker 1978, 237-240; cf. Stolper 2000, 670f. and Jursa 2004, no. 13.

[297] Stolper 2000, 668.

[298] *ú-ru i-šá-an-na*/ bat-qu šá *a-sur-ru-ú i-ṣab-bat* /*ù ṭi-it* é *gab-bi i-šak-kan.*

[299] *ta-aṣ-li-li* <*la*>*-bi-ri*/ *i-di-ki-ma ta-aṣ-li-li ma-aq-qu-tu*/ *ú-ṣal-lal* é im *i-šak-kan*.

[300] *ta-aṣ-ṣa-li-li la-bi-ri*/*i-di-ki-ma ta-aṣ-li-li ma-aq-qu-ú-tú*/ *ú-ṣal-lal* é.meš tùr im/ *i-šak-kan*, "he will remove the old portico (and) will seal the ruined portico." (CAD Ṣ 239). It cannot be excluded that the expression about removing the old portico and roofing the dilapidated portico describe in fact the same object if we accept the possibility that not whole portico was removed but only its roofing.

How often should a tenant renew the roof? According to TuM 2-3, 27 every year (*šattussu*). The same applies in L 1667[301] where the tenant should renew the roof every year during his three-year tenancy. However, NBC 8378[302] states that a two-year tenant should renew the whole roof, but only half of the roof if he rented the house for one year. Sometimes the obligation was different: in BRM 1, 43 the tenant is to renew one-third of the roof each year.

2.3.3 *gušūrē ina libbi ṣabātu*

The third expression *gušūrē ina libbi iṣabbat* may be translated "he will put the beams on it", i.e. on the roof, but CAD G 145 and CAD H 36 give the slightly different translation, "he (tenant) will cover the beams with laths." However, this clause occurs only in two documents (Nbn 48, no. 1 and Gordon Smith College 88: 6), which might suggest that this is non-mandatory, imposed on tenants in exceptional situations only. Such an interpretation is, however, doubtful, as many contracts mention *gušūru* beams in the context of charging for repairs made using of beams, reed and bricks. This suggests that the need to replace old, damaged beams with new came up quite often; the expression in Nbn 48, no. 1 and Gordon Smith College 88 could then refer to more specific matters. In majority of cases we can take it that beams for roof construction are probably meant, Dar 129 mentions that if the holder of the house, kept on antichretic terms, inserts the beams in the house wall maintaining the roof, he can remove them when the contract ends.

In a number of contracts there are no obligations on tenants to repair the house, which cannot be accidental. In such cases the owner took care of the house himsef, perhaps because he still occupied a part of the rented house. A second possibility is that certain circumstances might enable a tenant to refuse to accept this obligation (see below, p. 95). However, quite often it is stated that the tenant is responsible for repairs made with bricks, reeds and beams, but the question as who was charged with labour costs is left open. In TuM 2-3, 25 written in the twenty-second year of Nebuchadnezzar in Babylon all the tenant's expenditures (*telittu*) are covered by the owner. Sometimes costs were divided between owner and tenant, albeit resting more often on the owner. According to CTMMA 3, 97 from Babylon dated to the eighth year of Darius I, the costs of the usual materials are reckoned on the owner's account, but the work is to be done by the tenant.[303] At the end of the document there is an interesting note that, since the rent agreed in the previous contract has been changed, the tenant cannot expect the owner to

[301] Joannès 1989, 252f. and 39.

[302] Joannès 1989, 349 and 93.

[303] Also in MR 176 the cost of repair made by the tenants are paid by the owner.

pay him the builder's wages (*idi arad ekalli*) for the work done to put the house in good shape. This statement is important, because it suggests that additional liabilities could affect the amount of rent. In VS 5, 64 = Baker 2004, no. 99, it is said that if the cost of repair exceeded one shekel, it would be covered by the owner.[304] However, we are not sure if the owner was to cover the whole cost or only the part that exceeded one shekel. Such interpretation is suggested by JCS 28, no. 46 where all costs over two shekels are counted on the owner.[305] In general, it seems that whenever the appropriate information is missing, the cost of the repair was on the owner.

2.3.4 *sīra nasqa šakānu*

This obligation is known only from one tablet NCBT 178,[306] where Sîn-iddin, the king's resident (*qīpu*) in the Eanna temple in Uruk and owner of a house in Babylon in the vicinity of Esagila temple, rented it to certain Amēl-[Nanāya], son of Balāssu for one year, reserving for himself the right to dwell in it, should he visit the capital. The tenants were typically obliged to repair the footing of a wall and to seal the roof, but this clause followed by the obligation *si-*[*i*]*-ru na-as-qu i-šak-kan*, "he will apply a high-quality reed."[307] The formula is obviously related to tenant obligations to make necessary repairs with bricks, reeds and beams, but since it follows repairing the roof, it probably refers to some other task assigned to the tenant. In my opinion, the clause refers to the construction of a *gisallu*, "a reed fence or screen (along the edge of a flat roof)."[308]

2.3.5 The payment of *nūptu/šugarrû*

One of the obligations in a house rental contract was the payment of *nūptu* or *šugarrû*. The earliest expression is *nūpta nadānu*, next *nūpta nâpu*,[309] with the verb derived from the noun, and the younger *šugarrû nadānu*. While the two first expressions are known from the texts from all major centres, the third was

[304] VS 5, 64 = Baker 2004, no. 99: 9-11 *ma-la ina lìb-bi/ip-pu-uš ul-tu* ugu 1 gín kù.babbar *a-na* u[gu]/ᵐmu-ᵈag (the owner) *i-man-nu*; VS 5, 84+151 = Baker 2004, no. 103.

[305] *dul-lu šá* sig_4.ḫi.a gi *u* giš.ùr *ma-la ina lìb-bi ip-pu-šú* [*a*]*-na* ugu ᵐsum*-na-a i-man-nu*.

[306] Sack 1976, 282-283. It is not excluded that thc samc word occus in BM 31781 (Wunsch 1993, no. 311): 8 (a *si-ri i-šak-kan*). Such reading is accepted by Joannès 2016, 296 ({a}*si-ri i-šak-kan*) who thinks that the *sīru* and *ṭiṭṭū* were used interchangeably. Note that Jursa 1995/96, 261 suggests to read *a-gur*-ru*.

[307] Note that CAD N II 31, quoting this passage, translates *sīru* as "plaster", but in my opinion the second meaning "a reed structure" given in CAD S 320 (*sīru* B) is correct here.

[308] CAD G 97. Examples of the use of reed for the construction of the *gisallu* will be quoted elsewhere.

[309] The earliest use of this form is dated to the 3rd year of Nabonidus, see Kessler 1991, 133, no. 8: 10'.

used mainly in Borsippa, and seldom in other cities, namely in three texts from Babylon,[310] one from Ur,[311] and one from Uruk.[312] The rarity of the term *šugarrû* in those three cities might just be due to the small number of documents; but, importantly it does not occur before the Persian period. Additionally, the term is related to the feast on the "day of Enlil" in Borsippa only, while in Uruk Enlil was only a minor god and gained importance only in the Seleucid period.[313] As both terms *nūptu* and *šugarrû* were used in the same context, they must have had the same meaning.[314] The translation "additional payment" (CAD N II 343) or "supplementary payment" (Baker 2004, 55) is presumably due to the fact, that *nūptu*/*šugarrû* is not included in the rent house (*idi bīti*) agreed with the owner.[315] The only exception known to me is in BM 31273 (28.X.Dar 33+[x]).[316] The tenant, Marduk-nāṣir-apli/Itti-Marduk-balāṭu//Egibi should pay 35 shekels of white silver yearly including *nūptu* payment.[317]

As regards house rental,[318] *nūptu* was usually paid in three months of the year: Nisannu (I), Du'ūzu (IV) and Kislīmu (IX).[319] The late text from Uruk – BRM 2, 1 dated 5.IV.Sel 8 – mentions three payments yearly without mentioning the months, but comparison with other texts certainly suggests that the three months mentioned above are meant.

Divergences were rare, although they did happen. In TuM 2-3, 31 (Cyr 3, Nippur) the *šugarrû* is to be paid in Nisannu (I), Ulūlu (VI), and Kislīmu (IX). However, it cannot be excluded that Ulūlu is a mistake of the scribe or modern copyist for Du'ūzu (IV). Another divergence occurs in UET 4, 37 from Ur, dated to sixth year of Artaxerxes II, where *šugarrû* should be paid in Simānu (III) and Kislīmu (IX). According to a few texts *nūptu* or *šugarrû* should be paid

---

310 Dar 378 and VS 4, 146 = Baker 2004, no. 121 and UCLM 9-2919 = Stolper 2000, 668.

311 UET 4, 37.

312 BRM 2, 1.

313 Beaulieu 2003, 338.

314 This was already observed in Oppenheim 1936, 86 ("wohl eine ähnliche Bedeutung") and by Baker 2004, 55.

315 For more neutral meaning, see CTMMA 3, 201f.: "surcharge" and Waerzeggers 2014, 277: "gift." For older translation, see Oppenheim 1936, 86.

316 Bertin 2749.

317 [2]*a-na i-di* é *a-na* mu.an.na 3½ *ma-na* 5 gín kù.babbar babbar-*ú a-di nu-up-t*[*u*$_4$].Uncertain is MR 138, where the total sum is described as *idi bīti u šugarrû*, however, because it concerns outstanding debt, it is unclear whether *šugarrû* was included in rent or only exceptionally paid together with rent.

318 Sometimes *nūptu* was paid by a tenant to the owner of a field, by a renter of a boat or by a borrower to a creditor (for examples, see CAD N II 343). As the original meaning of the term was "a gift for cultic purposes," in the above contexts it might have been used in the broader meaning as a gift. Uniquely in MR 138 the sum due to the owner includes *idu* as well as *šugarrû*. There is no *nūptu* mention in TuM 2-3, 26, contrary Oppenheim 1936, 85.

319 Oppenheim 1936, 85. Many more texts are now known.

only in two months: Du'ūzu (IV) and Kislīmu (IX).[320]

Another possible divergence occurs in ZA 3, no. 14 (BM 34548): 9-10 where the *nūptu* should be paid in iti.⌜še⌝ u_4.2.[kam]/iti.šu *u* iti.gan, i.e. in the intercalary Addaru month (XIIb), Du'ūzu (IV) and Kislīmu (IX). Such a reading suggests that the first installment of *nūptu* was paid not in Nisannu (I), but already in the intercalary month ending the previous year. However, there are two problems with this interpretation. As I was kindly informed by Christopher Walker,[321] who has gathered a major file of intercalary dating, intercalary Addaru is written Addaru *arkû* or Addaru *šanû*, but never iti.še u_4.2.kam.[322] Additionally, according his understanding intercalary Addaru is unknown either in the sixth year of Seleukos, to which the text is dated, or the previous year. In fact the sign at the end of l. 9 is only partly preserved, and although its shape is a little strange, in Christopher Walker's opinion and mine the reading iti.⌜bár⌝ cannot be excluded.

Different terminology was used mainly in Borsippa and seldom in Babylon (one text) and in Sippar (three texts). The following variations are known:

***arah* Nisannu kīnajātu ūmu Enlil nūptu ša 1 šiqil inamdin** Peek 16 (Cyr 6, Babylon),

"he will make additional payment of 1 shekel in the month Nisannu (for) *kīnajātu* offerings and (gift on) the day of Enlil."

ūmu Enlil kīnajātu nūptu inamdin MR 167:10-11 (Dar 35, Sippar), BM 74949: 9-10 (22.VIII.Dar [x], [Sippar], (unp.); JCS 28, no. 9 (6.II.Dar 24, Sippar), "(on) the day of Enlil (and for) *kīnajātu* offerings he will make additional payment."

ūmu Enlil u kīnajātu šugarrû inamdin BRM 1, 68 = Joannès 1986, 325 (Camb 2, Borsippa); TuM 2-3, 30 ([Ach] 3, Borsippa), L. 1667 = Joannès 1986, 252-53 (Nbk IV, Borsippa; the same female owner as in BRM 1, 43, see below)

"(on) the day of Enlil (and for) *kīnajātu* offerings he will make additional payment."

---

[320] To three texts known to Oppenheim 1936, 85 (BRM 1, 78; VS 5, 77 and VS 5, 84, now VS 5, 84+151= Baker 2004, no. 103) we can add MR 99 (Dar 17); VS 5, 117: 16-17 = NRV 635 (Xer 0) and YBC 11599 = Stolper 2000, 673. Uncertain is how to understand VS 4, 146 = NRV 131 = Baker 2004, no. 121, written on 6.XII.Dar 17. This is a receipt for house rent for half a year from Addaru (XII) Dar 17 till Abu (V) Dar 18. It is said that *šugarrû* was paid *ina mišil šanāti* (mu.an.na.meš), translated in NRV, p. 171 "für die Mitte der (beiden) Jahre" while by Baker, "for the middle of the year". However, as the tenant paid the rent in Addaru, i.e. in advance for half a year, not "für die Mitte," the translation in NRV cannot be accepted. Baker's translation does not take into account the plural. It seems that the expression *ina mišil šanāti* should be translated "for half of the years" where *šanāti* stresses the fact that the payment comprises one month of the previous and five months of the current year. Another, simpler option is that the sign meš was written by mistake. In this period (Addaru till Abu), only two "installments" of *šugarrû* are due, i.e. in Nisannu (I) and Du'uzu (IV).

[321] I thank Ch. Walker here for discussion of the text with me and information on intercalary datings.

[322] Note also the redundant u_4 before the numeral.

nūptu ša ūmu Enlil u kīnajātu inamdin VS 5, 67, no. 119 (Dar 5, Babylon); VS 4, 137 = NRV 125 (Dar 10, Babylon); Barton 1900, no. 24 (Dar 34, Sippar); BM 82668 ([Ach], Borsippa),

"(on) the day of Enlil (and for) *kīnajātu* offerings he will make additional payment."

šugarrû ša ūmu Enlil u kīnajātu inamdin BRM 1, 43 (Nbk IV, Borsippa),

"he will make additional payment (on) the day of Enlil and (for) *kīnajātu* offerings."

ūmu Enlil u kīnajātu [*šugarr*]*û inamdin* L. 1667 = Joannès 1989, 252f. (the same female owner as in the previous text) and BRM 1, 68 = Joannès 186, 325,

"(on) the day of Enlil (and for) *kīnajātu* offerings she will make additional payment."

It is important that in the last two entries the term *šugarrû* occurs at the beginning or at the end of the phrase. A similar situation is in VS 5, 67, no. 119 and in two additional texts where *nūptu* is at the beginning, while in MR 167 at its end. This suggests that *nūptu* or *šugarrû* both functioned as generic terms describing payments on the day of Enlil and *kīnajātu* offerings on other days. It seems that although a different wording is used, the payment in "the day of Enlil" was made in Nisannu while the *kīnajātu* offerings were in Du'ūzu and Kislīmu.[323]

It should be noted that the earliest mention of *kīnajātu,* constituent of *nūptu* and later of *šugarrû,* is dated to the 35th year of Nebuchadnezzar (VS 4, 25 = NRV 298; Baker 2004, no. 1), in an antichretic agreement with a house taken as a pledge. It is said there the *kīnajātu* will be paid together by the owner and the tenant[324]. It means that *nūptu* as an additional obligation was known already in the last decade of Nebuchadnezzar. However, as texts before the time of Nabonidus omit this obligation altogether, it seems likely that – if paid at all – it was an obligation on the owner, not tenant. The earliest certain record of the payment of *nūptu* and *kīnajātu* by a tenant comes from the time of Nabonidus (VS 5, 23, no. 109 = NRV 113). From then on it occurs quite regularly until the first year of Xerxes I and the time of Artaxerxes I and II. The absence of the *nūptu/šugarrû* in earlier house rental documents and its presence in later documents suggests that, although the obligation existed already in the time of Nebuchadnezzar, in the early period of the Neo-Babylonian empire it was not paid by tenants, and for this reason was not mentioned in the documents. From the time of Nabonidus on, the *nūptu* was

[323] Note, however, a different sequence in Peek 16, which suggests that the *kīnajātu* and gift for *ūm Enlil* were all paid in Nisannu. Perhaps such a strange sequence is a scribe's mistake or that the tenant paid *kīnajātu* offerings and gift for "day of Enlil", together with first installment, in advance.

[324] *itti aḫameš ippulū.*

quite often paid by tenants,[325] although the recipient is not indicated. However, in VS 4, 25 = NRV 298, Baker 2004, no. 1 where both partners are responsible for the payment of *kīnajātu*, it is clear that it was not intended for the owner but to a third party not involved directly in the contract. In the light of this case it seems that two documents where *šugarrû* is paid by tenants to the owner[326] indicate that, although the payment of *nūptu/šugarrû* was transferred from owners to tenants, the obligation itself was to be paid by the owner.

The first part of the obligation is named in Borsippa *ūm Enlil*, i.e. it was meant for "the day of Enlil." As with the *kīnajātu*, recognised by scholars as a kind of offering,[327] it seems that the addressee was the temple. At least in the case of house rental we might recognise in *nūptu/šugarrû* a kind of "liturgy" imposed in favour of the temple on wealthy people, for whom house rent meant regular income over many years.[328] At least since the reign of Nabonidus house owners were able to transfer this obligation onto tenants. In unstable political situations some tenants refused to accept the *nūptu* oligation and this fact was sometimes clearly noted in the documents.

The amount of *nūptu* obligation is unclear as it occurs so rarely in texts. In VS 5, 23, no. 109 = NRV 114 (Nbn 13) the tenant is to pay half a shekel, while the yearly rent is 10 shekels, i.e. 5% of the rent. In Peek 16 (Cyr 9) the *nūptu* is one shekel, while the rent 8 shekels yearly, i.e. 12.5%. In BM 26689[329] (Borsippa, Nbk IV,1) the *nūptu* is one shekel, while the rent 7 shekels, i.e. ca. 14%. In Cyr 231 the *kīnajātu* is 5 shekels while the rent 1 mina 10 shekels, i.e. ca. 7%. In Dar 378 the tenant is to deliver one sheep valued 10 shekels, while the rent is 50 shekels yearly, i.e. 20%. In BM 82741 (Borsippa, Dar I [x]) the annual rent is 1 shekel while *kīnajātu* and *šugarrû* half a shekel, i.e. 50% of annual rent.[330] The *šugarrû* is extremely high in YBC 11599:[331] 40 shekels while the annual rent is

[325] With a number of exceptions discussed above, when in a complicated political situation the tenant were able to refuse this obligation. In general, when *nūptu/šugarrû* is not mentioned in contract, it was not paid by tenant.

[326] BM 136872 (Walker 1978, 237-240; cf. Stolper 2000, 670f.; Jursa 2004, no. 13), and VS 5, 117 = NRV 635.

[327] Oppenheim 1936, 87, accepted by the dictionaries: "Pflichtopfer" (AHw 921, s.v. *qinītu*); CAD K 379 ("an additional payment, present, or offering"), CDA 158, s.v. *kinayyātu* "pl,. tant. (a present, payment, or offering)."

[328] Cf. Jursa 2010, 292, n. 1751. For the question of liturgy as public obligation undertaken by an individual at his own expense, which might have been established in Babylonia under Greek influence, see San Nicolò 1934 and McEwan 1982.

[329] Zadok 2009, 155, no. 507.

[330] Zadok 2009, 258, no. 59.

[331] Stolper 2000, 673.

3½ shekels.[332] The data do not allow us to calculate any relation between the *nūptu* and the house rent (*idi bīti*), and suggest that it was not strictly defined.[333]

2.3.6 Payment of penalty by contravener (*nabalkattānu*)

The term *nabalkattānu* denoted "contravener (of contract),"[334] who is obliged to pay a penalty to the partner(s) if he transgresses the agreement. Such a clause occurs only in 21 house rental documents known to me, presented in the table below. The clause occurs in different places in the documents, i.e. after the setting of the day when the house is put at the disposal of the tenant (no. 10, 13) or before this clause (no. 16, 18), after the *nūptu* clause (no. 14, 21), after the clause that the owner received half or yearly rent (7), before the list of witnesses (2, 5, 12, 17), or even at the very end of the document (no. 3, 21).

No.	Yearly rent (in shekels)	Penalty (in shekels)	The relation of penalty to rent	Date	Text
1	12 breads daily and ½ š yearly	10		28.XI.Nbk 22 (583 BC)	GC 1, 35 = BR 6, 29
2	1 shekel and building Works	5		1.VI.Nbk [x]	TuM 2-3, 27
3	3¼	10	ca. 308%	16.VII.Nbn 1 (555 BC)	HSM 1899.2.141[335]
4	8	10	80%	13.VI.Nbn 13 (545 BC)	VS 5, 32 = NRV 114

[332] Maybe a mistake for 4 shekels, i.e. a little over 10%.

[333] The idea expressed in notes to ll. 13-14 of CTMMA 3, 97 (p. 202) that "the sum of 10 shekels (…) for first half a year may include one of the triennial *nūptu* surcharges, the amount of which is not specified" cannot be correct, as the payment is 10 out of 18 shekels of rent, paid for a little more than the first half of the tenant's occupation of the house, beginning from 1st Simānu. Oppenheim 1936, 85 recognised some additional payments, such as reeds, onion, *namzittu*-jars (of beer?) and *tabilu*-herbs as *nūptu/šugarrû*, but except for sheep in Dar 378 in the other texts quoted by him the term is missing and for this reason it is doubtful if *nūptu/šugarrû* was meant there. An argument against this idea comes from Cyr 231 = Wunsch 1993, no. 303, mentioning first *kīnajātu* worth 5 shekels and separately 2 baskets of *tabilu* herbs.

[334] On this clause, see Oppenheim 1936, 18-19; the same translation is in AHw 694 ("Vertragsbrüchtiger"), CAD N I 9 ("violator (of a contract)" and CDA 227 ("contravener (of contract)." From the above lists Oppenheim knew of only eight such texts. The term is discussed by Jursa 2010, 714ff. (in his discussion of Late Babylonian apprenticeship contracts).

[335] Zadok 2008, 88*-89*.

5	13	10	ca. 77%	13.II.Nbn 17 (539 BC)	Nbn 1030
6	5	10	200%	7.[x].Camb 1 (538 BC)	Cam 97
7	2 *kurru* of barley, i.e. ca. 2 š	3 [š!]	ca. 150%	4.[x].Camb 0 (530 BC)	BM 25832[336]
8	70	60	ca. 86%	5.[V].Camb 2 (528 BC)	Cam 147[337]
9	3½ *	5	ca. 143%	19.VI.Nbk IV,1 (521 BC)	L. 1667[338]
10	20	20	100%	2.XII.Dar 1 (521/0 BC)	Dar 25
11	25	30	120%	10.3. Dar [x+?]3	BM 26566[339]
12	18	60	333%	21.IV. Dar 4 (518 BC)	VS 5, 64 = Baker 2004, no. 99
13	5½	5½	100%	5.IV.Dar 5 (517 BC)	Dar 163
14	bread	10 if he breaks the condition within two years		5.IX.Dar 10 (512 BC)	TCL 13, 187
15	5 and building Works	60		ca. 1.Dar 12 (510 BC)	BM 136872[340]
16	50	⅔ or ⅚ mina	80 or 100%	22.V.Dar 14 (508 BC)	Dar 378
17	20	60	300%	[x].V.Dar 18 (504 BC)	VS 5, 84+151 = Baker 2004, 103

336 Zadok 2009, 117, no. 886 reconstructs the penalty at 3 [minas], which is highly improbable.

337 Wunsch 1993, no. 330. Because the house is at the disposal of the tenant from the first day of the month Ulūlu, there is no doubt that the text has been written in the previous month.

338 Joannès 1989, 352f.

339 Zadok 2009, 141, no. 384.

340 Walker 1978, 237-240; cf. Stolper 2000, 670f.; Jursa 2004, no. 13.

18	32	[20] or [more]	[62.5%] or [more]	2.3.Dar 20 (502 BC)	Dar 499
19	36	20	55.5%	5.XII.Dar 22 (500 BC)	BM 21999[341]
20	14	20	143%	15.IV.Dar 36 (486 BC)	BM 42393, no. 128
21	10 kur yearly, i.e. ca. 10 shekels	30	300%	13.IV.Xer 1 (4985 BC)	BM 33980, no. 133

The penalty, compared with yearly rent, is high or extremely high, with the lowest amounting from ca. 55.5% and to 77%, 80%, 86%, 100%, 120%, 143%, 150%, 200%, 300%, 308% and even to 333% of the yearly rent. It is, thus, difficult to recognise in it a "Konventionalstrafe", as was suggested by San Nicolò;[342] rather it was an extraordinary penalty in an extraordinary situation. Although it is not easy to establish the relation between yearly rent and penalty, it seems that at least in a few documents the clause had been introduced in face of difficult political situation. Nbn 1030 was written in middle of the month Ayāru, the 17th year of Nabonidus, i.e. at the time when the question was not *whether* but *when* the Persian army of Cyrus the Great would attack Babylonia. Cam 97 was presumably written in 538 BC, the year when Cyrus held the title of "King of Lands" and Cambyses "King of Babylon."[343] But already by the New Year *akītu* festival celebrated in Babylon in the month Nisannu, about five months after the conquest of Babylonia, there was a sharp dispute between Cambyses – or rather (as was suggested by George)[344] between Cambyses and his father Cyrus on the one side – and the Babylonian priesthood on the other. At the end of his first year (538 BC) Cyrus assumed both titles and dismissed the son from exercising royal duty and presumably sent him away from Babylonia. It is not hard to believe that such a political situation could have encouraged the use of this additional clause in order to make the partners respect the obligations. The high penalty, equal to the annual rent, i.e. 100% in Dar 25, recorded in the first

[341] Zadok 2009, 94, no. 104.

[342] NRV, 157, n. 8. The opinion is valid for the purchase of fields, orchards, etc., where the standard penalty was 12 times the price. For the sale of a prebend it was 19 shekels, and in hiring workers half a mina.

[343] Zawadzki 1996.

[344] George 1996, 379-381.

year of Darius I, might be caused by political chaos in the preceding years (see above, p. 77); additionally the contract was concluded at the time of struggle in northern Babylonia and the conquest of the capital by the Persian army. A similar political instability must be taken into account for contracts dated to Dar 36 and Xer 1 (see above).

It is difficult to explain the high penalty in the case of three contracts from the time of Darius, i.e. VS 5, 64 = Baker 2004, no. 99 from Babylon dated to the fourth year from (333%), Dar 163 from Borsippa dated to the fifth year (100%) and VS 5, 84+151 dated to the 18th year (300%). A parallel occurs between the fourth and fifth years in the above cities and the situation in Sippar, where the then rent collector was unable to regulate his obligation towards the Ebabbar temple beginning with the first year of Darius (see below, p. 115-118). While more documents are needed to establish if there were some political or economic difficulties in those years, the view that this clause was used in extraordinary situations seems certain.

But the reason for establishing an extremely high penalty of 200% of the annual rent might be different; sometimes – like in Cam 97 – the clause was introduced under the pressure of the owner of the house. This is indicated by the clause according to which the party who breaks the agreement should pay the penalty to fNuptaya, the wife of Itti-Marduk-balāṭu, son of Nabû-aplu-iddin, of the Egibi family, the owner of the house, i.e. the clause is evidently aimed against the tenant. It suggests that the owner of the house planned to leave the city and the clause might be a kind of warranty for the terms of contract. In fact, Itti-Marduk-balāṭu undertook a trip to Persia already in the first year of Cyrus, returning probably in the second half of the second year.[345]

According to A. L. Oppenheim the *nabalkattānu*-clause was turned mainly against the house owner, who was in a privileged situation and could easily break the contract having received the rent in advance.[346] In fact when the contract was agreed the house owner received only half the rent, and in an extraordinary situation (journey abroad or political instability) the house owner could be worried about payment of the next installment(s). It seems that for these reason the penalty clause was usually directed not against the owner, but against the tenant, i.e. it was primarily the owner who was interested in including it in a contract.

345 Zawadzki 1994. Concerning the purpose of journey, see Stolper 1990, 171; Joannès 2005, 190-193 and Waerzeggers 2010a, 800-802. For last discussion, see Tolini 2011, 191-197.

346 Oppenheim 1936, 18-19: "Der zweite Klausel wendet sich in erster Linie gegen den Vermieter, dann dieser kann – da der Mieter den Zins *Praenumerando* bezahlen muss – am leichtesten vertragsbrüchig werden, indem er etwa trotz Empfang des Mietzinses dem Mieter die Gebrauchsnahme verweigert."

2.3.7 The day, when the tenant will move into a house

The question is discussed above in point 2.2.8. The last two elements of the house rental contracts are common for other type of documents and for this reason are not discussed here.

3. Rental of temple houses

As noted in the introduction, the scope of research on the lease of temple houses has been limited up till now by the small number of sources. Only one known document concerned the lease of a temple house by the temple authority to an individual, while two administrative documents contained a fairly long list of the names of renters and the amount of rent paid by them.[347] In a larger group of documents temple houses are mentioned only incidentally as these documents are focused on the purchase of or payment for different items with silver paid by the tenants of the temple houses. A number of new texts now opens new research perspectives on the organisation of leases, the relation between temple and tenants and on their economic, social and legal status. Let us begin the discussion with a short description of the subject of each type of document presently available.

3.1 Typology of texts

The documents are here placed in the following categories:

1. A contract for rental of a house by an individual. There is only one well-preserved document[348] (for discussion, see below) and few fragments of tablets.[349]

2. A contract appointing a house rent collector.[350] Although the institution of the "rent house collector" was already recognised by Bongenaar (see below), only now do we know how they were chosen or discharged from office.

3. Annual accounts of house rent collectors. Such documents begin with a fixed formula:

kaspu idi bītāte makkūr ^{d}*Šamaš ultu* iti.x mu.x.kam *adi/adi libbi* mu.x.kam KN *šar Bābili* (*šar mātāti*),

"Silver, the rent of the houses, property of Šamaš from the month x, year x till the month x year x of KN, king of Babylon, (king of Lands)."

---

347 Nbn 201, no. 29 and BM 75208, no. 28 known to scholars from an unpublished copy by Bertin.

348 Nbn 48, no. 1.

349 BM 50539+ = no. 6; BM 67707 = no. 2; BM 68721 = no. 5; BM 73069 = no. 3; BM 99901 = no. 4.

350 BM 63353, no. 10.

If a change on the throne occurred, between the beginnings of the accounting period and its end, this fact was reflected in the formula:

ultu iti.x mu.x.kam KN_1 *adi*/*adi libbi* iti.y *rēš šarrūti* KN_2.

"From the month x KN_1 to the month/to the month y of KN_2."

The heading is usually followed by the name of the rent collector or collectors responsible for the execution of the obligation, although sometimes this information is missing. Usually (so far, with few exceptions) the heading is closed by a date indicating when the document was written; it might also indicate the day of the settlement of the rent by the rent collector for a given period.

In the operating section, separated from the heading with a ruling line, the amount of rent and the names of tenants are specified; quite often lines separate the entry for a given tenant from the previous and next one. Only exceptionally the expression *kaspu idi bītāte makkūr* ᵈ*Šamaš* is followed by the information about the assignment of the obtained silver.[351]

3a. The settlement of accounts has similar structure. The formula – in comparison with the above-discussed documents – is supplemented with the expression *epēš nikkassi*:

epēš nikkassi ša kaspi idi bītāte makkūr ᵈ*Šamaš*,

"Settlement of account for silver, rent of the houses, property of Šamaš."

The heading is followed by the name of the person responsible for the settlement and the period covered by the settlement. Documents of this type cover longer accounting periods. BM 65748, no. 13 was written in Nbn 16, but evidently concerns also the arrears from the fourtheenth year;[352] BM 61244, no. 15 covers the period from the fourth to the seventh year of Darius and additionally mentions the arrears for the period from the first till the third year.[353] In settlements of this type only the sum due is given, but the names of tenants from whom the money was reclaimed are omitted. In such documents it is the rent collector is in place of the debtor, not the tenants. A text similar to BM 61244, no. 15 is BM 68911, no. 12 where the total sums of money are listed, presumably – as in BM 61244, no. 15 – paid over several years.

4. The fourth category of documents concerns the use of the silver earned from rent. BM 64489, no. 45 is unusual. According to the heading the text concerns "the silver from the servants who live in the houses", then it enumerates the sums paid by each person and then (on the tablet reverse) how the income was spent on various purposes. However, the amount of spent silver considerably exceeds the sum of the payments listed on the obverse.

[351] Discussed below, p. 138-142.

[352] And presumably from the 15th – information might be in the damaged part of the document.

[353] The same concerns JEOL 40, no.1, no. 16; see there the edition and discussion.

Presumably the expenses incorporate payments from other tenants not mentioned in the document, or sums acquired in previous year.

5. Numerous are documents mentioning small amounts of silver (just a few shekels) out of the rent with information as to the purpose for which it was used. Such documents were written by rent collectors or their accountants for interim settlements. In such documents neither the name of the lessor nor the accounting period are specified, limiting the possibilities of their interpretation by us.

3.2 The lease of the temple houses to private persons

There are only five documents from Sippar archives in which the owner of the rented houses is the Ebabbar temple. Four come from the pre-Persian period: Nbn 48, no. 1 (Nbn 1), BM 67707, no. 2 ([Nbn] 6), BM 73069 , no. 3 (Nbn 14) and BM 99901, no. 4 (ca. Nbn 8-15), while one (BM 68721, no. 5) is from the Persian period (time of Cambyses). It means that at least from the time of Nabonidus the Ebabbar temple owned, purchased or built houses with the intention of renting them to private persons.

Nbn 48, no. 1, reveals that, in concluding the contract with a private person the Ebabbar temple used the standard form of document with rent-collecting clauses between private persons, i.e. the tenant was obliged to pay fixed rent in two installments, one at the beginning and the other in the middle of the rental year, and to renew the roof and repair cracks of the footing. However, Nbn 48, no. 1 lacks information as to who will bear the costs of repairs. The next difference concerns *nūptu*, which is not mentioned in the documents, either.[354] This is probably due to the fact that *nūptu* was paid by owners to the temple, and since the house was the Ebabbar temple's property, such an obligation would make no sense. The tenant, as can be judged from the amount of the rent (24 shekels yearly) and the ancestral name (Rē'i-sīsê), was relatively wealthy. Certainly he was no dependent of the temple but a free, materially independent person.

Two rather badly preserved documents deserve our attention because they deal with renting of temple houses on special, unusual terms. If I understand correctly BM 99901, no. 4, Bēl-aḫḫē-iqīša, the king's resident of the Ebabbar (and) Mušēzib-Marduk, the administrator of Sippar, rented out a temple house to Tabnēa of Ṣāḫit-ginê family for five years without any rent, obliging him, however, to build 5 cubits, (ca. 2.5 meters) of the terrace yearly. After five years Tabnēa begins to pay rent if he continues to live there. The second document BM 67707, no. 2 is similar to Nbn 48, no. 1 as it also concerns the rental of *bīt*

[354] The same applies to the texts from Uruk.

makkūri-storehouse rented for the fairly long period of 10 years. The mention of a wall (*igāru*) and two loads of bricks suggest that the tenant was obliged to rebuild or enlarge the store house, which – interestingly – was also suitable as a dwelling.

Although such a small number of documents concerning the rental of temple houses to individuals might be no more than accidental, it might suggest – despite the fact house rental secured stable income over many years – that contracts of this type other than temple personnel were rather rare. The main documented source of income came from the rental of houses to the temple servants or slaves (see below).

The number of documents from centres other than Sippar is too small to allow valid conclusions but it may be useful to note that in two cases in Uruk it is the oblates (*širāku*) of Lady-of-Uruk (YOS 7, 2 and YOS 7, 45),[355] who leased houses. In the first, YOS 7, 2 (21.XI.Cyr 0), oblate Anu-aḫu-iddin, son of Mušallim-Marduk, was unable to pay the rent to the temple and the contract was invalidated or revised by mutual agreement and the house rented to Šamaš-kāṣir, son of Anu-aḫu-iddin. If this Šamaš-kāṣir was the son of Anu-aḫu-iddin and the grandson of Mušallim-Marduk, he may have decided to take over his father's obligation, maybe allowing him to stay in the house as Anu-aḫu-iddin put the house at Šamaš-kāṣir's disposal on the day of signing the contract. In YOS 7, 45 (26.XI.Cyr 4) Gimillu, son of Šākin-šumi, oblate of Lady of Uruk, rented one-third of a house to Innin-šum-ibni, son of Eanna-ibni for some amount of barley paid to him in two installments. There is no need to look for non-economic reasons behind that situation.

Transfer of a debtor's house in lieu of unpaid debt was not unusual in Uruk. In AnOr 8, 57 (12.XI.Cyr 7)[356] the house of two debtors was taken over by the Eanna temple in lieu of male and female goats and their skins and then rented to a woman for 9 shekels yearly. A similar case is AnOr 8, 58 (21.XI.Cyr 7):[357] the house is taken over by the Eanna in lieu of sheep and goats and is then rented for 10 shekels of silver yearly, but reduced for the first year by 3 shekels for the repair done by the tenant. In both documents the period of rental is not determined, which suggests that the temple retained the right to use the house until the full value of defaulted animals had been recovered. As both texts are dated to the seventh year of Cyrus it cannot be excluded that the debts were due to draught,[358] which might have begun already in the last years of Cyrus' reign.[359]

[355] Edited in BR 6, no. 31 and no. 32.

[356] Cf. Kozuh 2014, 113.

[357] Kozuh, *idem*.

[358] Kleber 2012.

[359] Zawadzki 2014, 436-437; Tarasewicz 2016.

3.3 The house rent of the temple servants

A glance at the typology of the documents related to temple houses reveals the lack of written agreements between the temple and its servants. Likewise, there are no written contracts on remuneration in kind given to temple servants. Additionally, the possibility that each temple worker or oblate agreed a written contract with the temple, obliging him to pay a fraction of shekel or a little more seems highly unlikely. Presumably the relations of the temple with its personnel were regulated on an administrative level, i.e. the temple official knew the size of a family and allocated to it appropriate lodging and determined the rent. Later, after the office of the house rent collector was established, the collector received a record of the amount paid by each servant with only a limited scope for manipulating its amount. It seems highly probable that the temple kept a register (maybe a wax tablet) with the names of all tenants and the sums due.

In essence, if we define the lease of a house as a voluntary agreement between two parties, the renting of temple houses to its servants cannot be described as a 'lease,' but rather as an administrative decision of the temple. This does not change the fact that the payment was rightly named as 'rent'.

3.4 The frequency of rent payment

The frequency of rent payment in the discussed documents differs from that known from contracts agreed between private persons or between the temple and a person not belonging to temple personnel. The first most important difference concerns the time due. Unlike in private contracts, the rent was paid to the temple once yearly. However, as the sums due were paid to the temple by the rent collector it is not clear if he collected the payment from the dwellers once a year or, as in the case of private contracts, twice yearly. The only argument for the former is that the rent was usually low or extremely low, which makes the likehood dividing it into two installments less probable. However, at least in one case, in a document dated to the accession year of Nabonidus, some persons paid the rent in two installments,[360] which leaves the question open.

The second, even more important difference is in the payment of rent not at the beginning of the year but for the period which usually began in the month Ulūlu (VI) and ended in Abu (V).

ultu (ta) iti.kin (...) *adi* (en) iti.ne
"from month Ulūlu (...) to the month Abu"

[360] See BM 79054 (p. 107).

In two documents the scribes used the preposition "including" (*adi libbi*), presumably to avoid doubt that the last month included the month Abu.[361]

ultu iti.kin (...) *adi libbi* iti.ne
"from month Ulūlu (...) to the month Abu including"

A slightly different formula occurs in BM 68911, no. 12

ultu qīt iti.kin mu.2.kam *adi qīt* iti.ne mu.4.kam
"from the end of the month Ulūlu (V) of the second year to the end of the month Abu (V) of the fourth year."

The first part of the formula *ultu qīt* iti.kin is slighty ambiguous, because it might be understood that the accounting period included a few days of the month Ulūlu. Rather it means "since the very end of the month Ulūlu," practically from month of Tašrītu (VII), i.e. the accounting period began in month Tašrītu (VII) of the second year and ended in month Abu (V), the fourth year of Nabonidus covering 24 months: six months of the second year, 13 months of the third year (including the intercalary month of Addaru (XII) in this year) and five months of the fourth year, i.e. exactly two accounting years if we include the intercalary month Addaru.[362]

Departures from the standard did, however, happen and the explanation suggested below is by no means conclusive. In BM 62168, no. 17 the accounting period began from month of Abu (V), the second year of Neriglissar and ended in the end of Ulūlu (VI), the third year (T: 4), i.e. if we take the text verbatim, the accounting period would have lasted 14 months.[363] A similar situation occurs in Nbn 428, no. 49, the document recording silver expenditures from the rent (*idi bīti*) for the accounting period lasting from month Abu (V), the ninth year to month Abu (V), the tenth year,[364] i.e. 13 months. However, in order to receive the accounting period of 12 months it is enough to add *qīt*, i.e. *ultu* <*qīt*> iti.ne mu.9.kam *a-di* iti.ne mu.10.kam, "from the <very end>of month Abu [that is from month Ulūlu], ninth year to the end of Abu, tenth year," and in BM 62168, no. 17 "from the <very end> of month Abu (V) [that is from month Ulūlu (VI)] to the <very beginning> of month Ulūlu (VI)", [i.e. to the end of Abu]. BM 62168, no. 17 covered presumably two accounting years from the half of the second till the half of the fourth year. This is, however, doubtful as the text was written in the third year and the sums paid by the

[361] BM 73044, no. 24 and BM 114748, no. 19.

[362] If this interpretation is correct, in this document there is deviation from the standard as usually the accounting period begun from the month Ulūlu.

[363] *ul-tu* iti.ne mu.[2.kam]/⌜*a*⌝-*di-i* iti.kin mu.4.kam.

[364] *šá ta*/iti.ne mu.9.kam *a-di* iti.ne mu.10.kam.

tenants were very low (one shekel; once two shekels). Presumably the scribe wrote mistakenly mu.4.kam instead of mu.3.kam.

If the suggested interpretation is correct it means that the commonly adopted accounting period began in the sixth month of one year and ended with the end of the fifth month of the following year. However, the reason for adopting such an accounting year remains elusive.

Although reports on the collection of rent were prepared on an annual basis, there is doubt as to whether the renters paid rent in such a cycle or whether the documents only reflect the accounting period of the rent collector with the temple. The latter possibility is suggested by BM 79054, no. 20, where six tenants paid the whole sum at once, while payments of four persons are divided into two installments (no. 10-11, 13-14). It is interesting that six out of seven renters are placed in the second column (although there is no dividing vertical line between left and right columns, nevertheless the division is clear), which suggests that they paid their obligation in the second half of the accounting year. One can say that the rent collector acknowledged the difficult situation of those renters and was at liberty to make decision of division of rent into two installments.

3.5 Delays in payment of rent

There exist a few texts indicating that sometimes the rent collector did not pay the temple on time, presumably hoping to avoid payment or because he had been unable to collect the rent from the holders. Again, there is clear evidence that such situations occurred during the time of disturbances in the country caused by a war or coup d'etat.

The only list of the rent payment dated to the accession year of Lābāši-Marduk (556 BC) is BM 84424, no. 18. The text, contrary to the standard, did not give the term of payment ("from month x ... to month y") but only the date of delivery by Uššāya, presumably the rent collector at that time. The accounting period for which the rent was collected and delivered to the temple is uncertain. Although Neriglissar, the father of Lābāši-Marduk ruled four years (560-556 BC), the last year of his reign[365] ended before the end of the accounting period lasting from Ulūlu, his third year, to Abu of the next year, when in Sippar Nabonidus, a new king was already recognised. This is confirmed by several lists of rent payment comprising exactly the period from Ulūlu, the third year of Neriglissar to Abu the accession year of Nabonidus. Obviously, BM 84424, no. 18, dated to the accession year of Lābāši-Marduk, should concern the rent for the same period.

[365] The last document mentioning him as ruling king is dated to the very beginning of his fourth Babylonian year (sixth day of Nisannu, see Parker and Dubberstein 1956, 12). On the reign of Neriglissar, see Sack 1994, 1-33; Zawadzki 1997, 112-113; MacGinnis 2000, 64.

This means either that some people in the Ebabbar temple accepted the reign of Lābāši-Marduk much longer, at least till Abu 556 BC, when the accounting period ended, or it was an individual decision of the scribe to date the document to Lābāši-Marduk's reign, even though that ruler had been overthrown. The fact that there are three lists of rent payment for the period Ulūlu (VI) Nrg 3-Abu (V) Nbn 0 suggests that the turmoil in the country caused tenants or the rent collector in Sippar to hope that they might avoid paying the rent. This is supported by the BM 114748, no. 19, a long list of the rent paid for the same period called *rēḫānu*, i.e. arrears. A chance to avoid the payment of the fee proved to be illusory and within a few months of 556 BC presumably all holders of the temple houses had to pay their due rent. The last such list was made in Araḫsamna, presumably the month when arrears were definitely settled.

BM 65748, no. 13, written in Tašrītu of the sixteenth year of Nabonidus, is a settlement of accounts made with two rent collectors (Bēl-ušallim/Šamaš-ibni and Šamaš-mudammiq/Šūzubu//Šangû-Sippar) for the outstanding sum due for the fourteenth and presumably fifteenth years. As at least in the fourteenth year the function of rent collector was in the hands of Nabû-šum-iddin/Šamaš-aplu-uṣur//Ile'i-Marduk, this means that Bēl-ušallim and Šamaš-mudammiq regulated arrears of their predecessor.[366] The document suggests that the replacement of the highest officials of the country ordered by Nabonidus after his return from Teima resulted in rent arrears for the fourteenth and presumably for the fifteenth year of his reign.[367]

A similar problem occured when Babylonia was conquered by Cyrus. BM 83110, no. 14 is the settlement regulating arrears for the period from the month of Ulūlu (VI), the 17th year of Nabonidus till Abu (V), the second year of Cyrus, i.e. for two consecutive years. BM 61555, no. 94 concerns almost the same period, i.e. from the [end] of Abu (i.e. from the beginning of Ulūlu), the 17th year of Nabonidus, till Abu, the second year of Cyrus, probably referring to a different group of renters. Clearly, the political situation disrupted again the functioning of temple administration, the fact well known from other categories of documents of that time.

CT 57, 78, no. 36 written in the fourth year of Cyrus and dealing with the rent payment for the accounting year from Ulūlu (VI), third year to Abu (V), fourth year, demonstrates that the situation has been brought again under control. Possibly some problems occured again also in the sixth year of Cyrus,

[366] The lack of documents does not allow determining who the rent collector was in the fifteenth year of Nabonidus.

[367] Note that as in the case of the prebendary bakers, when in the period from Nbn 9 to Cyr 2 (Bongenaar 1997, 177-179) the department was managed by two overseers (*šāpirus*), the same solution was used in the management of the temple houses; even if only for a short time from Nbn 16 (maybe already in the fifteenth year), but dropped already in the first year of Cyrus.

as according to BM 63994, no. 52, silver from the rent of the houses for the period which began in Ulūlu, the sixth year of Cyrus (533 BC), was paid only in the first year of Cambyses (529 BC). It is interesting that one of two persons involved in this is Šamaš-aplu-uṣur, son of Niqūdu, the well-known *ša muḫḫi ešrî*, the person in charge of tithes (Bongenaar 1997, 432, Jursa 1998, 55-57).

3.6 The house rent collectors

It was indicated by Bongenaar that the collection of payment for rented houses rested on the *ša muḫḫi bītāti*, "in charge of the houses," or "the rent collector." The full title was in fact a *ša muḫḫi idi bītāti*, "in charge of collecting the rent of the houses," or "the house rent collector," although this full form is known only from one document.[368]

BM 63353, no. 10 is the only known document which sheds light on the appointment of a house rent collector to office. They were appointed in the same way as the general tenants (*ša muḫḫi sūti*): a candidate presented his proposal to the temple authorities and if they accepted the terms, a document was composed in form of dialogue. The presence of the two highest officials, i.e. Ina-Esagila-lilbur, the administrator (*šangû Sippar*) and Šarru-lūdāri, the king's resident (*qīpu Ebabbar*), reveals that the temple authority recognised that the appointment of the right person was important. It is interesting that the document indicates the year when the contract came into force, but it does not specify when it expired. Such terms gives the temple administration the possibility of terminating the agreement at any time.

Because the earliest settlement of accounts on collecting the rent goes back to the third year of Neriglissar, it seems probable that such a method of collecting the rent was introduced already in the year 557 BC.

Bongenaar identified three individuals (Nabû-šum-iddin, Iqīša-Marduk and Lūṣi-ana-nūri) who occupied this position, but other persons at the office are now recognized. For the convenience of the reader the names and texts known earlier are marked below in cursive.

Period of office	Name	Texts
Lb-M 0	Uššāya[369]	BM 84424, no. 18
Nbn 0	Šamaš-iqīša	BM 101635, no. 25

[368] BM 73499, no. 93: 2-3.

[369] Without title, but as he is responsible for collection of rent his role as rent collector is highly probable.

II.Nbn 2 - 2.VI. Nbn 5	Arad-Bēl/ Nabû-aḫḫē-iddin	BM 68911, no. 12; CT 57, 74, no. 72; CT 57, 69, no. 59; CT 57, 72, no. 60 and CT 57, 83, no. 50.
XIIb.Nbn 6–I.14[370]	*Nabû-šum-iddin/Šamaš-aplu-uṣur//Ile'i-Marduk* and Nādin	BM 73955, no. 73; *CT 57, 84*, no. 48; *Nbn 428*, no. 49; *Nbn 651*, no. 75; *Nbn 717*, no. 82; *Nbn 728*, no. 77; *Nbn 752*, no. 84; *Nbn 824*, no. 97
9.VII.Nbn 16	Bēl-ušallim(/Šamaš-ibni) and Iddin-Nabû[371]	BM 74332 , no. 85
27.VII.Nbn 16 – 10.VII.Nbn 17	Bēl-ušallim/Šamaš-ibni and Šamaš-mudammiq/ Šūzubu//Šangû-Sippar[372]	BM 65748, no. 13; BM 63552, no. 98; BM 79611, no. 86; BM 61839, no. 87; BM 63873; CT 55, 191[373]
14.VII.Camb 1 (š. B.) – V.Cyr 2	Šamaš-mudammiq/ Šūzubu//Šangû-Sippar	BM 63996, no. 91; BM 61555, no. 94; BM 83110, no. 14
1.VI.Cyr 5 – VI.Camb 5	Ina-ṣilli-Nergal	BM 68342, no. 37; BM 101435, no. 90 (dupl. of Cyr 234, no. 89); Nbn 234, no. 88; BM 71178, no. 54; BM 63990, no. 92, and BM 64481, no. 56
Nbk IV	Šamaš-mudammiq	Nbk 445, no. 81
I Dar 1[?] – XII. Dar 7	*Iqīša-Marduk*/Etel-pī-Šamaš//Šangû Sippar	BM 61244, no. 15[374]; *CT 57, 82*, no. 53[375] JEOL 40, no. 1, no.16;[376]
[I].Dar 8 – Dar 10	*Lūṣi-ana-nūri*	BM 63353, no. 10[377]; BM 73499, no. 93, *CT 55, 25*;[378] BM 60407, no. 99

[370] Bongenaar 1997, 164.

[371] The verb, always in plural, clearly indicates their joint action.

[372] Šamaš-mudammiq/Šūzubu in also present in Nbn 464 (13.X.Nbn 10): 4 š of silver *ultu irbi* [*ana* ninda.ḫi.a. šuku.ḫi.a lúdam.meš *šá* lugal for Šamaš-mudammiq/Šūzubu; CT 57, 149: 2 (12.X.Nbk 41): 2½ š of silver for buying sheep for him; CT 57, 147: 9 (10.XI.AmM 1): total 4⅛ š of silver for *ḫuṣābi*, part for *ana epēš* x x x.

[373] For BM 63873 and CT 55, 199 and 10.VII.Nbn 17, respectively, see Sandowicz 2015, 208-209.

[374] Only here with the father's name.

[375] Bongenaar 1997, 10, n. 21, where he occurs with the title, but without filiation. The text is dated to the fourth year, but without ruler's name. In the light of our list of rent collectors and BM 61244, no. 15 (Dar 7) Bongenaar's proposal to date it to Dar 4 seems convincing.

[376] See below, n. 400.

[377] L. 18' where one reads [*ul-tu*] mu.4.kam é.meš *ina* igi-*šú* suggests that he was involved in the administration of the rental of the houses of the Ebabbar temple already in Dar 4; maybe he was the partner of Iqīša-Marduk/Etel-pī-Šamaš, but this cannot be proven.

[378] Bongenaar 1997, 10, n. 21, dated it to "ca. Dar"; it was written rather later than BM 73499, no. 93.

In five cases, the father's and the family name are given in addition to the name of the collector, which in most cases allows us to recognise their ancestral affiliation and position in the temple.

3.6.0.1 Uššāya

Although he is known only from one tablet, its content suggests that he was either the house rent collector or acted as the collector's agent.

3.6.0.2 Šamaš-iqīša

Like Uššāya he is known only from one tablet, however, its content suggests that he was either the house rent collector or acted as the collector's agent.

3.6.1 Arad-Bēl/Nabû-aḫḫē-iddin

Although he is never identified by the title *ša muḫḫi bītāte*, the content of the texts mentioned in the table above suggests that he really held the office. The beginning of his activity as house rent collector began no later than Ulūlu (VI) of the second year of Nabonidus, as in BM 68911, no. 12 he delivers rents from tenants to the Ebabbar for the period of two years from Ululu (VI) Nbn 2 till Abu (V) Nbn 4. His last document with well-preserved date is CT 57, 72, no. 60 where he used money from house rent to pay for oxen. He might be identified with a well-known member of the Isinnaya family, the owner of the baker's,[379] and brewer's prebends,[380] and possibly *ṭupšar* Ebabbar.[381]

3.6.2 Nabû-šum-iddin/Šamaš-aplu-uṣur//Ile'i-Marduk

Although not attested with the title he was identified by Bongenaar as *ša muḫḫi bītāte* active in the period Nbn 6-14,[382] but he was still alive at least until Cyr 4.[383] His last attestation in this role is dated on 5.I.Nbn 14 (Nbn 752, no. 84).

The family was well-known in Sippar; no less than 16 members of the family were engaged in temple activity. They acted as *ērib bītis* of Šamaš (Aqara and

[379] Bongenaar 1997, 186-7 (from Nbk 37 till Nbn 4).

[380] Bongenaar 1997, 210-11 (from Nbn 4 till Nbn 6).

[381] Bongenaar 1997, 91.

[382] Bongenaar 1997, 164 and Bongenaar 2001, 9, n. 3. Here belongs presumably the badly preserved BM 73955, no. 73.

[383] BM 74458 = Bertin 1689 (5.IX.Cyr 3), see Bongenaar 1997, 223 (the owner of the brewer's prebend) and BM 54225 (21.III.Cyr 4), see Bongenaar 1997, 164 and Jursa 1998, 61 (translation), 112f., no. 14 (transliteration) and 125 (copy) as the witness.

Arad-Šamaš, Itti-Marduk-balāṭu, Nabû-tultabši-līšir/Aqara, Šamaš-šākin-šullum/Šumā), *ṭupšar* Ebabbar (Itti-Marduk-balāṭu), *ša muḫḫi ešrî* (Arad-Bēl/Na'id-Marduk), scribes (Ardiya/Rēmūt, Libluṭ/Šūzubu, Marduk-ŠA-DI, Nidintu, Šūzubu/Zababa-aḫ-iddin), and *rab banê*, "(prebendary) orchard-keepers" (Arad-Bēl/Nā'id-Marduk and his three brothers: Arad-Bunene, Arad-Šamaš and Murašu).[384] The earliest known data about the Ile'i-Marduk family in Sippar goes back to Kandalānu, but their greatest influence dates to Nabopolassar's reign, when their representatives belonged to the *ērib bītis* and Itti-Marduk-balāṭu was a member of a small prestigious group of *ṭupšar Ebabbar*. However, no member of the family held the highest office of *šangû* of Sippar, showing that the family did not belong to the highest level of the city elite. In the time of Nabonidus Nabû-šum-iddin was active as rent collector, however he also owned the prebends of temple enterer, baker and brewer of Šamaš and his son inherited his income after him. The brother of Šum-iddin was Šamaš-šum-līšir, but the sources of his income are unknown. Another fairly influential person was Arad-Bēl/Nā'id-Marduk, who held the office of tithe collector (*ša muḫḫi ešrî*) in the period from the seventh year of Nabonidus till the fifth year of Darius.[385] From currently available data it can be concluded that Arad-Bēl was the last prominent person in the family, which subsequently lost influence; most other members of the family acted then only as private scribes.

3.6.3 Nādin

Nādin occurs only in Nbn 428, no. 49: 15 (Nbn 10) which concerns expenditure made by Nabû-šum-iddin and Nādin for 3 minas and 11 shekels, paying for different products (bitumen, wine, honey, *inzaḫurētu*-dye, bricks and iron) with silver from house rent for the period from Abu (V) Nbn 9 till Abu, Nbn 10. As they acted together it seems that Nādin, although, like Nabû-šum-iddin, without the title, occupied the position of house rent collector with Nabû-šum-iddin, at least from Abu, the ninth year of Nabonidus.[386] It cannot be excluded, moreover, that Nādin is a hypocoristicon of Iddin-Nabû, attested in BM 74332, no. 85 (9.VII.Nbn 16), this time together with Bēl-ušallim. If in Nbn 428, no. 49 and BM 74332, no. 85 the same person occurs, it means that Iddin-Nabû=Nādin was first in the office together with Nabû-šum-

384 See Jursa 1995, 72.

385 Jursa 1998, 38-40. Additionally he is also present in BM 67068 (3.XII.Dar 2). According to Jursa, idem 42, he might have acted together with his brother Arad-Šamaš, or Arad-Šamaš could have acted on his behalf.

386 Cf. already Bongenaar 2001, 10 suggested that they were "apperently rent collectors."

iddin/Šamaš-aplu-uṣur//Ile'i-Marduk, at least from Abu (V) Nbn 9, and next with Bēl-ušallim/Šamaš-ibni (at least on 9.VII.Nbn 16). About 15 days later according to BM 65748, no. 13 (24.VII.Nbn 16) the office was in the hands of Bēl-ušallim and Šamaš-mudammiq, i.e. Iddin-Nabû's activity in this role ended before the last date.[387]

3.6.4 Bēl-ušallim/Šamaš-ibni

Until now Bēl-ušallim was unknown and an attempt to find his family background failed. He might be mentioned in BM 62901 (<->.IV.Nbk [x]), where he delivers barley or dates for *maššartu* prebendary payment. His first attestation as the person who paid with silver from house rent is BM 74322, no. 85 (9.VII.Nbn 16), where he acted together with Iddin-Nabû. However, in the light of BM 65748, no. 13 (25.VII.Nbn 16) he might have been in office much earlier, already in the fourtheenth year of Nabonidus. This is the settlement of account of Bēl-ušallim/ Šamaš-ibni and Šamaš-mudammiq made on 27.VII.Nbn 16. As the operative section begins with an expenditure made in month Simānu (III), the fourtheenth year of Nabonidus, this suggests that he acted in this role already in Simānu and replaced Nabû-šum-iddin/Šamaš-aplu-uṣur//Ile'i-Marduk mentioned last time in this role in Nisannu (I), the fourteenth year.

Bongenaar recognised that Nabonidus introduced the standard of two supervisors (*šāpirus*) of the bakers (attested from Nbn 9 till Cyr 2).[388] The same standard was applied in case of house rent collectors (attested from Nbn 9 till the end of Nabonidus reign). It is interesting that when Bēl-ušallim/ Šamaš-ibni acted together with Šamaš-mudammiq, with exception of BM 65748, no. 13, Bēl-ušallim always took second position, i.e. he was at this time subordinate to Šamaš-mudammiq. When Cyrus decided to go back to the earlier administrative tradition with a single supervisor, the position was lost by Bēl-ušallim, which supports the idea that his position was weaker than his partner's Šamaš-mudammiq/Šūzubu//Šangû-Sippar.

3.6.5 Šamaš-mudammiq/Šūzubu//Šangû-Sippar

BM 83110, no. 14 (Cyr 2) makes it possible to identify Šamaš-mudammiq as a member of Šangû-Šamaš family. He was active in the years Nbk 41 – Cyr

[387] Note that Šamaš-mudammiq was the father of Iddin-Nabû (Bongenaar 1997, 451), but it seems that the son of Šamaš-mudammiq and the Iddin-Nabû, the possible rent house collector, are different persons.

[388] Bongenaar 1997, 177-179.

3,[389] and therefore also in the period in which Šamaš-mudammiq/Šūzubu held the office of rent collector. This is supported by CT 55, 191 in which Šamaš-mudammiq and Bēl-ušallim, presumably the rent collectors of that time, paid for a boat to be left at the disposal of Šamaš,[390] and the document is written by Iddin-Nabû/Šamaš-mudammiq//Šangû-Šamaš, proving that they sometimes acted together. The date presented in the table above suggests that Šamaš-mudammiq lost the office after Abu Cyr 2 and before Ulūlu Cyr 5, but regained it at the time of the revolt of Nebuchadnezzar IV, maybe Nebuchadnezzar III. His successor is known only from the fourth year of Darius but this is presumably accidental due to the lack of documents.

3.6.6 Ina-ṣilli-Nergal

Although Ina-ṣilli-Nergal held office for quite a long time (10 years), an attempt to identify his family background failed. As noted above, BM 63994, no. 52 suggests that his activity as house rent collector caused suspicion or was ineffective, since two other people acted instead of him. The extraordinary nature of their actions indicates a period of four years (from the sixth year of Cyrus till the first year of Cambyses) for which they collected rent.[391] However, he delayed with payment of rent also in later time. According to BM 64481, no. 56, rev. 2'-4', Ina-ṣilli-Nergal paid 12 minas 54 shekels of silver for the period from <Tašrītu??> (VII), the fourth year till the 14th day of Ulūlu (VI) of the fifth year of Cambyses, i.e., presumably for one accounting year. The comparison of this amount with the yearly rent which was obliged to pay Iqīša-Marduk/Etel-pī-Šamaš//Šangû Sippar (19 minas 15 shekels) and Lūṣi-ana-nūri (17 minas per year) makes sure that Ina-ṣilli-Nergal did not pay the full amount due as in Rev. 5' it is added that Lūṣi-ana-nūri did not pay 7 minas 6 shekels, presumably for the same accounting period, what suggests that total yearly rent was 22 minas, a quite realistic amount. Still this is not whole debt due from Ina-ṣilli-Nergal as rev. 7' mentions his earlier debts (*e-lat ri-ḫa-nu* igi.meš *šá ina* igi-*šú*). It means that during almost the entire period when Ina-ṣilli-Nergal held the office, the temple had serious problems in obtaining his obligations.

[389] See Bongenaar 1997, 456 and 406, who looked into the activity of Šamaš-mudammiq, carpenter at that time (Nbn 8-11), which raises the difficulty of separating between them in the surviving documents. Bongenaar is right when he points out that most of the documents rather refer to the buyer (or in my opinion, the officer of the temple) than to a carpenter. The tasks assigned to him suggest that he was not an influential member of the family and the function of rent collector was probably his greatest achievement.

[390] For the interpretation of the text, see Sandowicz 2015, 209.

[391] The extraordinary character of their action is suggested by the use of the verb *esēru*, "to exact payment" never used elsewhere for the description of the collection of rent.

3.6.7 Iqīša-Marduk/Etel-pī-Šamaš//Šangû-Sippar

Although Iqīša-Marduk has been known as the *ša muḫḫi bītāti* (CT 57, 82, no. 53) it is only now certain that he was son of Etel-pī-Šamaš (BM 61244, no. 15) and a member of the Šangû Sippar family (JEOL 40, no. 1, no.16), the second person of the family in the office. His career in the Ebabbar temple falls during the reign of Persian kings (Cyr-Dar). Arguments put forward by Bongenaar support the idea that he held the influential position of *tupšar Ebabbar*,[392] i.e. he was another member of the family (although from a different branch) in the central administrative board of the Ebabbar temple.[393] He also owned the prebend of temple enterers (*ērib bītūtu*),[394] and of brewers (*sīrāšûtu*); additionally he acted as the performer (*ēpišānu*) of the baker in the sanctuary of the Anunītu.[395] All this demonstrates that he and the Šangû Sippar family had a good, stable material position based on the income from prebends and other administrative positions. This is now supported by BM 68563+BM 68965, dated to the seventeenth year of Darius, dealing with the division of property of Iqīša-Marduk among his four sons. Although only a fragment of tablet is preserved, it demonstrates that the sons inherited a huge plot of ca. 30 ha in Tīl-gubbi and also one of the largest known urban plots of about 1200 m^2.[396] Evidently, Iqīša-Marduk was one of the wealthiest people of his time in the Sippar region, but in spite of that, neither he nor his sons had any chance to be appointed to the highest post of *šangû*, at least not until the very end of Darius I's reign.[397]

The beginning of the activity of Iqīša-Marduk as rent collector for Ebabbar temple's houses is not fully clear, but it seems that he took office already in the first year of Darius' reign. This is suggested by BM 61244, no. 15: 16-17 written in the end of the seventh year of Darius. According to it, Iqīša-Marduk paid arrears of three minas of silver for the period of the first, second and third years.[398] One can imagine that after the uprising of Nebuchadnezzar III

[392] Bongenaar 1997, 91.

[393] The position was held by Bēl-apla-iddin/(Bēl-)Baliḫu (Bongenaar 1997, 69) and maybe by Bēl-uballiṭ/Kiribtu (Bongenaar 1997, 74f.).

[394] Bongenaar 1997, 162.

[395] Bongenaar 1997, 248-49.

[396] I wish to thank Małgorzata Sandowicz for the access to her unpublished interpretation of the tablet and permission to quote the result of her research here.

[397] A member of this family held again the post of *šangû Sippar* in the period of Dar 33 – Xer 0 (Bongenaar 1997, 12, 33), i.e. after a gap of ca. 65 years when the office was in the hand of the members of the Šangû-Ištar-Bābili and Ša-nāšišu families (see Bongenaar 1997, 12).

[398] Although Iqīša-Marduk occurs there without the title, the context of the document shows without doubt that he held the post of the *ša muḫḫi bītāti*.

and IV there were some problems with the collection of rent in the first year of Darius, but there is no reason to believe that difficulties persisted also in the next two years. Moreover, it is highly doubtful that Iqīša-Marduk would have agreed to pay the rent for the years when the function of the *ša muḫḫi bītāti* was exercised by another person. It is, thus, very likely that the backlog was caused by no one else but by Iqīša-Marduk himself.[399] If this is true, then BM 61244, no. 15 relates to the activity of Iqīša-Marduk for the whole term of office that lasted from the first to seventh year of Darius I (521-516 BC). This is supported by another document, JEOL 40, no. 1, no. 16,[400] written on 28th day of Nisannu, eighth year of Darius, concerning the final settlement of the economic relations of the Ebabbar temple with Iqīša-Marduk. BM 61244, no. 15 and JEOL 40, no. 1, no. 16 are to some extent parallel, but the first concerns only the debts of Iqīša-Marduk in silver, while the second also mentions the debt in dates. Not only the date, but also the content suggest that Lābāši, son of Nabû-nāṣir, descendant of Aḫḫūtu, the scribe of JEOL 40, no. 1, no. 16 knew BM 61244, no. 15, where the debts resulting from the function of *ša muḫḫi bītāti* are presented with all necessary details. JEOL 40, no. 1, no. 16 omits the details present in BM 61244, no. 15, repeating only the total sum of debt amounting to 22 minas 4.5 shekels, but explains how the debt of 1 mina of silver arose and adds that the debt of 122 *kurru* of dates will be registered by Iqīša-Marduk with the scribes of the Etušgina temple and the document will be given to Ina-Esagila-lilbur, then the *šangû Sippar*. It seems that MacGinnis is right in his translation suggesting that one mina of silver is the price of four talents[401] of wool, which was at the disposal of Iqīša-Marduk, and in treating it separately from the debt of 122 *kurru* of dates, because one mina as the price

[399] Such a long period of accumulation of arrears caused by political instability (not reported, let us note, in the second and third year of Darius) seems unlikely.

[400] John MacGnnis, the editor of JEOL 40, no. 1, no. 16, interpreted it as an agreement concerning the termination of Iqīša-Marduk's activity as the general rent farmer, although he noted his absence in the list of general rent farmers composed by Jursa (Jursa 1995, 86). In Jursa's opinion the use of the term é.meš in JEOL 40, no. 1 confirms the termination of Iqīša-Marduk's activity as the collector of rent from the temple houses because "houses" never means "fields" in Sippar text (Jursa 2010, 256, n. 1532). MacGinnis' interpretation resulted probably from the presence of the term *sūtu* (giš.bán), typical for the contract for rental of the temple's fields and/or garden written usually in the form of a dialogue document. However, the same form of a dialogue document is used in BM 63353, no. 10 the first known contract for the lease of houses of the Ebabbar temple. Although the expression *ana sūti* is missing there, it is uncertain whether it was used in the missing beginning of the tablet. The presence of expression *ana sūti* in the Westminster document cannot be an argument for the lease of land as its exact meaning is "for fixed rent", which can also refer to the lease of houses for a fixed sum to be paid by the *ša muḫḫi bīti*. The uncertainty as to how to interpret JEOL 40, no. 1 is now definitely resolved by the identification of BM 61244, no. 15.

[401] Mistakenly written "mina" in his translation.

of four talents of wool and 122 *kurru* of dates would certainly be too low.[402] It is conceivable that the debt in dates is the same debt (or a part of it) mentioned in two documents: MR 37a and its duplicate MR 37b dated to 26th day of the month Ulūlu, fourth year of Darius. In this document a group of eight ērib *bītis*, among them Iqīša-Marduk, acting on behalf of all the *ērib bītis* of Šamaš, confirm borrowing 200 *kurru* of dates from Marduk-rēmanni, son of Bēl-uballiṭ, from the Ṣāḫit-ginê family, promising to repay it in a single delivery in the month of Araḫsamna (VIII), i.e. after about two months at the latest. The note at the end of this document proves that Iqīša-Marduk was also the debtor of Bēl-uballiṭ, presumably the father of Marduk-rēmanni, but the amount is not specified. Less than a month later a new document MR 38a (cf. its duplicate 38b) dated to eighth day of the month Tašrītu (VII) was drafted concerning 120 *kurru* of dates borrowed again in the name of all the *ērib bītis* of Šamaš, to be repaid also in the month Araḫsamna. It cannot be excluded that the debt of 122 *kurru* owed from Iqīša-Marduk according to BM 61244, no. 15 is a part of date loan from the fourth year of Darius. Evidently, both documents BM 61244, no. 15 and JEOL 40, no. 1, no. 16 reveal serious economic trouble on the part of Iqīša-Marduk.

According to JEOL 40, no. 1, no. 16 the contract for a lease of temple houses was relinquished "on his [Iqīša-Marduk's] will", although this seems doubtful. His forceful resignation is suggested by the occurrence of arrears since he took over the function. According to BM 61244, no. 15, Iqīša-Marduk paid three minas of silver for the first, second and third years only in the seventh year of Darius, although the arrears for those years were rather small and probably differed in particular years. Luckily, the document makes it possible to establish the total amount to be paid as agreed between the temple and Iqīša-Marduk. In the first place, since Iqīša-Marduk paid for the fourth year 17 minas 50 shekels (l. 6), we can assume that the yearly obligation could not have been lower than this sum, as it is highly unlikely that he paid more than the agreed sum. For the period from the fourth year till Du'uzu, the seventh year of Darius, Iqīša-Marduk paid the temple 54 minas 55.5 shekels, except for 3 minas of silver of the arrears paid for the first, second and third year. Those arrears were settled at the end of the seventh year when the contract was relinquished. They amounted to 22 minas 4½ shekels, which gives a total of 77 minas for four years, i.e. 19 minas 15 shekels per annum. However, the debt of 22 minas 4½ shekels according to JEOL 40, no. 1, no. 16 concerns only the

[402] Assuming that one mina of silver is the price of four talents of wool, it gives 4.5 minas of wool for one shekel of silver. This is to some extent in agreement with Jursa's opinion that the price of wool "exhibited a sharp increase from an early time in the reign of Darius onwards" (Jursa 2010, 618). Evidently the price is higher than in the time of Cambyses (see Jursa, 617, Table 96), although the increase was by no means sharp.

sixth and seventh year (*re-ḫi ša* mu.6.kam *u* mu.7.kam) while in BM 61244, no. 15: 18 only the lower limit is described ([*e-lat* 22 *ma-n*]*a* 4½ gín [en t]il iti.še), i.e. "apart from 22 minas 4.5 shekels (to be paid) for the period until the end of month Addaru".

Accepting that both texts mention the same sum of unpaid silver due from the performance of the function *ša muḫḫi idi bītāti*, the total of debts for Dar 4-7 amounts to 22 minas 4½ shekels.

Knowing the yearly rent agreed by Iqīša-Marduk in the contract with the temple, the following picture of the yearly arrears occurs:

The rent for the houses per annum	Sum paid by Iqīša-Marduk	Payment for of year	Arrears
19 m. 15 š.	17 m. 50.5 š.	Dar 4	1 m. 24.5 š.
19 m. 15 š.	9 m. 55 š.	Dar 5	9 m. 20 š.
38 m. 30 š. for two years	14 m. 15 š. and 12 m. 55 š. Total 27 m. 10 š.	First sum for Dar 6 Second sum for the rest of Dar 6 and four months of Dar 7	11 m. 20 š. for two years
Total unpaid sum for four years			22 m. 4.5 š.

It is evident from this that the scribe of JEOL 40, no. 1, no. 16 did not understand BM 61244, no. 15 and thought wrongly that the debt of 22 minas 4.5 shekels was just due for the last two years of holding the function. In fact during the first four years the debt was quite small (an average of one mina during Dar 1-3 and one mina 24.5 shekels in the fourth year), but grew rapidly in the fifth (9 minas 20 shekels, i.e. 48.4% of the expected sum was not paid) and in the next two years an average was 5 minas 40 shekels, or 28.5% yearly was unpaid. We do not know what caused it: either Iqīša-Marduk could not enforce the payment from the tenants or he used the silver collected from the tenants to cover his own losses in other fields of activity. It is very likely that the growing debt prompted the temple authority to deprive Iqīša-Marduk of his function, forcing him simultaneously to issue the debt note. All this undermines the declaration of the scribe of JEOL 40, no. 1, no. 16 that the contract of Iqīša-Marduk with the temple was relinquished of his [Iqīša-Marduk's] own will (read: initiative).

3.6.8 Lūṣi-ana-nūri

It is certain that Lūṣi-ana-nūri held the function already in the eighth year of Darius as BM 73499, no. 93 in which he occurs with full title is dated to the 28th day of the month Šabāṭu, the eighth year (of Darius). However, it seems that he took up his new duties from the very beginning of this year, because the activity of Iqīša-Marduk, the former *ša muḫḫi bītāti* was closed at the end of the seventh year. The agreement with Lūṣi-ana-nūri might have been concluded at the same time to enable him to fulfill his new duty from the very beginning of the eighth year.

This supposition concerning the date is supported by BM 63353, no. 10 the first example of a contract between the temple and the house rent collector from temple houses. The document shows that for the appointment to the position of the *ša muḫḫi bītāti* the same procedure and the same form of dialogue document was used as in the case of the general rent farmer (*ša muḫḫi sūti*). Lūṣi-ana-nūri turned to the temple authorities: the administrator (*šangû*), the king's resident (*qīpu*), the temple scribes, the royal official (*ša-rēš šarri*) and the alphabet scribe (*sepīru*) with a proposal to rent him "all [x] reeds,[403] property of Šamaš in the city [...] and in the harbour district" for 17 minas of silver per annum. The authorities accepted his proposal and gave him "all [reeds] except for house [...of x] reeds in which the oblates are living." The following part of the document is unclear, as we read there that "[... from] the fourth year the houses are at his disposal." The presence of four persons: Nidintu, the *sepīru* (attested in the period from Camb 6 till Dar 22), Tērik-šarrūssu (attested from Camb 1 till Dar 15), Ina-Esagila-lilbur, the administrator (attested from Dar 1 till Dar 12) and Šarru-lūdāri (attested as the king's resident from Cyr 6 to Dar 7),[404] definitely proves that only the fourth year of Darius should be taken into consideration. The problem is that according to BM 61244, no. 15 the houses were managed in this and the next three years by Iqīša-Marduk. Either contrary to our document the agreement had been annulled and did not come into life,[405] or – because it is certain that Lūṣi-ana-nūri exercised the role of the *ša muḫḫi bītāti* in the eighth year – a scribe wrote badly "year four" instead of "year eight". This is supported – as already stressed – by BM 73499, no. 93 from the end of the eighth year.

Lūṣi-ana-nūri used the difficult situation of the temple, which in the last four years had not received the expected income to obtain a reduction of rent to 17 minas, i.e. he had to pay 2 minas 15 shekels less. He held the position at

[403] "Reeds" means here "houses" measured in reeds.

[404] See Bongenaar 1997, 93-94; 49; 31; 49 respectively.

[405] It would be strange, and according to my knowledge no such case is known.

least to the tenth year of Darius (BM 60407, no. 99), although a longer period cannot be excluded. He is the known last person in a fairly long list of people occupying the office.

Summing up: at least three known rent collectors belonged to two influential families of the city of Sippar: Ile'i-Marduk and Šangû-Sippar. At the time of their appointment to the office, they owned many prebends, but this, nevertheless, was not sufficient for them to run for the highest office. This is clearly visible in the case of Ile'i-Marduk, a powerful family at the beginning of Neo-Babylonian period, which later was to lose its privileged position. Members of Šangû-Sippar, while maintaining some influence, were kept away from holding the highest offices by other families, mostly the Ša-nāšišu and Šangû-Ištar-Bābili families. Although other rent collectors cannot be identified, the importance of the function itself can be evaluated from the example of the two families discussed here. One can say that the office situated rent collectors in the upper middle class, but did not create an opportunity for a higher position.

It seems certain that the authority of the Ebabbar temple established the institution of house rent collector in order to free its administration from the arduous collection of the rent every year from hundreds of servants. However, one can say that the burden was taken off from the temple's shoulders but not always with the expected income. Quite often the house rent collectors paid the due rent with a delay of many years; additionally new house rent collectors were able to force the temple to reduce the yearly rent. The establishment of the new institution did not resolve the problem of rents, which presumably existed already before this time. It is difficult to say if it was the result of poor selection of people for this post, or the opposite, that the rent tax collectors delayed payment because they themselves had a significant problem – just like the temple administration earler – with collection of rents from temple servants, the majority of whom belonged to the lower social and material class of local society.

The institution of rent house collector, known up till now only from Sippar, is not, in fact, unique, as according to BM 120099, no. 132 (written in Babylon), a certain Nabû-ēṭir held the office of *ša muḫḫi bītāte* of Bēl, i.e., Marduk, in the first year of Xerxes (485 BC). Although documents similar to those known from Sippar are not yet known from Babylon, it seems likely, too, that the institution existed earlier, and was established at the same time as in Sippar. Despite the fact that BM 120099 is later than the last mention of *ša muḫḫi idi bītāte* in Sippar (tenth year of Darius), it seems that such a situation is accidental, and that the office existed also at the same time in Sippar.

4. The temple houses, their location and quality

4.1 Location of the Sun god houses

The available cuneiform sources leave no doubt that the Ebabbar temple was the owner of a large number of houses.[406] The texts suggest that the houses formed complexes located in one city district. In describing the postion of the houses, one of the most common topographical elements was the river or canal. Many houses were located *ša (muḫḫi)* íd ud.kib.nun[ki],[407] i.e. on the Euphrates, which presumably denotes houses in the city of Sippar. Many houses were situated in the *kāru*, "the harbour district".[408] The expression *ka-a-ri ša* ud.kib. nunki[409] occuring next to the *qabal āli*, "middle of the city" and the fact that all the texts belong to the Ebabbar archives leave no doubt that the harbour district of Sippar is meant.

Many houses were located *qabalti āli* ($murub_4$ uru),[410] i.e. inside the wall encircling the city. The house rented by the temple to Bēl-ušallim, son of Šamaš-udammiq, the descendant of the Rē'i-sīsê family, was located near the sanctuary of Šarrat Sippar, close to the great gate leading to the sanctuary.[411]

The Ebabbar temple also owned houses outside the city. Two documents mention the houses located in the village Bāb-nār-Šamaš,[412] and one on the Nār-mašenni canal.[413] One might suppose that the temple had its houses in the

---

406 Also the temples in other cities owned houses used by temple personel or rented to individuals. Some such texts from Uruk are discussed in this study, for instance AnOr 9, 17. It is worth bringing in BM 117469, presumably for Uruk (see Altavilla and Walker 2016, 131 (A. 144)) which mention houses of the overseer of the herds (é.meš *šá* [lú]gal *bu-lum*, l. 3) written on a writing-board (*ki-i ina muḫ-ḫi*/giš.da *šaṭ-ru*, ll. 5-6).

407 BM 114748, no. 19: 2; BM 63552, no. 98: 13-14; BM 63994, no. 52: 1-2; maybe in BM 83110, no. 14: [2] and in BM 68384, no. 38: 1 (*šá* ud.kib.nun[ki]).

408 BM 61555, no. 94: 9'; BM 63552, no. 98: 8; BM 83110, no. 14. r. 4'. Cf. *šá* ugu *kāri* in BM 63499, no. 42: 5.

409 BM 63353, no.10: 8 and Nbn 234, no. 88: 8'.

410 BM 63353, no. 10: 7'; CT 57, 78, no. 36: 1; Nbn 201, no. 29: 1; Nbn 234, no. 88-90; cf. BM 83110, no. 14, r. 6' ($murub_4$.tu_4 uru). Cf. BM 83611, rev. 2'-3' where 26 *kurru* 2 *pānu* 3 *sūtu* was delivered from Tīl-Gubbi for the *širkus* living in the *qabal āli*.

411 Nbn 48, no. 1: *abulli* (ká.gal[!]) *ša bīt Šarrat Sippar*.

412 BM 63967, no. 101: 1, r. 4', and CT 57, 26, no. 40: ⸢1⸣, 14.

413 CT 57, 75, no. 43: 2.

majority of villages where economic life flourished. Lack of documents from other villages – except for the two mentioned above – might be accidental.

Rented houses are almost always described in the simplest way, i.e. as *bītu* (é). This may describe the whole house or only a part of it, even one room. Only seldom can we be certain that the tenant leased more than one room, i.e. when he subleased part of the rented lodging. These documents allow to say that, as in the case of fields, sublease of houses was legal.

4.2 Condition of houses

A few documents describe the condition of houses by using the ideograph šub, if one house is meant, or šub.meš, if more. Bongenaar saw in this term the description of the extremely low condition. The best evidence that the term described a ruined house is in BM 75208, no. 28: 10-11 stating that a leatherworker lives in the half of the subleased house, while the other half is ruined (*ina a-ḫi áš-bi a-ḫi* šub). Similar descriptions occur in BM 83110, no. 14, r. 8'-10': šu.nígin 15½ *ma-na* 4⅓ gín kù.babbar *i-di* é.meš/šub.meš *u* un.meš é *ina* ⌜*lìb*⌝*-bi áš-ba šá* 2-*ta*/mu.an.na.meš níg.ka$_9$ *ép-šú*, "grand total 15½ minas, 4⅓ shekels of silver, the rent of the ruined houses in which the servants live, the balance account for two years has been made." In two texts the condition of the lodgings is described with an adjective, which clearly is used instead of ideographic writing šub.meš. BM 61555, no. 94: 6'-7' mentions rent (the word must occur in an earlier line) from [é] *na-di*^{meš} *u* é.meš *šá* ^{lú}erín.meš ⌜é⌝/[*ina lìb-bi*] *áš-ba*, "(rent) from *nadēti* houses and from houses, [in which] the servants are living." The same expression is found in BM 83110, no. 14, r. 3'-4': [*i-di* é]/ *na-di-e-ti šá ka-a-ri*, "rent from *nadēti* houses in the harbour district." In BM 64489, no. 45: 8 we read about *i-di* é *na-du-ú šá* PN. Evidently *nadû* replaces šub and this view is already present in CDA, s.v. *nadû* I, with the meaning "laid down, deserted, abandoned," while the more appropriate meaning "damaged" or "dilapidated" should be in place, or even "ruined." However, it is worth noting that the rent for many such *bītātu nadētu* is similar to that paid for other houses that are not described with the term.[414] Although the term certainly described the low condition of a house, it probably did not always denote a "ruined" house so much as one that required general renovation in near future or was to be demolished and built anew from its foundation. BM 83110, no. 14 might be understood in the sense that, although the house was no longer habitable, it might be used in a different

[414] However, as the area of rented house is not known, it seems rather likely that the price of rented "fallen" lodging compared to whole surface of a house was low.

way. Maybe the fact that the temple demanded rent may mean that the tenant had been responsible for bringing the house to ruin, i.e. that he neglected vital repairs. It seems beyond dispute that tenants of temple houses – just like the tenants of private houses – were obliged to care for the houses and prevent their destruction. The above-cited texts suggest that the ruined houses were situated in the harbour district of the city of Sippar. This is clearly stated in BM 83110, no. 14, r. 4' (*nadēti ša kāri*) and maybe in two additional texts.[415] As we see below in this suburb of the city of Sippar lived the poorest people of the city.

4.3 The tenants of the houses of the Sun god

The most surprising result of this new study is the identification of tenants. Earlier studies on temple personnel were focused on remuneration, i.e. solid (bread made mostly of barley flour, dates) and liquid food (beer, oil for cooking) or oil used for personal care (as ointment) and medical purposes, while the problem of providing housing was not considred. The personnel of higher and middle strata had to provide accommodation for themselves and their families on their own and this is supported by hundreds of contracts between private persons. Probably it was assumed that – just as in medieval Europe – the dependants of Babylonian temples were allocated very modest lodgings free of charge. According to my knowledge only Jursa has referred to this issue: "But serfs would normally not have been required to pay for housing (and possibly also not for fuel), and they would not have had to pay government taxes (or hire substitute labour to fulfill corvée duties required from them, as free men frequently did)."[416] In the light of the documents presented here this opinion must be subjected to a fundamental revision. The cuneiform documents, sometimes already in the heading, sometimes in the operative section, describe in general terms those who lived in the temple houses and had to pay for them. The tenants are named as *nīšē bīti*, "the temple servants",[417] *ṣabē bīti* (erín.meš é), "the temple workers",[418] or *širkē* (^{lú}rig$_7$.meš) "the oblates".[419] BM 66665, no. 57 where first the name and the sum paid by an individual person is given is closed with the sentence ⸢pap⸣ 12 é.meš *šá* ^{lú}*ši-ra-*

[415] Cf. BM 63552, no. 98: 7-8 [*i-di* é.meš *na-di-e-ti*]/*šá ka-a-ri ù* mu[rub$_4$ uru] and in BM 61555, no. 94: 8-9: *i-di* é.meš ⸢x⸣ [x x]/ [... *š*]*á* ugu *šá ka-a-ri*.

[416] Jursa 2010, 298. Cf. Weisberg in OIP 122, 190, note to line i 1: "Did some oblates pay rent and did others receive free housing?"

[417] BM 51817, no. 44: 1; BM 64489, no. 45: 1, r. 9'; BM 64481, no. 56, r. 7'; BM 61555, no. 94: 11'; BM 63552, no. 98: 10'; BM 83110, no. 14, r. 6', 9'; BM 63499, no. 42: 4 (there ^{lú}<un.meš>).

[418] BM 51817, no. 44: 1 and CT 57, 73, no. 26: [1].

[419] BM 63353, no. 10: 16'.

⌜*ku*⌝/[*ina*] *lìb-bi áš-bi*, "total 12 houses in which the oblates are living."[420] All the terms denote in fact a homogenous group of people given to the temples as prisoners of war, donated by rulers or private individuals or born from parents of the same low status. This was presumably the largest group paying fees for lodgings provided by the temple. The texts relating to the rent paid by them locate their lodgings inside the city (*qabal* or *qabalti āli*) or in the harbour district of the city (*ina kāri ša nār Sippar*), but presumably such houses were built in all settlements belonging to the Ebabbar temple. Quite often the social position and professions of the tenant is given. Among the tenants are builders (*arad ekalli*),[421] bakers (*nuḫatimmu*),[422] leatherworkers (*aškāpu*),[423] fishermen (*bā'iru*),[424] carpenters (*naggāru*),[425] barbers (*gallābu*),[426] people in charge of the bulls (*ša bīt alpē*),[427] in charge of the bird house (*ša bīt iṣṣurē*), in charge of the house of the chief musician (*ša bīt* [lú]*rab zammārē*),[428] fullers (*ašlākē*),[429] maybe a decurion ([lú]10?),[430] and a person with an unidentified title *húp-pa-na*.[431] The rent was paid also by an unnamed chief of the harbour or harbour district (*rab kāri*).[432] Seldom among the tenants there occurs a person who, like Mammītu-enqet, who lived in the house of Šamaš-ēreš but paid for her accommodation on her own.[433] The same text mentions the lady [f]Humištu, who might be a member of the Hindanu tribe.[434]

The number of people who are identified by profession is low, less than

[420] On the basis of this text we can safely identify two leatherworkers as oblates of the Ebabbar temple.

[421] BM 64489, no. 45: 6 (Gadia) and presumably the same person in BM 101853, no. 46: 8 (written [m]*ga-di-da*, but the title is damaged), BM 75208, no. 28: 14 (Arad-Bunene), 17 (Bānītu-ēreš), BM 101853, no. 46: 1' (name broken) and 4' (Bēl-ēṭir-Šamaš).

[422] BM 63499, no. 42: 6 (Bēl-ēṭir); BM 75208, no. 28: 8 (Arad-Anunītu); BM 84424, no. 18, r. 2' (Zēriya).

[423] Gimillu in BM 66665, no. 57: 5', Lābāši in BM 64489, no. 45: 4 and BM 75208, no. 28: 18, Mūrānu in BM 66665, no. 57: 4' and BM 75208, no. 28: 10, [DN]-apla-iddin in BM 114748, no. 19: 14.

[424] BM 79054, no. 20: 14 (Arad-Nabû); BM 75208, no. 28: 13 (Mušēzib-Bēl), 28 (Arad-Bēl).

[425] BM 75208, no. 28, 37: 8 (Nabû-kēšir).

[426] BM 50347, no. 71: 8 (*i-di / šá* [lú]šu.i).

[427] BM 64489, no. 45: 5; BM 75208: 6 and BM 101853, no. 46: 7' (in all texts Šamaš-erība).

[428] CT 57, 78, no. 36: 6 (Ardīa).

[429] BM 75208, no. 28: 32 ([x]-*du-ú-a*).

[430] BM 75208, no. 28: 21 (Ina-ṣil-x-a/A [lú]10?).

[431] BM 101635, no. 25: 12 (Šamaš-erība).

[432] CT 57, 26, no. 40: 8.

[433] BM 63499, no. 42: 7.

[434] The text states only that she paid rent for the house (situated) *ina ma-la-ku šá ḫi-in-da-a-a*, "in the walkway of the Hindaneans;" however, she is followed by Būr-iddin, another person with typical Hinadanean theophoric name element, so her belonging to that tribe is plausible.

1% of all named tenants. This should not, however, surprise us; the ordinary people at the bottom of the social ladder did the work which required no professional skill and 1% of qualified workers in this social group reflect rather well the number of people with professional skills.[435]

4.4 Living conditions of the temple tenants

Heather Baker noted a few years ago that little is known about the living conditions of slaves because documents only seldom mention their accommodation (she cites two examples).[436] The administrative documents, the object of this study, deliver no information about the size of the rented dwellings, the neighbours, or the streets in which the houses were located. However, at least two texts (BM 752078, no. 28 and Nbn 201, no. 290) are of great importance, as they include some general information about the physical conditions and additionally about sub-leasing of a part of the occupied dwelling.[437] The latter information is of especial importance because it suggests that the tenant occupied a minimum of two rooms, however the rent paid by subtenants suggests that at least some of them leased more than one room.

Other data[438] suggest that the average size of the dwellings of the oblates in the Neo-Babylonian Uruk was about 120 m^2, i.e. presumably no less than four rooms.[439] However, it is not certain if similar living conditions for oblates prevailed in the Ebabbar temple in Sippar, a smaller economic center of the temple economy. Some data suggest that conditions might be considerably worse in comparison with other centres.

As was established earlier, the majority of people on the list of tenants who paid rent to a rent collector, belonged to the lowest social group. It is important now to try to establish their living conditions. Although the documents quote the amounts of rent paid by individuals, no text (including private rent contracts) gives the area of the occupied lodging. The only possibility of assessing, at least to some degree, the quality of living is to analyze the information mentioned above on the condition of "houses" and about the amount of rent. The bad condition of the discussed houses is, as discussed,

[435] Some of them (like famous Gimillu in Uruk, see San Nicolò 1933; Jursa 2004a), who gained economic independence certainly did not occur in the lists, because they were able to hire more comfortable houses, presumably on the basis of individual contracts between them and the temples.

[436] Baker 2001, 23f.

[437] The last data occurs also in BM 68384, no. 38.

[438] Baker 2014, 19f. with comments in point 3.

[439] This is supported by the fact that houses measuring about 100 m^2 had four rooms, see Baker 2013, 20, comments no. 2. In her opinion it would be space for about five persons (parents and children), see idem, 14.

indicated by descriptions with the adjective *nadû/nadêti* (šub).[440] Interesting and useful information is provided by BM 75208, no. 28, the only document mentioning the bad condition of house. Out of 33 "houses" 16 are identified as "ruined"; however, in eight cases the end of the line is damaged and the actual condition of the house cannot be guaged. Still, we can say without risk that the condition of more than half of these cases was bad; in one it is clearly stated that half of the house was not fit for living in.[441] The second indication of housing condition is the rent paid. The lowest fee is almost symbolic: one-fourth shekel yearly, which in itself suggests very modest accommodation. A majority paid one shekel or two shekels, though higher fees of four shekels or more are also recorded. One may suspect that such lodgings were rented by large families with several children, maybe with other relatives.

4.5 The question of sublease

For many holders of the Ebabbar temple houses even such low rent was too high and they decided to sublease a part of the house.[442] The understanding of sublease of the temple's lodging is based on two documents, BM 75208, no. 28, and BM 64489, no. 45. There is also third document, AnOr 9, 17, from the Eanna archive, which, however, has been interpreted differently and we begin discussion from this last text. It is a long list of "houses, property of [Ištar] of Uruk", similar to lists from the above-mentioned documents from Sippar. In Sippar texts the data concerning each house are presented in a separate entry. First the amount of rent is given, followed by "house of PN1, PN2 lives in the house."[443] Out of 28 entries in AnOr 9, 17, a similar structure is observed in 13 entries: "house of PN1, PN2 lives in it for x shekels of silver", while in six entries "house of PN1, PN2 (once profession is given) lives in it," and the amount of rent is omitted. On the basis of these entries Janković conjectures that PN1 "in all likelihood refers to the previous owners, who for some reason, probably indebtedness, had to cede their property to the temple."[444] If we accept this line of reasoning, a similar interpretation should be accepted for the Sippar text. There are, however, some doubts about the acceptance of this idea. First, in BM 64489, no. 45 the relation between the first and second person is expressed in a slightly different way, i.e. instead of *ina libbi ašib*, "he lives in it" (i.e. in a

[440] See above, p. 122-123.

[441] *ina a-ḫi áš-bi a-ḫi* šub (l. 11).

[442] For possibile case of sub-lease of private house, see p. 51.

[443] Additionally, sometimes PN1 or PN2 is identified by title, sometimes the house location is given ("near a huge well," "bordering a canal," "in the garden," "under/near the bridge of Nergal").

[444] Janković 2013, 187, n. 665.

house) there is *ina pān* "(house) is in disposal PN." Luckily, in both texts BM 75208, no. 28 and BM 64489, no. 45, the year is preserved; the first was written in the second year, the second in the sixth year of Nabonidus. In the second text the same 11 pairs of names occur again. It is difficult to explain why, after four years had elapsed, the house would still be identified by the name of its former holders. Janković leaves unexplained the eight entries in which only one holder ("house of PN1") is named. The same concerns the final entry *te-né-e šá* é ^{md}ag-numun-gál^{ši} /^{md}innin-du-igi *ina lìb-bi a-šib*, "replacement of the house of Nabû-zēr-ušabši, Innin-mukīn-apli lives in it"; presumably following an exchange Innin-mukīn-apli occupies the house which was previously in the hands of Nabû-zēr-ušabši.[445] Important is the entry in ll. 5-6, where the house taken as a pledge (*maškanu*) by one individual is in the hands of another for the rent of 10 shekels yearly. The former holder is not mentioned at all! This entry and the final entry about a replacement indicate that the temple did not interfere in relations between its servants unless it infringed its interests. It seems to me that in all three texts when PN2 follows PN1 described as living in the house, is proof of sublease of a part of PN1's house.[446]

It should be noted that ruined houses were never the subject of sublease, presumably because nobody wished to live in a dangerous property. In BM 75208, no. 28, if we exclude ruined houses, out of ten well preserved entries, in five, maybe six,[447] i.e. 50% or a little more, the tenants subleased part of houses rented by them from temple. It is interesting to know that among subtenants is a person in charge of birds, a leatherworker and two builders. The other text which gives an insight into sublease is BM 64489, no. 45, a document in which the names of tenant and – if subleased – subtenant are given. Out of ten tenants of a house rented from the temple, six decided to sublease part of their lodgings. Again, as in BM 75208, no. 28, a little over a half of all tenants decided to sublease, obviously because of a difficult material situation and trouble with payment of the required fee.

[445] However, in the animal offering lists *tenû* is used to describe the replacement of a bull by one bull of slightly lower quality. It means that the entry in AnOr 9, 17: 47-48 is not about depriving him of the house, but refers to exchange for another.

[446] Possibly sublease occurs also in BM 114748, no. 19 where the expression PN1 é PN2 is used, which might be understood as "PN1 (the tenant), the house is (at hands of) PN2 (sub-tenant)." However, because in three cases the first name changes, while the second is the same (for similar situation, see AnOr 9, 17: 11-14), possibly an opposite interpretation would be correct, as it seems unlikely that one person sub-leased three houses or part of three houses, i.e. in this document first the subtenants would be named, while the person who subleased the house to three different families was the same. Because the interpretation is not certain, they have not been taken into account when drawing conclusions. See also above, p. 51-52.

[447] In l. 17 the only the name of the subtenant is given (^{md}dù-*tú*-[kam] ^{lú}ìr é.gal *ina* lìb-bi áš*-bi**) while in other first the name of the tenant, then the subtenant is given.

Although the material on which our conclusion is based is limited to two documents and might be subject to doubt, a contrary interpretation, that sublease was seldom practised, is undoubtedly even less justified. It is interesting to note that there were women among the tenants and few subtenants.[448] Three women paid half shekel, (a very low fee),[449] one three-eigth shekel,[450] one two-third shekel,[451] one one and half shekels,[452] one two shekels.[453] ᶠLi'itu, presumably the same woman present in two texts, paid 3¼ shekels and 3½ shekels, respectively.[454] The highest rent paid by a woman is four shekels (BM 64489, no. 45: 1), however, the tenant, presumably a widow, had to sublease part of the house to another woman, presumably a bird-catcher.[455] The great differences in fee suggest that their material situation differed substantially, although their presence in the documents, instead of their husbands, is presumably related to their status of widows. An unusual situation is in Cam 28, no. 34 and Cam 29, no. 35, in which Ina-tēšê-ēṭir leases a house (or part of it) for ᶠĒṭirtu, his wife for two shekels of silver (yearly). It is interesting to note that a majority of women bear West-Semitic names, i.e. probably they belong to the people deported to Babylonia; their material and legal status expresses well this situation. Parallel to their names, male West-Semitic names or names with West-Semitic elements are on the list of tenants: names with Adad (presumably spelled Hadad/Haddu/Addu: -iabi, -natanu, -rapa'; Ahu-iabi, Basuru, Iltama (written also Altama), names with theophoric element Būr (but second element Akkadian) Haiammu, Hamadia, Harruru, Karea, Niri'immi, Sinû.[456] Generally, a majority of names are Akkadian but the conclusion that only a small percentage of the temple servants represented the deported people would be rather misleading, as most deported people quickly adopted Akkadian names.

[448] The sub-tenant ᶠ*su-ut-tur* is certainly identical with ᶠ*su-dir-tu*$_4$/*su-ud-dir-tu*$_4$, the bird-catcher (*ušandû*), active already during the third and fourth decades of Nebuchadnezzar II, see Janković 2004, 106f. and Tarasewicz 2009, 192.

[449] ᶠḪipta and ᶠBānītu-ēreš in BM 114748, no. 19: 3, 10; ᶠḪabarṣītu, daughter of Ina-māti/šādi-ia in BM 63499, no. 42: 4.

[450] ᶠḪummuštu in BM 63499, no. 42: 9.

[451] ᶠMammītu-enqet in BM 63499, no. 42: 7.

[452] ᶠTabātu in BM 63266, no. 41, r. 10'.

[453] ᶠḪaggia in BM 79054, no. 20: 16.

[454] BM 114748, no. 19: 18 (Nbn 0) and BM 73044, no. 24: 8 (Nbn 1). In BM 64489, no. 45 both the tenant and subtenant are women.

[455] See above, n. 448.

[456] For texts, see *Index of Personal Names.*

4.6 Economic importance of house rental for the Ebabbar temple

The very existence of official rent collectors, the engagement of the temple authority including the temple administrator of Sippar, the king's resident, temple scribes, the *sepīru*-interpreter scribe, and a royal official (*rēš šarri*)[457] indicates clearly the importance of the rental of houses for the temple economy. Luckily, the documents make it possible for us to establish the size of the income from this source for the temple economy. As was demonstrated above Iqīša-Marduk, rent collector in the period Dar 1-8, should have paid 19 minas 15 shekels of silver yearly, while his successor a little less, 17 minas of silver. Other texts, although they concern only to a part of the debt, provide numerous data about the payment of the rent:[458]

Number of text	Period	Amount	Commentary
BM 54956, no. 31	Time of Nbn	2 m 9 š	Total of individual payments
BM 75208, no. 28	Nbn 2	2 m 9¼ š[459]	Total of individual payments
CT 57, 83, no. 50	Nbn 5	2 m 13½ š	The rent received from Arad-Bēl/Nabû-aḫḫē-iddin, the then rent collector
Nbn 717, no. 82	Nbn 3	2 m 55 š	Part of tax delivered by the rent collector Nabû-šum-iddin
CT 57, 69, no. 59	Nbn 3	3 m	The text mentions the sum given *ana alpi*, i.e. to buy[?] oxen
Nbn 428, no. 49	V.Nbn 9 till V.Nbn 10[460]	3 m 11 š	Total of individual expenditure based on the house rent
BM 73499, no. 93	dated to <Dar> 8	5 m	
Nbn 234, no. 88	[...] till 1.VI.<Cyr> 6	5 m 20 š	Rest of silver from oblates living in the harbour district and inside the city

[457] On this office, see Jursa 2010a, 87f. and Jursa 2015, 599-602.

[458] Only sums over 2 minas are included in the table. The data are given from the lowest to the highest sums with exception of texts concerning the same or almost the same period.

[459] This is a subtotal, which is close to the preserved sum of individual payments; the next line gives total amounting to 4 minas 15½ shekels, but it is not clear how the scribe calculated this amount.

[460] Presumably "the very end," see above, p. 106.

BM 51817, no. 44	[Not preserved]	6?½ m	Total of individual payments
BM 61555, no. 94	5.Nbn 17 till Cyr 2	7 m	Presumably only from houses located in the harbour district
BM 83110, no. 14	6.Nbn 17 till 5.Cyr 2	35½ m	The sum presumably concerns the period of two years mentioned in the heading. In the body of the document 11 m 9 shekels *idi bītāte nadēti ša karē* and 4 m 16 shekels *idi bītāte ša qabal āli* are quoted.
BM 64481, no. 56	<5>.Camb 4 till 6.Camb 5	12 m 54 š	Additionally the text mentions 7 m 6 š, "the remainder" (*reḫi*) at disposal of Ina-ṣilli-Nergal, the then rent collector
CT 57, 82, no. 53	(Dar) 4	13 m 1 š	The sum delivered to the <*bīt*> *makkūri*-storehouse[461]
BM 63552, no. 98	6.Nbn 13 -5.16	18 m 15 š[462]	*idi bītāte ša karē u ša qabal āli*
BM 65748, no. 13	Nbn 14[?]-16	31½ m	It is impossible to establish the amount of arrears from each year of the accounting period
BM 61244, no. 15	1.Dar 4 till 12. Dar 7	54 m 55½ š	Note the highest payment for the fourth year (17 m 50½ š)

From the table it is evident that, presumably during the whole discussed period, the temple regularly received from the rent collectors quite important sums of silver, close to 17 minas agreed between the temple and the new rent collector in BM 63353, no. 10. The sum demanded from the tenants was certainly higher to guarantee the rent collector's income, however, nothing is known how he was rewarded, or what his cut was.

The table below gathers all data from the entries where the amount of rent paid is well preserved. The value of this data lies in the reasonable assumption that the tenant's decision to hire a larger or smaller house was influenced by his financial situation, and so the data give insight into his material and social situation.

[461] However, it is not certain if the sum comes exclusively from rent payment. The interpretation is based on the heading stating that the document concerns *i-di* é.

[462] Additionally 2 m 9 š are mentioned as *idi bīti* of the 16th year and 52 š as *idi bīti* from the houses located on the Euphrates.

Tab. 1a. The rent from the lowest (¼ shekel) to 5 shekels.

Number	Year	¼	⅓	½	⅔	¾	⅜	1	1 ¼	1 ½	2	2 ¼	2 ⅓	2½	3	3¼	3½	4	4½	4¾	5
BM 84424, no. 18	Lb-M 0							2			2							1			
BM 62168, no. 17	Nrg 3							12			1										
BM 114748, no. 19	Nbn 0	1		3		2		4	1	2	2	1		2	3	1	1	3			
BM 79054, no. 20	Nbn 0							3			3	1			1					1	
CT 57, 77, no. 21	Nbn 0							1?										1			
BM 73044, no. 24	Nbn 1		1?								2	1					1				
CT 57, 73, no. 26	(Nbn 1)																				
BM 59708, no. 27	Nbn 2																				
BM 75208, no. 28	[Nbn?] 2		1					1		1	11				2			8	1	1	1
Nbn 201, no. 29	Nbn 5							7			6	1			2						
BM 64489, no. 45	[Nbn] 6									3	2				1?			2			3
BM 68900, no. 30	Nbn 14										2										

BM 54956, no. 31	Nbn [x]													2							
BM 71910, no. 32	Nbn [x]										4							1			
BM 68342, no. 37	(Cyr 6)										1										
Cam 28, no 34 and Cam 29, no. 35	Camb 1							2[463]			1										
BM 68384, no. 38	(Camb 3)																1				
BM 74311, no. 39	[KN] ⸢5⸣										1	2									
CT 57, 26, no. 40	Und.																				
BM 63266, no. 41	Und.			5	2		1		2	2	1	1			1						
BM 66665, no. 57	Und.								1		1		1								2
BM 63499, no. 42	Und.			4	1	1	3			1											
CT 57, 75, no. 43	Und.										1			4							
BM 51817, no. 44	Und.							3			1				1?						
Total of cases		1	2?	12	3	3	4	35	4	8	42	7	1	8	11	1	2	16	1	2	6

463 Two shekels for two houses, i.e. one shekel for each house.

Tab. 1b. The rent over 5 shekels.

Number	Year	5½	5¾	6	6 ⅓	6 ¾	7	8	10	11	12	15	18
BM 84424, no. 18	Lb-M 0												
BM 62168, no. 17	Nrg 3												
BM 114748, no. 19	Nbn 0			2	1		1	1		1			
BM 79054, no. 20	Nbn 0												
CT 57, 77, no. 21	Nbn 0		1										
BM 73044, no. 24	Nbn 1												
CT 57, 73, no. 26	(Nbn 1)							2					
BM 59708, no. 27	Nbn 2			1									
BM 75208, no. 28	[Nbn?] 2			1					1				
Nbn 201, no. 29	Nbn 5	1											
BM 64489, no. 45	[Nbn] 6			1									
BM 68900, no. 30	Nbn 14												
BM 54956, no. 31	Nbn [x]											1	
BM 71910, no. 32	Nbn [x]												
BM 68342, no. 37	(Cyr 6)					1							
Cam 28, no. 24 and Cam 29, no. 35	Camb 1												

BM 68384, no. 38	(Camb 3)												
BM 74311, no. 39	[KN] ⌜5⌝						+						
CT 57, 26, no. 40	Und.			2							6		1
BM 63266, no. 41	Und.												
BM 66665, no. 57	Und.			2									
BM 63499, no. 42	Und.												
CT 57, 75, no. 43	Und.												
BM 51187											1		
Total of cases		1	1	9	1	1	1	3	1	1	7	1	1

In 24 texts the rent paid by 198 tenants in the period from the accession year of Lābāši-Marduk till about the third year of Cambyses' reign is preserved,[464]

[464] More names of tenants are known, but the sums of rent paid by them are damaged. Obviously, it cannot be excluded that undated documents or those with damaged date were written later, in the time of Darius. Possibly in BM 68420 (but maybe also in BM 74411) the house rent was owed by the tenants of the houses of the Ebabbar temple. In BM 68420 this is suggested by the expression "property of Šamaš" (níg.ga ^{d}utu). The text was edited by Bloch 2014, 154-156. As my reading differs from his, after collation a new transliteration is presented below:

Obv. 1. [x gí]n kù.babbar *ina* šu^{ii} ^{m}*mar-duk-*⌜*a**⌝ [*a-šú šá* ^{m}*a-r*]*i**-*iḫ**
2. [x gín] *i-di* é ^{md}ag-tin-*su*-e
3. [x]+ ⌜1⌝ gín *i-di* é ^{m}*ka**-*re-e-*⌜*a**⌝
4. [pap x *m*]*a**-⌜*na*⌝ 18 gín kù.babbar níg.ga ^{d}utu
5. [*a-na* x g]ín kù.gi *ina* ugu
6. [x x x ^{m}*Mar-du*]*k*-⌜*a*$^{?}$⌝ *a-šú šá* ^{m}*a-ri-iḫ*
7. [x x x x] ⌜*a**⌝-*na** ^{d}utu
8. [*it-ta-din*]

Rev. 9. [^{lú}*mu-kin-nu* PN1 *a*]-*šú šá*
10. [PN2 a ^{lú}sanga *si*]*p-par*^{ki}
11. [PN3 *a-šú šá* ^{m}]su*-^{d}amar*.utu*
12. [a ^{lú}sanga ^{d}mùš tin.ti]r^{ki}
13. [*u* ^{lú}umbisag ^{md}a]g*-⌜mu⌝*-si.sá *a-šú šá*
14. [ti]n*-*su** a ^{lú}sanga ^{d}mùš tin.tir^{ki}
15. [u]d*.⌜kib.nun⌝^{ki} iti.sig$_{4}$

L.e. 16. [u$_{4}$.x.kam] mu.11.kam ^{md}ag-[i lugal e^{ki}]

i.e. for the period of about 30 years (556-527 BC), when the majority of tenants were active for the whole or at least for most of the period. The rent differed substantially from the lowest ¼ shekel to the highest of 18 shekels yearly. If we recognise the rent as representative of material situation of the tenant, this huge differentiation is striking. There are twenty-five tenants (12.6% of the whole group) who paid the lowest rent between ¼ to ¾ shekel yearly. This can be compared with twenty-nine tenants who paid from over 5 to 18 shekels (14.6% of whole group) yearly, i.e. the poorest and wealthiest groups were almost equal. The difference between the poorest paying ¼ shekel and the wealthiest is extremely high, 1:72! This is also seen on comparing the income of the temple from the first and second group. The first paid 12⅔ shekels, the other ca. 253⅔ shekels, i.e. the second group paid 20 times more. The difference in the material situation of both groups is really shocking. Among the tenants the largest was the group paying 2 shekels (fourty-two people, 21.2% of the whole group), then those who paid 1 shekel (thirty-five people, 17.7% of the whole group); to both these groups thus belonged almost 39% of all tenants. Quite large is the group of fifteen tenants who paid 4 shekels (7.6% of all); however, four of them decided to sublease part of the house, which raises doubt that their material situation was really good. Intriguing is CT 57, 26, no. 40, with a list of nine tenants living in Bāb-nār-Šamaš,[465] who paid an extremely high fee: two tenants paid 6 shekels each, six 12 shekels each, and a woman with foreign name who paid 18 shekels; in total they paid 1 mina 42 shekels.[466] Unfortunately, because the document is not dated and it is impossible to identify the tenants unambiguously,[467] it is impossible to say

L. 1. Bloch wrongly recognised the last sign of the line written on rev. as ud after sig$_4$ in l. 15. Note that from ⌜*a**⌝ only the trace of one vertical wedge is preserved. After a damaged gap the trace of sign, almost certainly *ri*, is preserved. The last sign read as *iḫ* is badly preserved and has a strange shape, but the context makes the reading highly probable.

L. 3. For the name, see NBN 88.

L. 6. The sign following the rest of [*du*]*k* is probably written over erasure and it is not certain if double a was really written.

L. 8. I added the line for three reasons: a. there is a space for an additional line; b. without a verb at the end of the main part of document its sense is difficult to understand; c. in contract (as properly recognised by Bloch) rev. begins usually from the list of witnesses.

L. 11. Although I do not attempt a reconstruction of the name of first witness, most probably it is the name of Šamaš-tabni-uṣur (= Tabnēa), son of Erība-Marduk, descendant of Šangû-Ištar-Bābili, although the name of one of his brothers: Kī-Bēl, Kī-Nabû or even Marduk-šum-iddin, the future *šangû Sippar* cannot be ruled out.

L. 13. For *Nabû-šum-līšir*, son of Balāssu, descendant Šangû-Ištar-Bābili, see Bongenaar 1997, 85-87.

[465] Concerning this settlement, see Zadok 1985, 60 and Jursa 1995, 204.

[466] Note a mistake in the total: 1 mina 32 shekels.

[467] Arad-Anunītu might be identified with *rab būli*, however this is simply a guess based on his name; the title of Zumbā is damaged, while the unnamed *rab kāri* subleased the rented house to

why the rent was so extremely high. This situation demonstrates that despite the abundance of the administrative documents from Sippar, many situations are not reflected in them. It is obvious that the preserved list of names of 198 tenants is incomplete.

However, we can try to estimate the actual number of tenants by taking into account 17 minas, or 1020 shekels of silver that the rent collector Ina-ṣilli-Nergal was obliged to pay every year. In total 198 leaseholders paid almost exactly 550 shekels, i.e. statistically each paid about 2.77 shekels. It means that those tenants who did not occur in the known texts should pay 470 shekels. Assuming that each tenant pay 2.77 shekels in average, the missing amount should be paid by ca. 170 tenants. It means that during the period when Ina-ṣilli-Nergal was house rent collector the temple houses were in the hands of about 370 tenants, members of the personnel of the Ebabbar temple. This makes it possible to calculate the total number of temple servants, described in the analysed texts by the two terms *širāku* or *nīšē bīti*, living within the city (*qabal āli*) and in the harbour district, to 1850 people.[468] Such a calculation is based on the premise that all tenants who paid rent were fully grown persons, and that a family consisted on average of five people: two parents and three children.[469]

However, as it is not certain whether tenants living in Bāb-nār-Šamaš paid rent to Ina-ṣilli-Nergal or to the other *ša muḫḫi idi bītāte*, the total number of 198 tenants can be reduced to 189, and the sum paid by them to 458 shekels of silver yearly, i.e. on average 2.2 shekels per tenant. The rest of 562 shekels have to be paid by 255 tenants, i.e. the total number of tenants from the inner city and from the harbor district should be calcuated at about 450, the chief of families or ca. 2250 people with wife and three children (ca. 1350 children). If we accept the norm known from Roman Egypt, ca. 290 children were exempted from work.[470] However, BM 73261[471] and a few other texts divide workmen

Bēl-uballiṭ, son of Šamaš-nāṣir, unknown from other documents. It is uncertain if the *ša muḫḫi idi bīti* who collected the rent from temple servants living *qabal āli* and *ša kāri Sippar* were also responsible for collection of rent from houses in other towns and settlements. It cannot be excluded that in towns like Bāb-nār-Šamaš the people mentioned in CT 57, 26, no. 40 acted as agents of the temple or of the *ša muḫḫi idi bīti*, i.e. such high payment might constitute rent from a group of people, but at present this can be neither confirmed nor rejected.

468 Assuming that parents (total 1100) have in average three children.

469 When the rent was paid by a woman we assume that the husband was dead, i.e. the total number might be a little lower.

470 See MacGinnis 2004, 34 who quotes the result of reaearch according to which children aged 0-4 formed ca. 13% of the population.

471 Edited by MacGinnis 2004.

into adult (*rabû*) and young (*ṣeḫru*) not fully fit for work.[472] Such a division has sense only if we assume that children were not able to fulfill the requirement ascribed to fully-grown persons. 93 children out of total 284 persons in BM 73261 consist ca. 33% of the total, but this number should be enarged by 13% of children aged 0-4 years free of work. It means that from the estimated total of family of tenants only 54% were persons able to fulfill the standard norm.[473]

It means that only a little more than half of servants (including women) were fully capable of work, although already very young children and old, partly disabled people had to work.[474] If we compare these data with the great scale of work undertaken both in the city and outside it, especially during the reign of Nabonidus (renovation of all main temples, and the huge project of building new canals), but also, before him, the rebuilding of the temple at the beginning of the reign of Nebuchadnezzar, then the huge project of construction of the Median wall, the rebuilding of the *zikkurat* (from the last year of Nebuchadnezzar to the beginning of the reign of Nabonidus), there can be no doubt that the number of temple workers was far too small. The lack of sufficient workforce is confirmed in a variety of documents about the employment of hirelings (lúḫun.ga.meš = *agrūte*) working side by side with the temple workers (erín.meš = *ṣābē*).[475] Escape on massive scale (about 20%) demonstrates that the temple expectation exceeded the capabilities of its workers. In this context it is surprising that the temple did not provide dwellings for free, and did not give up even so low an income as one-fourth shekel yearly. While this can be seen as an expression of the extreme greed of the temple, another reason, associated with the shortage of labour cannot be ruled out. One method was to make the temple workers seek additional employment to pay for the rent forced on them. A few texts suggest that such a situation did in fact take place, for example, the fuller and gardener producing bricks were paid by the temple with wool for work recognised as being outside their duties.[476] In a broader sense also the prebend was a form of remuneration for service done for the temple. However, the most important argument lies in the fact that they had to pay for their lodging. Although the majority of renters received remuneration from the temple sufficient to maintain the elementary needs of the family, it is probable that the necessity of paying for lodgings

[472] See Zawadzki, 2018, 427-428.

[473] In other text this number of "children" was even higher.

[474] Jursa 1995, 8-9, Baker 2001, 22f., MacGinnis 2003, 99f., Zawadzki 2018, 428.

[475] The term is often replaced by the term *urāšu*, translated as "state labourers," which might denote "forced person".

[476] BM 61761: 15-16: 1 gú.un *šá* 2 lim 4 me sig$_4$.ḫi.a *šá* 5 *na-da-[ba-ka]*/m*ṣil-la-a* lútúg.babbar, "one talent (of wool) for 2400 bricks for 5 courses (for) Ṣillaya.

(one shekels, more often a few shekels of silver) put the family in difficulty and forced the workers to undertake extra work for extra money.[477]

4.7 Way of use of silver obtained from rental of houses

The texts provide numerous details indicating the use of money from the rental of temple houses. A few texts concern the issue of silver, presumably for the manufacture of the container for performing the *ḫarû*-ritual.[478] According to Nbn 728, no. 77: 2-3 (Nbn 13) Basuru, son of Altama' received 12 shekels of silver *a-na ḫa-ri-e šá ḫar-ri*. The same expression *a-na ḫa-ri-e šá ḫar-r*[*i-e*] occurs in BM 63391, no. 79: 7'-8' (Nbn 14) where the same Basuru, son of Iltama' occurs again receiving the same amount of silver. The use of three shekels of silver from the rental of the temple houses for the same purpose is also mentioned in CT 57, 83, no. 50: 6-7, but the content is badly preserved. The small amount of silver suggests that it was not destined for the manufacture of the cultic container,[479] but rather *idu*-payment for the work done. Although the function of Basuru is unknown, it seems that he was a jeweller or a goldsmith. It is worth to note that the first two texts mention the 11th day of Kislīmu, which might be the day of the performance of the ritual in Sippar.[480] Another text from the Sippar archives is BM 101080: 9, mentioning sheep for the *ḫarû* ceremony performed by the *mār šarri*, presumably Belshazzar, son of Nabonidus.[481] This text is important as it supports the picture drawn from two texts from Uruk, where the ceremony is named *ḫarê ša šarri*, i.e. it was probably performed by

[477] As noted by Jursa (Jursa and Garcia 2015, 137) "taxation system was geared primarily towards mobilization of manpower"; the necessity of bearing the cost of living may have fulfilled similar function.

[478] For a brief overview, see Linssen 2004, 119.

[479] Note, however, that the *šiddatu*-stands and *namzātu*-vats for fermenting beer used during *ḫarû* ceremonies were also made of silver (YOS 6, 62: 7, 15, 18; YOS 7, 185: 21-22). Larger *ḫarû*-containers were made of bronze (YOS 7, 89: 6; cf. Mayer 1983, 109: 397 (the booty from Musasir used as container for wine).

[480] Note that other texts suggest that in Assyria the ceremony was held also on the seventh day of an unknown month (ADD 1077), in Babylonia on eighth day of Nisannu (see Linseen 2004, 119 and n. 731) and eighth (YOS 3, 3: 16) and 15th-16th days of unknown months (YOS 3, 60: 11), and on 17th day of Kislīmu (BRM 4, 25, rev. 43, quoted by Linssen 2004, 119, n. 736).

[481] The text refers to ceremonies beginning from the second day of Kislīmu, tenth year. As the line preceding the description of *ḫarû* ceremony refers to the sheep for the fifth day of Addaru, the next line might refer to the following month, presumably Nisannu. The day number is poorly preserved, but the eighth day (the day when *ḫarû* ceremony was held in Babylon) cannot be excluded. It is highly probable that the text was written in the tenth or eleventh year of Nabonidus and that Bēl-šar-uṣur (Belshazzar) performed the ritual in place of the king absent in Teima.

the king or in his honour.[482] Unclear is ABL 42 where the king is informed that the person responsible for filling the *ḫarû* container neglected his obligation and now the proper kind of wine (called *ṣurāru*) is not available. It is not certain if the ceremony was to take place without the participation of the king or if the king was informed in advance (before his coming) that it was not properly prepared because of the negligence of certain individuals. Only the Cleveland document[483] suggests, despite interpretation problems, that although the ritual was performed in the temple it might be led by a person whose priestly title is unknown. According to this text the wife of the deceased, after putting on a *dīdû*-garment, entered the *bīt ḫilṣi*-sanctuary and performed the *ḫarû* ritual herself. This caused a reaction from the highest authorities of Eanna (the *šatammu*, *bēl piqitti*, *ērib bīti* and *kiništu*) who discussed the question during an assembly.[484] We may assume that the widow could feel responsible for performance of the ritual because of the lack of male offspring of her deceased husband. During the ceremony performed before the statues of the gods, presumably in their chapels, offerings made of liquids (wine, beer),[485] cereals (barley),[486] animals (bulls[487] and sheep[488]) were served. Silver obtained form house rental might have been used to purchase these products.

Only a few additional texts might relate to cultic ceremonies. In the tenth year of Nabonidus 46 shekels were spent on buying 18 jars of pure wine and seven shekels for 5 *sūtu* of pure honey.[489] Bronze was bought for 11 shekels for producing a *gandû* of the *balaggu*, presumably used during a cultic ceremony.[490] Money from house rent was also used to purchase animals for offerings: sheep,[491] and bulls.[492] Only two texts mention the use of silver spent

[482] Cf. also YOS 3, 60: 7, 11 (sheep) and GC 2, 269: 9 (a bull).

[483] Published by Geller 1995 and discussed lately by Janković 2013, 160-163 with important improvements.

[484] However, as is stressed by Janković 2013, 161 the final verdict of the body is not preserved.

[485] Libation offerings is mentioned in KAR 146, rev. col 2', beer in ADD 1077, VIII 14 and wine (cf. above, n. 479).

[486] Jursa 1997, no. 19: 2.

[487] GC 2, 269: 8.

[488] BM 101080: 9; Iraq 45, 190: 85 (four lambs and four female kids for *harû* (and *šalam bīti*) and l. 86 ([seven] female lambs and seven female kids for *harû* and for another ceremony).

[489] Nbn 428, no. 49: 6-7.

[490] Cyr 234, no. 89 and its duplicate BM 101435, no. 90. It is interesting to note that two copies of the text were written which suggests that the expenditure was recognised as important. For the purchase of bronze Liblut the blacksmith received six shekels of silver (BM 63996, no. 91, Camb 1 [538 BC]).

[491] BM 59164, no. 66 (Nbn 14): *a-na* ki.[lam]; later it is stated at least three times that the sheep are for offerings (*ana sattukki*).

[492] CT 57, 69, no. 59 (Nbn 3): 3 minas of silver were given to the *rab būli* and a small sum of 1½ shekels of silver for the workers of the fattening house; CT 57, 68, no. 63 (Nbn [x]): more than one

by rent collectors for purposes which belonged to the prebendaries, i.e. the prebendary brewers (*sattuk sirašūtu*) of the sanctuary of Anunītu and Šamaš.[493] It is not known why the temple had to support them.

Many texts concern expenditures on the temple's building activities. In the tenth year of Nabonidus the enormous amount of 500 talents of bitumen (15 tons) was purchased for 20 shekels for the work on the construction of the temple tower (*zikkurat*) carried out by people from Opis.[494] One might suspect that also bricks bought for 1 mina and iron for 8 shekels, given to the smith were used for the same purpose.[495] The *abattu*-reeds for 10 shekels were bought in Nisannu of the 14th year of Nabonidus.[496] A few months later that year, in Kislīmu, BM 68900, no. 30 was written which enumerates the rent of individual tenants used exclusively for the purchase of *abattu*. Evidently, intensive works were carried out that created high demand on reeds. Such purchase is witnessed in the 16th year of Nabonidus.[497] All these purchases might be related to the works in Gilūšu, which began in the 13th year and were continued until at least the 16th year. According to BM 65748, no. 13 (Nbn 16) *abattu* was bought for half a mina of silver and only a week later a part of the collected 1 mina 27 shekels was spent on works in Gilūšu. The building works were continued in the last year of Nabonidus's reign, as one text dated to the very end of month Simānu (i.e. three and half months before the conquest of Babylon by Cyrus) mentions silver *ana dullu ša bīt* [...][498] while the second text written in an unknown month speaks of the payment for baked bricks, maybe used for the work on the temple of Lady of Sippar.[499] Two other texts mentioning the purchase of *abattu* are later: BM 83110, no. 14 from the second year of Cyrus and BM 64481, no. 56 from the fifth year of Cambyses, both witness the ongoing building works, in the second text in the

mina of silver was used to buy bulls and given to the person of the same name as in the previous text, presumably the same *rab būli*; CT 57, 70, no. 61 (Nbn 9): six-year old bull bought for 22 shekels was delivered to the fattening house; BM 72990, no. 62 (Nbn 10): a few bulls bought for silver were delivered to the fattening house; BM 67021, no. 68 (Nbn 12+[x]): one black castrated bull was sold to the temple for 12½ shekels.

493 Cf. CT 57, 82, no. 53 (<Dar> 4), r. 5'-6' (one mina was issued) and 7'-8' (20 shekels). In the second case the name of Šamaš is not mentioned, but the destination is recognised on the basis of prosopography, because Šamaš-nāṣir/Šellibi owned only the brewer's prebend of Šamaš. A fairly important sum of 3 minas of silver was given.

494 Nbn 428, no. 49.

495 Nbn 428, no. 49: 9-13.

496 Nbn 752, no. 84. Presumably for the same work two iron spades were purchased.

497 BM 63552, no. 98.

498 BM 79611, no. 86.

499 BM 61839, no. 87.

sanctuary of Lady of Sippar. *Abattu*-reeds were also purchased for some work in the *bīt immēre*.[500]

Probably the most important part of silver from house rent was used for the manufacture of uniforms for soldiers and police forces who protected the flocks and, by state order, were drafted into the military. The earliest data are already from the 18th year of Nabopolassar when the temple paid for one kur.ra garment[501] and three jerkins.[502] The list of purchases is long: 19 kur.ra and six jerkins in the third year of Nabonidus for one mina (ca. 2.4 shekels per one),[503] then two kur.ra and one jerkin in the 12th year,[504] and again in the same year 17 kur.ra for 1 mina 30 shekels, but this time at a very high price suggesting best quality.[505] In the 13th year Nabû-šum-iddin, the rent collector, paid for 16 kur.ra and *iltapi* garments.[506] Interesting is BM 74332, no. 85 (16th year of Nabonidus), according to which a small sum out of house rent was used to pay for sacks, pack-saddles (and) *ilḫu*-clothes. Connection of that expediture with the expected war against Cyrus cannot be excluded.

A connection between the expenses and the current military situation is also possible in the case of a text written in the fifth year of Cambyses.[507] This document deals with the purchase of one dyed kur.ra for 12 shekels (a very high price, presumably to be worn by military officers) and additionally 14 kur.ra and 17 jerkins, presumably all given to the chief of the bowmen. As the fifth year of Cambyses is the year of his expedition against Egypt, police forces from Sippar might have been mobilized for it.[508] A similar situation occurs in CT 57, 82, no. 53 dated to the fourth year of Darius, when again important expenditures were based on the income from the rent of the temple houses. First, the enormous sum of 4 minas was issued to Arad-Anunītu, the chief of bowmen and his soldiers, then 28 shekels to people responsible for bringing horses from Egypt and 1 mina 50 shekels for kur.ra and jerkins for the bowmen. No doubt, the document reflects expenditures related to the Egyptian campaign of Darius.

[500] BM 63564, no. 58 (dated to year 3+x unknown king).

[501] On the function of this type of garment and possible Akkadian reading, see Malatacca 2017, 108-113.

[502] BM 50347, no. 71 for an average price a little over 3 shekels. For jerkin (*širam*), see Malatacca 2017, 116-119.

[503] CT 57, 74, no. 72 (but only 50 shekels was taken from idu).

[504] BM 64807, no. 74, for 6 shekels for an average price of 2 shekels.

[505] Nbn 651, no. 75.

[506] Nbn 703, no. 76.

[507] The use of money from house rent occurs in Cam 27 no. 80 to cover the purchase of three very expensive kur.ra (each 4.5 shekels) purchased out of *irbu*-income and house rent.

[508] BM 64481, no. 56.

Other payments in silver from temple house rent are much smaller and happened infrequently, such as 5 shekels for dying skins by leatherworkers,[509] for oil for workers of the king's residence,[510] for wool,[511] sesame,[512] dates,[513] rental of a boat,[514] and travel costs.[515]

The money which the temple received from house rental was used for expenses that usually did not correspond to regular spending that could be planned in advance. Rather they were used for unexpected needs, which occurred irregularly.

The activity of the house rent collectors was not limited to the collection of rent from individual holders of the temple houses and issue of the yearly rent to the temple. Quite often they purchased different products and delivered them to the temple or to recipient(s) mentioned in the text. Although only one published letter order is addressed to the house rent collector (CT 55, 25), it seems that all cases of purchase were made at the order of temple officials. The absence – except one – of letter orders addressed to the *ša muḫḫi idi bītāte* may result from the fact that – as the texts suggest – their activity was focused on collection of rent from houses located inside the city (*qabal āli*) or, if outside the city, located in the harbour district close to the city. It seems that house rent collectors lived in the city and for this reason they received the orders orally.[516]

509 CT 57, 72, no. 60.

510 BM 63996, no. 91.

511 BM 63990, no. 92 (for workers of the horse stall; see also BM 63564, no. 58).

512 BM 73499, no. 93.

513 CT 57, 84, no. 48.

514 BM 73499, no. 93.

515 CT 57, 72, no. 60.

516 According to MacGinnis 1995, 20 "normally the *šangû* and/or the scribes will have given an order by word of mouth."

5. Summary

In the first millennium BC houses were leased by private persons as well as by the temples. The contract of house lease had a fairly strictly established form, with such important elements as the amount of yearly rent, term of payment of rent, and certain additional obligations of lessor and tenant. Some lessors belonged to the wealthiest and most influential families in their cities, but many houses were owned by members of ordinary families, which suggests that tenants had the opportunity to rent a house that suited their needs. Healthy individuals bought or built houses with the intention of renting them and earning profit over a long time. But some people (usually women) leased houses because it was the only way to provide the family with basic food (usually bread).

According to the commonly occurring clause, rent should be paid in two equal installments yearly: the first at the beginning and the second in the middle of the rental year. Only occasionally the tenants paid part of the first installment before entering the house; many tenants paid it after a delay of a few weeks or even months. Quite often the tenant paid the rent only in the last month of the half-year period, presumably apprehensive that the owner would remove him from the house. Cases of not paying rent for a longer period of one to few years are also known.

Although the standard was payment of rent in two installments per year, in a number of contracts a tenant was obliged to pay it monthly or even daily. Additionally, while the standard was payment of rent in silver, when the tenant was obliged to pay rent monthly, or daily, the means of payment also changed, i.e. bread, flour, barley or even bricks were accepted instead of silver. Our research has shown the relationship between short periods for rent payment and political turmoil, such as changes on the throne, wars, revolts, or natural disasters (drought). However, such changes might also result from family reasons, such as the death of a husband, when the widow was obliged to lease part of the house to secure food for herself and her children. Usually they received *kusīptu*-bread, a kind of small flat bread, comparable to our pitta, most often ca. 20 per day.

Two additional obligations, *nūptu/šugarru* and the penalty for breaking the contract, have been discussed in detail. As for the former, I share the opinion that these synonymous terms refer to charges for cultic ceremonies but I argue that the charge was imposed on the lessors. Only in later time (at least from the time of Nabonidus if not earlier) the transfer of this obligation from the house owners to tenants can be observed. However, the tenants paid it not to the temple, but to the lessor, which clearly supports the conclusion that payment of *nūptu* was the duty of the lessors, who transferred it to tenants. In some contracts there is a penalty clause to be paid by him, who breaks the obligations agreed in the contract. The majority of texts with this clause are dated to a year of political instability: supporting the idea that this clause was added at the owners' request, targeted against tenants.

This raises a question about the position of owners and tenants in their commercial relation. By using contemporary economic terms we may ask whether in the first millennium Babylonia the producer's or consumer's market predominated, or – in other words – whose position was stronger: house owner or tenant. Whether we are dealing with the producer's market or the consumer's market is determined primarily by supply and demand. When the supply is lower than the demand, we are dealing with the producer's market, but when the demand is lower than supply, we meet the customer's market because customers (in our case, tenants) have different options.

It seems that in Babylonia of the VI-V centuries BC – the period for which we have sufficient documentation to try to answer the question – the position of tenants was stronger than the lessors as the supply certainly exceeded demand. The large price range of house rent from one shekel to over one mina yearly shows that tenants had great variety of choice, which limited the possibility of imposing high rental price by house owners. Houses for rental were in hands of rich and influential families as well as many people outside this group, which supports the idea of large number of houses for rental. Other arguments support this opinion. According to the clause present in majority of the house rental contracts the tenant should pay the first installment for half a year at the beginning of rental year and the second installment at the beginning of the second half (seldom: at the end) of the rental year. However, the clause was quite often ignored and many tenants paid the rent with a delay from a few weeks till many years. Quite often – as was mentioned above – the tenants paid rent not at the beginning of rental year but close to the end of first half of rental year. Impressive are two cases when tenants did not pay rent for three years and three months (MR 138) and for four years and five month (Dar 554, no. 124).[517] These cases suggest that it was not so easy to find trustworthy tenant. But even if the tenant did not pay rent for a long time, the owners neither decided to terminate the contract nor to go to court. In cases of breaking contract, the recovery of unpaid installments would be highly

[517] Cf. also BM 82620 (Baker 2010, 132f.; a debt for one year).

difficult, in practice impossible without a trial. In only one case was resolving the problem by legal procedure applied and that was only after 22 years! (AnOr 8, 70). Cases of termination of contract were rare, or even extremely rare.[518] Rather, other ways of soliciting the case were sought. In VS 4, 99 = NRV 117 the tenant issued a promissory note for unpaid rent, and paid it after some time, i.e. both partners were interested in continuing the contract. The owners of rented houses tried to protect their profits by introducing the clause according to which contraveners (*nabalkattānu*) should pay high penalty. Because such clauses occur quite often in documents from turbulent years, it seems that it was introduced by lessors fearing that tenants will break the terms of the contract.[519] Cases of forcing tenants to make a solemn oath obliging him to carry out the agreed earlier obligations are also known. Except for VS 4 99 = NRV 117 (interest bearing promissory note) I do not know a case of penalties for delay in paying the rent. All this suggest that the position of tenants was stronger than the position of house owners, which is supported by the fact that in contracts concerning the same house the price was the same or almost the same.

The documents from Sippar show that the Ebabbar temple was the owner of many houses, but only a few documents concern the rental of temple houses to private persons. In such situations the same standard document known from contract between private contractors was used. However, when the houses belonged to the temple the clause about *nūptu/šugarru* was omitted.

The rich materials concerning payment of rent researched here demonstrate that the majority of temple servants lived in the city or in the harbour district, while the most important understanding is that they did not receive their dwelling free, but they were obliged to pay rent regularly. No contract or any other document is known to indicate that the temple signed an individual contract with the temple servants. Rather the servants received the oral decision of the temple administration, and were informed in the same way about the amount of annual rent.

In cases of private persons as contracts were agreed in different months so the rental year began in different months. In cases of rent paid by Ebabbar servants the situation is completely different: the rental year began usually in Ulūlu (VI) in the middle of the year and ended in Abu (V). Only seldom it began in Tašrītu (VII) and ended in Ulūlu (VI). There is no doubt that such a structure of the rental year was established by the administration of the Ebabbar temple. The reason for such a shape is, however, unknown.

[518] Such a case of termination of contract between the Sippar temple and the *ša muḫḫi idi bītāti* is discussed in the second part of this book.

[519] In fact the tenant was usually meant, see above, p. 99.

All known documents of the collection of rent from the temple servants are dated to the quite short period of about 30 years (556-527 BC). In this period the rent was collected by the *ša muḫḫi idi bītāte*, "the rent house collector". The organization of rent collection before this time is unknown. The house rent collector was appointed in the same way as the field rent collector (*ša muḫḫi sūti*). The contract between the temples authorities represented by the temple administrator (*šangû*), the king's deputy (*qīpu*), the scribes (*ṭupšarrē*), the royal officer (*reš šarri*) and the interpreter-scribe (*sepīru*) defined the amount of yearly rent and then the house rent collector began his job. The documents left open its final term, i.e. it was valid as long the temple accepted the collector. The rent was paid in silver. In two known cases the collector was obliged to pay 19 minas 15 shekels and later only 17 minas of silver. The role of house rent collector was not limited to the collection of rent from individual servants; the temple could oblige him to pay for some work or to buy materials using the money from the house rent and deliver them to an indicated place.

At least some house rent collectors were members of well-known Sipparean families, but it seems that for them this was highest achievable position. The temple administration watched carefully the activity of rent collectors, and if he were assessed negatively it invalidated the contract, obliging him to settle the whole debt.

The institution of a house rent collector was not unique to Sippar, as the newly published document confirms its existence in Babylon during the time of Xerxes (485 BC). It is very likely that it was established in Babylon in the same time like in Sippar.

The rent paid by the temple servants – in comparison with the rent paid by tenants of private houses – was much lower and ranged from ¼ shekel (the lowest) to 18 shekels (the highest), but about half the servants paid 1 or 2 shekels yearly. Quite often the servants sub-leased part of their dwellings; the quality of dwellings was quite frequently very low, so they could be described as "ruined." This expressed emphatically the lowest position of the servants in the temple hierarchy.

6. Texts edition

6.1 Contracts between individual persons and the Ebabbar temple

1. Nbn 48 = BM 92769 (83-1-18, 836); Sippar, 21.XI.Nbn 1

Obv. 1. é níg.ga ^{d}utu *šá ina* ká.gal^{i} *šá* é
2. ^{d}gašan *sip-par*^{ki} 2 *ni-ri-bi*^{meš} *šá su-ú-tu*$_{4}$
3. *tar-ba-ṣu* ká-*a.ni* é im.mar.tu
4. *ni-ri-bi šá tar-ba-ṣu* gal^{ú} é *pa-ni*
5. *šá* é im.u$_{18}$.lu *u pa-rak-ka-šú*
6. *a-di* 6-*ta* mu.an.na.meš *a-na*
7. mu.an.na ⅓ 4 gín kù.babbar *a-na i-di*
8. é *ina* igi ^{md}en-gi a-*šú šá* ^{md}utu-sig$_{5}^{iq}$
9. a ^{lú}sipa anše.kur.ra *bat-qa*
10. *i-ṣab-bat ú-ru i-šá-an-ni*
11. ^{giš}ùr *še-bir-ri ú-ḫal-lap*

Edge 12. *a-ḫi* kù.babbar *ina re-eš* mu.an.na
13. *a-ḫi* kù.babbar *ina mi-šil* mu.an.na

Rev. 14. *i-nam-din ta* u$_{4}$.1.kam *šá* iti.še
15. é *ina* igi ^{md}en-gi^{na} *ina* gub^{zu}
16. ^{md}u+gur-lugal-*bul-liṭ* ^{lú}*qí-i-pi é-babbar-ra*
17. ^{lú}*mu-kin-nu* ^{md}ag-*ni-ip-šá-ru*
18. a-*šú šá* ^{md}u-numun a ^{md}kaskal.kur^{i}
19. ^{m}*mu-šib-ši*-^{d}amar.utu a-*šú šá* ^{md}en-*na-din*-ibila
20. a ^{lú}sanga ^{d}utu ^{md}ag-mu-mu a-*šú šá*
21. ^{md}en-numun a ^{lú}*man-di-di u* ^{lú}šid
22. ^{md}ag-mu-gar^{un} a-*šú šá* ^{m}*lu*-ud.du-*a-na*-zálag
23. a ^{m}*šá-na-ši-šú sip-par*^{ki} iti.zíz
24. u$_{4}$.21.kam mu.1.kam ^{md}ag-i
25. lugal tin.tir^{ki}

Notes

For previous edition, see Joannès 1992, 166.

L. 4. The reading *pa-rak-ka* instead of *ma-rak-ka* (Joannès) is after CAD P 85a. Note that the document was written only in the presence of *qīpu Ebabbar*, while the *šangû Sippar* is missing. It is not excluded that Mušallim-Marduk, the previous *šangû* Sippar, attested for the last time on [x].VIII.Nrg 3 (BM 63239, see MacGinnis 2000, 63) or later in Lb-M 0 (Bongenaar 1997, 28), had died or been removed from office by Nabonidus and in Šabāṭu (XI) Nbn 1 his successor was not yet appointed.

Translation

The document concerning the house of Šamaš (located) at the great gate of the temple of Šarrat Sippar (with) two entrances (facing) south, with an outer enclosure of the west house, (with) an entrance of the great enclosure, the front building of the south house, and its outbuilding, was leased for six years for a yearly rent of 24 shekels of silver. The house is (given) at disposal of Bēl-ušallim, son of Šamaš-udammiq, the descendant of the Rē'i-sīsê. He will carry out the repairs, renew the roof (and) cover the beams with laths. He will pay half of the silver at the beginning of the year and the half of the silver in the middle of the year. From the first day of Addaru the house is at the disposal of Bēl-ušallim.

In the presence of Nergal-šar-bulliṭ, the king's resident.

Witnesses:

Nabû-nipšarri, son of Mukīn-zēri, descendant of Balīḫu

Mušibši-Marduk, son of Bēl-nādin-apli, descendant of Šangû-Šamaš

Nabû-šum-iddin, son of Bēl-zēri, descendant of Mandidi, and the scribe, Nabû-šum-iškun, son of Lūṣi-ana-nūri, descendant Ša-nāšišu

Sippar, month Šabātu, 21st day, first year of Nabonidus, king of Babylon.

2. BM 67707 (82-9-18, 7705); 6.8 x 5.1 cm; [Sippar], 27.[4].[Nbn] 6

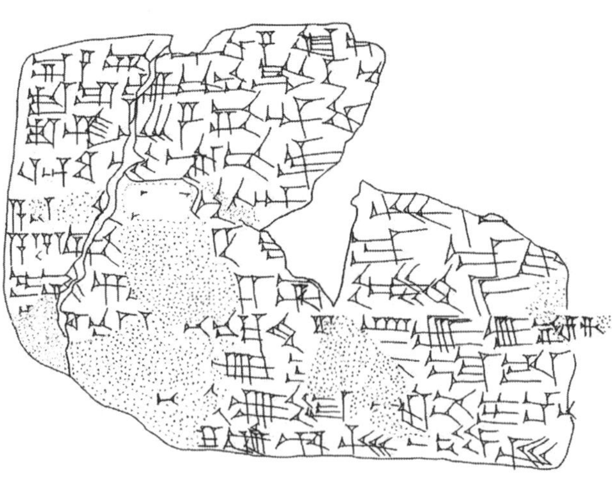

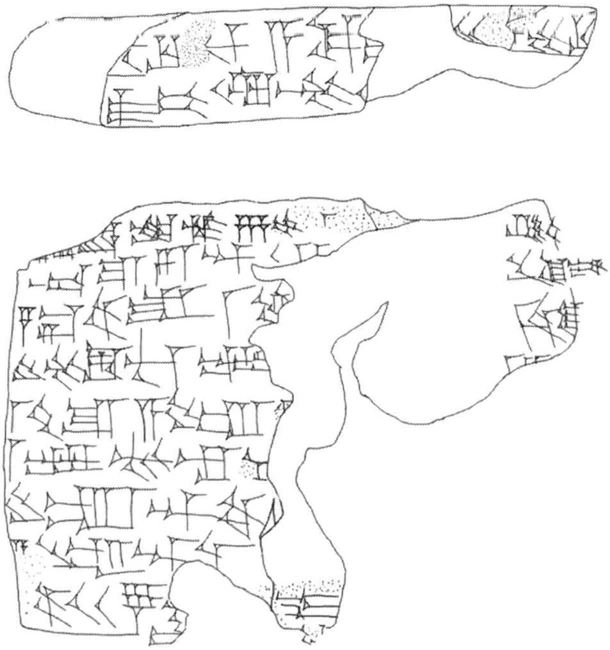

Obv. 1. é níg.ga ⸢^{d}⸣utu *šá qé-r*[*eb* ud.kib.nun^{ki}]
2. da *su* (T: *zu*)-*ú-qu rap-šú m*[*u-taq* ...]
3. da gi.meš níg.ga ^{d}utu [....]
4. *u* ^{md}utu-⸢mu⸣ *ina lìb-bi áš*-[*bi* ...]
5. *a-na* x (ras.) 10+[x$^{?}$] x (ras.) mu.an.[na].meš ⸢^{m}x⸣ [...]
6. a-*šú šá* ^{m}⸢*ga*⸣-[x] ⸢x x⸣-ma *iṣ-ba-t*[*u*]
7. *i-ga*-⸢*ri*⸣ [x x] 2-*ta* sig$_4$.ḫi.a
8. ⸢*ú* ka⸣ *ina muḫ-ḫi* ⸢3$^{?}$-*u*$^{?}$⸣ ú ú *ga-ṣa z*[*i*$^{?}$]
9. [...] *ú* ⸢x (x)⸣ tap-šu da
10. [giš.ùr] *pít*-⸢*nu*$^{!}$⸣-*ú-tu ina lìb-bi i-ṣab-bat*
11. [giš.ig.meš] ⸢*zu*⸣-*uḫ-ḫu*^{meš} *ina* ká.meš

Edge 12. [*i-za*]*q*-⸢*qáp*⸣ *a-di*-⸢*i* 20$^{?}$⸣ mu.m[eš]
13. [*ina lìb-bi*] *áš-bi ù ina* mu ⸢10⸣+[x x x] ⸢x⸣

Rev. 14. ⸢*ù* ta⸣ iti.ne mu.6 kam ^{m}[^{d}ag-i lugal e^{ki} *i-di i*]-*nam-din*
15. *ina* gub^{zu} *šá* ^{md}u+g[ur-lugal-*bul-liṭ*] ^{lú}*qí-i-pi*
16. *é-babbar-ra* ^{m}ka[r-^{d}amar.utu ^{lú}sanga] *sip-par*^{ki}
17. ^{lú}*mu-kin-nu* ^{md}ag-[mu-si.sá a]-⸢*šú šá*⸣
18. ^{m}tin^{su} a ^{lú}sanga [^{d}mùš tin.tir^{ki}]
19. ^{md}ag-numun-si-s[á a-*šú šá* ^{m}tin a ^{lú}pa.še ^{ki} *u*]
20. ^{lú}šid ^{md}⸢utu-x⸣ [...]

21. a ^{lú}sanga ^{d}utu [*sip-par*^{ki} iti.x]
22. u$_{4}$.27.ka[m mu].⸢6⸣.k[am ^{d}ag-i]
23. lu[gal tin].ti[r^{ki}]

Notes

The sense of lines 8-9 is unclear to me.

L. 10. For known nB examples, see Joannès 2016, 295.

L. 11-12. for *zuḫhu*, see CAD S 347: "1. reed matting used for doors." For all known examples, see Joannès 2016, 295-296.

L. 14. The sign mu is written over erasure (traces of two vertical wedges are clearly visible).

L. 18. The tiny of sign trace following sanga is unlike dingir, but reconstruction of line seems certain.

Although the king's name is not preserved, we can safely say that the tablet was written in the sixth year (written horizontally) of Nabonidus, as Nergal-šar-bulliṭ, the *qīpu* of the Ebabbar, held office in the period Nbn 1-6 (Bongenaar 1997, 47-48), while Mušēzib-Marduk, the *šangû* Sippar in the period Nbn 2-15 (Bongenaar 1997, 28-29). The reconstruction of the month is based on the fact that according to l. 14, the tenant should pay rent from the month Abu (V) of the sixth year, and usually the contract were composed a few days or weeks earlier.

Translation

A house, property of Šamaš, (located) insi[de of Sippar], adjacent to the broad street, pas[sage of ...], adjacent to a plot, property of Šamaš [..., which PN] and Šamaš-iddin liv[e …] for 20$^{?}$ years [to PN], son of Ga-...] wall […], two (loads$^{?}$) of bricks […] … . He will put in [so]lid [beams], he will [se]t up reed mat doors in the doorways. Until 20$^{\text{th?}}$ year [he will] live (there) and in the 20/$^{?}$ year[…] and from the month Abu, sixth year of [Nabonidus, king of Babylon] he will pay the house rent.

In the presence of Ner[gal-šar-bulliṭ, the *qīpu*] of the Ebabbar and Mušēzib-[Marduk, the šangû] Sippar.

Witnesses:

Nabû-[šum-līšir], son of Balāssu, descendant of Šangû-[Ištar-Bābili]

Nabû-zēr-līš[ir, son of Balāṭu, descendant of Isinnaya, and] the scribe Šamaš-[...], descendant of Šangû-Šamaš

[Sippar, month x], 27th day, sixth y[ear of Nabonidus], ki[ng of Babylon].

3. BM 73069 (82-9-18, 1307); 6.5 x 4.1 cm; Sippar, 27.IV.Nbn 14

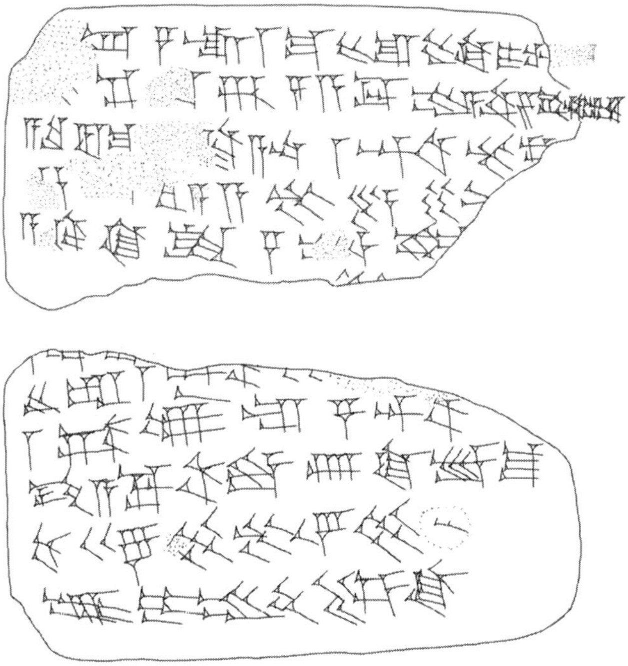

Obv. 1. [*šá*] é *šá ina* šu^{ii} ^{m}*ba-lat-su* ^{lú}*qí-i-pi* [*šá é-babbbar*]-⸢*ra*?⸣
2. [*ù*$^{?}$ ^{lú}]*si*-⸢*pir*⸣-*ri šá* íd lugal *a-na* níg.ga ^{d}utu *ab-ka*
3. *a-na* ⅚ *ma*-[*na* kù].babbar *a-na* ^{md}utu-mu-si.[sá]
4. ⸢a⸣-[*šú šá* ^{md}]⸢utu$^{?}$⸣-a-mu sum^{in} [ta iti.kin]
5. *a-di qí-it šá* ⸢iti⸣.ne [...]
6. (line erased with traces of three signs)

Rev. 1'. ⸢^{md}x⸣ [...]
2'. ^{lú}šid ^{md}⸢utu-numun⸣-[dù a-*šú šá*]
3'. ^{m}*ta-qiš* uru *šá* ^{d}utu
4'. gú íd ud.kib.nun^{ki} iti.šu
5'. u$_{4}$.27.kam mu.14.kam
6'. ^{d}ag-i lugal tin.tir^{ki}

Notes

The text is mentioned in the unpublished dissertation of M. Weszeli and in MacGinnis 2000, 64, n. 4

L. 1. The title of Balāssu (^{lú}*qí-i-pi*) is well preserved, but it is evidently the scribe's mistake as in the 14th year of Nabonidus the office was held by Bēl-aḫḫē-iqīša (from Nbn 8 till Cyr 5, see Bongenaar 1997, 48-49).

Rev. 2' The scribe was known previously in the time of Cambyses, see Bongenaar 1997, 498.

Rev. 3'-4'. Cf. Ālu-(ša)-Šamaš *šá né-ber-ti* íd ud.kib.nunki in BM 63900 = Jursa 1995, no. 45 (p. 135 and 207), where the identity with Ālu-(ša)-Šamaš located on the Pallukat canal is suggested. The term *kišādu* (gú), "bank" is used interchangeably with *nēbertu*, "far side, opposite bank" of the river.

Translation

[Concerning the] house, which was taken to the property of Šamaš by Balāssu, the king's resident [of the Ebabba]r$^{?}$ (sic!) [and?] the interpreter-scribe (located) on Nār-šarri canal, which was rented to Šamaš-šum-lī[šir], son of Šamaš-aplu-iddin for ⅚ mina of silver. [From the month Ulūlu] till the end of the month Abu [...]

[...], the scribe, Šamaš-zēr-[ibni, son of] Taqīš.

Ālu-(ša)-Šamaš on the opposite bank of Euphrates. Month Du'ūzu, 27th day, fourteenth year of Nabonidus, king of Babylon.

4. BM 99901 (83-1-21, 2263); 3.8 x 3.6 cm; (Time of Nbn 8-15)

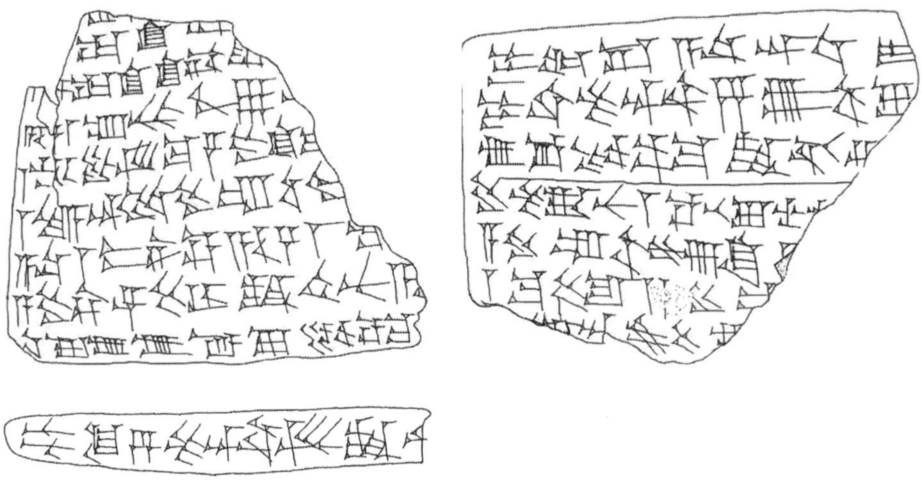

Obv. 1'. [x (x)] ⸢é *šá*$^{?}$⸣ [...]
2'. [x kùš] sag.ki an.[ta ...]
3'. ⸢x kùš$^{??}$⸣ sag.ki ki.ta i[m...]
4'. a-*šú šá* dub-numun pap 9 g[i$^{?}$.meš...]
5'. ^{md}en-šeš.meš-ba^{šá} ^{lú}*qí*-⸢*i*⸣-[*pi é-babbar-ra*]
6'. ^{m}kar-^{d}amar.utu ^{lú}sanga ud.ki[b.nun^{ki}]
7'. *a-na* ^{m}*tab-ni-e-a* a-*šú šá* ^{md}[...]

	8'.	a ^{lú}ì.sur *sat-tuk id-din-nu a-n*[*a*]
	9'.	*tam-lu-ú ú-mál-*{*lu*}*-li-e-ma*
Edge	10'.	*ár-ki* 5 mu.an.na.meš *it-t*[*e-et-qu*]
Rev.	11'.	*i-di* é *a-na* ^{d}utu *i-*[*nam-din*]
	12'.	*i-na* mu.an.na 5 kùš *tam-lu*
	13'.	*ú-mál-li-ma it-ti r*[*i*? ...]
	14'.	^{lú}*mu-kin-nu* ^{m}*e-tel-lu-pi-*⸢^{d}⸣[utu a-*šú šá* ^{md}utu-mu-giš]
	15'.	a ^{lú}sanga ud.kib.nun^{ki} ⸢^{m}⸣[...]
	16'.	^{m}*ba-laṭ-su* a ^{lú}sa[nga ...]
	17'.	⸢dumu ^{m}⸣^{d}kaskal.kur⸢^{ú}⸣ [...]

Notes

The presence of Bēl-aḫḫē-iqīša, the *qīpu* in office from Nbn 8 till Cyr 5 (Bongenaar 1997, 47-48) and Mušēzib-Marduk, the *šangû* Sippar, in office from Nbn 3 till Nbn 15 (Bongenaar 1997, 28-29) narrows document to the period Nbn 8-15.

Ll. 2'-3'. Filling the gap depends from that what was at the end of first and second lines.

L. 7'. Tabnēa, the descendant of Ṣāḫit-ginê family, occurs here for the first time.

L. 14'. For Etel-pî-Šamaš, son of Šamaš-šum-līšir, descendant of Šangû-Sippar, the *ērib bīt* Šamaš, possibly *aḫu rabû* and maybe the owner of the brewer's prebend of Šamaš, see Bongenaar 1997, 162, 215, 451.

Translation

... house ...

[x cubits?], the upper front on the [north ...]

⸢cubits⸣, the upper front on the [south ...]

[...], son of Šāpik-zēri, total 9 r[eeds? ...] Bēl-aḫḫē-iqīša, the king's res[ident of the Ebabbar (and)] Mušēzib-Marduk, the administrator of Sippar gave (this house?) to Tabnēa, son [of ...], descendant of Ṣāḫit-ginê for filling the terrace. After five years pa[ss] he will pay the rent for the house. Each year he will fill 5 cubits of terrace with [...]

Witnesses:

Etel-pî-[Šamaš, son of Šamaš-šum-līšir], descendant of Ṣāḫit-ginê

[...], son of Balāssu, descendant of the [...] Šan[gû ...]

[...], descendant of Balīḫu [...].

5. BM 68721 (82-9-18, 8720); 5.9 x 3.5 cm; Camb [6-8]

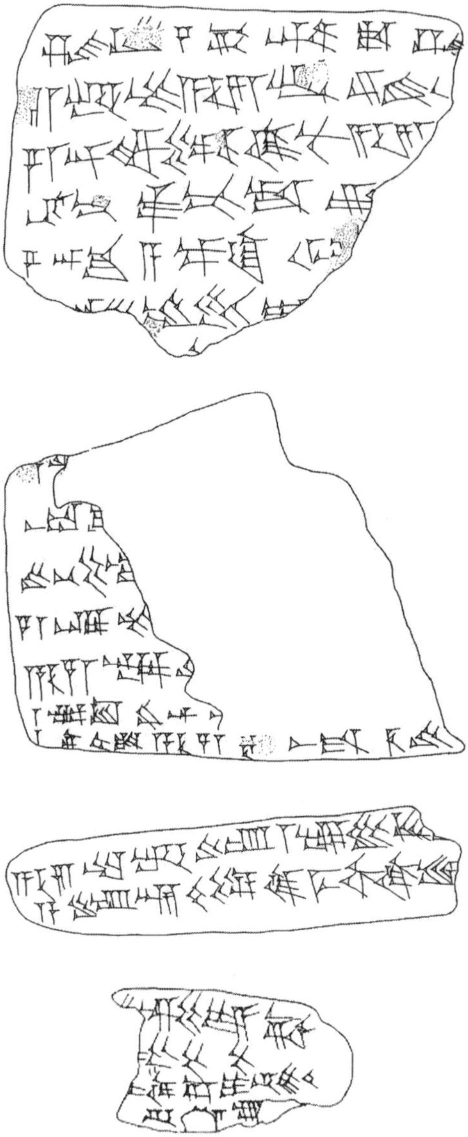

Obv. 1. gi.⸢meš⸣ níg.ga ^{d}utu da ⸢gi⸣.[meš]
2. *šá* ^{md}en-mu a-*šú šá* ^{md}⸢en⸣-gi *u* [gi.meš]
3. *šá* ^{md}im-*li-ki-nu* a-*šú šá* ^{m}[…]
4. *ina lìb-bi áš-bi* da ⸢x⸣ […]

5. *šá* ^{d}gašan *a-gada*^{ki} *ù* [...]
6. ⸢^{m}⸣⸢^{d}30⸣-lugal-ùru ⸢*i*⸣-[...]
7. [...] ⸢x⸣ [...]
Rest lost

Rev. 1'. ^{m}*s*[*i*$^{?}$-...]
2'. *ina* gub^{z}[*u* ^{md}lugal-*lu-da-ri*]
3'. ^{lú}til.gíd.d[a é-*babbar-ra* ^{md}en-mu a-*šú*]
4'. *šá* ^{md}ag-mu-[si.sá a ^{lú}sanga ^{d}mùš tin.tir^{ki} PN]
5'. a-*šú šá* ^{md}ag-m[u$^{?}$...]
6'. ^{md}ag-*bul-lit-an-n*[*i* ...]
7'. ^{m}*ni-din-it* a-*šú šá* ^{m}⸢*ḫa*⸣-*aš*$^{?}$-*da*$^{?}$-⸢*šú*⸣ ^{lú}[...]
L.e. 8'. a-*šú šá* ^{m}ìr-^{d}en ^{lú}šid ^{md}ag-šeš.meš-g[i a ^{m}kar-^{d}šú]
9'. a ^{lú}sanga ^{d}mùš tin.tir^{ki} *sip-par*^{ki} iti.[x]
L.h.e. 10'. [u$_{4}$.x.kam mu.x.kam ^{m}*kam-b*]*u-zi-ia* {ta}
11'. [lugal tin.tir^{ki} lu]gal kur.kur
12'. [... *i*]-*di é i-nam-din*
13'. [...] *ri* ⸢x⸣ *ú*

Notes

L. 3. Presumably Adad-līkin, cf. Schwemer 2001, 654 and notes 5348-5349.

L. 6. It cannot be excluded that the last sign instead of ⸢*ab*⸣ should be read ⸢*ab*⸣.

Rev. 2'. The reconstruction of the name Šarru-lūdāri is certain because he held the office of *qīpu Ebabbar* in the period Cyr 6-Dar 7, see Bongenaar 1997, 49.

Rev. 3'-4' is reconstructed on the basis of the fact that Bēl-iddin/Nabû-šum-līšir//Šangū-Ištar-Bābili is the first witnesses in the documents dated to the period Camb 6-8 (Bongenaar 1997, 97).

Rev. 7'. Nidintu, maybe the *sepīru*, mentioned regularly as the last witness. (Bongenaar 1997, 97). He is never mentioned, like all but one *sepīru* (see Bongenaar 1997, 93-96) with the name of his father. The published text might be an exception but the name is badly preserved and reading is uncertain.

L.e. 8'-9'. For Nabû-aḫḫē-šullim/Mušēzib-Marduk//Šangū-Ištar-Bābili, see Bongenaar 1997, 84 (as *ṭupšar ša Ebabbar* from Camb 6), but earlier as scribe of private documents (Bongenaar 1997, 490) and owner of different prebends (see Bongenaar 1997, Index, 527).

Translation

Reeds, property of Šamaš, adjacent to the reeds [...] of Bēl-iddin, son of Bēl-ušallim and [the reeds of...] Adad- līkin, son of [...] in it lives (and) adjacent to x [...] of Bēlet-Akkad and [...] Sîn-šar-uṣur

In the pres[ence of Šarru-lūdāri], the king's resident of the Ebabbar
[Bēl-iddin son of] of Nabû-šum-[līšir, descrendant of Šangū-Ištar-Bābili]
[PN], son of Nabû-š[um ...]
Nabû-bulliṭann[i ...]
Nidintu, son of ⌜Ḫašdašu⌝(?)
[PN], son of Arad-Bēl (and)
the scribe Nabû-aḫḫē-š[ullim, son of Mušēzib-Marduk], descendant of the Šangū-Ištar-Bābili.

Sippar, month [x, day x, year x of Cam]byses, [king of Babylon, ki]ng of Lands.

[...] he will deliver the rent for the house ...

6. BM 50539+ 50833 (82-3-23, 1530+1827); 6.2 x 3.8 cm; 2.VII.Nbp 16?

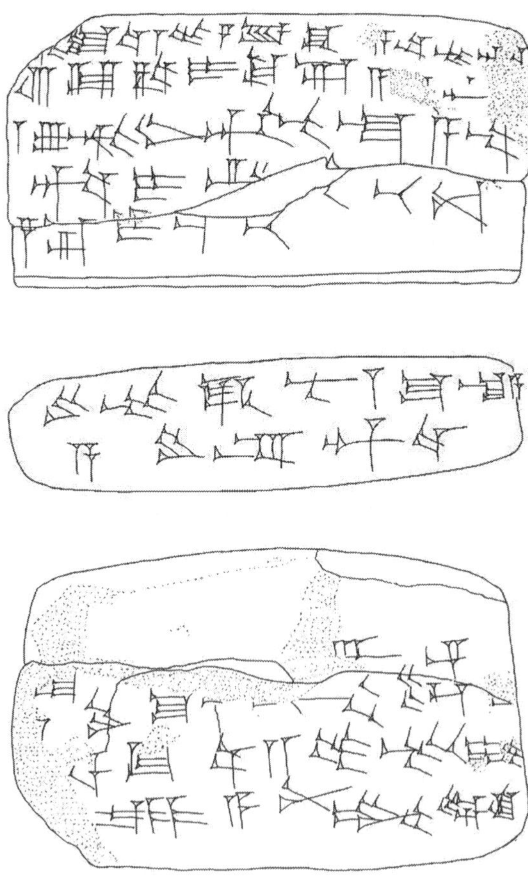

Obv. 1. [*ul*]-*tu* u$_{4}$.1.kam *šá* iti.kin ⸢*a-na*⸣ mu.an.na
2. 13 gín kù.babbar *i-di* é {x x}
3. ^{m}*ú-bal-liṭ-<su>-*^{d}*gu-la a-na*
4. ^{d}utu *i-*⸢*nam-din*⸣ *bat-qa*
5. *šá* é *i-*⸢*ṣab-bat*⸣

Edge 6. ^{lú}*mu-kin-nu šu-la-a*
7. a ^{lú}sanga ^{d}utu

Rev. One blank line
8. ⸢*ù*$^{?}$⸣ [^{lú}šid ^{md}a]g-sur
9. ⸢a⸣ ^{lú}gal.⸢dù⸣ tin.tir^{ki}
10. [it]i.⸢du$_{6}$⸣ u$_{4}$.2.kam mu.16$^{?}$.kam
11. [^{m}]^{d}ag-a-pap lugal tin.tr^{ki}

Notes

Da Riva 2002, 441 suggests that Nabû-ēṭir the scribe was descendant of Šangû-Ištar-Bābili; however, the sign is certainly not sanga, rather gal. Additionally, the reading Šangû-Ištar-Bābili does not accord with her suggestion that the text was drafted in Babylon, as there is no place for repeating Bābili, first in the family name and next as place name. It is highly interesting that although Uballissu-Gula will pay rent to Šamaš, i.e. he rented a house of the Ebabbar temple, the document was drafted in the capital city. The fact that there is only one witness suggests that Uballissu-Gula was influential and trustworthy person.

Kennedy 1986, 204 (T.17.32) who knew only BM 50833, and Da Riva 2002, 441, 465 suggest that the text was dated to the 17th year of Nabopolassar. In my opinion the 16th year is more probable, but not certain.

Translation

From the first day of the month Ulūlu Uballissu-Gula will pay to Šamaš 13 shekels of silver yearly. He will repair the house.

Witness:
Šulā, descendant of Šangû-Sippar
and [the scribe Na]bû-ēṭir, the descendant of Rab-banê.

Babylon, [mon]th Tašrītu, second day, 16$^{th?}$ year of Nabopolassar, king of Babylon.

Appendix
Rental of the temple houses of the Ištar of Uruk and Nanāya

7. BM 114446; Copied by Radosław Tarasewicz; 8.1 x 4.6 cm; 24.XII.Cyr 0 Uruk

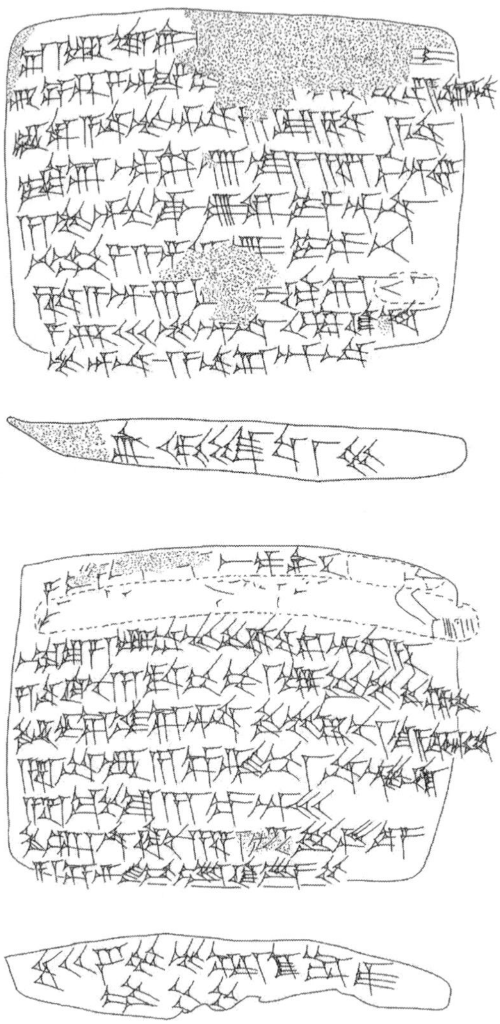

Obv. 1. é <*šá*> ^{md}en-kar^{ir} [...] ⸢*i*$^{?}$⸣

2. *re-e-ḫu šá* ^{d}gašan *šá* un[ug^{ki} x] ⸢x x x⸣ *šá a-na é-an-na*

3. *maḫ-ru a-na* mu.an.na 6 gín kù.babbar *a-na*

4. *i-di* é *ina pa-ni* ^{m}*ṣil-la-a* a-*šú šá* ^{m}dù-^{d}15

5. a ^{m}mu-^{d}kur.gal *ú-ru i-šá-an-na*
6. *bat-qu šá u-sur-*⸢*ru-ú*⸣ *i-ṣab-bat*
7. kù.babbar-a_4 6 g[ín *šá*] ⸢*i*⸣-*di* é ⸢x⸣ (ras.)
8. *šá re-eš* mu.an.na *u qí-it*
9. mu.an.na *a-na é-an-na*

Edge 10. [*iṭ-ṭi*]-*ir ul-tu* u_4.1.kam

Rev. 11. *šá* ⸢iti.bár é⸣ *ina pa-ni-šú* x (ras.)
One line erased
12. *ina* gub^{zu} *šá* ^{md}ag-du-numun ^{lú}*šà-tam é-an-na* a-*šú*
13. *šá* ^{m}*na-di-nu* a ^{m}*da-bi-bi* ^{md}ag-šeš-mu ^{lú}sag lugal
14. ^{lú}en *pi-qit-tu*$_4$ *é-an-na* ^{lú}*mu-kin-nu* ^{m}*la-a-ba-ši*-^{d}amar.utu
15. a-*šú šá* ^{m}ìr-^{d}en a ^{m}*e-gi-bi* ^{m}ìr-^{d}*in-nin*
16. a-*šú šá* ^{m}*ba-laṭ-su* a ^{m}zálag-^{d}30
17. ^{lú}šid ^{m}*na-di-nu* a-*šú šá* ⸢^{md}en⸣-šeš.meš-ba^{šá}
18. a ^{m}*e-gi-bi* unug^{ki} iti.še

L.e. 19. u_4.24.kam mu.sag ^{m}*ku-ra-áš*
20. lugal kur.kur

Notes

L. 2. Expected is ^{d}gašan *šá* un[ug^{ki} *u* ^{d}*na-na-a-a*], however, the sign traces do not support such a reading.

Although the first two lines of the document are only partly preserved, it seems rather certain that it concerns debt owed by Bēl-ēṭir to the Eanna temple. He regulated part of his debt but was unable to pay the outstanding balance and the temple has therefore taken his house, renting it to Ṣillaya. Because the document does not mention that the court was involved it seems that an agreement was accepted by both parties more or less voluntarily.

Translation

The house of Bēl-ēṭir [… for?] the outstanding balance of Lady of Ur[uk] ⸢x x x⸣ was received by the Eanna (and) for yearly house rent of 6 shekels (was given) at disposal of Ṣillaya, son of Ibni-Ištar, descendant of Iddin-Amurru.

He will seal the roof and repair the (cracks) of the wall footing.

That 6 [shekels] of the house rent he will [pa]y to the Eanna in the beginning and in the end of the year.

From the first day of the month [Nisan]nu the house is at his disposal.

In the presence of Nabû-mukīn-zēri, the administrator of Eanna, son of Nādin, descendant of Dābibī

Nabû-aḫ-iddin, the royal office, the representative for Eanna.

Witnesses:

Lābāši-Marduk, son of Arad-Bēl, descendant of Egibi

Arad-Innin, son of Balāssu, descendant of Nūr-Sîn

The scribe Nādin, son of Bēl-aḫḫē-iqīša, descendant of Egibi.
Uruk, month Addaru, 24th day, the accession year of Cyrus, king of Babylon.

8. BM 114551 (1920-6-15, 147); 5.4 x 4.8 cm; Uruk, ⸢2⸣3.[x].Cyr 5

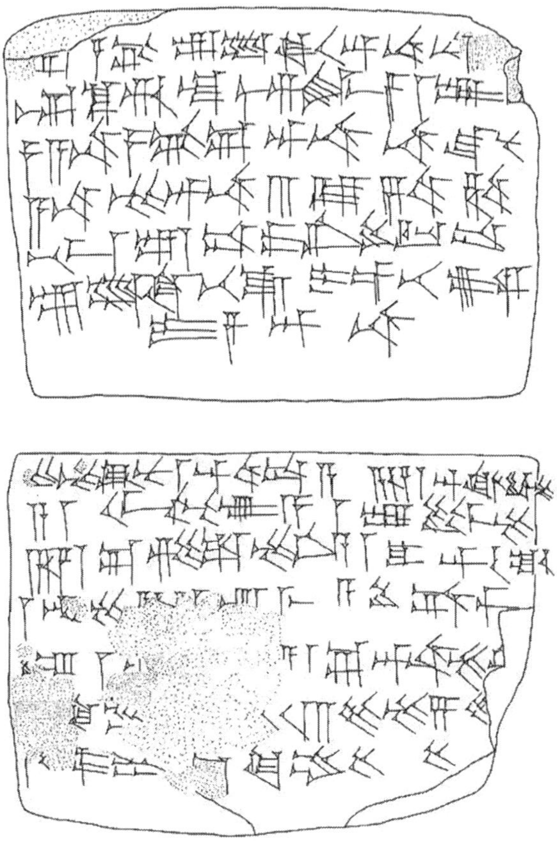

Obv. 1. é níg.ga ^{d}mùš unug^{ki} *u* ^{d}*na-na-*[*a*]
2. *ina* é *ku-tal-la ina* gi.me *šá* ^{md}ag-m[u-x]
3. *šá a-na* níg.ga *é-an-na na-šu-nu*
4. *a-na* mu.an.na 3 gín 4-*tú* kù.babbar
5. *ina* igi ^{md}innin-du-*pa-ni* ^{lú}<pa>.kab.du
6. ^{d}mùš unug^{ki} *bat*-šu^{ii} *i-ṣab-bat ú-ru*
7. *i-šá-an-na*

Rev. 8. ^{lú}*mu-kin-nu* ^{md}utu-du-a a-*šú šá* ^{md}di.kud-šeš.me-mu
9. a ^{m}*ši-gu-ú-a* ^{md}ag-šeš.me-mu
10. a-*šú šá* ^{m}*e-zi-da*-mu-dù ^{m}:dumu dingir-*šú*-ad-*šú*

11. ^{md}⌜en⌝-mu ⌜a-*šú šá* ^{m}abgal⌝ a ^{lú}uš.bar
12. ⌜^{lú}⌝šid ^{m}⌜x⌝ [x x] a ^{m}*e-an-na*-mu-⌜dù⌝
13. [unug]^{ki} iti.[x u$_4$].⌜2⌝3.kam mu.5.kam
14. ^{m}⌜*kur*⌝-*áš* lugal ⌜e⌝^{ki} lugal kur.kur

Notes

L. 8. Šamaš-mukīn-apli, son of Madānu-ahhē-iddin, descendant of Šigûa, see Kümmel 1979, 133, 151.

L. 11. Bēl-iddin, son of Apkallu, descendant of Išparu, see Kümmel 1979, 131, n. 168, 191.

L. 12. Eanna-šum-ibni was the father of Ardiya and Pir'u, see Kümmel 1979, 113.

Translation

The storehouse, property of Ištar-of-Uruk and Nanāya, in the rear house in the reeds of Nabû-šu[m-x], that was brought to the property of Eanna, (given at disposal) of Ištar-ālik-pāni, the oblate of Ištar-of-Uruk for 3¼ shekels yearly. He will carry out the repairs and renew the roof.

Witnesses:
Šamaš-mukīn-apli, son of Madānu-aḫḫē-iddin, descendant of Šigûa
Nabû-aḫḫē-iddin, son of Ezida-šum-ibni, descendant of Ilušu-abīšu
Bēl-iddin, son of Apkallu, descendant of Išparu
The scribe [PN], son of Eanna-šum-ibni.
[Uruk], month [x], 23rd day, fifth year of Cyrus, king of Babylon, king of Lands.

9. BM 114472 (1920-6-15, 68); 5.4 x 3.8 cm; 19.XII.Camb 1 Uruk

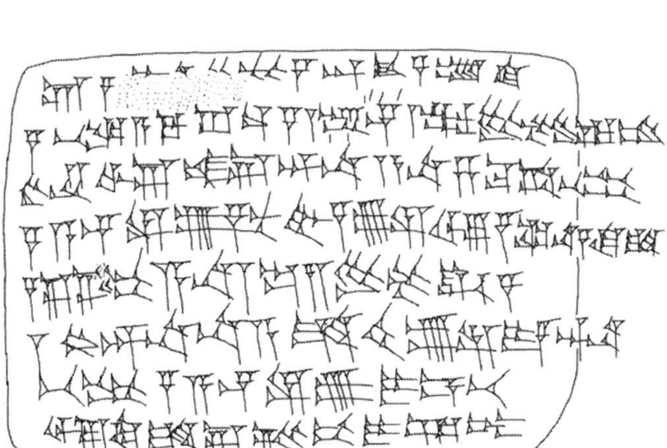

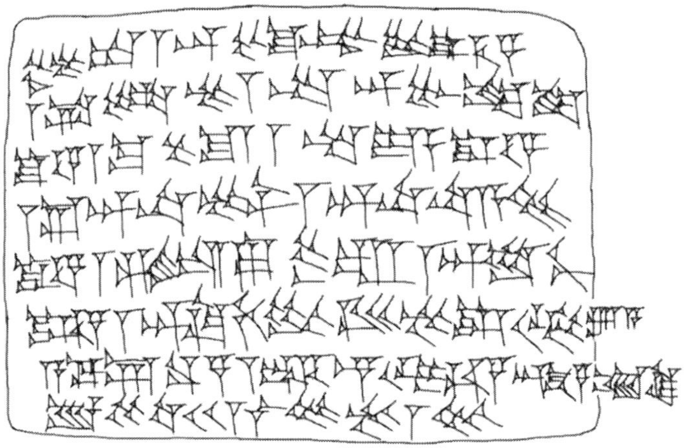

Obv. 1. é *šá* ⌜*i-na* še⌝.numun *šá* ^{d}gašan unug^{ki}
2. *šá ina* ugu ^{íd}*bit-qa šá* ^{md}en-sur ^{md}ag-šeš-mu ^{lú}sag lugal
3. ^{lú}en *pi-qit-tu*$_{4}$ *é-an-na a-na ṣa-ba-ta bat-qu*
4. *šá a-sur-ru-ú šá-nu-' šá ú-ru ù šá-ka-na šá ṭi-iṭ*
5. *šá* é *gab-bi a-na* ^{md}mùš-šeš-mu dumu-*šú šá*
6. ^{m}lú-^{d}*na-na-a id-din ú-ru i-šá-an-na*
7. *bat-qu šá a-sur-ru-ú i-ṣab-bat*
8. *ù ṭi-iṭ* é *gab-bi i-šak-kan*

Edge Two lines erased (rest not copied)

Rev. 9. ^{lú}*mu-kin*$_{7}$ ^{md}kur.gal-lugal-ùru dumu-*šú šá*
10. ^{m}*ta-li-mu* ^{m}ìr-^{d}*bu-ne-ne*
11. dumu-*šú šá* ^{m}*ba-laṭ-su* ^{m}ìr-*ia* dumu-*šú šá*
12. ^{m}*é-an-na*-mu-dù ^{md}*na-na-a*-kam
13. dumu-*šú šá* ^{m}*gi-mil-lu* ^{lú}šid ^{md}amar.utu-pap
14. dumu-*šú šá* ^{md}di.kud-šeš.meš-mu dumu ^{m}*ši-gu-ú-a*
15. ^{íd}*bit-qa šá* ^{md}en-sur *ši-i-ḫu šá* ^{d}gašan šá unug^{ki}
16. iti.še u$_{4}$.20.1.lal.kam mu.1.kam

L.e. 17. ^{m}*kam-bu-zi-ia* lugal tin.tir^{ki}
18. lugal kur.kur

Notes

Note that according to the text the tenant is not obliged to pay rent, a situation unknown from other documents.

Ll. 6-7 repeats in different grammatical form the same clause expressed in ll. 3b-5a. Cf. *ṣa-ba-ta bat-qu* in NBC 8378: 5 (Joannès 1989, 349).

L. 9 Amurru-šar-uṣur, son of Talīmu is mentioned in YOS 6, 109: 15 and in YOS 6, 159: 26 with the title *sepīru.* On this basis it seems certain, that Amurru-šar-uṣur, the *sepīru* mentioned in YOS 6, 118: 22 and YOS 6, 164: 21 is the same person. He occurs also in GC 2, 120: 21 and its duplicate BM 113339, with the title ^{lú}sag according to Kleber 2008, 258, n. 257. In GC 2, 120: 21, although the line is partly damaged, the last wedge at the very end of the line is vertical, suggesting the reading [sa]g. Such a situation when the same person is identified in some texts by one title, in others by another, is atypical.

Ll. 13-14. Marduk-nāṣir, son of Madānu-aḫḫē-iddin, descendant of Šigûa. He was active in the period from Cyr 7 till Dar 2 (Kümmel 1979, 117; Kleber 2008, 36), and as the scribe of Eanna from 22.IV.Cam 4 to 13.VI.Dar 2 (Kleber 2008, 36).

Translation

The house located in the arable field of Lady of Uruk on Bitqa-ša-Bēl-ēṭir canal, Nabû-aḫḫē-iddin, the king's official and the representative for Eanna, gave (it) to Ištar-aḫ-iddin, son of Amēl-Nanāya to repair (the cracks) of the wall footing, sealing the roof and covering whole house with clay.

He will repair (the cracks) of the wall footing, seal the roof and cover the whole house with clay.

Witnesses:

Amurru-šar-uṣur, son of Talīmu

Arad-Bunene, son of Balāssu,

Ardiya, son of Eanna-šum-ibni

Nanāya-ēreš, son of Gimillu

The scribe, Marduk-nāṣir, son of Madānu-aḫḫē-iddin, descendant of Šigûa

Nār-bitqa-ša-Bēl-ēṭir, the *šīḫu* of Lady of Uruk, month Addaru, 19th day, first year of Cambyses, king of Babylon, king of Lands.

6.2 The contract between the temple authority and Lūṣi-ana-nūri appointing him *ša muḫḫi bītāti*

10. BM 63353 (82-9-18, 3320); 6.4 x 5.3 cm; [ca. end of Dar 7]

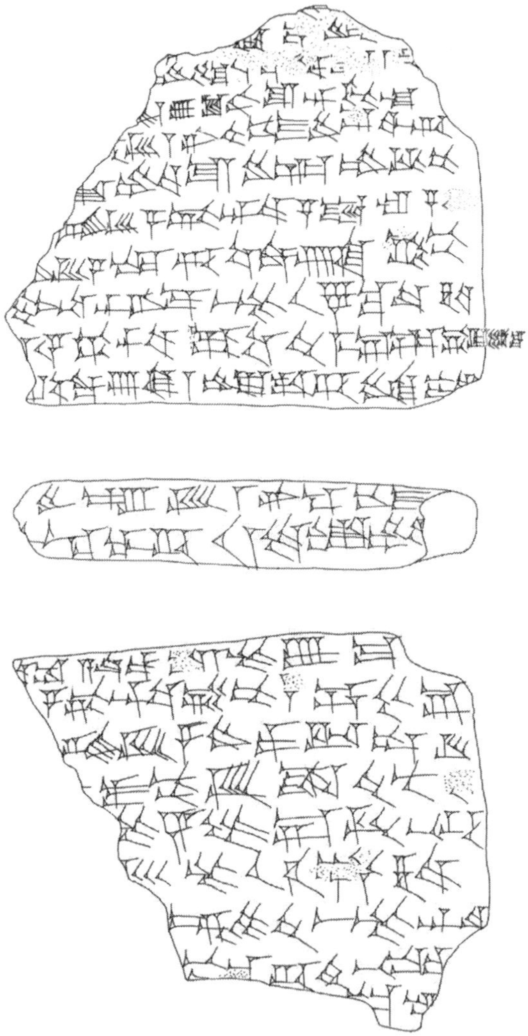

Obv. 1'. [.....] ⸢x⸣ [x x]

2'. [^{m}*ina-é-sag-ila*]-⸢*li-bur*⸣ ^{lú}s[anga *sip-par*^{ki}]

3'. [^{m}lu]gal-*lú*$^{!}$-*da*-⸢*ri* ^{lú}*qí-i-pi*⸣ $^{\mathrm{m⸢d⸣}}$e[n-mu]

4'. [^{m}ag-šeš.meš-g]i ^{m}*ú-bal-liṭ-su-*^{d}*gu-la*

5'. [^{lú}*tup-šar-r*]*i*$^{\text{?meš}}$ ^{m}*ni-din-tu*$_{4}$ ^{lú}⸢*si*⸣-*pi-ri*
6'. [*u* ^{m}*te-r*]*ik*-lugal-*ut-su* ^{lú}sag lugal *iq-bi*
7'. [*um-ma* x] gi.meš níg.ga ^{d}utu *šá* murub$_{4}$ uru *šá* ⸢x⸣ [...]
8'. [*ù* x g]i.meš *šá ka-ri* ud.kin.nun^{ki} *gab-bi*
9'. [*i bi*]-*in-na-an-ni-ma ina* mu 17 *ma-na* kù.babbar
10'. [*a-n*]*a* níg$^{!}$.ga ^{d}utu *lu-ud-din* ^{m}*ina-é-sag-ila-li-bur*
11'. [^{lú}san]ga ud.kin.nun^{ki} ^{m}lugal-*lu-da-ri* ^{lú}*qí-i*-⸢*pi*⸣
Edge 12'. ^{lú}šid.meš ^{m}*ni-din*$^{!}$(T: si)-*tu*$_{4}$
13'. [^{l}]^{ú}*si-pi-ri u* ^{m}*te-rik*-lugal-*ut*-[*su* ^{lú}sag lugal]
Rev. 14'. [^{m}*lu*]-ud.du-*a-na*-zálag ⸢*iš*⸣-*mu-šum-ma*
15'. [gi.meš] níg.ga ^{d}utu *gab-bi* ⸢*šá*⸣ *e-lat* é
16'. [x x (x)] gi.meš *šá* ^{lú}riq$_{7}$^{meš}
17'. [*ina lìb-bi*] *áš-bi*^{meš} *id-din-nu*-⸢*šú*$^{?}$⸣
18'. [*ul-tu*] mu.4.kam é.meš *ina* igi-*šú*
19'. [*ina ri-e*]*š* mu *u* ⸢*mi-šil*⸣ kù.babbar
20'. [*a-na* níg.ga ^{d}utu] ⸢*i*⸣-*nam-din ina* mu.an.na
21'. [x x x x] ⸢x⸣ *ri-ḫi ina* ugu-[*šú*]
22'. [.......] ⸢x x⸣

Notes

L. 10' the níg looks like šid.

L. 21' *ri-ḫi* might be preceded by ⸢*mim-ma*⸣. Maybe "the remaining which is due from him..."

Uballissu-Gula, son of Aḫḫē-iddin-Marduk, descendant of Šangû-Ištar-Bābili, *ṭupšar* Ebabbar attested from Dar 0 to Dar 36 (Bongenaar 1997, 87-90).

Nidintu *sepīru* attested from Camb 6 to Dar 22 (Bongenaar 1997, 93-94).

Tērik-šarussu, *ša rēš šarri* attested from Camb 1 to Dar 15 (Bongenaar 1997, 49).

Ina-Esagila-lilbur, *šangû* Sippar, attested from Dar 1 to Dar 12 (Bongenaar 1997, 31).

Šarru-lūdāri, *qīpu* Ebabbar from Cyr 6 to Dar 7 (Bongenaar 1997, 49). His presence shows that the tablet was drafted not later than in Dar 7.

Translation

[... Lūṣi-ana-nūri] said to [Ina-Esagila]-lilbur, the ad[ministrator of Sippar, Ša]rru-lūdā[ri], the king's resident, [Bēl-iddin, Nabû-aḫḫē-šu]llim, Ubalissu-Gula, [the scrib]es, Nidintu, the interpreter scribe [and to Tēr]ik-šarussu, the royal officer [as follows: "[G]ive me all [x] reeds, property of Šamaš which are in the city centre [... and x re]eds, which are in the harbour district of Sippar, [...]. Yearly 17 minas of silver I will give to the property of Šamaš." Ina-Esagila-lilbur, [the adminis]trator of Sippar, Šarru-lūdāri, the king's resident, the scribes, Nidintu, the interpreter scribe, and Tērik-šarus[su, the royal officer] consented to {his} [Lū]ṣi-ana-nūri and they gave him [reeds], all property of Šamaš except for [x] reeds of the oblates [where?] they live. [From] the fourth year the houses are at his disposal. [In the beginni]ng and in the middle <of the year> he will give silver [to the property of Šamaš. Yearly ..., the rest is on his account [...].

11. BM 72524 (82-9-18, 12530); 6.6 x 4.7 cm

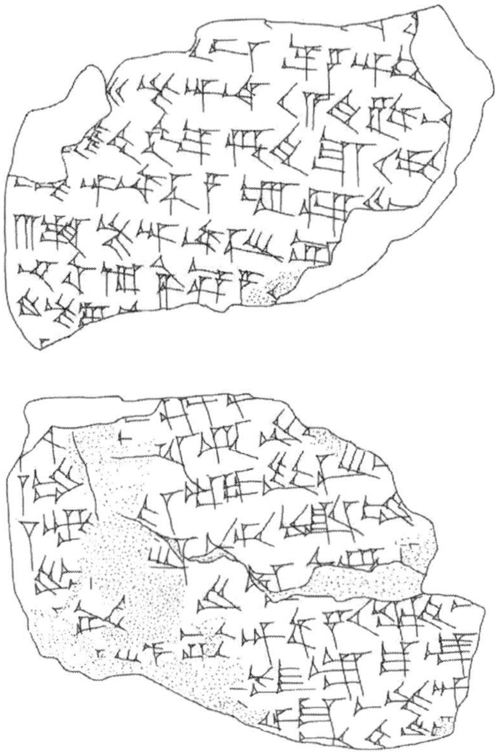

Obv. 1'. ⸢*a-na*⸣ [^{m}*ina*]-⸢*é-sag*⸣-[*gil-lil-bur* ^{lú}sanga *sip-par*^{ki}]
2'. ^{m}lugal-[*lu-d*]*a-ri* ^{lú}*q*[*í-i-pi é-babbar-ra*]
3'. ^{md}en-[m]u ^{md}ag-šeš.meš-g[i]
4'. ^{lú}š[id.m]eš ^{m}*te-riq*-lugal-[*ut-su* ^{lú}sag lugal]
5'. ⸢^{m}⸣*ni-din*-[*tu*$_{4}$] ^{lú}*si-p*[*ir*]-⸢*ri* x⸣ [x x]
6'. [x gi]⸢$^{meš?}$⸣ níg$^{!}$.ga ^{d}utu *šá muḫ-ḫi* ⸢x⸣ [x x]
7'. [...]-*tu*$_{4}$ ^{uru}*ma-la*-[...]
8'. [...] *ù*$^{?}$ *ina* mu.an.[na ...]
9'. [... *it-t*]*a-din* ^{lú}⸢x⸣ [...] 1'.

Rev. 1'. [...] ⸢x x x x⸣
2'. [... *ina*] igi ^{m}ba^{šá}-^{d}ama[r.utu ...]
3'. [*ina ri-e*]*š* mu.an.na *u a-ḫi* kù.babbar *ina m*[*i-šil* mu.an.na]
4'. [*i-n*]*am-din mim-ma ri-ḫi-su ul* [...]
5'. *ina* mu.an.na-*šú* níg.ka$_9$ *ip-p*[*u-uš* ... *a-na*]
6'. 3^{it} mu.an.na.meš é.[meš...]
7'. en ud diri *né-e šá* ⸢x⸣ [...]
8'. ^{lú}*mu-kin-n*[*u* ....] ^{m}[...]
9'. ⸢x⸣ [...]

Notes

Although only a fragment of the document is preserved it cannot be excluded that Iqīša-Marduk mentioned in rev. 2' is the future rent collector. The payment of rent in two installments a year suggests that it is not a contract between the temple and Iqīša-Marduk as rent collector, but rather that he occurs here as a private person. However, one may ask if the mention of three years in rev. 6' have something in common with backlogs for three years (Dar 1-3) in BM 61244, no. 15, or not.

Rev. 7'. The sense of this line (kindly collated also by I. Finkel and R. Tarasewicz) is unclear to me. The possible reading: *adi ūm* diri-né-e *šá* ⸢x⸣ [...] is also unclear.

Translation

[...] to [Ina]-Esag[ila-lilbur, the administrator of Sippar], Šarru-[lū-d]ari, the ki[ng's resident of Ebabbar], Bēl-[idd]in (and) Nabû-aḫḫē-šul[lim], the scr[ib]es, Tērik-šaru[ssu, the royal officer], Nidintu, the interpreter scribe ... x reed]s, property of Šamaš on account ... town Mala-[...] and yearly ... [g] ave...

[....at] disposal of Iqīša-Mardu[k. He will pay half of silver] at the beginning of the year and half of silver in the mi[ddle of the year]. None of his backlogs [...] in his$^{?}$ year he will make the settlement of account. [For] three years the house[s ...].

Witnesses: [...].

6.3 Settlement of accounts made by the rent collector

12. BM 68911 (82-9-18, 8910); *10.1* x *4.8* cm; (V.Nbn 4)

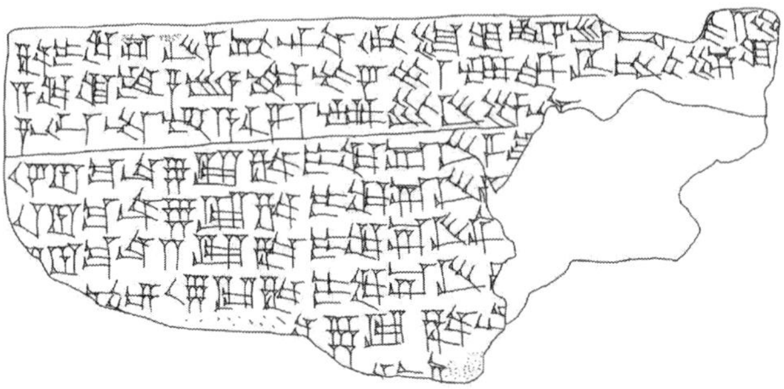

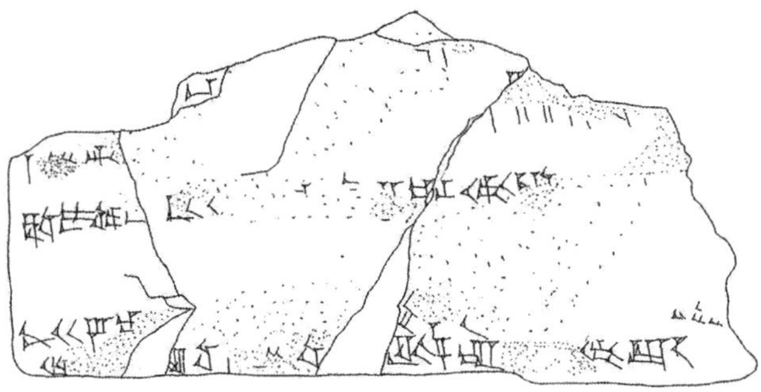

Obv. 1. kù.babbar *i-di* ⌜é⌝.meš níg.ga ^{d}utu *ul-tu qí-it* iti.⌜kin⌝ [*šá* m]u.2.kam
2. *a-di qí-it šá* iti.ne mu.4.kam ^{md}ag-im.tuku lugal.tin.tir^{ki}
3. *šá ina* igi ^{m}ìr-^{d}en a-*šú šá* ^{md}ag-šeš.meš-sum^{na}

---

4. 14⅚ *ma-na* 8 gín kù.babbar *i-di* é.meš *šá* ⌜x⌝ [..............]
5. 11⅚ *ma-na* 8 gín kù.babbar *i-di* é.meš ⌜*šá*⌝ [...............]
6. [x]+⌜2⌝⅚ *ma-na* 2 gín kù.babbar *i-di* é.meš *ni* [...........]
7. [pap x] ⌜gú⌝.un 18 gín kù.babbar *i-di* é.meš ⌜*šá*⌝ [..................]
8. [...... *ma-n*]*a* 8 gín kù.babbar ⌜*na*⌝-[*din*.........................]
9. [........................] ⌜x x x⌝ [........................]

Rev. 1'. ⌜x⌝ [.........................] ⌜x x x x x⌝
2'. Erased line
3'. kù.babbar *i-di* ⌜é.meš⌝ [x x] ⌜x x⌝ níg.ka$_{9}$ *ul* ⌜*ep*⌝-[*šú*]
Blank space for ca. two lines
4'. pap 24 *m*[*a-na* ....[*it-ta*]-*din* [.....] ⌜x x x⌝
5'. ⌜x⌝ [......*ri*]-*iḫ-tú* ⌜*šá*⌝ [^{m}]⌜^{d}⌝utu-[sig$_{5}$]^{iq} níg.ka$_{9}$ *ul ep-šú*

Notes

On the basis of the heading it seems that in ll. 4-6, the rent for the second, third and fourth years is enumerated.

Translation

Obv. 1-3. Silver, the rent of houses, property of Šamaš from the end of the month Ulūlu, the second year to the end of month Abu, the fourth year of Nabonidus, king of Babylon, which is at disposal of Arad-Bēl, son of Nabû-aḫḫē-iddin.

4. 14 minas 58 shekels of silver, rent of houses for [...]
5. 11 minas 58 shekels of silver, rent of houses for [...]
6. [x]+⌜2⌝ minas 52 shekels of silver, rent of houses [...]
7. [total x] talent 18 shekels of silver, rent of houses [...]
8. [... mi]na(s) 8 shekels of silver [he has gi]ven.
9. ...

Rev. 1'. ...
2'. Erased line
3'. Silver, rent of the houses [...] settlement of account has not been ma[de].
4'. total 24 mi[nas ...he ga]ve. [...]
5'. [..., the r]est has not been made by Šamaš-[udammiq].

13. BM 65748 (82-9-18, 5738); *6.5* x *7.0* cm; 27.VII.Nbn 16

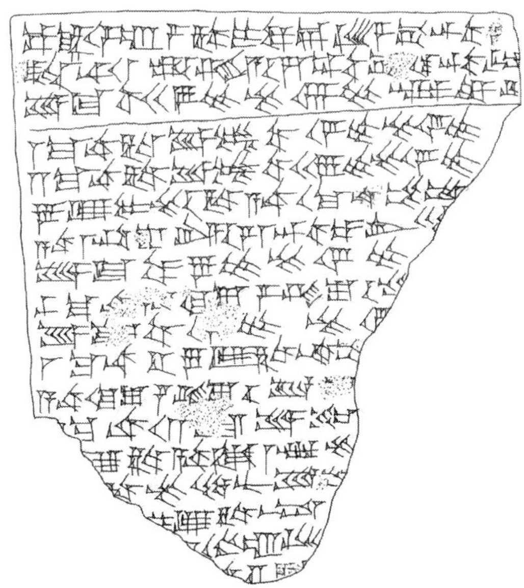

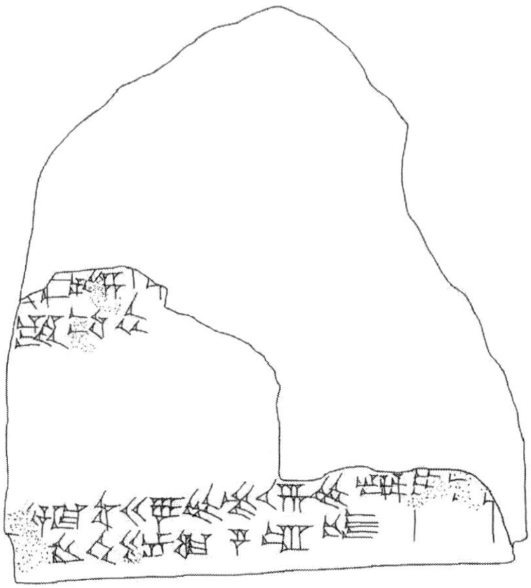

Obv. 1. *e-peš* níg.ka$_9$ *šá* kù.babbar *i-di* é.meš níg.ga ^{d}utu ⸢*šá*⸣
2. *it-ti* ^{md}en-gi a-*šú šá* $^{md!}$utu-⸢dù$^{!}$⸣ *u* $^{md!}$utu-sig$_5$[^{iq}]
3. iti.du$_6$ u$_4$.27.kam mu.16.kam ^{d}ag-im.tuku [lugal e^{ki} *ép-šú*]

---

4. 1 *ma-na* kù.babbar iti.sig$_4$ u$_4$.14.kam mu.14.kam
5. 2 *ma-na* kù.babbar iti.sig$_4$ u$_4$.27.kam mu.14.kam
6. 7 gín *lum-mu-šú* kù.babbar *a-na* 10 *ma-na* duḫ.làl [(…)]
7. *a-na* ^{md}utu-nigin^{ir} a-*šú šá* ^{md}utu-zálag^{ir} su[m$^{(na)}$]
8. iti.du$_6$ u$_4$.7.kam mu.14.kam
9. ½ *ma-*⸢*na a-na*⸣ *dul-lu šá gi-lu-šú* it[i …]
10. iti.⸢bár⸣ u$_4$.1⸢4⸣.kam mu.1⸢4⸣.kam
11. 1 *ma-na* ⅓ 7 gín kù.babbar *ina lìb-bi* […]
12. *a-na dul-lu šá gi-lu-šú* iti.⸢ne$^{??}$⸣ […]
13. [1] *ma-na* 12 gín iti.ne […]
14. [x] gín kù.babbar *a-na* <udu>.gukkal ^{md}ag-mu-[…]
15. [x x ^{m}]^{d}utu-mu sum^{na} iti.n[e …]
16. [x *ma-na* x g]ín kù.babbar *ina* gub[^{zu} …]
17. […] ^{lú}šid.meš […]
18. [… -*n*]*a* 2 ⸢gín$^{?}$⸣ […]

Rev. 1'. pap ½ gú.un ⸢1½⸣ [*ma-na*$^{?}$ ...]
2'. *it-ta-din* [*it-ti* ^{md}en-gi *u* ^{md}utu-sig$_5$^{iq} *sip-par*^{ki}]
3'. ⸢iti⸣.du$_6$ u$_4$.27.kam mu.16.kam ^{d}ag-i
4'. [lug]al tin.tir^{ki} níg.ka$_9$ *ép*-[*šú*]

Notes

L. 2. Note the atypical writing of the determinative dingir before the name of the god. The sign following ^{d}utu is partly damaged and looks like the beginning of *ni*, then dù. Also the determinative preceding the next ^{d}utu is written over three horizontal wedges. It seems the signs following ^{d}utu till the next ^{d}utu were written over erasures.

L. 14. Although the sign following *a-na* is clear, the reading <udu>.gukkal = *gukkallu* is uncertain, as such a writing is, to my knowledge, found only in cultic texts (CAD G 126). The alternative reading, dam = *aššatu*, is even less probable, because it is not related to the content of the text.

Translation

Obv. 1-3. Settlement of account of silver, the rent of houses, property of Šamaš [which] has been made with Bēl-ušallim, son of Šamaš-ibni and Šamaš-udammiq on the 27th day of the month Tašrītu, 16th year of Nabonidus, king of Babylon.

4. 1 mina of silver: month Simānu, 14th day, 14th year

5. 2 mina of silver: month Simānu, 27th day, 14th year

6-8. 7⅕ shekels of silver for 10 minas of honey (was given) to Šamaš-upaḫḫir, son of Šamaš-unammir. Month Tašrītu, seventh day, 14th year.

9-10. ½ mina for work in Gilūšu, mo[nth? ...]. Month Nisannu?, 14th day, 14th year.

11-12. 1 mina 27 shekels of silver, including [...] for the work in Gilūšu, month Abu?? [...]

13. [1] mina 12 shekels: month Abu [...].

14-15. [x] shekel(s) of silver for fat-tailed sheep(?) of Nabû-šum-[x] [x x] Šamaš-iddin was given. Month Ab[u ...]

16-17. [x mina x shek]el(s) of silver in the pres[ence of.......] scribes [...]

18. [x mi]na(s) 2 shekels [...]

Rev. 1'-4'. [...], total 31½ [minas?] he has given. [With Bēl-ušallim and Šamaš-udammiq] the settlement has been m[ade. Sippar], month Tašrītu, 27th day, 16th year of Nabonidus, king of Babylon.

14. BM 83110 (83-1-21, 273); 8.*1* x *6.3* cm; Cyr 2

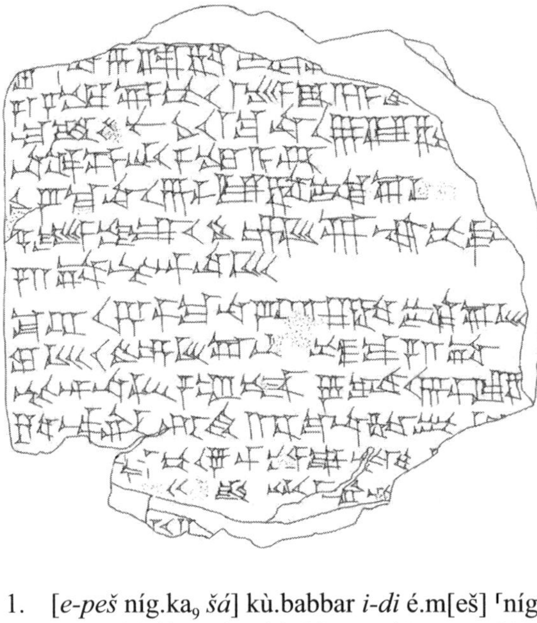

Obv. 1. [*e-peš* níg.ka$_9$ *šá*] kù.babbar *i-di* é.m[eš] ⸢níg.ga⸣ [^{d}utu]

2. [x x x (x)]^{ki} *šá ul-tu* iti.[kin u$_4$.1.k]am mu.[17.kam ^{d}ag-i lugal e^{ki}]

3. [*a-d*]*i lìb-bi* ⸢iti.ne mu.2.kam ^{m}⸣*ku-*[*ra-á*]*š* lugal t[in.tir^{ki} lugal kur.kur *šá*]

4. [^{m}] ^{d}utu-sig$_5$^{iq} a-⸢*šú šá*⸣ ^{m}*šu-zu-bu* a $^{⸢lú⸣}$sanga ^{d}utu *ép-šú* [iti.x mu.2.kam]

5. [^{m}]*ku-ra-áš* lugal tin.tir^{ki} lugal kur.kur níg.ka$_9$ [*ép-šú*]

---

6. ⸢8⸣⅓ *ma-na* 5½ gín kù.babbar *ri-iḫ-tu$_4$* ½ ⸢gú.un 5⸣½ *ma-na* [kù.babbar]

7. *šá* ⸢*i*⸣-*na* iti.ab mu.1⸢7⸣.kam ^{md}ag-⸢im.tuku⸣ [lugal tin.tir^{ki} *šá*]

8. *ina muḫ-ḫ*[*i-šu š*]*u*-⸢*uz-zu*⸣-*zu*
9. 2⅓ ⸢*ma-na* 4⸣ gín 4-*tú* kù.babbar ^{md}en-gi *u* ^{m}⸢mu⸣-[^{d}ag ...]
10. *a*-[*na*] *é-babbar-r*[*a*] ⸢*it-tan*⸣-*nu* iti.[x ...]
11. ⸢⅓⸣ *ma-na* 5 gín 4-*tú* k[ù.babbar *šá*] *a-na a-bat-ti* [sum^{na} ...]
12. [x x x] ⸢x⸣ [...]

Rest of obverse lost

Rev. 1'. ⅚ [*ma*]-*na* 6 gín kù.babbar *i*-⸢*di* é⸣.[meš ...]
2'. *šá* ^{m}*šá*-ka-*kal-bi u* iti.kin-*a-a* $^{l[ú}$ ...]
3'. *la id-din-nu* pap 11 *ma-na* 19 gín kù.babbar [*i-di* é.meš]
4'. *na-di-e-ti šá ka-a-ri*
5'. pap 4 *ma-na* 16½ gín kù.babbar *i-di* é.meš
6'. *šá* murub$_4$-*tu*$_4$ uru *u* ^{lú}un.meš é *ina lìb-bi áš-b*[*i*]
7'. *šá* 2-*ta* mu.an.na.meš
8'. šu.nigin 15½ *ma-na* 4⅓ gín kù.babbar *i-di* é.meš
9'. šub.meš *u* un.meš é *ina* ⸢*lìb*⸣-*bi áš-ba šá* 2-*ta*
10'. mu.an.na.meš níg.ka$_9$ *ép-šú* 7 *ma-na* 16½ gín kù.[babbar ...]
11'. kù.babbar *ina pa-ni-šú ri-ḫi* 2⅓ *ma-na* kù.babbar qu ⸢x⸣ [...]
12'. [x x *in*]*a* ⸢*lìb*⸣-*bi* 17½ iti.bár mu.1.kam ⸢m⸣[*ku-ra-áš*]
13'. [x x (x)] ⸢x x⸣ *it-ti ni*-⸢x⸣ [...]
14'. [x x (x)] ⸢x⸣ 12$^{?}$ [...]

Notes

L. 8. For possible parallel, see TEBR 66: 15.

L. 11. The sign is preserved in such way that the reading 2 instead of ⅓ is also possible; however, the sum of 2 minas seems to be too high for payment for reed.

Rev. 3'-4'. For [*i-di* é.meš] *na-di-e-ti*, cf. *i-di* é *na-du-ú* in BM 64489, no. 45: 8.

Translation

Obv. 1-5. [Settlement of account of] silver, the rent of houses, property of Šamaš, [...] from month [Ulūlu, first d]ay, [17th year of Nabonidus un]til month Abu, second year of Cy[ru]s, king of Babylon, king of Lands which Šamaš-udammiq, son of Šūzubu, descendant of Šangû Sippar has made.
[Month x, second year] of Cyrus, king of Babylon, king of Lands the settlement [has been made].

6-8. 8 minas 25½ shekels of silver, the rest of 35½ minas of [silver] from the month Ṭebētu, 17th year of Nabonidus, [king of Babylon,] which are re[glistered on him].

9-10. 2 minas 24¼ shekels of silver Bēl-ušallim and Iddin-[Nabû ....] have delivered to the Ebabbar. Month [x ...]

11-12. ⸢2⸣5¼ shekels of si[lver which] was [given] for (buying) *abattu* reeds [was given] ...

Big gap

Rev. 1'-7'. 56 shekels of silver, the rent of houses[...] which Ša-pī-kalbi and Ulūlaya, t[he ...] did not give, total 11 minas 19 shekels of silver, [the rent of houses for] dilapidated lodgings in the harbour district, (and) total 4 minas 16 shekels of silver for two years, the rent of houses (located) in the middle of the city in which the temple' servants live,

8'-10'. grand total 15½ minas, 4⅓ shekels of silver, the rent of the ruined houses in which the temple servants live, the balance account for two years has been made.

10'-11'. 7 minas 16½ shekels of sil[ver ... from] silver (which is) in his disposal; the rest of 2 minas 20 shekels of silver ...

12'-14'. [... in]cluding 17½ <shekels>. Month Nisannu, first year of [Cyrus ...] with [...] 12[?]....

15. BM 61244 (82-9-18, 1218); 7.0 x 6.6 cm; 23.XI[?].Dar 7

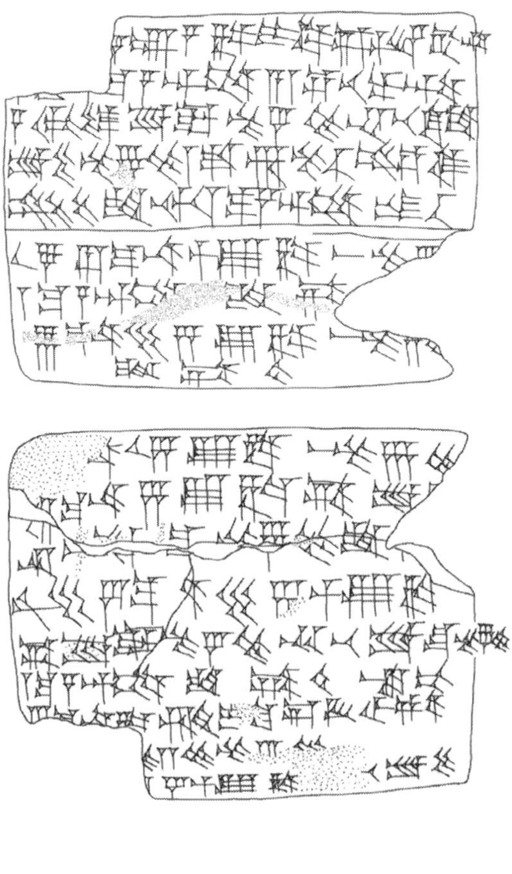

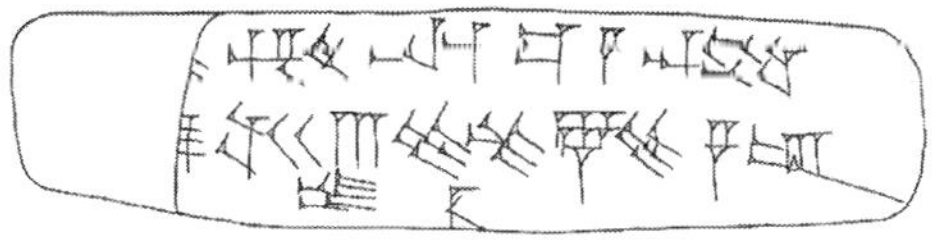

Obv. 1. [*e-peš*] níg.ka$_9$ *šá* kù.babbar *i-di* é.meš níg.ga ^{d}utu
2. ⸢*ina*? ugu? ^{m}⸣ba^{šá}-^{d}amar.utu a ^{m}*e-tel-pi-*^{d}utu
3. *šá ul-tu* iti.bár mu.4.kam en {til} *qí-it*
4. iti.še mu.⸢7⸣.kam ^{m}*da-ri-mu-šú* lugal e^{ki}
5. lugal kur.kur *it-ti* ^{m}ba^{šá}-^{d}amar.utu *ép-šú*

---

6. 17⅚ *ma-na* ½ gín kù.babbar *ina* mu.⸢4⸣.[kam]
7. ^{m}ba^{šá}-^{d}amar.utu *it-ta-*[*din*]
8. 9 *ma-na* 55 gín kù.babbar *ina* mu.⸢5.kam⸣
9. *it-ta-din*

Rev. 10. [14 *ma*]*-na* 15 gín kù.babbar *ina* mu.6.kam
11. ⸢12⸣ *ma-na* <5>5 gín kù.babbar ta iti.[bár mu.7.kam]
12. en ⸢til iti.šu mu.7⸣.kam *it-t*[*a-din*]
13. pap 54 *ma-na* 55½ gín kù.babbar
14. ta iti.bár mu.4.kam en til iti.šu mu.7.kam
15. ^{m}ba^{šá}-^{d}amar.utu *it-ta-din ina lìb-bi*
16. ⸢3 *ma-na* kù⸣.babbar *ri-ḫi i-di* é.meš igi-*e-tú*
17. [*šá* mu.1.kam m]u.2.kam mu.3.kam
18. [*e-lat* 22 *ma-n*]*a* 4½ gín kù.babbar [en t]il? iti.še

L.h.e. 19. [*ù* 1 *ma-n*]*a ri-ḫi ina* igi ^{m}ba^{šá}-^{d}amar.utu
20. [iti.z]íz? u$_4$.23.kam mu.7.kam níg.ka$_9$
21. *ép-šú*

Notes

L. 11. The idea that the scribe forgot to write the number 50 is supported by the fact that only with such an emendation will a total of 54 minas 55 shekels be reached.

L. 15. *ina libbi* means "including," "of this amount" or similar, however, it seems that the scribe made a mistake in writing *ina libbi* instead of *elat*, "in addition to". For such understanding of the text, see above, p. 115-118.

Translation

Obv. 1-5. [Settlement] of account of silver, the rent of houses, property of Šamaš ⸢on account?⸣ of Iqīša-Marduk, son of Etel-pī-Šamaš which (for the period) from month Nisannu, fourth year till the end of month Addaru, seventh year of Darius, king of Babylon, king of Lands has been made with Iqīša-Marduk.

6-7. 17⅚ minas ½ shekels of silver in the fourth year Iqīša-Marduk has given
8-9. 9 minas 55 shekels of silver in the fifth year he has given
Rev. 10. [14 mi]nas 15 shekels of silver in the sixth year
11-12. 12 minas <5>5 shekels of silver from month [Nisannu, seventh year] till the month Du'ūzu, seventh year he has gi[ven],
13-15. total 54 minas 55½ shekels of silver from month Nisannu, the fourth year till the end of month Du'ūzu, seventh year Iqīša-Marduk has given. *Apart from* (?!)
16-17. ⸢3 minas of silver⸣, the rest of an earlier house rent [for first], second (and) third year.
18-19. [This is apart from 22 min]as 4½ shekels of silver [till the end$^{?}$] of month Addaru [and 1 mi]na, the remainder, which is at disposal of Iqīša-Marduk.
L.h.e. 20-21. [Month Šabā]ṭu$^{?}$, 23rd day, seventh year, the settlement has been made.

16. JEOL 40, no. 1; 23.I.Dar 8

Obv. 1. ^{m}ba$^{\textit{šá}}$-^{d}amar.utu a ^{m}*e-tel-pi-*^{d}utu a ^{lú}sanga ^{d}utu
2. *ina mi-gi*-ir** [šà-*bi*]-*šú* é.meš níg.ga ^{d}utu *šá a-na*
3. ^{giš}bán *ina* igi-*šú ul-*⸢*tu*⸣ iti.bár mu.8.kam ^{m}*da-ri-ia-muš*
4. lugal é^{ki} lugal kur.kur *ina* níg.ga ^{d}utu *ina* igi ^{m}*ina*-é-sag-íl-lil-bur*
5. ^{lú}sanga ud.kib.nun^{ki} *u* ^{lú}šid.meš *un-da-ši-*⸢*ir*⸣
6. *e-lat* 22 *ma-na* 4½ gín kù.babbar *re-ḫi šá* mu.6.kam
7. *u* mu.⸢7⸣.kam *ù* 1 *ma-na* kù.babbar babbar-⸢*ú*⸣
8. šám 4 gú.un síg.ḫi.a *šá ina* igi-*šú* ⸢*u*⸣
9. 1 me 22 kùr zú.⸢lum⸣.ma ⸢*it-ti*⸣
10. ^{lú}šid.meš *šá* é.ki$^{!}$.tuš$^{!}$.gi.na *ú-*[*šá*]*-az-za-ma*
11. *a-na* ^{m}*ina*-é-sag-íl-li*[*l-bur*] ^{lú}sanga ud.kib.nun^{ki} *u*
12. ^{lú}šid.meš *i-nam-*[*din*]
13. ^{lú}*mu-kin-nu* ^{md}am[ar-utu-mu-dù] ⸢a⸣-*šú šá* ^{m}kar-^{d}šu
14. a ^{lú}sanga ^{d}mùš é[^{ki} ^{md}x x]-mu a-*šú šá*
15. ^{m}*gi-mil-lu-*^{d}ut[u a ^{m}dù]$^{\textit{eš}}$-dingir ^{md}utu-⸢mu⸣
16. [a]-*šú šá* ^{md}en-a-mu a ^{lú}sanga ^{d}utu ^{md}utu-*na-ṣir* a-*šú šá*
17. ^{m}*mu-šal-lim-*^{d}amar-utu a ^{lú}sanga ^{d}utu ^{m}*ba-su-*⸢*ru*⸣ *šá ina muḫ-ḫi qu-úp*
18. ^{m}*la-ba-ši* [a-*š*]*ú šá* [^{md}]ag-*na-ṣir* a ^{m}šeš^{ki}-*ú-tu*
19. *u* ⸢^{lú}⸣šid ^{md}[utu-k]ád a-*šú šá* ^{md}ag-du-a a ^{lú}pa.še^{ki}
20. ud.kib.nun^{ki} iti.bár u$_{4}$.23.kam

21. mu.8.kam ^{m}*da-ri-ia-muš* lugal é^{ki}
22. [lu]gal ⸢kur⸣.[kur]

Translation

Iqīša-Marduk, son of Etel-pī-Šamaš, descendant of the Šangû-Šamaš, the houses, property of Šamaš, which he has leased on the fixed rent, he will relinquish (them back) on his own will into the property of Šamaš from (the very beginning) of Nisannu, the eighth year of Darius, king of Babylon, king of Lands, to Ina-Esagila-lilbur, the administrator of Sippar and the scribes. This is apart from the 22 minas 4½ shekels of silver, outstanding of the sixth and seventh year and 1 mina of white silver the price of 4 talents of wool, which is in his disposal; and (apart from) 11 *kurru* of dates, which he will register with the scribes of the Etušgina temple and give (the receipt) to Ina-Esagila-lilbur, the administrator of Sippar and the scribes.

Witnesses:

Marduk-šum-[ibni], son of Mušēzib-Marduk, descendant of Šangû--Ištar-Bābili

[...]-iddin, son of Gimil-Šam[aš, descendant of Epp]eš-ili

Šamaš-iddin, son of Bēl-aplu-iddin, descendant of Šangû-Šamaš

Šamaš-nāṣir, son of Mušallim-Marduk, descendant of Šangû-Šamaš

Basuru, in charge of the cash box

Lābāši, son of Nabû-nāṣir, descendant of Aḫḫūtu,

and the scribe [Šamaš-kā]ṣir, son of Nabû-mukīn-apli, descendant of Isinnaya

Sippar, month Nisannu, 23rd day, eighth year of Darius, king of Babylon, [ki]ng of Lan[ds].

6.4 The House Rent Payment Lists

17. BM 62168 (82-9-18, 2137); 4.1 x 5.3 cm; [x].VI.Nrg 3

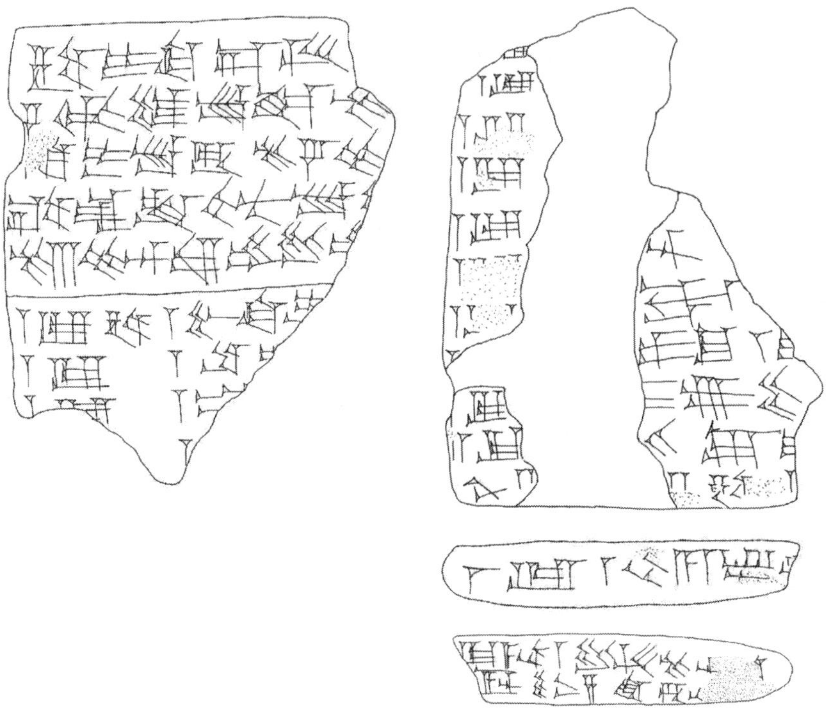

Obv. 1. kù.babbar *i-di* é.meš [níg.ga ^{d}utu]
2. *šá ul-tu* iti.ne mu.[2.kam]
3. ⸢*a*⸣*-di-i* iti.kin mu.3$^{!}$ (T: 4).kam [*a-na*]
4. *é-babbar-ra id-din-nu* iti.k[in$^{?!}$ u$_{4}$.x.kam]
5. mu.3.kam ^{d}u+gur-lugal-ùru lu[gal e^{ki}]
6. 1 gín kù.babbar ^{m}*pu-di-ia*
7. 1 gín ^{m}ìr-*i*[*a*]
8. 1 ⸢gín⸣ ^{m}du[b-numun]
9. [x gín] ^{m}[…]
Rest lost

Rev. 1’. [1] gín […]
2’. 1 gín […]
3’. 1 gín […]
4’. 1 gín […]
5’. 1 ⸢gín⸣ […]
6’. 1 g[ín ^{m}]^{d}[…]

7’. 1 gín]x ^{m}[...]
8’. 1 [gín]sipa$^{?}$ ^{m}⸢x⸣[...]
9’. ⸢1⸣ [gín ^{md}a]g-*ú-še*-[*zib*]
10’. 2 [gín ^{md}e]n$^{?}$-*lu-d*[*a-ri*]
11’. pap ⸢⅓$^{?}$⸣ [*ma-na* x g]ín kù.babbar ⸢x⸣ [x x]
L.e. 12’. 1 gín ^{m}⸢tin⸣ a ^{md}ag-⸢x⸣ [(x)]
L.h.e. 13’. [x x x g]ín *a-na* ^{m}šeš-meš-mu-^{d}[amar.u]tu
14’. [x x š]ám *in-za-ḫur-ri-t*[*i* sum^{na}]

Notes

Obv. 3. ⸢*a*⸣-*di-i* iti.kin mu.4.kam suggests that in l. 2 the [second] year has to be reconstructed. However, the document is evidently dated to the third year (l. 5), which might suggest that, exceptionally, the rent was paid for the period from month Ulūlu, the third to end of Abu, the fourth, i.e. at least half a year in advance, which is hardly probable. Presumably the scribe made a mistake in l. 2 where instead of iti.kin mu.4.kam should be iti.kin mu.3$^{!}$.kam.

Obv. 3. The tiny trace of the month sign looks like two *Winkelhaken*, i.e. like beginning of the month of Simānu; however, because usually the reports were written after the end of or in the last month of the accounting year I suggest emending to iti.k[in].

Rev. 11’. The reading pap ⸢2⸣ [*ma-na* x g]ín kù.babbar cannot be excluded.

Rev. 13’. In gín one vertical wedge is not drafted.

Translation

Obv. 1-5. Silver, the rent of houses, [property of Šamaš] which was delivered [to] the Ebabbar temple (for the period) from the month Abu, [second year] to the month of Ulūlu, third$^{!}$ (T: 4) year. Month U[lūlu$^{!}$, nth day], third year of Neriglissar, ki[ng of Babylon].

	6.	1 shekel	Pudia
	7.	1 shekel	Aradiy[a]
	8.	[x] shekel(s)	Šāp[ik-zēri]
	9.	[x shekel(s)]	PN
Rev.	1’.	[1] shekel	PN
	2’.	1 shekel	PN
	3’.	1 shekel	PN
	4’.	1 shekel	PN
	5’.	1 shekel	PN
	6’.	1 shekel	PN
	7’.	1 shekel	x [x (x)]
	8’.	1 shekel	]-rē’û$^{?}$ ^{m}[x x x]

9'. 1 [shekel Na]bû-ušē[zib]
10'. 2 shekels [Bē]l-lūd[āri]
11'. Total ⌜⅓?⌝ [minas x she]keels of silver [...]
L.e. 12'. 1 shekel: Balāṭu, son of Nabû-[x (x)]
L.h.e. 13'-14'. [x sheke]ls for Aḫḫē-iddin-Ma[rdu]k ..., pr]ice of *inzaḫurētu*-dye was given.

18. BM 84424 (83-1-21, 1587); 4.0 x 3.9 cm; 12.[x] Lb-M 0

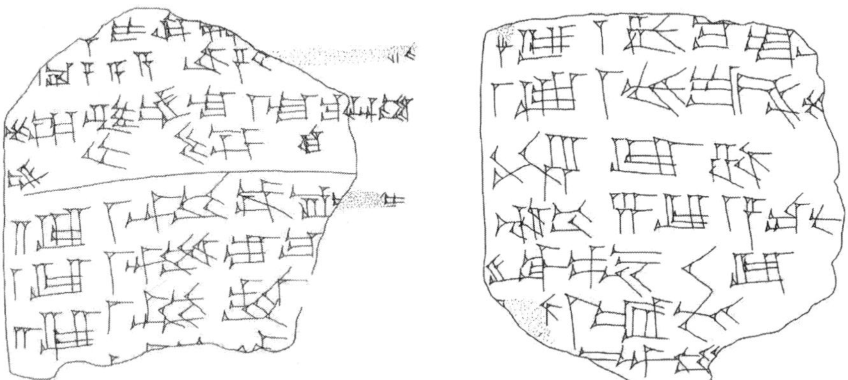

Obv. 1. [kù.babbar *š*]*á i-di* ⌜é⌝.[meš níg.ga ^{d}utu *šá*]
2. ^{m}*uš-šá-a-a na-šá-'* [iti.x u_4].⌜12.kam⌝
3. mu.sag.nam.lugal.la ^{m}*la-ba-ši-*^{d}amar.utu
4. lugal tin.tir^{ki}

5. 2 gín ^{md}amar-*e-ṭir-*⌜x⌝ [x x] *i*
6. 1 gín ^{md}amar.utu-*eri*$_4$*-ba*
7. 2 gín ^{md}amar-*it-*[*tan-nu*]
8. [x gín] ⌜^{m}⌝[x x] ⌜x⌝
Rest lost

Rev. 1'. ⌜4⌝ gín ^{m}*ḫa-ba-ṣi-r*[*u*]
2'. 1 gín ^{m}numun-*ia* ^{lú}mu
3'. pap 15 gín kù.babbar
4'. *ina lìb-bi* 5 gín ^{m}*šá-du-nu*
5'. ^{lú}gal giš.ban 10 gín
6'. [*a-n*]*a* ^{m}dub-numun
7'. [*u* ^{m}]⌜i?⌝-^{d}amar.u[tu]

Notes

Rev. 5'. Šadûnu, chief of bowmen active in Sippar, see Bongenaar 1997, 132. Add also BM 79665, dated to Nbk 36 (courtesy R. Tarasewicz).

Rev. 7'. Or ⌈ a ^{m}]⌈i$^{?}$⌉-^{d}amar.utu.

Translation

[Silver, o]f the rent of houses, [property of Šamaš], which was brought.
[Month x], 12th [day], the accession year of Lābāši-Marduk, king of Babylon.

2 shekels	Būr-ēṭir [...]
1 shekel	Marduk-erība
2 shekels	Būr-ittannu
[x shekel(s)	[PN]

Rest lost

Rev.

4 shekels	Ḫabaṣīru
1 shekel	Zēriya, the cook

total 15 shekels of silver, including 5 shekels (for) Šadûnu, the chief of bowmen (and) 10 shekels [fo]r Šāpik-zēri [and$^{?}$] Nā'id-Mard[uk].

19. BM 114748 (1920-12-13, 40); 5.3 x 8.7 cm; (V.Nbn 0)

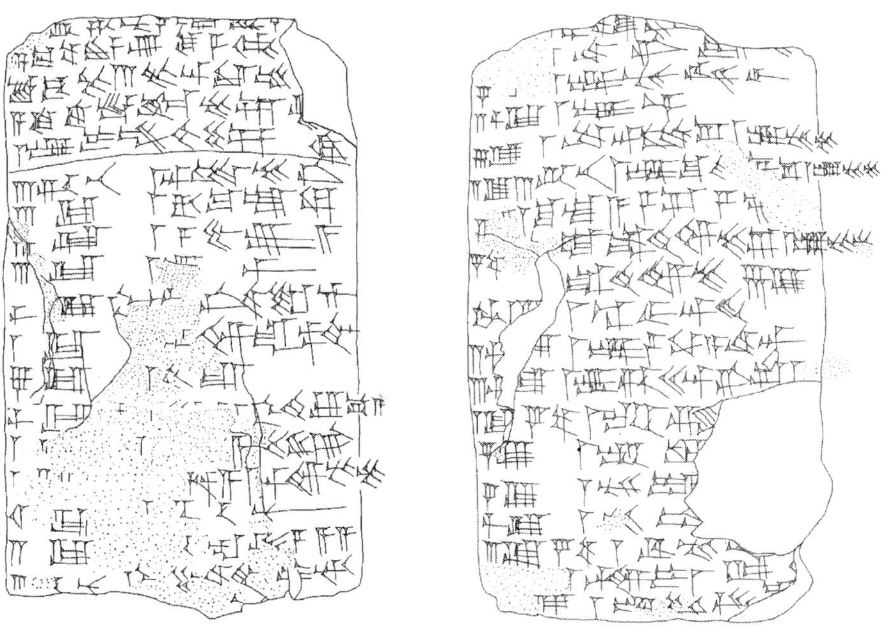

Obv. 1. [kù.babbar] *ri-ḫa-nu šá ina* é.meš *šá* [ugu]
2. íd ud.kib.nun^{ki} *šá ul-*[*tu*]
3. iti.kin mu.3.kam ^{d}u+gur-lugal-[ùru]

4. *a-di* šà iti.ne mu.sag.n[am.lugal.la]
5. ^{md}ag-i lugal tin.tir^{ki}
6. 3 *ri-bat* ^{md}amar.utu-mu-dù
7. 3 gín ^{m}*ḫa-ba-ṣi-ru*
8. ⸢3$^{?}$⸣ gín ^{m}*šá-bu-ú-a*
9. 3 gín ^{m}⸢*ú*⸣*-bar*
10. ½ gín ^{fd}dù-*tú-šar-rat*
11. 1 gín [^{m}]^{d}im-*ra-pa-'*
12. 7 gín ^{m}[ti]n-⸢*su*⸣
13. ½ gín [^{m}x x (x)] ^{f}*ḫi-ip-ta-a*
14. 1 g[ín [^{md}DN]-a-⸢mu⸣ ^{lú}ašgab
15. 1 g[ín [^{m}x x]-*qa-a*/a ^{md}im-numun-mu
16. 11 gín ^{m}⸢en$^{?}$⸣-*šú-nu*
17. 2 gín [^{m}x]-*um-meš-šá-a-a*
18. 3 ⸢*ri*⸣*-bat* ⸢^{f}*li-'-i*⸣*-ti*
19. [...] ⸢x x⸣ [...]
Rest lost

Rev. 1'. [x gín ^{md}]utu-su ^{lú}⸢x⸣ [...]
2'. [x gín] ^{m}*na-ni-ia* ⸢x⸣
3'. 4 ⸢gín⸣ ^{md}ag-numun-gál^{ši}
4'. 2½ gín ^{md}ag-sur
5'. 6 gín ^{m}ìr-^{d}amar.utu é ^{md}ag-numun-mu
6'. 2 gín 3 *ri-bat* ^{md}ag-*šu-zi*[*b-an-n*]*i* é ^{md}ag-numun-mu
7'. ⸢2⸣ [gí]n ^{m}*šu-la-a šá* é níg.g[a] ⸢x⸣ [(x x]
8'. 4-*tú* ⸢x⸣ ad <m>*ra-ḫi-im-mu* é ^{md}ag-numun-⸢mu⸣
9'. [*u*$^{?}$ ^{m}]*ra-ḫi-im-mu* 6 gín
10'. *šal-šú* ⸢gín⸣ ^{m}*si-lim*-^{d}šár
11'. 2½ ⸢gín⸣ ^{md}ag-*šá-qa-a-na*-dingir
12'. 3½ ⸢gín⸣ ^{md}ag-*ri-man*^{an}*-ni* ⸢é⸣ ^{m}[...]
13'. 1 gín 4-*tú* ^{md}en-gi [(...)]
14'. 4 gín ^{md}en-*ka*-[*ṣir* ...]
15'. 4 gín ^{m}numun-*ia* [(...)]
16'. ½ gín ^{m}⸢mu$^{?}$-du⸣ [...]
17'. 3 gín 4-*tú* ^{m}*tuk-kul-t*[*i* ...]
18'. ^{md}im-i 1 gín ⸢x⸣ [...]
19'. [x] ⸢gín⸣^{md}en-šeš.meš-⸢su⸣

L.e. 20'. pap 1 *ma-na* 5 gín kù.babbar

Notes

Rev. 16'. The reading ^{m}⸢numun?-du⸣ cannot be excluded.

Translation

Obv.	1-5.	[Silver], rest of (the rent of) houses (located) on the Euphrates, for the period from month of Ulūlu, third year of Neriglissar until month of Abu, the accession year of Nabonidus, king of Babylon.	
	6.	3¼ (shekels)	Marduk-šum-ibni
	7.	3 shekels	Ḫabaṣīru
	8.	3$^{?}$ shekels	Šabûa
	9.	3 shekels	Ubāru
	10.	½ shekel	Bānītu-šarrat
	11.	1 shekel	Adad-rapa’
	12.	7 shekels	[Uba]llissu
	13.	½ shekel	[PN] ^{f}Ḫiptā
	14.	1 [shekel	DN]-aplu-iddin, the leatherworker
	15.	1 [shekel	x]qa, son of$^{?}$ Adad-zēr-iddin
	16.	11 shekels	Bēlšunu
	17.	2 shekels	[x]ummeššaya
	18.	3¼	^{f}Li’iti
	19.	…	
Rev.	1’.	[x shekel(s)]	Šamaš-erība, the […]
	2’.	[x shekel(s)]	Naniya
	3’.	4 [shekels]	Nabû-zēr-ušabši
	4’.	2½ shekels	Nabû-ēṭir
	5’.	6 shekels	Arad-Marduk, the house of Nabû-zēr-iddin
	6’.	2¾ shekels	Nabû-šūz[iban]ni, the house of Nabû-zēr-iddin
	7’.	2 shekels	Šulā, from the storehouse […]
	8’.	¼	[x] the father of Raḫimmu, the house of Nabû-zēr-iddin
	9’.		[and$^{?}$] Raḫimmu,
	10’.	6 shekels (and) one-third of shekel	Silim-Ašur
	11’.	2½ shekels	Nabû-šaqa-ana-ili
	12’.	3½ shekels	Nabû-rēmanni […]
	13’.	1¼ shekels	Bēl-ušallim
	14’.	4 shekels	Bēl-kā[ṣir …]
	15’.	4 shekels	Zēriya
	16’.	2½ shekels	Šum$^{?}$-uk[īn …]
	17’.	3¼	Tukult[i-DN]
	18’.		[Ad]ad-nā’id, 1 shekel …
	19’.	[x] shekel(s)	Bēl-aḫḫē-erība
L.e.	20’.	Total 1 mina 5 shekels of silver.	

20. BM 79054 (Bu 89-4-26, 3510); 5.4 x 7.7 cm; 10+[x].VII.Nbn 0

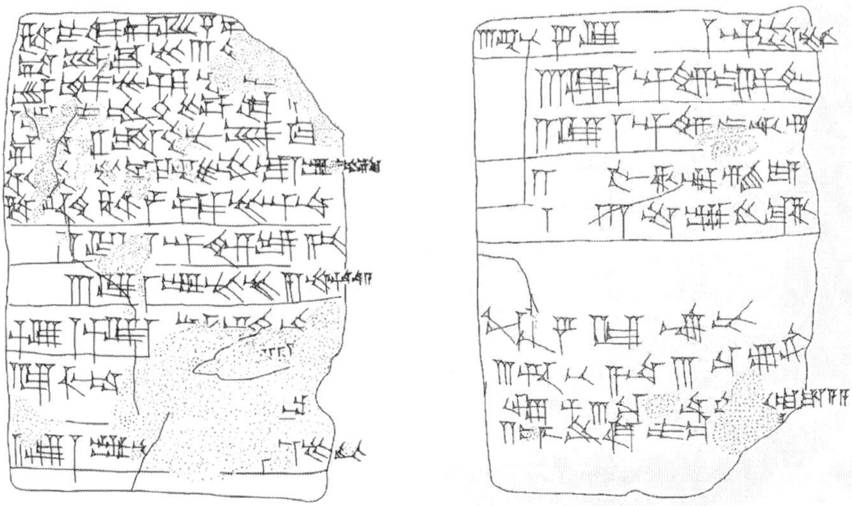

Obv.	1.	kù.babbar *i-di* é.meš níg.g[a ^{d}utu *šá*]	
	2.	ta iti.kin mu.3.k[am ^{d}u+gur-lugal-ùru lugal e^{ki} *a-di*]	
	3.	iti.ne mu.sag.⸢nam.lugal⸣.[la]	
	4.	^{md}⸢ag-i⸣ lugal.tin.tir^{ki} ⸢*a*⸣-[*na*]	
	5.	*é-*[*babb*]*ar-*[*r*]*a id-din-nu* iti.du$_{6}$	
	6.	u$_{4}$.10+[x].⸢kam⸣ mu.sag.nam.lugal.la ^{md}ag-[i] lugal e^{ki}	
	7.	kù.babbar *ri-ḫi* kù.babbar *šá* sag mu.an.na	
	8.		2 gín ^{md}im-*ia-a-bi*
	9.		3 gín ^{md}ag-numun-mu a ^{m}ìr-^{d}*na-na-a*
	10.	½ gín	1½ gín $^{m⸢d}$en$^{?⸣}$-gi.na
	11.	1 gín IGI.DU	[.....]
	12.		[.....] ⸢x⸣
	13.	⸢2⸣ gín ^{md}ag-m[u$^{?}$ x x x] ⸢x⸣-mu-⸢ùru⸣	
Rev.	14.	3 *ri-bat*	4 gín^{md}amar.utu-mu-dù
	15.		3 gín^{md}im-*ra-pa-*'
	16.	2 gín	^{md}im-⸢*i*$^{?}$⸣-*ṭì-ri*
	17.	2 gín	^{f}*ḫa-ag-gi-ia*
	18.	1 ⸢gín⸣	^{m}ìr-^{d}ag ^{lú}šu.ḫa
	19.		pap ⅓ 4 gín *ina lìb-bi*
	20.		3 *ri-bat a-na* 3 sìla *šam-ni*

21. *ù* 1 bán 3 sìla [*a*]-*na q*[é$^{?}$-*me*$^{?}$ x]-⸢x⸣-*ad-da-a-a*
22. 2 ⸢pi⸣ ^{lú}*qí-i-p*[*i*]

Translation

Obv. 1-7. Silver, the rent of houses, prop[erty of Šamaš] which was delivered to the Ebabbar (for the period) from month Ulūlu, third year [of Neriglissar, king of Babylon till] month Abu, the accession year of Nabonidus, king of Babylon.
Month Tašrītu, 10+x day, the accession year of Nabo[nidus], king of Babylon. The silver, the rest of silver for the beginning of the year.

	8.		2 shekels Adad-iābi	
	9.		3 shekels Nabû-zēr-iddin, son of Arad-Nanāya	
	10.	½ shekel	1½ shekel	⸢Bēl?⸣-ukīn
	11.	1 shekel IGI.DU [ ]		
	12.		[...]⸢x⸣	
	13.	2 shekels Nabû-šu[m-x son of x]-šum-uṣur		
Rev.	14.	¾	4 shekels	Marduk-šum-uṣur
	15.		3 shekels	Adad-rapa'
	16.		2 shekels	Adad-ēṭir
	17.		2 (shekels)	^{f}Ḫaggia
	18.		1 [shek]el	Arad-Nabû, the fisherman

19-22. Total 24 shekels, of it ¾ shekels for 3 *qû* of oil and 1 *sūtu* 3 *qû* for fl[our$^{?}$ x]-addaia; 2 *pānu* (for) the king's resident.

21. CT 57, 77 = BM 56726 (82-7-14, 1134) Collated; *4.2 x 5.2* cm; 25.VII.Nbn 0

Obv. 1. [kù.babbar *šá i-d*]*i* é.meš *šá* ^{d}utu
2. [*šá* x x] *ul-tu* iti.kin
3. [mu.3.kam] ^{d}u+gur-lugal-ùru luga[l e]^{ki}
4. [*a-di-i* it]i.ne mu.sag.nam.lugal.la
5. [^{md}a]g-i lugal.tin.tir^{ki}
6. ⸢*a-na*⸣ *é-babbar-ra id-din-nu* iti.du$_{6}$
7. u$_{4}$.25.kam mu.sag.nam.lugal.la ^{md}ag-i lugal e^{ki}
8. kù.babbar *ri-ḫi* kù.babbar ⸢*ina*⸣ sag mu.an.na

9.	[(…)]	4 gín ^{md}utu-mu a ^{m}*ab-da-mil-ki*
10.	[(…)]	5 gín ⸢3⸣-[*ta ri-bat* …] ⸢*na*⸣
11.	[(…)]	⸢1⸣ +[x gín ....]
	Rest lost	

Rev. 1'. [.....] ⸢x x⸣
2'. […] ⸢x⸣ […] udu.n[íta$^{?}$]
3'. ⅔ gín 4-*tú* kù.babbar ⸢x⸣

Translation

Obv. 1-8. [Silver, the re]nt of houses, property of Šamaš [located ...] from month Ulūlu [third year] of Neriglissar, king of Babylon [to the m]onth Abu, the accession year of Nabonidus, king of Babylon he(?) delivered to the Ebabbar temple. Month Tašrītu, 25th day, the accession year of Nabonidus, king of Babylon. Silver the rest of silver (paid) in the beginning of the year.

9. 4 shekels: Šamaš-iddin, son of Abda-milki

10. 5⅔ shekels: [...]-*na*$^{?}$

11. ⸢1⸣+[x? shekels ...]

Rest lost

Rev.1'-2'. [...]sh[eep$^{?}$]

3'. 40¼ shekels ⸢x⸣

22. CT 57, 76 = BM 57732 (82-7014, 2140) Collated; 25.VIII.Nbn 0

Obv. 1. kù.babbar *šá i-di* é.meš níg.<ga> ⸢^{d}⸣[utu]

2. *ul-tu* iti.⸢kin⸣ mu.sag.n[am.lugal.la]

3. ^{md}ag-i lugal.tin.tir^{ki} *a-d*[*i* iti.ne]

4. mu.sag.nam.lugal.la *a-na é-babbar*-[*ra* sum^{in}]

5. iti.apin u$_4$.28.kam mu.sag.na[m.lugal.la]

6. [^{md}ag]-i lugal.tin.tir[^{ki}]

7. [...] ⸢x⸣ [...]

Rest lost

Rev. uninscribed

Notes

Pinches' copy is accurate, however, because the accounting period lasted one year, it is not excluded that in l. 4 the scribe made a mistake and wrote mu.sag.nam.lugal.la instead of expected mu.1.kam. The translation expresses the suggested emendation.

Translation

Silver, the rent of houses, property of [Šamaš], from the month Ulūlu, the acces[sion year] of Nabonidus, king of Babylon to [the month Abu], the first$^{!}$ year was delivered to the Ebabbar temple.

Month Araḫsamna, 28th day, the accessi[on year of Nabo]nidus, king of Babylon.

23. BM 66344 (82-9-19, 6337); 4.3 x 5.4 cm; 25.VIII.Nbn 0

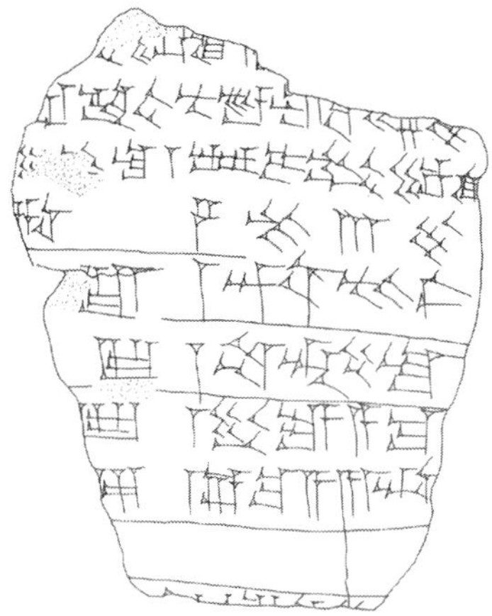

Obv. 1’. [....lugal ti]n.tir^{ki} ⸢*a*⸣-[*na* ...]
2’. [*é-babbar-r*]*a id-din-nu* iti.apin u$_4$.25.kam
3’. [mu.sag].⸢nam.lugal⸣.la ^{md}ag-i lugal.tin.tir^{ki}
4’. [...] kù.babbar *šá* mu.3.kam
5’. [x] gín ^{md}utu-numun-dù
6’. [x] gín ^{m}ìr-^{d}*gu-la*
7’. [x] gín ^{m}šeš-*ia-a-ba*
8’. [x] gín ^{m}*kal-ba-a* a ^{md}utu-[x x]
9’. [x gín] ⸢^{md}x xx⸣-[...]

Notes

Maybe the name of the rent collector occurred in the missing part of the tablet, but it is not certain as it is sometimes omitted (see next text below).

L. 4’. “Silver of the third year” concerns presumably the third year of Neriglissar.

Translation

Obv. 1’-4’. [Silver, the rent of houses, property of Šamaš ... king of Baby]lon, [.....] delivered to the [Ebabb]ar.
Month Araḫsamna, 25th day, [the access]ion year of Nabonidus, king of Babylon.
[...] silver of the third year.

5’. [x] shekel(s) Šamaš-zēr-ibni
6’. [x] shekel(s) Arad-Gula
7’. [x] shekel(s) Aḫu-iaba
8’. [x] shekel(s) Kalbā, son of Šamaš-[x x]
9’. [x shekel(s)] [...]

24. BM 73044 (82-9-18, 13054); 5.0 x 5.4 cm; 12$^{?}$.V.Nbn 1

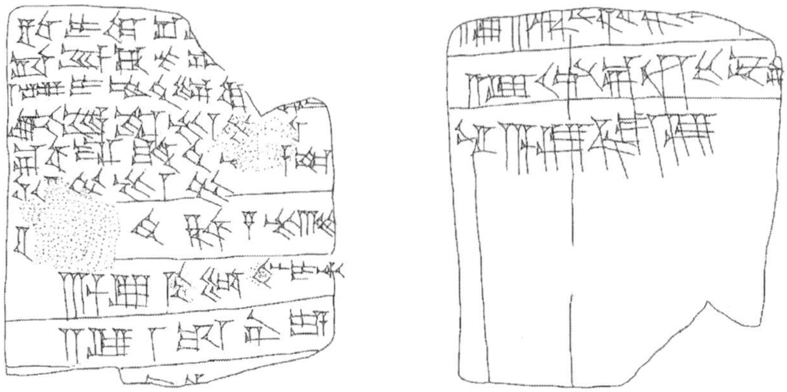

Obv. 1. kù.babbar *i-di* é.m[eš níg.ga ^{d}utu *šá*]
2. ta iti.kin mu.sa[g.nam.lugal.la]
3. ^{md}ag-i lugal.tin.tir^{ki} [*a*]-⌜*di-i*⌝
4. *lìb-bi* iti.ne mu.1.⌜kam⌝ [*a*]-⌜*na*⌝
5. *é-babbar-ra id-din*-⌜*nu*⌝ [it]i.ne
6. u_4.1⌜2⌝.kam mu.1.kam

7. ⌜⅓$^{?}$⌝ [*ma-na ri*]-*ḫi* kù.babbar *šá* mu.3.kam

8. 3½ gín ⌜^{f}⌝*li*-⌜ʾ⌝-*i-ti*

9. 2 gín ^{m}*da-ni-ia*

10. [x x] ⌜x x⌝ [...]

Rest lost

Rev. 1'. ⌜2 gín 3 *ri-bat* kù.babbar x x⌝

2'. 2 gín *mi-šil bit-qa* ^{m}*kur-ba-ni*

3'. pap ⅓ 2½ gín *šul*-<*lul*>1 gín

Translation

Obv. 1-6. Silver, the rent of houses, prop[erty of Šamaš, wh]ich they delivered to the Ebabbar (for the period) from month Ulūlu, the accessi[on y]ear of Nabonidus, king of Babylon as until month Abu of the first year including.
Month Abu, 12th day first year.

7. ⅓$^{?}$ [mina, re]st of silver of the third year

8. 3½ shekels ^{f}Li'iti

9. 2 shekels Dannêa

10. [...]

Rest lost

Rev. 1'. 2¾ shekels of silver [...]
2'. 2⅝ (shekels) Kurbanni
3'. total 22⅚ shekels.

25. BM 101635 (83-1-21, 3296); 3.8 x 4.3 cm; (V.Nbn 1)

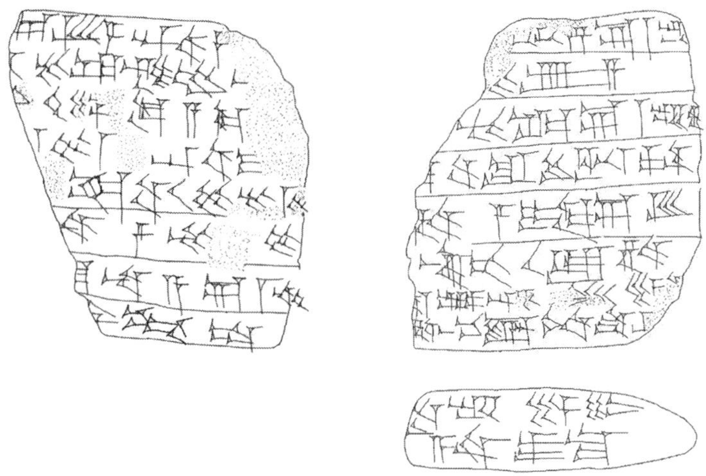

Obv. 1. [kù.babbar *i-di*] é.meš níg.<ga> ^{d}utu ⸢*šá*⸣ [ta]
2. [iti.ki]n mu.sag.nam.lugal.l[a]
3. [^{md}ag-i luga]l tin.tir^{ki} *a-di-*[*i*]
4. [iti.ne mu].1.kam ^{md}utu-b[a^{šá} *a-na é-babbar-ra*]
5. [*id-din-nu* iti].ne u$_4$.10.kam mu.1.[kam]
6. [x *ma*]*-na šá* mu.[x].kam
7. [x x ^{m}*k*]*i-na-a* é ^{m}*na-din*
8. [x x (x) é ^{m}*n*]*i-qu-du*

Rev. 9. [x x x]-⸢*ti-iá*⸣ é ^{md}en-[x]
10. [x x x]-⸢*mu*⸣*-ú-a*
11. [x x x] numun sag é ^{md}en-kád
12. [x x x^{m}]⸢$^{d?}$⸣utu-su ^{lú}*ḫúp-pa-na*
13. [x x x] kù.babbar *šá i-di* é.meš
14. [x x x] *ina lìb-bi* 10 gín kù.babbar
15. [x x x *n*]*a* ^{md}ag-⸢en-kam$^{?}$⸣^{eš} sum$^{⸢na⸣}$
16. [x x] kù.babbar *ina* šám na$_4$.ur$_5$ ⸢x⸣ [...]

Edge 17. [x x x ^{m}ì]r-^{d}en sum^{in}
18. [x x x] *a-na áš-la*

Notes

L. 12. The only parallel might be nA *ša ḫupānišu*, cf. CAD Ḫ 238, s.v. *ḫupānu* or less probably Pl. of *ḫuppû,* cf. CAD Ḫ 240 "acrobat" or "cultic dancer" (CDA 121), but such a form of Pl. is unknown.

Translation

Obv. 1-5. [Silver, the rent] of houses, property of Šamaš, which Šamaš-iqīš[a has delivered [to the Ebabbar temple] (for the period) from the month [Ulū]lu, the accession year of [Nabonidus, king] of Babylon, to the month [Abu] the first [year].
[Month] Abu, tenth day, first year

6. [x mi]na(s) for the [x] year
7. [x shekel(s) K]īnā, the house of Nādin
8. [x shekel(s) PN], the house of [N]iqūdu

Rev. 9. [x shekel(s) …]-tiya, the house of Bēl-[…]
10. [x shekel(s) …]-mua
11. [x shekel(s) …]-zēri SAG, the house of Bēl-kāṣir
12. [x shekel(s)] Šamaš-erība, the *ḫuppana*
13. […] of silver from the rent of houses
14. […] in it 10 shekels of silver
15-18. [… t]o$^?$ Nabû-bēl$^?$-ēreš was given [...] of silver, for the price of a grindstone [… to A]rad-Bēl was given.

26. CT 57, 73 = BM 56557 (82-7-14, 933) Collated; (Nbn 1)

U.e. 1. [^{lú}erín.m]eš *šá* ^{m}⸢*re*⸣-[*mut* x x]

Obv. 2. [x gín] *i-di* é *šá* ^{md}ag-a-[x]
3. [x g]ín *i-di* é *šá* ^{m}zálag-^{d}utu
4. 8 gín *šá* ^{md}ag-numun-du
5. 8 gín *šá* ^{m}*na-din ina* ká.gal
6. *a-di* iti.ab mu.1.kam
7. ^{md}ag-i lugal tin.tir^{ki}
8. ⸢*i*⸣*-di* é *it-te-*[*ṭir*]

Rev. 9. *i-di* é.meš šá ^{lú}[gal]
10. *ka-a-ri* ^{md}utu-⸢dù$^?$⸣
11. *a-di* iti.ab mu.1.⸢kam⸣
12. ^{md}ag-i lugal tin.tir^{ki}
13. *i*[*t-t*]*e-ṭir*

Translation

U.e. 1-3. [The worker]s(?), which Rē[mūt x x]

Obv. [x shekels], the rent of house of Nabû-aplu-[x]
[x shek]el(s), the rent of house of Nūr-Šamaš

4. 8 shekels of Nabû-zēr-ukīn
5. 8 shekels of Nādin, <that> in the gate

6-8. until month Ṭebētu, first year of Nabonidus, king of Babylon, the house rent has been paid.

Rev. 9-13. The rent of houses of the [chief] of the harbour district, until month Ṭebētu, first year of Nabonidus, king of Babylon, has been paid (by) Šamaš-⸢ibni?⸣.

27. BM 59708 (82-9-18, 4118); 3.0 x 3.3 cm; (5.Nbn ⸢2⸣)

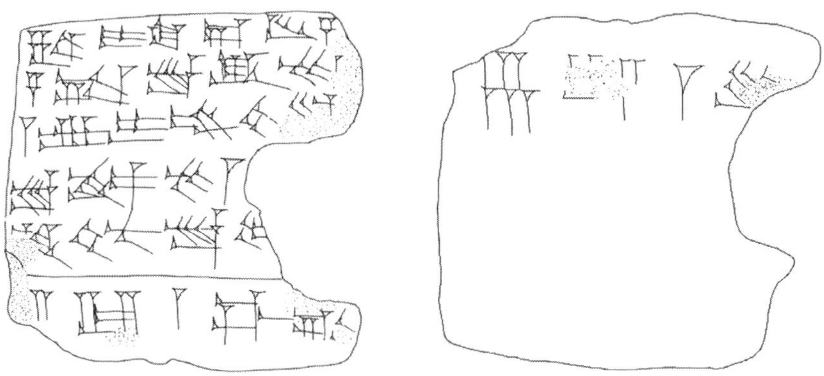

Obv. 1. kù.babbar *i-di* é.meš níg.[ga ^{d}utu]
2. *šá* ta iti.kin mu.1.[kam]
3. ^{md}ag-i lugal.tin.t[ir^{ki} *a-di*]
4. iti.ne mu.1+[1.kam ...]
5. ⸢*id*⸣-*din-nu* iti.si[g$_4$ ...]
6. [x]+2 gín ^{m}*mar-duk*

Rev. 7. 6 ⸢gín⸣ ^{m}šeš.[meš-...]

Translation

Obv. 1-5. Silver, the rent of houses, the prop[erty of Šamaš] (for the period) from the month Ulūlu, first year of Nabonidus, king of Babylon, [till] the month of Abu, the ⸢second⸣ [year] they has given.
Month Sim[anu [...]

6. [x]+2 shekels Marduk

Rev. 7. 6 shekels Aḫḫē-[...]

28. BM 75208 (83-1-18, 538) = Str. ii 263/3-4; 6.1 x 11.8 cm; [x].V.[Nbn] 2

Obv.	1.	[kù.babbar] níg.⸢ga⸣ [^{d}utu …]		
	2.	[x x] ⸢x⸣ […]		
	3.	[x] ta it[i.kin mu.1.kam KN]		
	4.	[(x) it]i.ne mu*.2*.kam* […]		
	5.	4½ gín	é	^{md}utu-⸢dù*⸣ [x] ^{md}ag-[…]
	6.	5 gín	é	^{md}⸢utu⸣-su *šá* é gu$_4$
	7.	2 gín	é	^{m}tin a [^{m}]*bu-un-na-an**-[*nu*]
	8.	4* gín 3 ri-bat	é	mìr-^{d}*a-nu-ni-tu*$_4$ ^{lú}mu šub
	9.	4 gín	é	^{m}*ú*-bar ^{md}utu-mu *šá* é mušen* *ina lìb-bi áš-bi*
	10.	2 gín	é	^{m}numun-*ia* ^{m}*mu-ra-nu* ^{lú}ašgab
	11.			*ina a-ḫi áš-bi a-ḫi* šub
	12.	2 gín	é	*ri-mut* a ^{m}šeš-*šú-nu** šub
	13.	3 gín	é	^{m}kar-^{d}en ^{lú}šu.ḫa
	14.			⸢^{m}ìr⸣-^{d}ḫar ^{lú}ìr é.gal *ina lìb-bi áš-bi**
	15.	6 gín	é	^{md}en-ba^{šá} ^{md}utu-*lu-da-ri*
	16.			*ina lìb-bi áš-ba*
	17.	1½ gín	é	^{md}dù-*tú*-[kam] ^{lú}ìr é.gal *ina** *lìb-bi áš**-*bi**
	18.	3 ⸢gín	é⸣	[^{m}]*la-a-ba-ši* ^{lú}ašgab
	19.	4 g[ín	é]	^{md}e[n-kád] ^{m}*ina*-giš.mi-^{d}⸢a*-a*⸣
	20.			*ina lìb-bi* [áš]-*ba*
	21.	⸢1⸣½ gín	é	^{m}⸢*ina**-*ṣil**⸣[x x]-*a*/a ^{lú}10$^{?}$ […]
	22.	1½ gín	é	^{m}[ìr]-^{d}u+gur š[ub (...)]
	23.	4 gín	é	[^{md}x]-ad-ùru [(...)]
	24.	4 gín	é	^{m}[x x]-*a-qar*-⸢x⸣ [x]
	25.	2* gín*	[é	x x (x)] ⸢x⸣
Rev.	26.	2* gín	é	^{md}amar.utu-kam [(x x)]
	27.	4 gín	é	^{m}*ina*-sùḫ-sur [(x (x)]
	28.	2 gín	é	^{m}⸢ìr⸣-^{d}en ^{lú}šu.ḫa
	29.	1 gín	é	⸢x *ḫi*/it⸣-*ṣu**-*ú* šub
	30.	2 gín	é	⸢^{md}en-dù?.an.ki šub
	31.	4 gín	é	^{md}en-šeš-⸢mu⸣ šub
	32.	2 gín	é	^{m}⸢x (x)⸣-*du-ú-a* ⸢^{lú*}túg*.babbar*⸣ šub
	33.	⸢2⸣ gín	é	^{m}⸢*šad*⸣-*din-nu* šub
	34.	[x]+1½ gín	é	^{m}⸢x⸣-*di**-*ia* šub
	35.	[x]+2 gín	é	^{m}a-*a* šub
	36.	2 gín	é	^{m}⸢^{d}en⸣-*tuk**-⸢*te**⸣-*e-tir-ri* šub
	37.	10 gín	é	^{m}⸢*šu-la-a*⸣ šub
	38.	2 gín	é	^{m}⸢ba$^{?}$⸣[$^{šá-a?}$]-*a* ^{md}ag-*ki-šìr* ⸢^{lú}⸣nagar
	39.	⅓ gín	é	^{m}⸢^{d}en⸣-*tak-lak* šub
	40.	4 gín	é	^{md}⸢ag-lugal$^{?}$-x [1$^{?}$]^{it}⸣ mu.an.na šub
	41.	4 gín	é	^{m}*mar-duk-a* šub

42. pap 2 *ma-na* 9 gín 4-*tú* kù.babbar *šá* ^{m}⌜mu$^{?}$⌝-[ ]
43. pap.pap 4 *ma-na* 15½ gín ⌜kù.babbar x⌝ [...]

Notes

Note that upper and lower edges are preserved and the tablet is in fact complete. The dividing line between the fifth and sixth line is almost invisible.
L. 5. One missing sign might be [*u*] or [*a*].
L. 13. Not Mušēzib-Ea (Kleber 2004, 140).
L. 25 is missing in Strassmaier's copy.

Translation

[Silver], property [of Šamaš ...] from the mon[th Ulūlu, first year ... to the mon]th Abu, second year [...].

4½ shekels — the house of Šamaš-ibni [x] Nabû-[...]
5 shekels — the house of Šamaš-erība of the sheep shed
2 shekels — the house of Balāṭu, son of Bunanu
4¾ shekels — the house of Arad-Anunītu, the baker, ruined
4 shekels — the house of Ubār; Šamaš-iddin of the bird stall lived in it
2 shekels — the house of Zēriya; Mūrānu, the leatherworker lived in the half of it; the half is ruined
2 shekels — the house of Rēmūt, son of Aḫušunu
3 shekels — the house of Mušēzib-Bēl, the fisherman; Arad-Bunene, the master-builder live in it
6 shekels — the house of Bēl-iqīša; Šamaš-lūdāri lived in it
1½ shekels — the house of Bānītu-[ēreš], the master-builder who lived in it
3 shekels — the house of Lābāši, the leatherworker
4 shek[els — the house of Bē[l-kāṣir]; Ina-ṣilli-Aya lived in it
1½ shekels — the house of Ina-ṣil$^{?}$[-DN], the [...]
1½ shekels — the house of [Arad]-Nergal, ru[ined]
4 shekels — the house of [DN]-aba-uṣur [...]
2 shekels — [the house of PN]

Rev.

2 shekels — the house of Marduk-ēreš
4 shekels — the house of Ina-tēšê-ēṭir
2 shekels — the house of Arad-Bēl, the fisherman
1 shekel — the house of [x x]-ṣū, ruined
2 shekels — the house of Bēl-x x, ruined
2 shekels — the house of Bēl-aḫ-iddin, ruined
2 shekels — the house of [...]-dūa, the washerman, ruined
2 shekels — the house of Šaddinu, ruined
[x]+1½ shekels — the house of [x]dia, ruined
[x]+2 shekels — the house of Aplā, ruined

2 shekels	the house of Bēl-tuktē-tirri, ruined
10 shekels	the house of Šulā, ruined
2 shekels	the house of Iqīšā, ruined
⅓ shekel	the house of Bēl-taklak, ruined
4 shekels	the house of Nabû-šar$^{?}$-x, [for one?] year, ruined
4 shekels	the house of Marduka

Total 2 minas 9¼ shekels of silver which …; grand total 4 minas 15½ shekels of silver…

29. Nbn 201 = BM 92724 (82-9-18, 57a) Collated; 4.7 x 6.6 cm; 15.IX.Nbn 5

Obv.	1.	kù.babbar *i-di* é.meš *šá* murub$_4$ uru	
	2.	*šá a-na a-bat-tu$_4$* sum^{na} iti.gan	
	3.	u$_4$.15.kam mu.5.kam ^{md}ag-i	
	4.	lugal tin.tir^{ki}	
	5.	5½ gín	^{md}utu-numun-dù
	6.	3 gín	^{md}utu-lugal-ùru
	7.	2 gín 4*-*tú**	^{m}*ni-qu-du*
	8.	2 gín	^{m}*kal-ba-a*
	9.	2 gín	^{md}im-*na-ta-nu*
	10.	2 gín	^{m}*pu-di-iá*
	11.	1 gín	^{m}*ina*-sùḫ-sur
	12.	a ^{md}en-ba⸢*šá*⸣	
Rev.	13.	1 gín	^{m}*ka-ri-e-a-'**
	14.	1 gín	⸢^{m}*ina*⸣-sùḫ-sur a ^{md}utu-šeš-mu
	15.	1 gín	^{m}⸢*la-a-ba*⸣-*ši*
	16.	3 gín	^{m}a-*a* a ^{md}utu-šeš-mu
	17.	1 gín	^{m}mu-mu a ^{md}ag-dù-šeš
	18.	2 gín	^{m}*ḫaš-di-ia* a ^{md}im-ad-tin
	19.	2 gín	^{m}*šu-la-a* a ^{md}en-šeš.meš-gál^{ši}
	20.	1 gín	^{md}utu-su a ^{md}ag-kád
	21.	2 gín	^{m}*ki-na-a*
	22.	1 gín	^{md}en-gi
	23.	pap ½ *ma-na* 2 gín 3 *ri-bat*	

Notes

L. 15. Judging by the Strassmaier copy the signs are well preserved and reading of the name in this line is certain. In fact the signs following the determinative are now damaged, and the reading possible but not certain.

Translation

Obv. 1-4. Silver the rent of houses in the middle of the city, which was given for *abattu* reeds.

Month Kislīmu, 15th day, fifth year of Nabonidus, king of Babylon.

	5.	5½ shekels	Šamaš-zēr-ibni
	6.	3 shekels	Šamaš-šar-uṣur
	7.	2 shekels	Niqūdu
	8.	2 shekels	Kalbā
	9.	2 shekels	Adad-natanu
	10.	2 shekels	Pudia
	11-12.	1 shekel	Ina-tēšê-ēṭir, son of Bēl-iqīša
Rev.	13.	1 shekel	Karea'
	14.	1 shekel	Ina-tēšê-ēṭir, son of Šamaš-aḫ-iddin
	15.	1 shekel	Lābāši
	16.	3 shekels	Aplā, son of Šamaš-aḫ-iddin
	17.	1 shekel	Šum-iddin, son of Nabû-bān-aḫi
	18.	2 shekels	Ḫašdia, son of Adad-abu-uballiṭ
	19.	2 shekels	Šulā, son of Bēl-aḫḫē-ušabši
	20.	1 shekel	Šamaš-erība, son of Nabû-kāṣir
	21.	2 shekels	Kīnā
	22.	1 shekel	Bēl-ušallim
	23.	total 32¾ shekels	

30. BM 68900 (82-9-18, 8899); 5.6 x *5.0* cm; X.Nbn 14

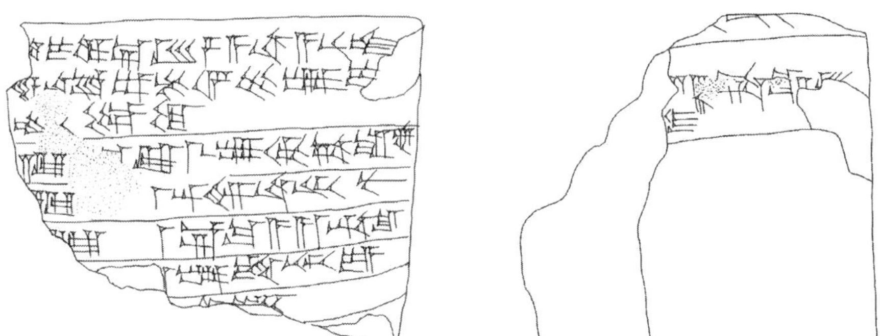

Obv. 1. [kù].babbar *i-di* é.meš *šá a-na a-bat-tu*$_4$
2. [s]um^{na} iti.ab mu.14.kam ^{d}ag-i
3. lugal [ti]n.tir^{ki}
4. 2 gín [x] 1 gín ^{m}*ina-*^{d}ag-*ul-ta-ra-aḫ*
5. ⌜2⌝ gín [(x)] ^{md}im-*na-ti-nu*
6. [x] gín ^{m}*kal-ba-a* a ^{md}utu-su

	7.	[x gín] ^{md}ag-*it-ti-iá*
	8.	[x gín ^{m}]⸢x⸣-^{d}en
		Rest lost
Rev.	1'.	[...] ⸢x x⸣ [...]
	2'.	[... x gí]n 3$^{!}$-*ta* šu^{i}[$^{i.meš}$] [...]
	3'.	[... *t*]*u*$_{4}^{?}$

Notes

Cf. Jursa 2010, 512, 525.

Rev. 2'. The *Winkelhaken* is redundant.

Translation

Obv.	1-3.	[Si]lver, the rent of houses, which was given for (purchase) *abattu* reeds.
		Month Ṭebētu, 14th year of Nabonidus, king of [Ba]bylon.
	4.	2 shekels [x] 1 shekel Ina-Nabû-ul-taraḫ
	5.	2 shekels Adad-natinu
	6.	[x] shekel(s) Kalbā, son of Šamaš-erība
	7.	[x shekel(s)] Nabû-ittia
	8.	[x shekel(s)] [x]-Bēl
		Rest lost
Rev.	1'.	[...] ⸢x x⸣ [...]
	2'.	[... x shek]el(s) (and) three-fourth [...]
	3'.	[...]

31. BM 54956 (82-5-22, 1286); 3.5 x 4.6 cm; Nbn [x]

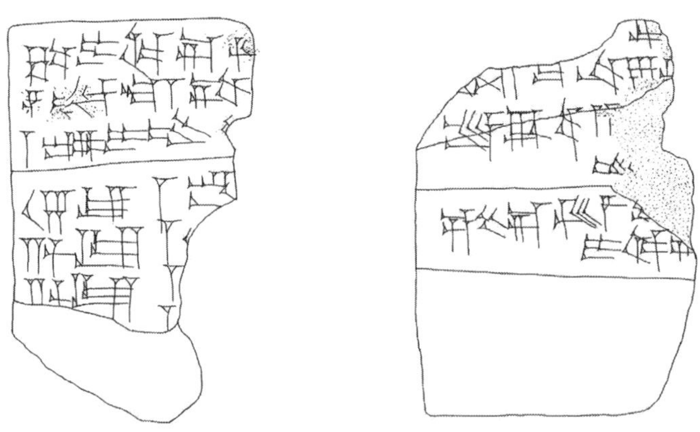

Obv.	1.	kù.babbar *i-di* é.m[eš níg.ga ^{d}utu]
	2.	*šá* ⸢iti⸣.apin ta [...]

3. ^{md}ag-i lugal.t[in.tir^{ki} ...]
4. 15 gín ^{md}⸢en⸣-[...]
5. 2½ gín ^{m}⸢x⸣-[...]
6. 2½ gín ^{m}[...]
7. [x gín] ^{m}[...]

Rev.
1'. [.......] ⸢gín⸣ [...]
2'. [pa]p.pap 2 *ma-na* ⸢9⸣ g[ín kù.babbar ...]
3'. iti.kin u_4.2.[kam mu.x kam ^{md}ag-i]
4'. lugal t[in.tir^{ki} ....]
5'. *e-lat* é.meš *šá* ⸢[ú?...]
6'. *i-di* ⸢é⸣.[meš ...]

Notes

L. 2. It seems that the scribe mistakenly wrote the sign ta after ⸢iti⸣.apin instead after *šá*.

Translation

Obv. 1-3. Silver, the rent of houses, [property of Šamaš], which from the month of Arahsamna [...] of Nabonidus, king of Ba[bylon ....].
4. 15 shekels ⸢Bēl⸣-[...]
5. 2½ shekels [...]
6. 2½ shekels [...]

Rev. 1'. [x] shekel(s) [...]
2'. Total 2 minas 9 shekels of silver [...]
3'-4'. Month Ulūlu, second day, [x year of Nabonidus], king of Ba[bylon]
5'-6'. This is except for houses of [... which] ... rent of house[s...]

32. BM 71910 (82-9-18, 11913); 4.2 x 4.0 cm; [x].X.Nbn [x]

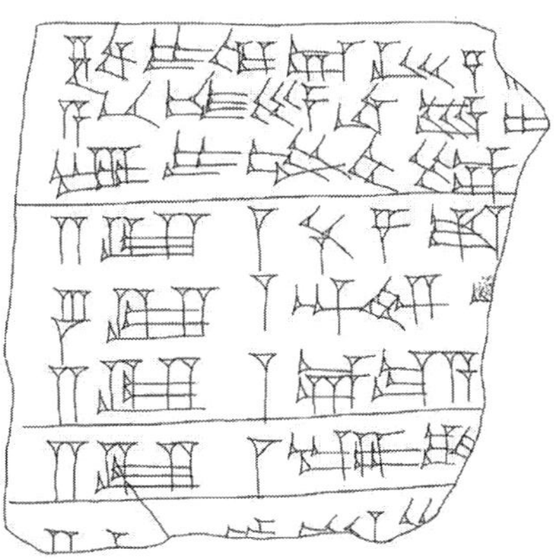

Obv.	1.	kù.babbar *i-di* é.meš *šá* ⌜a⌝-[na]	
	2.	*a-bat-tu*$_{4}$ sum^{na} iti.a[b u$_{4}$.x.kam mu.x.kam]	
	3.	^{d}ag-i lugal.tin.tir[^{ki}]	
	4.	2 gín	^{m}*ḫaš-šá-da-*[*a*]
	5.	4 gín	^{md}im-⌜x⌝
	6.	2 gín	^{m}*kal-ba-a*
	7.	2 gín	^{md}ag-*i*[*t-tan-nu*]
	8.	⌜2⌝ g[ín]	⌜^{md}amar.utu$^{?}$-mu$^{?}$⌝
		Rest lost	
Rev.		in preserved lower part the tablet is uninscribed.	

Translation

Obv.	1-3.	Silver, the rent of houses, which was given [for] *abattu* reeds. Month Ṭebētu, [x day, x year] of Nabonidus, king of Babylon.	
	4.	2 shekels	Ḫašdāya
	5.	4 shekels	Adad-[...]
	6.	2 shekels	Kalbā
	7.	2 shekels	Nabû-it[tannu]
	8.	2 shekels	Marduk$^{?}$-iddin$^{?}$

33. CT 56, 590 = BM 57369 (82-7-14, 1777) Collated; 16.II.Nbn 14

Obv.	1.	[k]ù.babbar *šá a-na i-di* é.meš
	2.	[su]m^{nu} iti.gu$_{4}$ u$_{4}$.16.kam mu.14.kam
	3.	^{d}ag-i lugal tin.tir^{ki}
	4.	⅓ gín ^{md}en-kád a-*šú šá* ^{md}en-sur
	5.	*a-di* ⌜4½$^{?}$ gín⌝ *ri-e-ḫi* ⌜*ù*$^{?}$⌝
	6.	15 g[ín ...]
	7.	[...] ⌜x x x⌝ [...]
	8.	[...] ⌜x sig$^{?}$⌝.ḫi.a ⌜x⌝ [...]
		Rest lost

Translation

Silver, which for the rent of the houses was given. Month Ayāru, 16th day, 14th year of Nabonidus, king of Babylon.

20 shekels: Bēl-kāṣir, son of Bēl-ēṭir including 4½ shekels, the remainder 15 she[kels ....] bricks$^{?}$ [......]

34. Cam 28 = BM 60004 (83-1-18, 768); 3.I.Camb 1

Obv.	1.	2 gín kù.babbar *šá* ^{md}utu-tin^{iṭ} a-*šú šá* ^{m}*ina*-sùḫ-sur *šá* 2-*ta* é.meš
	2.	2 gín é ^{m}*ina*-sùḫ-sur

3. *šá* ^{f}*e-ṭir-tu*$_4$ *ina lìb-bi*
4. *áš-ba-tu*$_4$ iti.bár
5. u$_4$.3.kam mu.1.kam

Rev. 6. ^{m}*kam-bu-zi-ia*
7. lugal tin.tir^{ki}

Translation

2 shekels of silver from Šamaš-uballiṭ, son of Ina-tēšê-ēṭir for two houses.
2 shekels: the house of Ina-tēšê-ēṭir, in which ^{f}Ēṭirtu lives.
Month Nisannu, third day, first year of Cambyses, king of Babylon.

35. Cam 29 = BM 60065 (83-1-18, 17); 3.I.Camb 1

Obv. 1. kù.babbar *i-di* é.meš *šá* ⸢x x x⸣
2. 2 gin é ^{m}*ina*-sùḫ-sur *ina* šu^{ii}
3. ^{f}*e-ṭir-tu*$_4$ dam-*šú*
4. 2 gín ^{md}utu-tin${}^{\text{iṭ}}$ *šá* 2-*ta* é.meš
5. iti.bár u$_4$.3.kam
6. mu.1.kam ^{m}*kam-bu-zi-ia*

Edge 7. *šá a-na* igi

Rev. 8. ^{lú}šid.meš *ir-ru-ub-bu*

Translation

Silver, the rent of houses, which …
2 shekels: the house of Ina-tēšê-ēṭir, from ^{f}Ēṭirtu, his wife.
2 shekels (from) Šamaš-uballiṭ for two houses.
Month Nisannu, third day, first year of Cambyses, king of Babylon, which were *transferred* to the scribes.

36. CT 57, 78 = BM 56273 (82-7-14, 644) Collated; (V.Cyr 4)

Obv. 1. kù.babbar *i-*⸢*di*⸣ é.meš *šá* murub$_4$* uru níg.ga ^{d}⸢utu⸣
2. [*šá* t]a iti.kin [m]u.3.kam *a-di-i* iti.ne mu.⸢4.kam⸣
3. [^{m}*ku-r*]*aš* lugal tin.tir^{ki} lugal kur.kur *a-na é-babbar-ra*
4. [*id-di*]*n-nu* iti.gu$_4$ u$_4$.28.kam mu.4.kam
5. [x g]ín ^{m}*kal-ba-a* a-*šú* ^{m}*šá-*^{d}en-*ni*-⸢x⸣
6. [x gín] ^{m}ìr-*ia šá* é ^{lú}gal *za-am-ma-ru*
7. [x gín ^{m}]⸢^{d}⸣utu-a-⸢ùru⸣ [x x] ⸢x x⸣

Presumably only one line is missing.

Rev. 1'. [x x] ⸢x x⸣ [...]
2'. [x x] [x x x] ⸢x x⸣

3'. [(x) *a*]-*na nam-zu-ú* ud.ka.bar sum^{na}
one blank line
4'. [x x] ⸢*ma*⸣-*na* 3 gín kù.babbar 1^{en} túg.kur.⸢ra⸣
5'. [x x x iti].gu$_4$ u$_4$.28.kam

Translation

Obv. 1-4. Silver, the rent of houses (located) in the middle of the city, property of Šamaš, which they delivered to the Ebabbar for the period from month Ulūlu, third year to month Abu, fourth year of Cyrus, king of Babylon, king of Lands. Month Abu, 28th day, fourth year.

	5.	[x shek]el(s)	Kalbā, son of Ša-Bēl-ni-[...]
	6.	[x shekels]	Ardiya of the household of the chief singer
	7.	[x shekels]	Šamaš-aplu-uṣur
Rev.	1'.	…	
	2'.	…	
	3'.	… for the bronze *namzû*-vats? was given	

One blank line

4'-5'.[… x] mina(s) 3 shekels of silver, one kur.ra-garment, [… mon]th Ayāru, 28th day.

37. BM 68342 (82-9-18, 8340); *5.8* x *5.5* cm; (1.VI.Cyr 5)

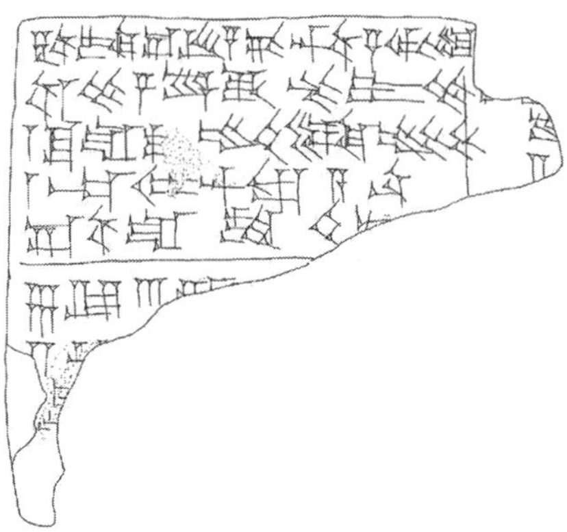

Col. I			Col. II?
Obv.	1.	kù.babbar *i-di* é.meš níg.ga ^{d}utu *šá ul-tu*	[…]
	2.	u$_4$.1.kam *šá* iti.kin mu.5.kam ⸢x x⸣	[…]
	3.	^{m}*ku-ra-áš* lugal tin.tir^{ki} lugal kur.kur	it[i …]
	4.	^{m}*i-na*-gissu-^{d}u+gur *a-na*	2 […]
	5.	*é-babbar-ra id-din* i[ti? …]	
	6.	6 gín 3 ⸢*ri*⸣-[*bat* kù.babbar …]	

7. 2 g[ín$^{?}$ …]
8. ⌞x⌟ g⌞ín …⌟
Rest lost

Rev. only one sign pap (not copied) is preserved

Translation

Silver, the rent of houses, property of Šamaš from first day of month Ulūlu, fifth year of Cyrus, king of Babylon, king of Lands, Ina-ṣilli-Nergal has delivered to the Ebabbar temple. M[onth …]

6¾ shekels [of silver PN]
2 she[kels PN]
[x] sh[ekel(s) PN]

38. BM 68384 (82-9-18, 83382); 7.5 x 5.8 cm; (9.I. Camb 3)

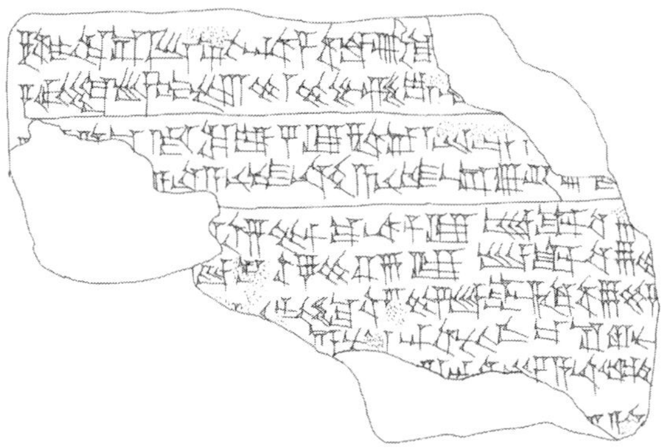

Obv. 1. kù.babbar *i-di* é.meš níg.ga ^{d}utu *šá* ud.kib.nun^{ki} […]
2. *šá ul-tu* iti.gan mu.3.kam ^{m}*kam-bu-zi-ia* ⌜lugal⌝ [e^{ki} lugal kur.kur …]
3. ⌜2⌝+[x gí]n ⌜kù.babbar é⌝ ^{m}*da-di-ia* 4 gín kù.babbar é $^{md⌜}$ìr-*ia* x⌝ […]
4. [x gín kù.babbar] *a-na a-bat-tu*$_4$ *na-din a-bat-tu*$_4$ *ina* é *ú-ri-*⌜*e it*$^{?}$⌝ [x x]
5. [.........] ⌜*šá*⌝ u$_4$.5.kam ½ *ma-na* ½ gín iti.bár u$_4$.⌜6⌝.[kam]
6. [............] iti.kin u$_4$.7.kam ⅓ 6 gín iti.bár u$_4$.9.kam [*šá* x x x]
7. [...............] *ul-tu* u$_4$.⌜6⌝.kam *šá* iti.bár *a-di* u$_4$.9.kam *šá* [iti.bár]
8. [................. *it*]-⌜*tan-nu*⌝ ^{md}utu-numun-dù *is-si-ru-nu*
9. [..........................] *šá* ^{md}utu-⌜mu⌝ *šá a-na muḫ-ḫi*
10. [................. ....] ⌜*šá*⌝ *a-*⌜*na*⌝ [...]

Notes

L. 1. It is not excluded that *šá* ud.kib.nun^{ki} concerns the location of the houses.

Translation

Obv. 1-2. Silver, the rent of houses, property of Šamaš at Sippar […] from the month Kislīmu, third year of Cambyses, [king of Babylon, king of Lands …]

3-4. ⸢2⸣+[x shekels] of silver: house of Dadia;
4 shekels: house of Ardiya [...]
[x shekels of silver] for *abattu* reeds was given (and then) *abattu* reeds were [dispatched] to the fattening house

5. […] of the fifth day
5. 30½ shekels: month Nisannu, sixth day
6. [x shekels]: month Ulūlu, seventh day
6. 26 shekels: month Nisannu, ninth day [of…]
7. [....... from the sixth day of month Nisannu till ninth day of month [Nisannu …]
8. [.....-it]tannu (and) Šamaš-zēr-ibni collected.
9. [....] which Šamaš-iddin, who in addition [...]
10. [................. ....] that for [...]

39. BM 74311 (82-9-18, 14334); 3.6 x 4.5 cm; [x.I.KN] ⸢5⸣

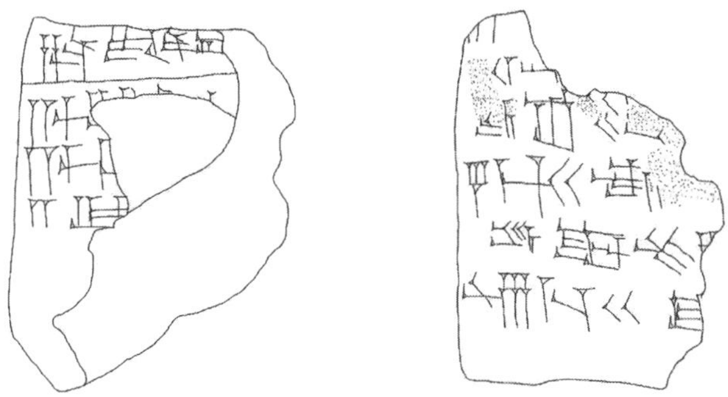

Obv. 1. kù.babbar *i-di* é.[meš níg.ga ^{d}utu …]
2. 2½ gín ⸢kù.babbar⸣ […]
3. 2½ g[ín …]
4. 2 gín […]
Rest lost

Rev. 1’. ⸢3⸣ […]
2’ *u* ^{md}[…]
3’ ⸢iti.dirig.še.kin⸣.[kud …]
4’ 4 me 80 *ina* šu^{ii} […]
5’. iti.bár mu.⸢5⸣.k[am …]
6’ pap 6 me 80 *ku*-[…]

Translation

Obv. 1. Silver, the rent of house[s, property of Šamaš …]
2. 2½ shekels o silver […]
3. 2½ sh[ekels …]
4. 2 shekels […]
Rest lost

Rev. 1'. 3 […]
2'. and [PN …]
3'. Intercalary month Addaru …
4'. 480 from […]
5'. Month Nisannu, fifth year […]
6'. Total 680 […]

40. CT 57, 26 = BM 56696 (82-7-14, 1105) Collated; 3.8 x 5.8 cm

Obv. 1. ⸢kù⸣.[babbar ní]g.ga ^{d}utu *šá* ⸢ká⸣-[íd]-⸢^{d}utu⸣
2. 12 gín kù.babbar ^{m}ìr-^{d}*a-nu-*[*ni*]-⸢*tu*$_{4}$⸣
3. 10+[2] gín kù.babbar ^{m}*ki-i-*^{d}[ag/en]
4. 12 gín kù.babbar ^{m}*zab-di-ia* ⸢x x⸣
5. 18 gín kù.babbar ^{f}*ni-ri-'-im-mi-i*
6. 6 gín ^{md}en-dù-*šu-tur*
7. 12 gín ^{m}*zu-um-ba-*⸢*a* ^{lú}x⸣
8. 6 gín é ^{lú}gal *ka-a-ri*
9. *ina* igi ^{md}en-tin^{it} a ^{md}utu-pap
10. 12 gín ⸢kù$^{?}$⸣.babbar ⸢*ir*$^{?}$-*bi*$^{?}$⸣ *šá* x *be-lit*
11. 1⸢2⸣ gín ^{lú}ga[l$^{?}$ x]
12. pap 1½ *ma-na* 2 gín

Edge 13. kù.babbar *i-di* é.meš

Rev. 14. *šá* ^{uru}ká-íd-^{d}utu

Notes

L. 10. The reading is highly uncertain.

L. 11. Or ^{lú}*ma*-[x].

L. 12. Note the total of all entries is higher: 1 mina 42 shekels.

Translation

Obv. 1. Si[lver, the pro]perty of Šamaš, (located in) Bāb-nār-Šamaš

2.	12 shekels	Arad-Anu[nī]tu
3.	1[2] shekels	Kī-[Bēl/Nabû]
4.	12 shekels	Zabdiya ⸢x x⸣
5.	18 shekels	Niri'immī
6.	6 shekels	Bēl-bāni-šūtur

7. 12 shekels Zumba, the [...]
8. 6 shekels the house of the chief of the harbour district,
9. at disposal of Bēl-uballiṭ, son of Šamaš-nāṣir
10. 12 shekels of silver, the income of […]
11. 12 shekels the […]
12. Total 1 mina 32 shekels of silver, the rent of houses (located) in city of Bāb-nār-Šamaš

41. BM 63266 (82-9-18, 3235); 3.8 x 4.6 cm

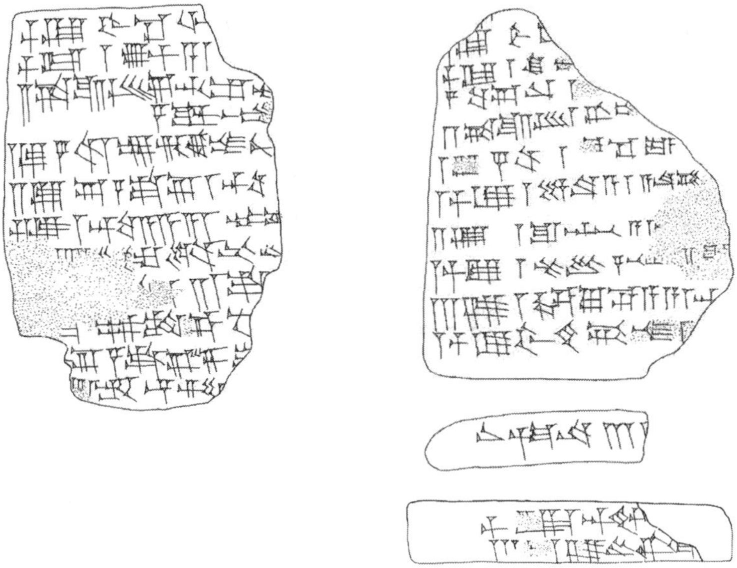

Obv. 1. ½ gín ^{f}*si-lim*-[…]
2. ½ gín ^{m}*ú-bar* a ^{m}[…]
3. 2-*ta* šu$^{ii.meš}$ é ⸢^{md}⸣u+gur-m[u …]
4. *šá* <iti.>bár *ina* ⸢x⸣ […]
5. 1 gín 4-*tú* ^{md}ag-*ri-iḫ-tu*$_{4}$ pap [(…)]
6. 2 gín é *šá* da é ^{md}utu-[…]
7. ½ gín ^{md}utu-*a-a* a ^{m}*ina*-x-k[a ….]
8. [x gín ^{m}]⸢*še-el*⸣-*li-bi* ^{lú}[…]
9. [x gín ^{m}x] ⸢x⸣ a ^{m}da-[…]
10 [x gí]n$^{?}$ ^{md}ag-*it-tan-nu* [(…)]
11. [x gín] é *šá* da é x x […]
12. [x gín é] ^{md}en-sur-zi.[meš …]

Rev. 1'. ⸢x⸣ […]
2'. [x gí]n ^{f}⸢x⸣ […]

3'. ½ gín ^{m}ki-^{d}⸢...⸣
4'. 4-*tú bit-qa* ^{m}[...]
5'. 2-*ta* šu$^{ii.meš}$ ^{m}*ni-q*[*u-du*]
6'. 1 ⸢gín⸣ 4-*tú* ^{m}⸢*ba*⸣-*si-ia* [...]
7'. 1½ gín ^{m}sum^{na} a ^{m}*a-na-gab*-[...]
8'. 2 gín ^{m}su-^{d}idim a ^{m}⸢x⸣ [...]
9'. 1½ gín ^{m}mu-ùru *šá ina* ⸢ugu$^{?}$ x x⸣
10'. 3 gín ^{m}*šul-lu-e-a* a ^{md}[...]
11'. 1½ gín ^{f}dùg.ga-*tu*$_{4}$ ⸢x⸣ [...]
L.e. 12'. pap ½ *ma-na* 3 g[ín kù.babbar
L.h.e. 13'. ½ gín ^{md}im-[...]
14'. 3 ⸢x⸣ 1 gín ^{lú}*šir*$^{!?}$-*k*[*i*$^{?}$ ...]

Translation

Obv. 1. ½ shekel: ^{f}Silim-[...]
2. ½ shekel: Ubāru, son of [...]
3. ⅔ shekel: the house of Nergal-šu[m-x]
4. of <the month> Nisannu in [...]
5. 1¼ shekel: Nabû-rēḫtu-uṣur [...]
6. 2 shekels: the house adjacent to the house of Šamaš-[...]
7. ½ shekel: Šamšaya, descendent of Ina-x$^{?}$-[...]
8. [x shekel(s)]: Šellibi, the [...]
9. [x shekel(s): PN], son of Lē'i-[...]
10. [x shekel(s): Nabû-ittannu
11. [x shekel(s)]: the house adjacent to the house ... [...]
12. [x shekel(s): the house of] Bēl-ēṭir-napš[āte]

Rev. 1'. ⸢x⸣ [...]
2'. [x sheke]ls: ^{f}[...]
3'. ½ shekel: Itti/Kī-[...]
4'. ⅜ shekel: [...]
5'. ⅔ shekel: Niq[ūdu]
6'. 1¼ shekels: Basia
7'. 1½ shekels: Idinnaya, son of Ana-gabbi-[...]
8'. 2 shekels: Erība-Ea, son of [...]
9'. 1¼ shekels: Šum-uṣur ...
10'. 3 shekels: Šullea, son of [...]
11'. 1½ shekels: ^{f}Ṭābātu [...]
L.e. 12'. total 33 [shekels of silver]
L.h.e. 13'. ½ shekels: Adad-[...]
14'. 3 ⸢x⸣1 shekel: the obla[tes$^{!?}$... ...]

42. BM 63499 (82-9-18, 3466); *5.0* x *5.3* cm;

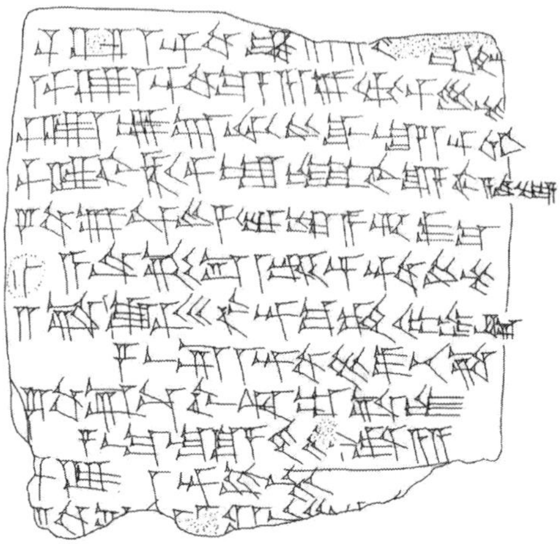

Obv. 1. ½ gín ^{md}utu-⌜da$^{!?}$ a ^{m}*a-ḫi*⌝-*ra-'*
2. 1½ gín ^{md}utu-ba^{šá} a ^{m}*é-ul-maš*-šeš-mu
3. ½ gín ^{md}ag-*kit-ti* ^{lú}*qal-la šá* ^{md}utu-dù
4. ½ gín ^{f}*ḫa-bar-ṣi-tu*$_4$ dumu.mí-*su šá* ^{f}*a-na*-kur-*ia*
5. 4-*tú bit-qa* ^{lú}<un.meš> *šá* ugu *ka-a-ri áš-ba*
6. x (ras.) *a-na gab-*<*bi*> é ^{md}en-sur-^{d}utu ^{lú}mu
7. 2-*ta* šu^{ii}.meš ^{fd}*ma-am-mi-tu*$_4$*-en-qet*
8. *šá ina* é ^{md}utu-kam *áš-bat-ta*
9. 4-*tú bit-qa* ^{f}*ḫu-um-uš-tu*$_4$
10. *šá ina ma-la-ku šá ḫi-in-da-a-a*
11. ½ gín ^{md}amar-mu
12. ⌜4⌝-*tú bit-*⌜*qa* kù⌝.babbar $^{m⌜}$mu-$^{d⌝}$[DN]
Rest lost

Rev. uninscribed

Notes

L. 1. The sign following utu looks like id, but probably da migh be read; or su?

L. 10. For similar use of the word *mālaku*, see Dar 378: 1; Dar 379: 10, 33; BE 8/1. 3: 8 (cf. BE 8/7, p. 41).

Translation

Obv.	1.	½ shekel	Šamaš-nā'id, son of Aḫira'
	2.	1½ shekels	Šamaš-iqīša, son of Eulmaš-aḫ-iddin
	3.	½ shekel	Nabû-kitti, the slave of Šamaš-ibni
	4.	½ shekel	^{f}Ḫabarṣītu, the daughter of ^{f}Ana-mātīja

5-6.	⅜ (shekel)	the temple' servants who live in the harbour district, for the whole house: Bēl-ēṭir-Šamaš, the baker
7-8.	⅔ (shekel):	fMammītu-enqet who live it the house of Šamaš-ēreš
9-10.	⅜ (shekel):	fḪumuštu, (the house) which is situated in the walkway of the Hindaneans
11.	½ shekel:	Būr-iddin
12.	⅜ (shekel):	Iddin-[DN]

43. CT 57, 75 = BM 56662 (82-7-14, 1071)

Obv. 1. kù.babbar *i-di* é.meš *šá ina* ugu
2. íd lúagrig níg.ga dutu
3. 2½ gín mdag-mu
4. 2 gín mdamar.utu-[x (x)]
5. 2½ gín m*zab*-[*di-ia*]
6. 2½ gín m[x x x]
7. 2½ gín [x x x]
8. pap [12 gín *i-di* é.meš …]

Rev. uninscribed

Translation

Obv. 1-2. Silver, the rent of houses situated on the Nār-mašennu canal, property of Šamaš

3.	2½ shekels	Nabû-iddin
4.	2 shekels	Marduk-[…]
5.	2½ shekels	Zab[dia]
6.	2½ shekels	[PN]
7.	2½ shekels	[PN]

8. Total [12 shekels, rent of the houses …].

44. BM 51817 (82-3-23, 2851); 6.7 x 3.2 cm

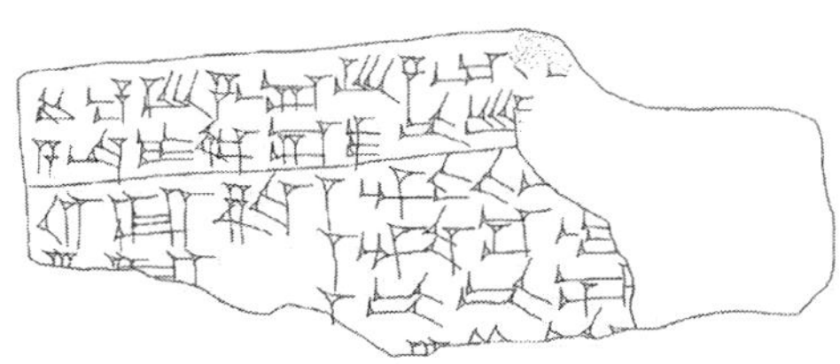

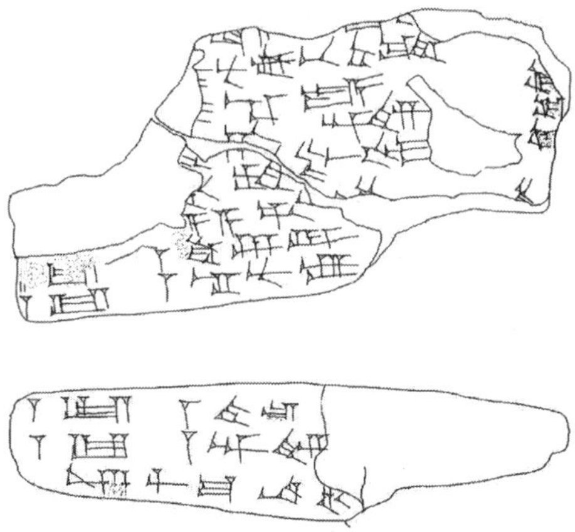

Obv.	1.	^{lú}erín.meš *šá* é.meš *ina šá ina* ⸢x⸣ [....]		
	2.	*a-na i-di* é *áš-bi* iti.[x u_4.x.kam KN]		
	3.	12 gín kù.babbar	^{md}amar-⸢x⸣-[...]	
	4.	⸢3$^{?}$⸣ gín	^{md}utu-*kil-l*[*a-an-ni*]	
	5.	[x x]	^{m}*bi-bi-e-*[*a*]	
	6.	[x x]	[^{md}]⸢ag$^{?}$-mu$^{?}$-du$^{?}$⸣	
		Rest lost		
Rev.	1'.	[x x]	[x]-⸢*na-a*⸣ [x] ⸢x⸣	[ki.min$^{?}$]
	2'.	[x x]	[*l*]*i-nu-uḫ*-be-tin$^{!!}$	[ki.min$^{?}$]
	3'.	[x x]	[^{m}*b*]*a-si-ia*	k[i.min]
	4'.	[x x]	[^{m}dù]g.⸢ga⸣-^{d}im	k[i$^{?}$.min]
	5'.	[x x]	[^{m}*ḫ*]*a-am-bu-ṣu*	k[i.min]
	6'.	[x x]	[^{m}x]-*a-a-am-*⸢*mu*⸣	⸢$^{\text{lú?}}$⸣[...]
	7'.	⸢2 gín⸣	^{m}⸢*ḫar*⸣*-ru-ru* [...]	
	8'.	1 gín	^{m}*si-nu-ú* [...]	
L.e.	9'.	1 gín	^{m}*ḫi-*⸢x⸣ [...]	
	10'.	1 gín	^{md}im-[...]	
	11'.	pap ⸢6$^{?}$⸣½ *ma-na* kù.[babbar]		

Translation

Obv. 1-2. Servants, who are living in the houses (situated in) [...] for the rent of houses.

Month [x, nth day, nth year of KN]

3.	12 shekels of silver	Būr-[...]
4.	3$^{?}$ shekels	Šamaš-kill[anni]
5.	[x shekel(s)]	Bibē[a]
6.	[x shekel(s)]	Nabû$^{?}$-šum$^{?}$-ukīn$^{?}$
	Rest lost	

Rev.	1’.	[x shekel(s)]	[x]-nā	
	2’.	[x shekel(s)]	[L]inūḫ-mīṭa-uballiṭ	[ditto?]
	3’.	[x shekel(s)]	[B]asia	di[tto]
	4’.	[x shekel(s)]	[Ṭ]āb-Adad	di[tto]
	5’.	[x shekel(s)]	[Ḫ]ambūṣu	di[tto]
	6’.	[x shekel(s)]	[Ḫa]iammu	the [...]
	7’.	⸢2 gín⸣	Ḫarruru	
	8’.	1 shekel	Sinū	
L.e.	9’.	1 shekel	Ḫi-⸢x⸣ [...]	
	10’.	1 shekel	Adad-[x (x)]	
	11’.	total ⸢6?⸣½ minas of sil[ver]		

45. BM 64489 (82-9-18, 4469); 9.0 x *6.8* cm; (2.IV.[Nbn] 6)

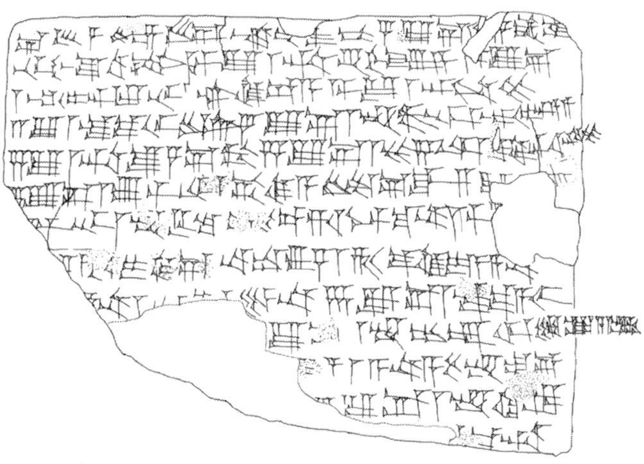

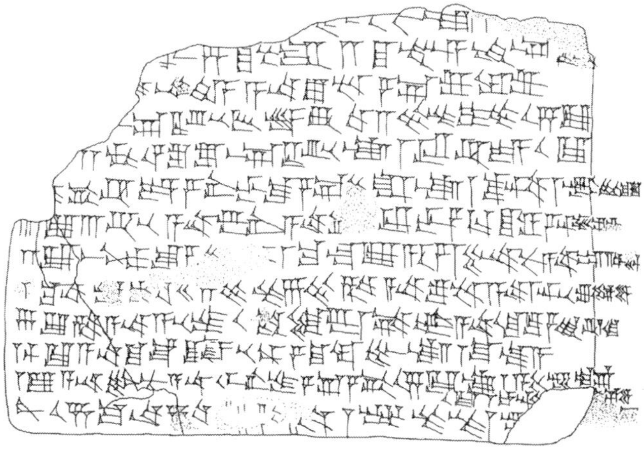

Obv. 1. é.meš *šá* ^{lú}un.meš é *ina lìb-bi áš-bi* 4 gín é ⸢^{f}⸣[*z*]*a*$^{?}$*-ra-tu*$_{4}$

2. *ina* igi ^{f}*su-ut-tur* 1½ gín ^{md}utu-*ri-ṣu-ú-a* 1⸢½⸣ gín é

3. ^{m}*i-na*-gissu-^{d}uraš *ina* igi ^{m}*muk-ki-e-a* 1½ gín ^{md}dù-*tú*-kam

4. 2 gín ^{m}*la-ba-ši* ^{lú}ašgab 4 gín é ^{md}en-kád *ina* igi ^{m}*i-na*-gissu-^{d}*a-a*

5. 5 gín ^{md}utu-su *šá* é gu$_{4}$ 5 gín é ^{m}numun-*iá ina* igi ^{m}⸢*ma*⸣-*di*-dingir *u* ^{md}utu-mu

6. ⸢5⸣ gín é ^{m}*ú-bar ina* igi ^{m}*ga-di-a* ^{lú}ìr é.gal 2 gín x(ras.)

7. [^{m}ú-*b*]*ar*$^{?}$ *ina* igi ^{md}en-*tuk-te-*⸢*e-tir*⸣*-ri* pap ½ *ma-na* 2½ g[ín kù.babbar]

8. [x x] ⸢x⸣ kù.babbar *i-di* é *na-du-ú šá* ^{m}*ḫa-ma-ki-ia a-na*

9. [x x] ⸢*a*⸣*-na* ^{m}⸢x x⸣ sum^{na} 6 gín é ^{m}*la-ba-a-ši*

10. [......... x] gín ⸢é⸣ ^{md}en-*tak-lak ina* igi ^{m}*li-šìr* a ^{md}ag-pap

11. [............] ⸢gín⸣ *šá* ^{m}*a-na-a-mat-*^{d}en-*at-kal*

12. [............] ⸢3$^{?}$ gín⸣ é ^{md}en-*ki-šìr*

13. [...................] ^{m}zálag-^{d}utu

Rest lost

Rev. 1'. [.........] ⸢x *šú*$^{?}$*-nú*$^{?}$⸣ *ina* šu^{ii} ⸢^{m}⸣[...]

2'. [.......] ⸢x⸣ 5 túg.kur.ra 2 ^{túg}*šìr-a-am ina* é.g[ur$_{7}$.meš]

3'. [x x x *ma-n*]*a* mun.ḫi.a *a-na* udu.níta *šá* é *ú-ru-ú*

4'. [pap x] *ina* é.gur$_{7}$.meš iti.kin u$_{4}$.2.kam mu.6.kam 15 gín

5'. [šám$^{?}$] 2 gu$_{4}$ *šuk-lu-lu ina* é.gur$_{7}$.meš *ina* šu^{ii} ^{m}*ip-ri-ia* 10 gín

6'. [*a-n*]*a ga-ri-iá šá ni-pi-šú šá* é.⸢kur⸣.ra *ina* šu^{ii} ^{m}šu-^{d}utu ^{md}ag-dù-šeš *šu-bul*

7'. 3 gín 3 *ri-bat a-na šam-ni a-na* [x x]-*ip-pi šá sik-ku-ru šá* ^{d}*ziq-qur-rat*

8'. 2 gín *ina pap-pa-su šá* ⸢^{lú}⸣[mu.meš] ^{m}*ba-la-ṭu a-šú šá* ^{m}*bu-na-nu a-na* 2 kùr 2 pi ⸢še⸣.bar

9'. 1 *ma-na* ⸢iti.gu$_{4}$⸣ u$_{4}$. 2⸢5⸣.kam mu.6.kam *a-na* udu.níta *a-na* ^{md}idim-*ú-ṭir*$_{5}$ sum

10'. 6 gín kù.babbar *a-na a-bat-tu*$_{4}$ *u iṭ-ṭú-ú* ^{m}*ta-qiš a-na dul-lu šá ḫar-ri šá* du$_{6}$

11'. 1½ gín *a-na ku-pur* {*ku-pur*} *bat-qa šá ku-ru-pu ina* šu^{ii} ^{m}*šu-la-a*

12'. 1 gín *a-na* in.nu *a-na ši-ni-tu*$_{4}$ *šá* é níg.ga 15 gín *ina* šu^{ii} ^{m}*a-na-a-mat-*^{d}en-*at-kal*

12a'. 10 gín ^{m}zálag-^{d}utu [x x] ⸢x⸣ e sum

13'. pap 15 *ma-na* 4-*tú* x x(ras.) kù.babbar ⸢*a*⸣*-na* ^{md}ag-mu-mu ^{md}⸢ag/en⸣-[x x]

L.h.e. 14'. é ⌜*šá*⌝ da sila ⌜*la*?⌝ [.....]
15'. ⌜é⌝ ᵐ*pir-šu-ú* [...]
16'. ᵐ*nu-ri-iá* [.....]

Notes

Note that the same 11 tenants occur in BM 75208, no. 28.

Translation

Obv. Houses in which the temple' servants are living:
4 shekels: the house of ᶠZaratu at disposal of ᶠSuttur
1½ shekels: (the house) of Šamaš-ruṣûa
1½ shekels: the house of Ina-ṣilli-Uraš, at disposal of Mukkēa
1½ shekels: (the house) of Bānītu-ēreš
2 shekels: (the house) of Lābāši, the leatherworker
4 shekels: the house of Bēl-kāṣir, at disposal of Ina-ṣilli-Aya
5 shekels: (the house) of Šamaš-erība of the cattle shed
5 shekels: the house of Zēriya, at disposal of Madi-ili and Šamaš-iddin
⌜5⌝ shekels: the house of Ubāru, at disposal of Gadia, the builder
2 shekels: [(the house) of Ub]ār?, at disposal of Bēl-tuktê-tirri
total 32½ she[kels of silver out?] of silver, the house rent (of) the ruined house of Hamakia for [...] was given to [PN].
6 shekels: the house of Lābāši, [at disposal of PN](?)
[x] shekel(s): the house of Bēl-taklak, at disposal of Līšir, son of Nabû-nāṣir
[x] shekel(s): the house of [PN]
[x] shekel(s): the house of Ana-amat-Bēl-atkal
[x shekel(s): the house of PN]
3? shekels: the house of Bēl-kēšir
[x shekel(s): the house of PN]
[x shekel(s)]: the house of Nūr-Šamaš

Rev. [x]-*šunu*? from[PN]
[...] 5 kur.ra-garments, 2 jerkins at the harbour storehouse
[... min]as of salt for (salting) sheep in the fattening house
[total x x] at the harbour storehouse. Month Ulūlu, second day, sixth year.
15 shekels, [the price] of 2 fattened bulls (which are) at the harbour storehouse (sent) by Ipria.
10 shekels ... for construction in the small temple send by Gimil-Šamaš (and?) Nabû-bān-aḫi.
3¾ minas for oil for [smea]ring the bars of the temple tower
2 shekels as the prebendary income of the beakers (to) Balāṭu, son of Bunanu for 2 *kurru* 2 *pānu* of barley

1 mina (on the) 25th day of Ayāru, sixth year for sheep to Adad-uṭer.
6 shekels of silver for *abattu* reeds and bitumen (to) Taqiš for work on the water canal at hill
1½ shekels of silver for dry bitumen for repair of basket by the hand of Šulā
1 shekel for straw for roof-sealing of the *bīt makkūri*-storehouse
15 shekels from Ana-amat-Bēl-atkal
10 shekels (to) Nūr-Šamaš […] … is given
total 15¼ minas one-fourth (mina?) of silver to Nabû-šum-iddin (and) Nabû/Bēl-[x x]

L.h.e. a house adjacent to the n[o-through?] street […]
a house of Piršû [...]
Nūrêa [...]

46. BM 101853 (83-1-21, 3514); 5.2 x 4.8 cm

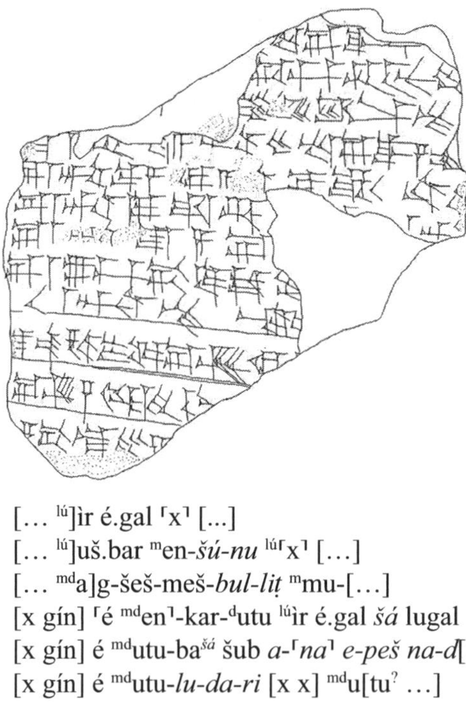

Obv. 1'. [… ^{lú}]ìr é.gal ⌜x⌝ [...]
2'. [… ^{lú}]uš.bar ^{m}en-*šú-nu* ^{lú}⌜x⌝ […]
3'. [… ^{md}a]g-šeš-meš-*bul-liṭ* ^{m}mu-[…]
4'. [x gín] ⌜é ^{md}en⌝-kar-^{d}utu ^{lú}ìr é.gal *šá* lugal
5'. [x gín] é ^{md}utu-ba^{šá} šub *a-*⌜*na*⌝ *e-peš na-d*[*in* (…)]
6'. [x gín] é ^{md}utu-*lu-da-ri* [x x] ^{md}u[tu? …]
7'. [x gín] é ^{md}⌜utu⌝-su *šá* é [gu$_4$ …]
8'. […] é ^{m}*ú-bar* ^{m}*ga-di-da* ^{lú}[…]
9'. […] *u* ^{md}utu-mu *ina lìb-*[*bi áš-bi*]
10'. [pap x *m*]*a-na*! kù.babbar *i-di* é.meš šub.m[eš …]
11'. […] é.meš *šá muḫ-ḫi* ^{f}[…]

12'. [...] ⸢níg⸣.ga *la* sum ⸢x⸣ [...]
Rest lost

Rev. Lost

Notes

Ll. 4'-7'. In the missing part there is insufficient space for more than [x gín].
L. 10'. The *na* is written over erasure.

Translation

Obv. 1'. [...] the builder
2'. [... the] weaver, Bēlšunu, the [...]
3'. [... Nab]û-aḫḫē-bullit, Mu[...]
4'. [x shekel(s)] the house of Bēl-ēṭir-Šamaš, the king's builder
5'. [x shekel(s)], the house of Šamaš-iqīša, ruined, for rebuilding is gi[ven]
6'. [...] the house of Šamaš-lūdāri [x x] Šamaš-[...]
7'. [x shekel (s)] the house of Šamaš-erība of the [cattle] shed
8'. [...] the house of Ubāru, Gadida, the [...]
9'. [...] and Šamaš-iddin, <who> [lives in i]t
10'. [total x mi]nas of silver, the rent of houses (from) the ruined [houses]
11'. [...] houses, which on ^{f}[...]
12'. [...] property, not given ... [...]
Rest lost

Rev. Lost

6.5 Redistribution of silver from the rental of houses

47. BM 92723 (82-9-18A, 50) = Stevenson, ABC, no. 30. Collated; 8.X.Nbn 8

Obv. 1. [kù.babbar] *i-di* é.meš *šá a-na a-ba-*⸢*at*⸣*-tu*$_4$
2. sum^{na} iti.ab mu.8.kam
3. ^{md}ag-i lugal tin.tir^{ki}
4. [x] ⸢gín⸣ ^{m}*kal-ba-a* a-*šú šá* ^{m}*re-mut*
5. [x gín] ^{m}*kal-ba-a* a-*šú šá* ^{md}utu-su
6. [x gín] ^{md}im-*na-ti-en*-dingir
7. [x gín ^{m}]^{d}ag-*it-ti-ia*
8. [x gín ^{m}]*da-di-ia*
9. [x gín ^{m}]⸢ìr⸣*-*ia*
10. [x gín ^{m}ki]-^{d}en-*a-dag-gal*

11. [x gín ^{m}ìr]-⸢^{d}⸣me.me
12. [x x x x x x] ⸢x⸣

Rev. 1'. [x gín ^{m}]⸢gi*-mil$^{?*}$ x x⸣
2'. [x gín ^{m}i]r*-^{d}en
3'. [pap x *m*]*a-na* 5 gín 2-*ta* šu$^{ii.meš}$
4'. [kù.babbar *i-di*] é.meš *šá a-na*
5'. *a-ba-at-tu*$_4$

Translation

Silver, the rent for houses, which was given for (purchase) of reeds. Month Ṭebētu, the eighth year of Nabonidus, king of Babylon.

[x] shekels Kalbā, son of Rēmūt
[x shekels] Kalbā, son of Šamaš-erība
[x shekels] Adad-naten-ili
[x shekels] Nabû-ittiya
[x shekels] Dadia
[x shekels] Ardiya
[x shekels Itti]-Bēl-adaggl
[x shekels Arad]-Gula
[...]
[x shekels] Gimil-[...]
[x shekels Ar]ad-Bēl
[total, x m]inas, 5⅔ shekels [of silver, the rent] of the houses for (purchase) of reeds.

48. CT 57, 84 = BM 58285 (82-7-14, 2694) Collated; 4.4 x 3.5 cm; [x].XIIb.Nbn 6

Obv. 1. kù.babbar *šá i-di* é.[meš níg.ga ^{d}utu]
2. [*šá* ^{md}a]g-mu-mu
3. [x x] *šá a-na* zú.lum.ma
4. [*šá* š]u^{ii} ^{m}*mar-duk na-šá-a*
5. [x x] ⸢x⸣ *ir-bi* igi-⸢*ú*⸣

Rev. 1'. [... *i*]*a* ⸢sum⸣ [...]
2'. [... iti].dirig.še.kin.k[ud]
3'. [u$_4$.x.kam] mu.6.ka[m]
4'. [^{md}ag]-⸢i⸣ lugal tin.t[ir^{ki}]
5'. [kù.babbar] *ir-bi a-na i-d*[*i* (x x)]

L.e. 6'. [x x x] ⸢x⸣-*ḫu a-na* ^{m}⸢*di*$^{?}$⸣-[...]

Notes

L. 5. Only the head of a vertical wedge is preserved, presumably [t]a.

Translation

Silver, the rent of house[s, property of Šamaš, which] Nabû-šum-iddin, [x x] for dates [which was] carried by Marduk [...] an earlier income [. . .] was given.

Rev. [......] Intercalary month Addaru, [x day], sixth ye[ar of Nabon]idus, king of Babylon.

[Silver], income which for rent [...] for [...]

49. Nbn 428 = BM 92750 (83-1-18, 69) Collated; 6.4 x 4.6 cm; 10.V.Nbn 10

Obv. 1. [kù.bab]bar *i-di* é.⌜meš⌝ níg.ga ^{d}utu *šá* ta
2. iti.ne mu.9.kam *a-di* iti.ne mu.10.kam
3. ^{d}ag-i lugal tin.tir^{ki}
4. ⅓ gín kù.babbar *a-na* 5 me gú.un *ku-pur a-na*
5. *dul-lu šá* ^{d}*ziq-qur-at* ^{lú}erín.meš *šá ina* bad.an^{ki}
6. ⅔ *ma-na* 6 gín kù.babbar *a-na* 18 *šap-pa-tu*$_4$ *šá** geštin* kù
7. 7* gín kù.babbar *a-na* 5 bán *di-iš-pi el-lu*
8. 50 gín kù.babbar *a-na* 40*½* *ma-na* 15 gín *in-za-*⌜*ḫur-ri*⌝*-tu*$_4$
Edge 9. 1 *ma-na a-na* sig$_4$.ḫi.a ^{md}utu-⌜šeš.meš⌝-su
10. *e-lat* kù.babbar *šá* mu.9.kam
Rev. 11. 8 gín kù.babbar *a-na* 1* gú.un an.bar
12. *a-na dul-lu a-na* ⌜^{m}ìr⌝-^{d}me.me
13. ^{lú}simug sum⌜^{in}⌝
14. pap 3* *ma-*[*na*] ⌜11 gín⌝ kù.babbar ^{md}ag-mu-mu
15. *u* ^{m}*na-din-nu it-tan-nu*
16. iti.ne u$_4$.10.kam mu.10.kam
17. ^{d}[ag]-⌜i⌝ lugal tin.tir^{ki}

Notes

Cf. Bongenaar 2001, 10.

Translation

Obv. 1-3. Silver, the rent of houses, property of Šamaš, which (is) from the month Abu, ninth year until month Abu, tenth year of Nabonidus, king of Babylon.
4-5. 20 shekels of silver for 500 talents of bitumen for work on the temple towe (for) workers of Opis
6. 46 shekels of silver for 18 *šappatu*-jars of pure wine
7. 7 shekels for 5 *sūtu* of pure honey
8. 50 shekels of silver for 40 minas 45 shekels of *inzaḫurētu*-dye
Edge 9. 1 mina for bricks (to) Šamaš-aḫḫē-erība
10. except for silver from the ninth year.
Rev. 11-15. 8 shekels of silver for one talent of iron for work was given

to Arad-Gula, the smiths, total 3 minas 11 shekels of silver Nabû-šum-iddin and Nādin have given.
16-17. Month Abu, tenth day, tenth year of [Nabo]nidus, king of Babylon.

50. CT 57, 83 = BM 56959 (82-7014, 1367) Collated; 5.5 x 4.1 cm; 21.[x].Nbn 5

Obv. 1. […] ⸢x⸣
2. […] ⸢x⸣
3. *a-na* ^{md}en-pap a ⸢^{m}x⸣ […]
4. ^{m}*šu-la-a* [x] a ⸢x x⸣ [x x]
5. *u* ^{m}*ap-la-a* a ^{m}⸢x⸣ […]
6. 3 gín kù.babbar *a-na* ⸢*šá*$^{?}$ *ḫa*$^{?}$⸣-[*ri*]
7. *šá ḫa-ri-*⸢*e*⸣ *šá* ⸢é$^{?}$⸣ [x x]
Rev. 8. 1½ gín [x x] ⸢x x x⸣
9. *a-na* ^{lú}*um-man-nu šá ina* é *ú-r*[*u-ú*]
10. pap 2 *ma-na* 13½ gín kù.babbar
11. *i-di* kù.babbar *šá i-na* é.meš
12. *ina* š[u^{i}]^{i} ⸢^{m}⸣ìr-^{d}en a ^{md}ag-šeš.meš-mu
13. [iti.x] ⸢u_4⸣.21.kam mu.5*.kam
14. [^{md}ag-i lugal tin.ti]r^{ki}

Translation

... to Bēl-nāṣir, son of [...], Šulā [...] and Aplā, son of [...]
3 shekels of silver for *ḫarû*-container for *ḫarû*-ceremony of the temple$^{?}$ [...]
1½ shekels [...] for qualified workers which are in the fattening house,
total 2 minas 13½ shekels of silver, the rent of the rented houses from Arad-Bēl, son of Nabû-aḫḫē-iddin.
[Month x], 21st day, fifth year of [Nabonidus, king of Baby]lon.

51. CT 57, 909 = BM 58047 (82-7-14, 2456) Collated; 4.8 x 2.1 cm

Obv. 1. [kù.babbar *i-di* é.meš] níg.ga ^{d}utu ús*sa*.d[u* …]
2. *šá* ^{d}utu *šá* ^{md}en-gi a-*šú šá* $^{md!?}$utu$^{?}$-⸢x⸣ [x (x) *šá*]
3. *ina lìb-*⸢*bi*⸣ *áš-bi a-na* mu.an.[na]
4. 2+[x gí]n kù.babbar *a-na i-d*[i* …]
5. [x x (x)] ⸢gi-^{d}en⸣ dumu-*šú šá* ^{m}[…]
Rest lost

Translation

[Silver, the rent of houses], property of Šamaš, adjacent to [...] of Šamaš, which Bēl-ušallim, son of Šamaš-[...] who live there, for 2+[x] shekels yearly for rent [... to$^{?}$] Mušēzib-Bēl, son of [...].

52. BM 63994 (82-9-18, 3963) = Bertin 1866 Collated; (Camb 1)

Obv. 1. kù.babbar *i-di* é.meš níg.[ga] ^{d}utu *šá* u[gu]*
2. íd ud.kib.nun^{ki} *šá* ta iti.kin mu.6.kam
3. ^{m}*ku-raš* lugal e^{ki} lugal kur.<kur> *ina lìb-bi šá* ^{lú}erín*.meš
4. *ina* iti.bár mu.1.kam ^{m}*kam-bu-zi-iá* lugal e^{ki} *u* kur.kur*
5. ^{md}utu-a-ùru a ^{m}*ni-qu-du u* ^{m}mu-mu a
6. ^{md}ag-dù-šeš *i-si-ir*
7. 5*4 gín 4-*tú* kù.babbar ta <iti>.bár u$_4$.4.k[am]
8. *a-di* iti.bár u$_4$.6.<kam>
Rev. 9. kù.babbar *ina* igi ^{md}utu-a-ùru *u* [^{m}mu-mu]
10. *ina* gub^{zu} *šá* ^{m}*mu-ra-nu* ⸢x⸣ [x (x)]

Translation

Silver, the rent of houses, property of Šamaš (located) on the Euphrates from the month Ulūlu, sixth year of Cyrus, king of Babylon, king of Lands, including (rent) of the servants which Šamaš-apla-uṣur, son of Niqūdu and Šum-iddin, son of Nabû-bān-aḫi exacted in the month Nisannu, first year of Cambyses, king of Babylon and Lands.

54¼ shekels of silver from the fourth day to sixth day of month Nisannu. Silver at disposal of Šamaš-apla-uṣur and [Šum-iddin]. In the presence of Mūrānu…

53. CT 57, 82 = BM 57222 (82-7-14, 690) Collated; (Dar) 4

Obv. 1. [kù.babbar *i-d*]*i* é.meš *šá* mu.⸢4⸣.kam
2. ⸢*šá*⸣ [*ina* i]gi ^{m}ba-^{d}amar.utu *šá* ugu é.meš
3. *šá a-na é-babbar-ra id-di-nu*
4. 4 *ma-na* ^{m}ìr-^{d}*a-nu-ni-tu*$_4$
5. ^{lú}gal giš.ban *ù* ^{lú}erín.meš *na-di-in*
6. ½ *ma-na* 8 gín kù.babbar *a-na* ^{md}utu-mu
7. *ù* erín.meš anše.kur.ra.meš
8. *šá* ta ^{uru}*mi-ṣir iḫ-ḫi-su-nu*
9. 1 *ma-na* 50 gín kù.babbar *a-na* túg.kur.ra.meš
10. *ù* ^{túg}*šìr-a-am*^{meš} *a-na* ^{lú}erín.[meš]
11. *šá* giš.ban sum^{na} iti.du$_6$ u$_4$.[x.kam]
12. 1 *ma-na* kù.babbar ⸢x⸣ […]
Rest lost
Rev. 1'. 1⸢4$^{?}$⸣ […]
2'. [^{md}DN]-mu-ùru *u* […]
3'. 1^{en} [x x *ṣ*]*u*$^{?}$ *u* ⸢te x⸣ […]
4'. *a-na*$^{!}$ [^{m}*ri*]-*ḫi-e-t*[*u*$_4$ x x x]
5'. 1 *ma-na* kù.babbar *a-na sat-tuk* ^{lú}⸢bappir⸣-*ú-tu*

6'. *šá* é^{d}*a-nu-ni-tu*$_4$ sum^{in}
7'. ⅓ *ma-na* ^{md}utu-*na-ṣir* a-*šú šá*
8'. ^{m}*še-el-li-bi*
9'. pap 13 *ma-na* 1 gín kù.babbar
10'. *šá a-na* <é> níg.ga sum

Notes

Rev. 7'. Šamaš-nāṣir/Šellibi, is identified by Bongenaar 1997, 225 with <*sirāšu ša* Šamaš> and the member of the Šangû-Šamaš family.

Translation

[Silver, the r]ent of houses for the fourth year, which is at disposal of Iqīša-Marduk, the house rent collector, who gave it to the Ebabbar temple.

4 minas is given (to) Arad-Anunītu, the chief of bowmen and his servants;

38 shekels of silver (was given) to Šamaš-iddin and horse grooms who withdrew them from the Egyptian city.

1 mina 50 shekels of silver was given for kur.ra-garments and jerkins for the bowmen. Month Tašrītu, [nth] day [...]

1 mina of silver [...]

Rev. (translated from l. 5')

1 mina of silver was given for *sattukku*-offerings of the prebendary brewers of the Anunītu temple; 20 shekels (for) Šamaš-nāṣir, son of Šellibi, total 13 mina 1 shekel of silver, which was deposited to *bīt makkūri*-storehouse.

54. BM 71178 (82-9-18, 11180); 2.5 x 2.5 cm; (1.I.[KN] 1)

Obv. 1. [x x] ⸢x x udu⸣.níta [x x x]
2. [iti].bár u$_4$.1.kam mu.1.ka[m …]
3. [x x x] *i-di* é.meš *a-na* […]
4. […] ⸢x⸣ ^{m}*i-na*-gissu-^{d}u+g[ur …]
5. […] ⸢x⸣ *ina* é *ú-ri-e* […]
6. […] sum⸢^{in} x x⸣ […]

Translation

[…] sheep -[…]

[…] rent of the houses for [… month] Nisannu, first day, first year [...]

[...] the rent of houses for[...] Ina-ṣilli-Nergal […] has given to the fattening house […].

55. BM 69293 (82-9-18, 9291); 3.6 x 5.4 cm; [x.x KN] 6

Obv. 1. [........] *a-n*[*a*$^{?}$ ....]
2. [.....*i-d*]*i* é.m[eš ......]

3. [........] *a-na* 1 me gu$_4$ m[eš......]
4. [...] ⌜4⌝ gín kù.babbar *šá ir-bi šá* [...]
5. [... g]ín kù.babbar *šá a-na muḫ-ḫ*[*i* ...]
6. [...] *i-di* é.meš [....]
7. [... *ma-n*]*a* 1 gín kù.babbar *a*-[*na* ...]
8. [...] mu.6.kam su[m^{na} ...]
9. [...] *ir-bi š*[*á* ...]

Translation

Too fragmentary to be translated.

56. BM 64481 (82-9-18, 4461); 9.7 x 6.0 cm; [x].VI.Camb 5

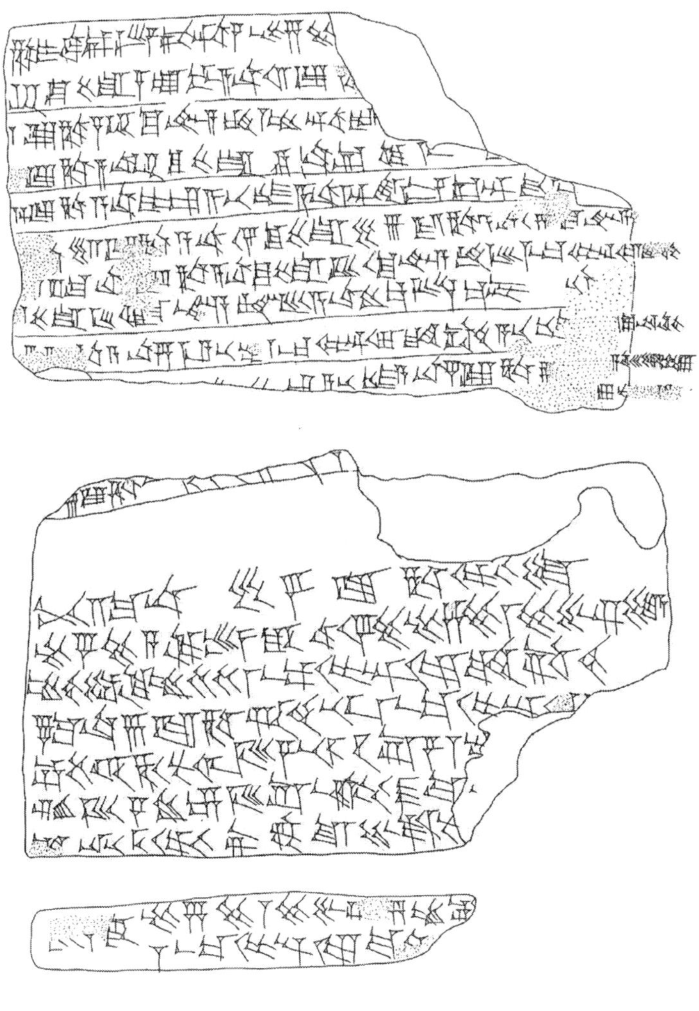

Obv. 1. kù.babbar *i-di* é.meš níg.ga ^{d}utu *šá* mu.5.kam [^{m}*kam-bu-zi-iá* lugal e^{ki} lugal kur.kur]
2. 1^{en} túg.kur.ra *šá ṣi-pi a-na* 12 gín k[ù.babbar …]
3. 1 gín kù.babbar *šá* 1^{en} ^{túg}*šìr-a-am* ^{m}lugal-^{d}utu-*ia* […]
4. [1$^{?}$] gín kù.babbar *a-na* 1^{en} túg.kur.ra *a-na* é *qé-me* ⸢x⸣ […]
5. 1½ gín kù.babbar *a-na* 5 kùr *a-bat-tu*$_4$ *a-na* ^{md}ḫar-dù *šá* é ^{d}gašan ⸢*sip*⸣-[*par* ^{ki}]
6. [1$^{?}$ *ma-n*]*a* 52 gín ⸢kù⸣.babbar *a-na* 14 túg.kur.ra 56 gín kù.babbar *a-na* 15 ^{túg}*šìr-a-*[*am*]
7. [x]+1⅔ *ma-na* [x] ⸢gín⸣ kù.babbar *a-na* túg.kur.ra.meš *u* ^{túg}*šìr-a-am*^{meš} ^{m}*i-na-*gissu-^{d}u+gur ⸢*it-ta-din*⸣
8. [tú]g.kur.ra^{meš} *ù* ^{túg}*šìr-a-am*^{meš} *a-na* ^{lú}erín.meš *šá* giš.ban *na-*[*din*]
9. ⸢4$^{?}$ gín kù.babbar⸣ *a-na* 5 me *a-bat-tu*$_4$ ^{m}*i-na-*giš.mi-^{d}u+gur *it-ta-din a-bat-tu*$_4$ ⸢*a*$^{?}$⸣-[*na* é] udu.níta *na-din*
10. [......] ⸢x kùr *a-bat*⸣-*tu*$_4$ *a-na* 4 gín kù.babbar ⸢9$^{?}$⸣ [x (x)] *a-na* 30 *il-qu-ú*
11. [..........]-*ú-nu* x x ⸢x⸣ [x]

Rev. 1'. 6 gín kù.babbar ⸢x x x x⸣ […]'
Blank space for 1 or even 2 lines
2'. pap 12 *ma-na* 54 gín kù.babbar *ul-tu*
3'. mu.4.kam *a-di* iti.kin u$_4$.14.kam mu.⸢5⸣.kam ^{m}*kam-bu-zi-ia*
4'. lugal tin.tir^{ki} lugal kur.kur ^{m}*i-na-*gissu-^{d}u+gur *it-ta-din*
5'. 7 *ma-na* 6 gín kù.babbar *ri-ḫi ina* igi ^{m}*i-na-*gissu-^{d}⸢u+gur⸣
6'. *e-lat ri-ḫa-nu* igi.meš *ina* igi-*šú* é *šá* ^{md}[x x x]
7'. gi.meš *šá* ^{lú}un.meš é *ina lìb-bi áš-ba* ⸢x⸣ […]
8'. ⸢*it*⸣-*ti-šú ul ni-ḫu-su* gíd.da nu [x x]

L.e. 9'. ⸢iti⸣.kin mu.5.kam ^{m}*kam-bu-zi-iá* lugal e^{k}[^{i} lugal kur.kur]
10'. ^{m}*i-na-*gissu-^{d}u+gur ⸢*it*⸣-[*ta-din* …]

Notes

L. 5. For Bunene-ibni *ša bīt Šarrat Sippar*, see Bongenaar 1997, 247.

Rev. 8. The sense of the line is unclear and a different reading cannot be excluded: *it*⸣-*ti-šú ul ne-ḫu* ^{kuš}gíd.da nu. This reading suggests that such documents were written also on parchment. The *giṭṭu* might be transalted also as "receipt" (Jursa 2005, 6). The problem is that the sense of *neḫu* is unknown.

Translation

Obv. 1. Silver, the rent of houses, property of Šamaš for the fifth year of [Cambyses, king of Babylon, king of Lands].
2. 1 dyed kur.ra-garment for 12 shekels of si[lver …]
3. 1 shekel of silver for one jerkin: Šarru-Šamšaya […]
4. [1$^{?}$] shekel of silver for one kur.ra-garment to the flour storehouse […]

5. 1½ shekels of silver for 5 *kurru* of *abattu* reeds for Bunene-ibni of the temple Šarrat Sip[par]

6. [1$^?$ min]a(s) 52 shekels of silver for 14 kur.ra-garments; 56 shekels for 15 jerkins;

7. [x]+ 1 minas 40+ x shekels of silver for kur.ra-garments and jerkins (which) Ina-ṣilli-Nergal has given.

8. The kur.ra-garments and jerkins are giv[en] for the bowmen.

9. 4$^?$ shekels of silver for 500 (bunches) of *abattu* reeds (which) Ina-ṣilli-Nergal has given.

10-11. [...] *kurru* of *abattu* reeds for 4 shekels of silver 9$^?$... for 30 was taken.[...]

Rev. 1'. 6 shekels of silver [...]

2'-4'. Total 12 minas 54 shekels of silver from the fourth year till the 14th day of the month Ulūlu, the fifth year of Cambyses, king of Babylon, king of Lands, Ina-ṣilli-Nergal has given.

5'-6'. 7 minas 6 shekels of silver, the remainder at disposal of Ina-ṣilli-Nergal, except for earlier arrears at his disposal; a house of [PN ...].

7'-8'. [x] reeds of the temple'servants who live in (them) which is not withdrawn from him

8'. The *giṭṭu*-parchement document is not [received$^?$].

L.e. 9'-10'. Month Ulūlu, fifth year of Cambyses, king of Babylon, [king of Lands], Ina-ṣilli-Nergal has gi[ven].

57. BM 66665 (82-9-18, 6659); 5.4 x 4.6 cm; Dar

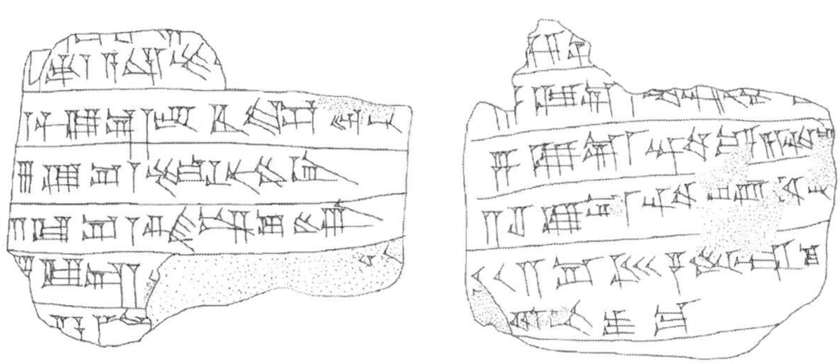

Obv. 1'. [(x) it]i.⌜x u$_4$.15⌝.[kam mu.x.kam]

2'. [^{m}]*da-a-ru-mu-š*[*ú* lugal tin.tir^{ki} lugal kur.kur]

3'. 1½ gín é ^{md}en-*tuk-te-e-*⌜*tir-ri*⌝

4'. 6 gín é ^{m}*mu-ra-nu* ^{lú}ašgab

5'. 2 gín é ^{m}*gi-mil-lu* ^{lú}ašgab

6'. ⌜5⌝ gín é ^{m}[x x x] ⌜x x⌝

7'. [x] ⸢x *šá a-na*⸣ [...]
Rest lost

Rev. 1'. [x] gín ⸢é⸣ [...]
2'. ⸢6⸣ gín é ^{m}ìr-^{d}⸢*a-nu-ni-tu*$_{4}$⸣
3'. 5 gín é ^{md}utu-ba^{šá} a ^{md}utu-⸢su⸣
4'. 2⅓ gín é ^{md}utu-⸢*lu-ú-da-ri*⸣
5'. ⸢pap⸣ 12 é.meš *šá ši-ra-ku*
6'. [*ina*] *lìb-bi áš-ba*
Rest lost

Translation

Obv. 1'-2'. [..., mon]th ⸢x⸣, 15th [day, x year of] Dariu[s, king of Babylon, king of Lands].
3'. 1½ shekels: the house of Bēl-tuktē-tirri
4'. 6 shekels: the house of Mūrānu, the leatherworker
5'. 2 shekels: the house of Gimillu, the leatherworker
6'. 5 shekels: the house of [PN]
7'. [...], which for [...]
Rest lost

Rev. 1'. [x] shekel(s): the house of [PN]
2'. 6 shekels: the house of Arad-Anunītu
3'. 5 shekels: the house of Šamaš-iqīša, son of Šamaš-erība
4'. 2⅓ shekels: the house of Šamaš-lūdāri,
5'-6'. total 12 houses, in which the oblates are living.
Rest lost

58. BM 63564 (82-9-18, 3531); 4.0 x 5.2 cm; 6.III.[KN] 3[+x]

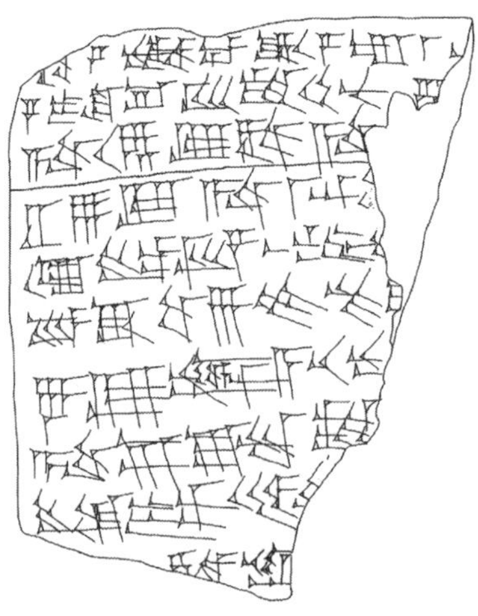

Obv. 1. ⸢kù⸣.babbar *šá* egir *e-peš* níg.ka$_9$ $^{\text{m⸢d?⸣}}$[x x]
2. *šá i-di* é.meš *id-din-nu* ⸢5⸣ [...]
3. *a-na* 19 gín kù.babbar *a-na* [...]
4. ⅓ 9 gín kù.babbar ^{md}ut[u ...]
5. *ù* ^{lú}erín.meš *šá* {*ina*} anše.k[ur.ra]
6. iti.kin u$_4$.6.kam mu.3+[x$^?$.kam
7. 7 gín šám *a-bat-t*[*u*$_4$ ... *šá*]
8. *a-na* é udu.níta *id*-[*din-nu* ...]
9. ^{lú}*qí-i-pi* sum^{n}[^{a} ...]
10. [x x] kù.babbar šá[m ...]

Rev. Uninscribed in preserved lower part of the tablet.

Notes

L. 5. For *ṣabê ša sīsê*, see MacGinnis 2012, 12 and note 64. In his opinion at present it is impossible to recognize if they "were professional cadre or the wider levy."

Translation

Silver from the former settlement of account, [... from$^?$] the rent of houses which [PN1 and PN2) have given.

5 [...] for 19 shekels of silver for [...]

29 shekels of silver: Šam[aš- ...] and workers of hor[ses ...]

Month Ulūlu, sixth day, 3[+x$^?$] year

7 shekels, the price of *abattu* reeds [... which] for the sheep shed they have gi[ven]

[...] was given [by?] the king's resident.

[...] of silver, the pr[ice of ...]

59. CT 57, 69 = BM 56932 (82-87-14, 1340); 21.IV.Nbn 3

Obv. 1. 3 *ma-na* kù.babbar *i-na* kù.babbar
2. *šá i-di* é.meš *ina* šu^{ii}
3. ^{m}ìr-^{d}en a-*šú šá* ^{md}ag-šeš.meš-mu
4. a-*na* gu$_4$.meš *a-na*
5. ^{md}utu-ba$^{\textit{šá}}$ ^{lú}gal *bu-ú-lu*

Edge 6. sum^{in}

Rev. 7. iti.šu u$_4$.21.kam
8. mu.3.kam ^{md}ag-i
9. lugal tin.tir^{ki}

Translation

3 minas of silver from silver from the rent of houses was given for oxen to Šamaš-iqīša, the overseer of the herds by Arad-Bēl, son of Nabû-aḫḫē-iddin.

Month Du'ūzu, 21st day, third year of Nabonidus, king of Babylon.

60. CT 57, 72 = BM 57582 (82-87-14, 1993) Collated; 2.VI.Nbn 5

Obv. 1. ½ *ma-na* 8 gín kù.babbar *šá i-di* é.[meš]
2. 2 gín kù.babbar ta é.gur$_7$.meš
3. ⌜x⌝ ½ [x *ina*] šu^{ii} ^{md}utu-numun-gál[^{ši}]
4. [*u* ^{md}ag-*ta-at-ta*]*n-nu*-ùru *a-na* ⌜x⌝-*bi*
5. ⌜*a*⌝-*na* tin.tir[^{ki} *it-ta-d*]*in*
6. ⌜1⌝ *ma-na* [...]
7. *a-na* [...]
8. ⌜½?⌝ [...]
Edge 9. ⌜½?⌝ [...]
Rev. 10. ⌜é⌝ [...]
11. *a-di* iti.ne mu.5.kam [^{md}ag-i]
12. lugal nun^{ki} ^{m}ìr-^{d}en *a-na é-ba*[*bbar-ra* sum]
13. 5 gín kù.babbar ta *lìb-bi šá* é ^{d}*a-nu-ni-tu*$_4$
14. *u* ^{d}*gu-la* x (ras.) *a-na ši-in-du*
15. *a-na* ^{m}*mu-ra-nu u* ^{md}utu-su sum^{in}
16. ½ gín *a-na ṣi-di-tu*$_4$ *šá* ⌜x x⌝
17. ^{md}utu-numun-gál^{ši} *u* ^{md}ag-*ta-at-t*[*a-nu*-ùru]
18. sum iti.kin u$_4$.2.kam mu.5.kam
19. ^{md}ag-i lugal tin.tir^{ki}

Notes

L. 4. The last but one sign in the line is preserved very badly and I cannot identify it.

L. 15. Mūrānu certainly (Bongenaar 1997, 413-414) and possibly Šamaš-erība were leatherworkers, who received silver for preparation of glue or varnish (for such meaning of *šindu*, see Bongenaar 1997, 399).

Translation

Obv. 1-5. 38 shekels of silver from the rent of houses, 2 shekels of silver from the *bīt makkūri*-storehouse [...] by hands of Šamaš-zēr-ušabši [and Nabû-tattan]nu-uṣur [was delivered] to Babylon [...]
6. 1 mina [...]
7. for [...]
8. ½? [...]
Edge 9. ½? [...]
Rev. 10. house [...]
11-12. to the month Abu, fifth year [of Nabonidus], king of Babylon, Arad-Bēl [has given] to the Ebab[bar temple]
13-15. 5 shekels of silver from the temple of Anunītu and Gula was given for glue to Mūrānu and Šamaš-erība.

16-18. ½ shekel of silver for travel provision was given [to] Šamaš zer-ušabši and Nabû-tattan[nu-uṣur].

18-19. Month Ulūlu, second day, fifth year of Nabonidus, king of Babylon.

61. CT 57, 70 = BM 56722 (82-87-14, 1130) Collated; 6.2 x 4.3 cm; 5.V.Nbn 9

Obv. 1. 1* gu$_4$ 6-*i a-na* ⅓ 2 gí[n kù.babbar]
2. *ina* kù.babbar *šá i-di* é.meš *a-na*
3. ^{m}šeš.meš-*šú* a-*šú šá* ^{md}ag-mu-⸢dù⸣
4. ^{m}[*ar*]-*ra-bi* a-*šú šá* ^{m}*ṣil-la-a*
5. [^{m}*mu-š*]*e**-zib* a ^{md}en-mu
6. [^{m}še]š-*lu-mur* a ^{md}en-a-mu
7. sum^{in}

Rev. 8. gu$_4$ *i-na* é *ú-ru-ú ina* igi
9. ^{md}utu-su
10. iti.ne u$_4$.5.kam mu.9.⸢kam⸣
11. ^{m*d}ag-i lugal tin.tir^{ki}

Translation

One six-year old bull for 22 she[kels of silver] from silver from the rent of houses was given to Aḫḫēšu, son of Nabû-šum-ibni, [Ar]rabi, son of Ṣillaya, [Muš]ēzib, son of Bēl-iddin (and) [Aḫ]u-lūmur, son of Bēl-aplu-iddin.

The bull (was given) to fattening house at disposal of Šamaš-erība.

Month Abu, fifth day, ninth year of Nabonidus, king of Babylon.

62. BM 72990 (82-9-18, 12999); 5.7 x 6.9 cm; VII.Nbn 10

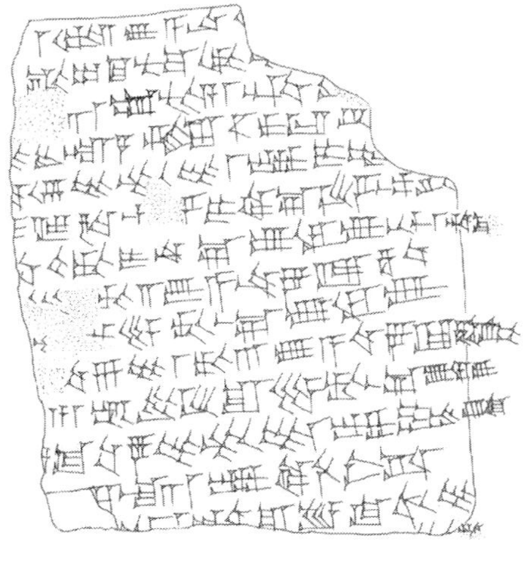

Obv. 1. [...] ⌜x⌝ 10 gu$_4$ 2-*ú a-na* 10+[x gín kù.babbar ...]
2. [...^{m}*mar*]-*duk ab-ku-nu-ma ul* ⌜x⌝ [...]
3. [... *ina* šu]^{ii} ^{m}dub-numun a ^{md}utu-⌜dù$^{?}$⌝ [...]
4. [...]-*zib* ^{lú}engar *šá gi-lu-šú šap-ri* [x x]
5. [...] u$_4$.16.kam mu.10.kam ^{md}ag-i luga[l nun^{ki}]
6. [... x]+$^{?}$⌜3⌝ gín kù.babbar *ina* ⌜kù⌝.[babbar] *šá i-di* é.meš *šá ina pa-*⌜*ni-šú*⌝
7. [... *it-t*]*a-din* gu$_4$ *ina* é *ú-ru-ú ina* igi ^{md}utu-⌜su⌝
8. [...] ⌜sum$^{?}$⌝ [1$^{?}$] gu$_4$ 2-*ú a-na* 7 gín kù.babbar
9. [...] ⌜mu$^{?}$-dingir$^{?}$⌝ sum gu$_4$ *ina* é *ú-ru-ú*
10. [...] u$_4$.6.kam 1 gu$_4$ 3-*ú a-na* 7 gín kù.babbar *ir-bi*
11. [...] ⌜a⌝ ^{md}en-šeš.meš-su sum gu$_4$ *ina* é *ú-ru-ú*
12. [... it]i.du$_6$ u$_4$.7.kam mu.10.kam ^{md}ag-i lugal nun^{ki}
13. [...] ⌜gín⌝ *ina* šu^{ii} ^{md}ag-di.kud-dù^{uš}
14. [...] ⌜*ina* igi ^{md}utu⌝-su iti.du$_6$ u$_4$.10.kam
15. [.................] ⌜x-^{d}utu⌝
Rest lost

Rev. is entirely lost.

Notes

L. 1 . Or [...] 70 gu$_4$

Translation

1-5. [...] 10 bulls for 10+[x shekels of silver ...] Marduk has bought (but) he did not [...] by the hands of Šāpik-zēri, son of Šamaš-ibni$^{?}$ [... Mušē]zib, the ploughman from Gilūšu sent [... month x], 16th day, tenth year of Nabonidus, king of [Babylon].

6-7. [... x]+3 shekels of silver from silver from the rent of houses, which is at his disposal [... PN has gi]ven. The bull is given to the fattening house at disposal of Šamaš-erība [...].

8-10. One bull two-years old for 7 shekels of silver [...]-šum$^{?}$-ili$^{?}$ has given (and) a bull in the fattening house [... for?] the sixth day.

10-12. One bull three-years old for 7 shekels of silver, the income [...] was given to [PN], son of Bēl-aḫḫē-erība. The bull is in the fattening house [... Mon]th Tašrītu, seventh day, tenth year of Nabonidus, king of Babylon.

13-15. [...] shekels from Nabû-dīni-ēpuš [...] at disposal of Šamaš-erība. Month Tašrītu, tenth day [...]-Šamaš.

63. CT 57, 68 = BM 56306 (82-7-14, 678); 30.I.Nbn [x]

Obv. 1. [x]+1 *ma-na* kù.babbar *ul-tu*
2. [kù.babb]ar *šá i-di* é.meš
3. [*a*]-*na* gu_4.meš *a-na*
4. ^{md}utu-ba^{šá} a-*šú*
5. *šá* ^{md}utu-šeš-mu sum^{in}
6. iti.bár u_4.30.⌜kam⌝
Rev. 7. m[u.x].kam ^{d}ag-[i]
8. lugal tin.tir[^{ki}]

Notes

Šamaš-iqīša/Šamaš-aḫ-iddin, presumably *rab būli* in the time of Nabonidus, see Bongenaar 1997, 130.

Translation

[x]+1 minas of silver from [sil]ver from the rent of houses was given to Šamaš-iqīša, son of Šamaš-aḫ-iddin for oxen.

Month Nisannu, 30th day, [x ye]ar of Nabo[nidus], king of Babylon.

64. BM 63966 (82-9-18, 3935) = Bertin 1443 Collated; 6.III.Nbn 11

Obv. 1. ½ *ma-na* kù.babbar *i-na*
2. *i-di* é.meš *ina* šu^{ii}
3. ^{md}ag-mu-mu *u* ^{m}*šu-la-a*
4. *a-na é-babbar-ra it-tan-nu*
5. kù.babbar *a-na* udu.níta *ina* šu^{ii}
6. ^{m}*na-ṣir u* ^{m}*šu-la-a*
Edge 7. *šu-bu-ul*
Rev. 8. iti.sig_4 u_4.9.kam
9. mu.11.kam ^{md}ag-i
10. lugal tin.tir^{ki}

Notes

Bertin's copy is perfect!

Translation

½ mina of silver from the rent of houses Nabû-šum-iddin and Šulā have given to the Ebabbar temple. Silver for (buying?) sheep was brought by Nāṣir and Šulā.

Month Simānu, ninth day, 11th year of Nabonidus, king of Babylon.

65. BM 66407 (82-9-18, 6400); 4.4 x 3.5 cm; 8.⸢II⸣.Nbn 12

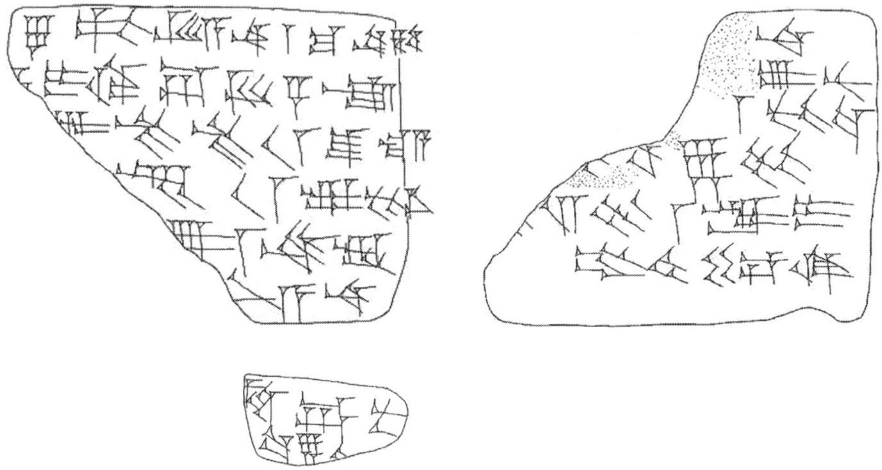

Obv. 1. 7 gu$_4$.meš *a-na* 1 *ma-na* kù.babbar
2. ⸢*šá*⸣ *i-di* é.meš *šá ina* šu^{ii}
3. [^{md}]ag-mu-mu *u* ^{m}*šu-la-a*
4. [x]-^{d}en *u* ^{md}ag-numun-dù
5. [x x x]-*ú* ^{m}ìr^{d}-en
6. [x x x]-pap *a-na*

Edge 7. [*é-babbar-ra i*]*t-tan-nu*
8. [iti.x] u$_4$.8.k[am]

Rev. 9. [x x x]-*na*
10. [x x x]-*ú-nu*
11. [x x x] ^{m}numun-*tú*
12. [sum iti.g]u$_4$ u$_4$.8.kam
13. [m]u.12.kam ^{md}ag-i
14. lugal tin.tir^{ki}

Translation

7 bulls for 1 mina of silver from the rent of houses from Nabû-šum-iddin and Šulā [x]-Bēl and Nabû-zēr-ibni [...] Arad-Bēl [...DN]-nāṣir have delivered to the [Ebabbar]

[Month Ayaru$^{?}$], eighth day [...]

[...]. Zērūtu [has delivered]

[Month Aya]ru$^{?}$, eighth day, 12th [ye]ar of Nabonius, king of Babylon.

66. BM 59164 (82-7-14, 3573); 4.9 x 6.5 cm; 14.III.Nbn 14

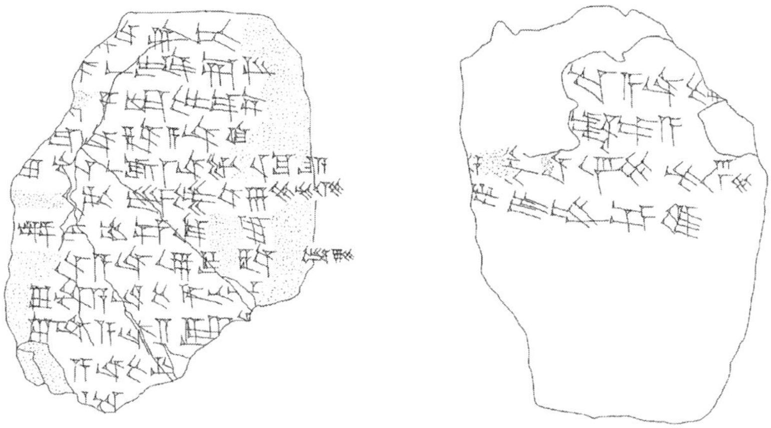

Obv. 1. [... k]ù.babbar *ir-bi* [...]
2. [x *ma-n*]*a ina i-di* é.meš [...]
3. [x]-⸢x⸣ *šá* zú.lum.ma ⸢*ni*?⸣-[...]
4. [x] *ma-na* kù.babbar *a-na* ki.[lam]
5. [x] ⸢udu.níta⸣ *ina* šu^{ii} ^{m}*na-ṣir u* ^{m}*šu-*⸢*la*⸣*-a*
6. [x (x)] ⸢10⸣ gu$_4$ iti.sig$_4$ u$_4$.6.kam mu.11.kam
7. [^{md}]ag-i lugal e^{ki} [x g]ín [kù.babbar ...]
8. [x x udu.ní]ta *a-na* 18 ⸢gín⸣ kù.babbar [iti].sig$_4$ u$_4$.8.kam
9. [x] udu.níta *a-na sat-tuk ina* igi [...]
10. [1] udu.níta *a-na* 2 gín [...]
11. [...] *a-na sat-tuk* [...]
12. [x x ud]u.níta [...]

Rev. 1'. [x x udu.ní]ta *a-na sat-t*[*uk* ...]
2'. [x x x] šem pa a
3'. [iti.s]ig$_4$ u$_4$.14.kam mu.14.kam
4'. [^{md}a]g-i lugal e^{ki}

Notes

The text is mentioned in Jursa 2010, 535.

Translation

1-3. [... s]ilver, the income [... x mi]nas from the rent of houses [...] dates [...]

4-7. [x] mina of silver for pr[ice of x] sheep from Nāṣir and Šulā [...] 10 oxen. Month Simanu, sixth day, 11th year of Nabonidus, king of Babylon.

8-9. [x she]kels of si]lv[er ...] [x she]ep for 18 shekels of silver, [Month] Simānu, the eighth day [x] sheep for *sattukku* offering

at disposal of [PN]
10-11. [one$^{?}$] sheep for two shekels [...] for *sattukku* offering [...]
12. [x sh]eep [...]
Rev. 1'-2'. [x sh]eep for *sattukku* offering [...]
3'-4'. [Month Si]mānu, 14th day, 14th year of [Na]bonidus, king of Babylon.

67. BM 64852 (82-9-18, 4833); 4.2 x 3. 3 cm; [x].I.Nb[n] 17

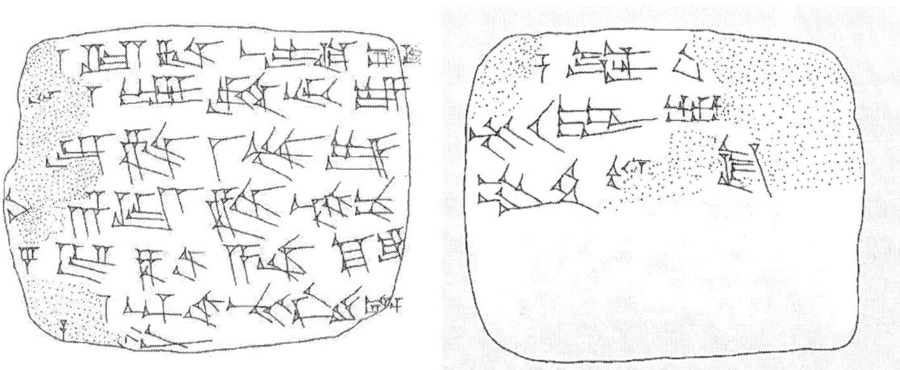

Obv. 1. ⸢⅓⸣ gín kù.babbar *ina i-di* ⸢é⸣.m[eš]
2. ⸢*ina* igi⸣ ^{md}ag-*it-ti-ia*
3. [6] gín kù.babbar ^{m}ìr-*ia*
4. pap [⅓] 6 gín kù.babbar *ina lìb-bi*
5. 4 gín kù.babbar *a-na ku-pur*
6. [*ina* igi] ^{md}utu-numun-dù ^{lú}⸢uš⸣.bar
7. [su]m^{in}

Rev. 8. [it]i.bár u_4.[x.kam]
9. mu.17.<kam> ^{md}ag-[i]
10. lugal tin.tir^{ki}

Notes

Regarding Šamaš-zēr-ibni the weaver, see Bongenaar 1997, 348 (three documents with broken data) and Zawadzki 2006, 229, where he is identified as son of Nūrêa active in the period from Nbn 5 to Cyr 8.

Translation

20 shekels of silver from the rent of the houses at disposal of Nabû-ittiya;

[6] shekels of silver (from) Ardiya, total [2]6 shekels of silver in it 4$^{?}$ shekels of silver for bitumen [(which) was giv]en at disposal of Šamaš-zēr-ibni, the weaver.

Month Nisanu [x day], 17th year of Nabo[nidus], king of Babylon.

68. BM 67021 (82-9-18, 7016); 5.2 x 3. 7 cm; 16.II$^{?}$.Nbn 12+x

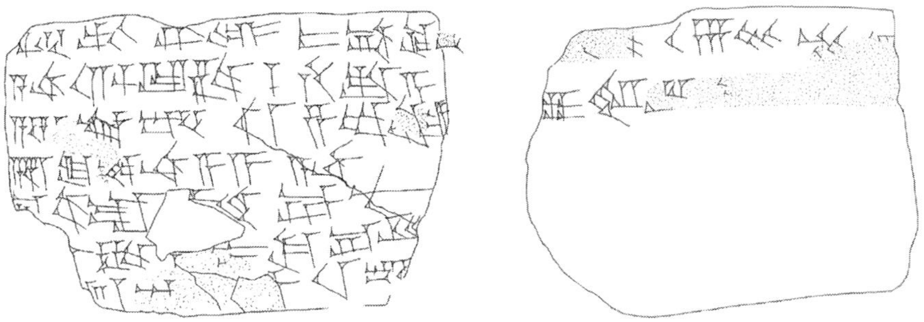

Obv. 1^{en} gu$_4$ *ṣal-lam tap-*{*ta*}*-ṭi-*⸢*ri*⸣
a-na 12½ gín kù.babbar ^{m}*haš-da-a*
a-*šú šá* ^{m}kar-^{d}en *u* ^{m}*za-ab-*⸢*di*⸣*-ia*
a-*šú šá* ^{m}ki.⸢ne⸣*-na-a-a a-na*
⸢*é*⸣*-babbar-ra* ⸢*it*⸣*-tan-nu*
[x gín$^{?}$] kù.babbar ⸢*šá i*⸣*-di* é.meš
[*ina* š]u^{ii} ^{md}[x]-⸢zálag$^{?}$⸣ *u* ^{md}en-[x (x)]

Rev. [iti.g]u$_4^{?}$ u$_4$.16.kam mu.⸢12⸣+[x.kam]
[^{d}a]g-im.tuku l[ugal tin.tir^{ki}]

Notes

L. 4. The *u* is written over a vertical wedge.

Translation

One black castrated bull Ḫašdāya, son of Mušēzib-Bēl and Zabdiya, son of Kinūnaya sold to the Ebabbar for 12½ shekels of silver. [x shekels?] of silver that is from the rent of houses [fro]m [DN-nū]ri and Bēl-[x x]. [Month Aya]-ru$^{?}$, 16th day, 12th+x year of [N]abonidus, ki[ng of Babylon].

69. CT 55, 790 = BM 56744 (82-7-14, 1152) Collated; ⸢2$^{?}$⸣.+[x.x].<Nbk> 40

Obv. 1^{en} túg.kur.ra
a-na 3 gín kù.babbar
ina i{me}*-di* é
ina igi ^{md}idim-kád
ina šu^{ii} ^{m}*šú-la-a*

Rev. iti.šu u$_4$.⸢2$^{?}$⸣.+[x$^{?}$kam]
mu.40.k[am ...]

Notes

The script suggests dating the text to the time of Nebuchadnezzar.

Translation

One kur.ra-garment for 3 shekels of silver from the house rent (given) at disposal of Ea-kāṣir from Šulā.

Month Du'ūzu, day 2+[x], 40th year of [...]

70. BM 67991 (82-9-18, 7989); 4.4 x 3.9 cm; 14.[x]. Nbk 41

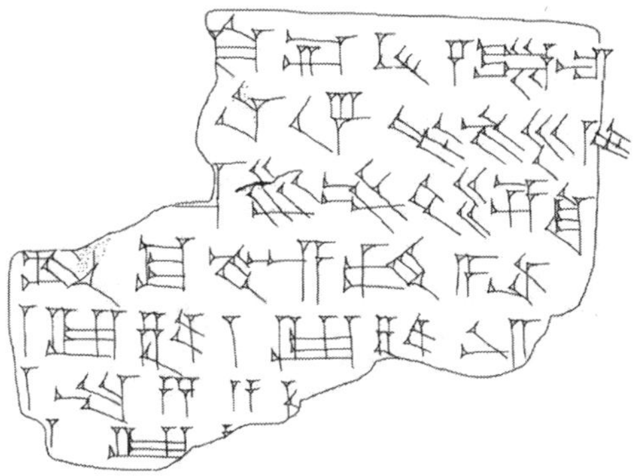

Obv. 1. [kù.babbar *i*]-*di* é.meš *šá* murub$_4$ uru
2. [ta iti.x] u$_4$.14.kam mu.41.kam
3. [^{md}ag-níg.d]u-ùru lugal tin.tir^{ki}
4. ⌜1^{it}⌝ ^{túg}*šir-a-am a-na*
5. 1 gín kù.babbar 1 gín kù.babbar pap 2 [gín]
6. ^{m}ìr-*iá a-šú* [...]
7. [1]+1 gín k[ù.babbar ...]
Rest lost

Rev. completely damaged

Translation

[Silver, the re]nt of houses (located) in the middle of the city [from month x], 14th day, 41st year of [Nebucha]dnezzar, king of Babylon.

One jerkin for 1 shekel of silver, (plus) 1 shekel of silver, total [2 shekels] Ardiya, son of [...].

⌜2⌝ shekels of si[lver ...]

71. BM 50347 (82-3-23, 1338); 4.5 x 2.2 cm; 26.VIb.<Nbp> 18

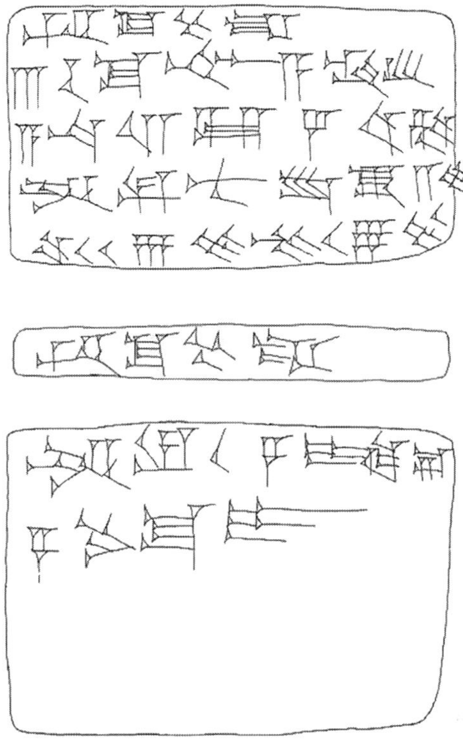

Obv. 1. 1^{en} túg.kur.ra
2. 3-*šú* ^{túg}*šir-a-am*^{meš}
3. *a-na* 12 gín 4-*tú* kù.babbar
4. *maḫ-ru-nu* iti.kin.2.kam
5. u$_4$.26.kam mu.18.kam

Edge 6. 1^{en} túg.kur.ra

Rev. 7. *maḫ-ru-u šá i-di* é
8. *šá* ^{lú}šu.i

Translation

One kur.ra-garment, 3 jerkins bought for 12¼ shekels of silver.
The intercalary month Ulūlu, 26th day, 18th year.
One old kur.ra-garment (was bought) for house rent of the barber.

72. CT 57, 74 = BM 56315 (82-7014, 687) Collated; 2.III.Nbn 3

Obv. 1. 19 túg.kur.ra 6-*ta*
2. ^{túg}⸢*šir-a*⸣-*am a-na*
3. 1 *ma-na* kù.babbar *ina lìb-bi* 50 gín
4. kù.babbar *i-di* é.meš *ina* šu[^{ii}]
5. ^{m}ìr-^{d}en [kù.babbar] ta
6. *ir-bi š*[*á* x] túg.kur.ra
Edge 7. [*a*]-*na* 13 gín 3 *ri-bat*
Rev. 8. [*i-n*]*a* šu^{ii} ^{md}ag-šeš.meš-*bul-liṭ*
9. [*n*]*a-šu-nu*
10. iti.sig$_4$ u$_4$.2.kam mu.3.[kam]
11. ^{d}ag-i lugal tin.tir^{ki}

Notes

L. 5 . Or [x x]-*ta*.

Translation

19 kur.ra-garments, 6 jerkins for 1 mina of silver, including 50 shekels of silver (from) the rent of houses from Arad-Bēl.

[Silver] from income of [x] kur.ra-garments, which for 13¾ shekels has been brought by Nabû-aḫḫē-bulliṭ.

Month Simānu, second day, third year of Nabonidus, king of Babylon.

73. BM 73955 (82-9-18, 13966); Not copied; *4.5* x 3.7 cm; [x].IV.Nbn 11

1. túg.kur.ra.meš *šá i-di* é.[meš (...)]
2. *a-na* kù.babbar *ina muḫ-ḫi* iti.šu u[$_4$.x.kam]
3. mu.11.kam ag-i lugal tin.tir[^{ki} sum^{na}⸣]

---

4 1^{en} túg.kur.ra *a-na* 2 g[ín kù.babbar]
5. ^{m}*ḫa-ba-ṣi-*[*ru*]
6. 1^{en} k[i.m]in *a-na* 2 g[ín kù.babbar]
7. ^{md}im-*ú-še-*[*zib*]
Rev. 8. ⸢x⸣ [ki.min] *a-n*[*a* ....]
9. [x x] ⸢x⸣ ba ⸢x⸣ [...]
10. [x ki.min] *a-na* 2 gín [kù.babbar ....]
11. ⸢x⸣ [tug].kur.⸢ra⸣ 2-⸢*ú*$^{??}$⸣ [...]
12. pap ⸢6⸣ túg.kur.ra.m[eš]
13. *a-na* 12½ gí[n kù.babbar *šá*]
14. ^{md}ag-mu-mu [*u* PN]
15. *it-tan-nu e-*⸢*lat* kù⸣.[babbar]
L.e. 16. igi-*tu*$_4$

Translation

The kur.ra-garments, which were [bought] for silver from the rent of houses on [x] day, 11th year of Nabonidus, king of Babylon.

---

1 kur.ra-garment for 2 sh[ekels of silver (for)] Ḫabaṣīru
1 [ditt]o for 2 sh[ekels of silver (for)] Adad-ušē[zib]
[x ditto] fo[r x shekels of silver …]
[x ditto] for 2 shekels [of silver …]
[x] kur.ra-garment(s) …,

total 6 kur.ra-garments for 12½ shekels of silver, which Nabû-šum-iddin [and PN] have delivered.

This is except for the previous sil[ver].

74. BM 64807 (82-9-18, 4788); 4.3 x 3.3 cm; 25.VIII.Nb[n] 12

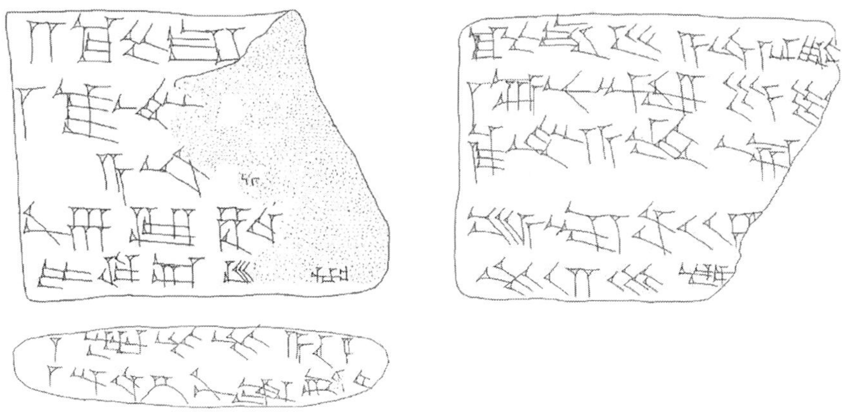

Obv. 1. 2 túg.kur.ra.[meš]
2. 1 ^{túg}*šir-*[*a-am*]
3. *a-na* ⸢x⸣ […]
4. pap 6 gín kù.babbar [*šá*]
5. *i-di* é.meš [x] ⸢x⸣

Edge 6. ^{md}ag-mu-mu a-*šú šá*
7. ^{md}utu-⸢a⸣-pap *it-ta-din*

Rev. 8. túg.kur.ra.meš *a-na* ^{md}ḫar-dù
9. ^{m}*dan-nu-*^{d}u+gur sum⸢*in*⸣
10. ^{túg}*šir-a-am ina* é […]
11. iti.apin u$_4$.2⸢5?⸣.[kam]
12. mu.12.kam ^{md}ag-[i lugal e^{ki}]

Translation

2 kur.ra-garments, one jerkin for ⸢x⸣ [...], total 6 shekels of silver [from] the rent of houses [...] Nabû-šum-iddin, son of Šamaš-aplu-uṣur has paid.

The kur.ra-garments were given to Bunene-ibni (and) Dannu-Nergal. The jerkin is in the house [...].

Month Araḫsamna, 25$^{th?}$ day, 12th year of Nabo[nidus, king of Babylon].

75. Nbn 651 = BM 60451 (82-9-18, 419) Collated; 6.0 x 4.0 cm; IX.Nbn 12

Obv. 1. 1*7* t[úg.kur.ra ...]
2. *a-na* 1½ *m*[*a-na* kù.babbar]
3. [*ina*] *i-di* é.meš ⸢x⸣ [...]
4. ^{md}ag-mu-mu [...]
5. [(x)] 12 túg*.kur*.ra* *a**-⸢*na**⸣ [x x]
6. [x x x 1]^{it*} ⸢^{túg}*šir**-a⸣-[*am*]
7. [x x x] *šá* šuku.ḫi.a lugal

Rev. 8. [...] ^{md}amar.utu-⸢numun-giš⸣
9. [x x (x)] ⸢^{lú}kab.sar$^{?}$⸣
10. [1] túg.kur.ra ^{md}amar.utu-mu-⸢dù*⸣
11. ^{lú}nagar
One blank line
12. pap 37 túg.kur.ra 1 ^{túg}*šir**-*a**-*am**
13. iti.gan mu.12.kam ^{d}ag-i [lugal e^{ki}]

Notes

Note that l. 9 is missing in the Strassmaier's copy; however, all three signs are badly preserved and the reading is not certain.

L. 10. The last sign is badly preserved, but ùru (uṣur) as read by Bongenaar 1997, 402, or mu (Strassmaier) are less probable.

L. 13. The title was presumably written over right side of the damaged lower edge.

Translation

1-4. 17 k[ur.ra-garments ...] valued 1½ mi[nas of silver], from the rent of houses [...] Nabû-šum-iddin, [...]

5-9. 12 kur.ra-garments for [... o]ne jerkin [...] in charge of royal rations [...] Marduk-zēr-līšir, the stone-carver$^{?}$

10-13. [1] kur.ra-garment (for) Marduk-šum-ibni, the carpenter, total 37 kur.ra-garment(s), one jerkin.

14. Month Kislīmu, 12th year of Nabonidus, [king of Babylon].

76. Nbn 703 = BM 60573 (82-9-18, 548) Collated; 5.9 x 4.1 cm; 28.II.Nbn 13

Obv. 1. [túg.kur.r]a$^{?}$.meš *šá* ^{md}ag-mu-mu
2. $^{lú!?}$[*šá* ug]u *i-di* é.meš níg.g[a]* ⸢^{d*}⸣[ut]u*
3. *id-di-nu* iti.gu$_4$ u$_4$.28.kam
4. mu.13.kam ^{md}ag-i lugal e^{ki}
5. 5 ^{kuš}*il-ta-pi la ḫi-ri*
6. 6 túg.kur.ra *la ḫi-ri*
7. ⸢5$^{?}$⸣ túg.kur.ra *ḫi-ri*

Rev. 8. ⸢pap.pap 1⸣6 túg.kur.ra[^{meš}]

Notes

L. 7. Traces of two wedges are preserved, which might be interpreted as numeral 5.

Translation

Obv. 1-4. The [kur.r]a-garments, which Nabû-šum-iddin, the house rent collector, property of Šamaš, has given. Month Ayāru, 28th day, 13th year of Nabonidus, king of Babylon.
5. 5 *iltapi*-garments without *ḫiru*
6. 6 kur.ra-garments without *ḫiru*
7. 5$^{?}$ kur.ra-garments with *ḫiru*,

Rev. 8. total 16 kur.ra-garments.

77. Nbn 728 = BM 75749 (83-1-18, 1099) Collated; 5.2 x 3.9 cm; 11.IX.Nbn 13

Obv. 1. 12 gín kù.babbar *ina* kù.babbar
2. *šá i-di* é.meš *a-na*
3. *ḫa-ri-e šá ḫar-ri*
4. ^{md}ag-mu-mu a-*šú šá* ^{md}utu-a-ùru
5. *a-na* ^{m}*ba-su-ru* a-*šú* ⸢*šá*⸣
6. ^{m}*al-ta-ma-*' *ina qí-bi*
7. *šá* ^{m}kar-^{d}amar.utu ^{lú}sanga ⸢*sip**-*par**^{ki*}⸣

L.e. 8. *it-*⸢*ta-din*⸣

Rev. 9. iti.gan u$_4$.11.kam
10. ⸢mu⸣.13.kam ^{d}ag-⸢i⸣
11. [lugal t]in.tir^{ki}

Notes

Ll. 1-6, see below, BM 63391, no. 79: 7'-8'. Note that the same name is written with *al* or with *il*. Concerning the name and the discussion on its etymology, see PNAE, vol. 2, Part 1, 525, s.v. Iltama' (by M. Weszeli).

L. 3. Concerning the *ḫarû* ritual, see Geller 1995, Kessler 2002 and Kleber 2008, 285-287. The texts published here supports Kessler's idea that *ḫarû* described a type of container used during the ceremony of the same name. More probably is that a distinctive shape of a vessel used during ceremony resulted in naming it with the same term *ḫarû*. According to the text published by Geller (cf. Jankowić 2013, 161f.), ^{f}Bu'itu was the wife of Šum-ukīn/Bēl-zēri/Basia, but because she did not give him a son he married a second wife ^{f}Li'idu. After the death of Šum-ukīn, ^{f}Li'idu dressed in a garment suitable for the ritual and went to the *bīt ḫilṣi* to perform ritual, although as is stressed in the text she had no right to share in the income or to perform the ritual. The matter was so serious that the question had to be settled by the Eanna authorities. They decided that ^{f}Li'idu had no right to wear *didū* garment, or to enter into *bīt ḫilṣi* and perform ritual. Nbn 728, no. 77 (Nbn 13) and BM 63391, no. 79 (Nbn 14) where Basuru, son of Il/Altama' received a payment of 12 shekels of silver, equal to one-year wages of worker, allows us to conclude that it was a fixed remuneration. It is worth noting that in the last two texts the rite was held on the 11th Kislīmu.

Translation

12 shekels of silver from silver from the rent of houses for *harû*-container for *harû*-ceremony was given by Nabû-šum-iddin, son of Šamaš-aplu-uṣur to Basuru, son of Altama' at the order of Mušēzib-Marduk, the administrator of Sippar.

Month Kislīmu, 11th day, 13th year of Nabonidus, [king of Ba]bylon.

78. BM 62971 (82-9-18, 2940); 4.8 x 3.7 cm; 4.[VIII].Nbn 2

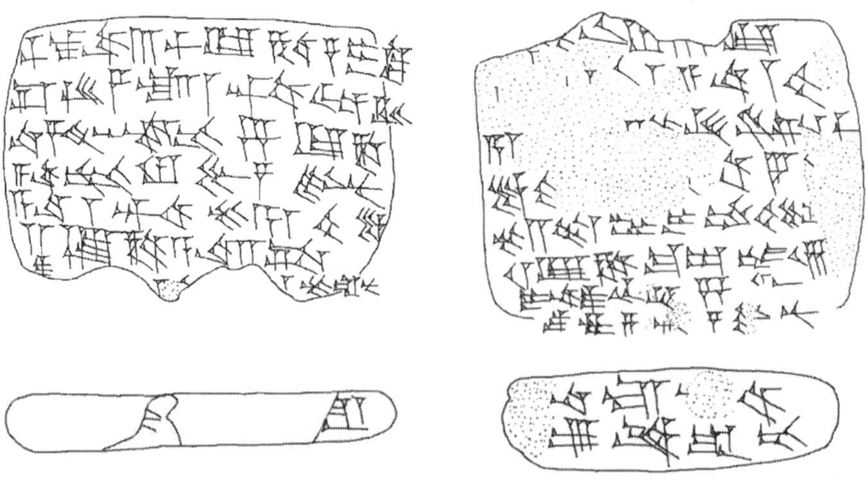

Obv. 1. ½ *ma-na* 3½ gín kù.babbar *šá i-di*
2. é.meš *šá ina* šu^{ii} ^{md}utu-sig$_5$^{iq}
3. *na-ša-a'* *ina lìb-bi* 5 gín kù.babbar
4. *a-na qu-ru-bu šá* in.nu
5. *a-na* ^{md}utu-mu a ^{m}tin sum[^{na}]
6. 2 gín kù.babbar *a-na* 2-*ta*
7. *áš*-[x x] ⸢x⸣ [x x] ^{m}*mu-ra-nu*

Edge 8. [x] ⸢x⸣ [x x x]-*su*

Rev. 9. [x] ⸢x⸣] pap ⸢5/6? 3?⸣ gín
10. ⸢x⸣ [x] ⸢x⸣ *a-na* ^{m}tin
11. a ^{m}[^{d}ag-e]n-[m]u.meš ^{lú}uš.bar
12. sum^{n}[^{a} iti.apin?] u$_4$.4.k[am]
13. mu.2.kam ^{md}ag-i lugal tin.ti[r^{ki}]
14. 11 gín kù.babbar *ba-ab-tu*$_4$ 16 [gín]
15. *i-na-áš-ši* ⸢en⸣ 5 *lim*
16. *ma-ak-ṣa-*⸢*ri*⸣ *šá* ⸢in⸣.nu

L.h.e. 17. [*a*]-⸢*na*⸣ uru-⸢d⸣utu
18. *ú-qar-ra-bi*

Notes

Šamaš-iddin, son of Balāṭu, probably the *rab ikkarāti* of the Ebabbar temple, see Jursa 1995, 24ff., who was active in Āl-Šamaš, mentioned in our text. Šamaš-udammiq is most probably identical with the person of the same name from Gilūšu or Til-qaqulli (Jursa 1995, 223 and 236, respectively).

L. 1. For Balāṭu/Nabû-bēl-šumāti, the weaver, see Bongenaar 1997, 320-321 and Zawadzki 2006, 212-213 and Zawadzki 2013, 522, no. 630a.

Translation

1-5. 33½ shekels of silver from the rent of houses Šamaš-udammiq has brought in month Araḫsamna; of it 5 shekels was given to Šamaš-iddin, son of Balāṭu for transportation of straw;

6-13. 2 shekels of silver for 2 ......[to?] Mūrānu ..., total 53? [shekels of silver for ...] to Balāṭu, [son of [Nabû-bē]l-[šu]māti, the weaver was given. [Month Araḫsamna?], fourth day, second year of Nabonidus, king of Babylon.

14-18. 11 shekels of silver, the due amount on 16 [shekels] he will bring (and) he will transport to Ālu-Šamaš with five thousand of bundles of straw.

79. BM 63391 (82-9-18, 3958); 6.2 x 6.6 cm; 21.III.[Nbn] 14

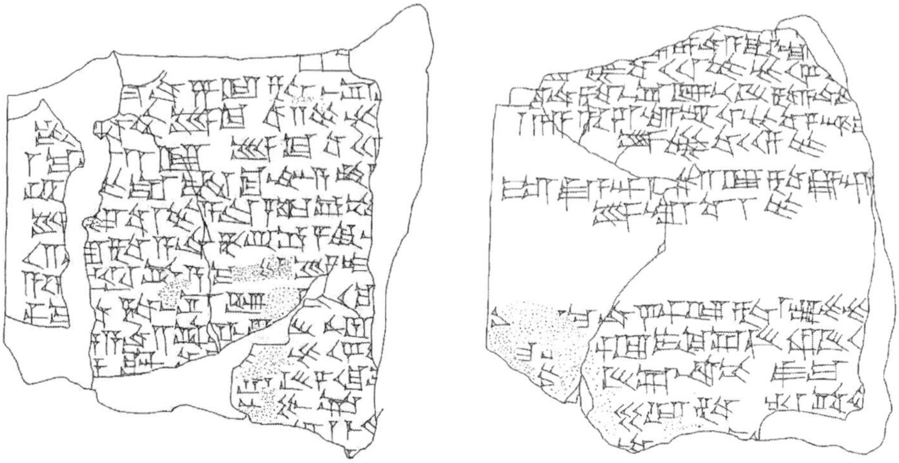

Obv. 1’. [.......] ⸢x⸣ [.....]
2’. [x x] *ma-na* 5 gín kù.babbar *ina* <*i-di*> é.m[eš ...]
3’. *it-*⸢*ta*⸣*-din* iti.du$_6$ u$_4$.2.kam mu.[x.kam ...]
4’. 1 *ma-*[*na*] 2 gín iti.du$_6$ u$_4$.21.kam [...]
5’. 1^{en} [túg].kur.ra <1>$^{it\ túg}$*šir-a-am* ⸢*šá*⸣ [...]
6’. iti.⸢ne⸣ u$_4$.1.kam *a-na* ^{m}*šá*-ka-*kal-bi* ^{l}[^{ú}….]
7’. 12 [g]ín kù.babbar *a-na ḫa-ri-e šá ḫar-r*[*i a-na* ^{m}*ba-su-ru*]
8’. a-*šú* š[á ^{m}]*il-ta-a-*⸢*ma*⸣-[’ su]m iti.gan [u$_4$.11.kam]
9’. ½ *m*[*a-n*]*a* kù.babbar *ina* é.gur[$_7$.me]š *dul-*[*lu* …]
10’. [.… *š*]*á a-na* 2-*ta mar-r*[*i*^{m}]^{eš} pap ⅚ [*ma-na* ...]
11’. [x x it]i.bár u$_4$.1+[x.ka]m mu.14.k[am] [...]
12’. [x *ma-na* kù.babbar *i-di*] é.meš *šá dul-l*[*u* ...]
13’. [.......................] ⸢*i*⸣*-pu-uš*
14’. [..................] ⸢x⸣ 1 me 20 [...]
15’. [...........] ⸢x⸣

Rev. 1’. [...] ⸢x⸣
2’. [*a-na* ^{f}*z*]*u-un-na-a* dumu.mí-*su* […]
3’. ⸢iti⸣.sig$_4$ u$_4$.21.kam mu.14.k[am]
4’. ⸢x⸣ *ma-na* kù.babbar *ina* é.gur$_7$.meš kù.babbar *a-na* ⸢^{lú}⸣[…]
5’. ^{m}a-*a* a-*šú šá* ^{m}kar-^{d}en *u* ^{m}numun-*tú šá pal-l*[*u-kat*]
6’. iti.sig$_4$ u$_4$.24.kam
7’. 3 kùr zíz.a.an ⸢*a-na*⸣ 2 gín kù.babbar zíz.a.an ⸢*šá*⸣
8’. iti.apin u$_4$.1.kam
Blank space for ca. two lines
9’. pap.[pap x] *ma-na* 4½ gín kù.babbar ^{md}ag-mu-mu

10'. [x] *ma-n*[*a* x]+ ½ gín *i-di* é.meš šub.meš *u*
11'. [x x] ^{lú}[un].meš é *ina lìb-bi áš-ba*
12'. [x x x] 50 gín kù.babbar *it-ta-din*
13'. [x x x]-*na* [x x] ⸢x⸣ [...]

Notes

Ll. 7-8, cf. Nbn 728, no. 77: 1-6.

Translation

Obv. [... x mi]na(s) 5 shekels of silver from the rent of houses [... PN] has given. Month Tašrītu, 10th+x day, year [...]
1 mi[na] 2 shekels, month Tašrītu, 21st day [...]
one kur.ra-garment, one jerkin of [...]; month Abu, 1st day for Ša-pī-kalbi, th[e ...]
12 [sh]ekels of silver [was gi]ven [to Basuru], son of Iltama' for *harû*-container of *harû*-ceremony, month Kislīmu, [14th day].
½ mina of silver from the harbour storehouse (for) wo[rk ...]
[... th]at for two spades, total ⅚ [mina ...; mon]th Nisannu, 1+[x] day, 14th year [...]
[x mina(s) of silver, the] rent of houses for work [...] has done [...]
[...] 120 [...]

Rev. [...] to Zunnā, daughter [of ...]; month Simānu, 21st day, 14th year.
⸢x⸣ mina of silver from the harbour storehouse; the silver is for the [...] Aplā, son of Mušēzib-Bēl and Zērūtu from Pall[ukat]; month Simānu, 24th day.
3 *kurru* of emmer for 2 shekels of silver; emmer for month Araḫsamna, first day.
[Grand?] total [x]minas 4½ shekels of silver (from?) Nabû-šum-iddin; [x] minas [x]+½ shekels of silver (from) the rent of the ruined houses and in which [x] temple' servants are living.
[...] 50 shekels of silver he has paid [...]

80. Cam 27 = BM 74695 (83-1-18, 12); 2.I.Camb 1

Obv. 1. 8½ gín kù.babbar *šá i-di*
2. é.meš ⸢5 gín ta⸣ *ir-bi*
3. pap 13½ gín kù.babbar
4. šám 3 túg.kur.ra.meš

Edge 5. sum^{na} sur

Rev. 6. iti.bár u_4.2.kam
7. mu.1.kam
8. ^{m}*kam-bu-zi-ia*

Translation

8½ shekels of silver, from the rent of houses, 5 shekels from the income, total 13½ shekels of silver, the price of 3 kur.ra-garments is given; is paid.

Month Nisannu, second day, first year of Cambyses.

81. Nbk 445 = BM 75189 (83-1-18, 515) Collated; Nbk (IV) [1]

Obv. 1. 3 túg.kur.ra.meš ⸢x⸣ [x x]
2. *šá i-na i-di* é.meš
3. *la-pa-ni* ^{md}utu-sig$_5$^{iq}
4. ⸢*na*?⸣-*šu-nu a-na* ^{lú}nu.kiri$_6$.meš
5. [x x x] sum^{in}
6. [.......]⸢kam*⸣

Rev. 7. [mu.1.kam ^{md}ag-níg].⸢du-ùru*⸣
8. ⸢lugal⸣ tin.tir^{ki}

Notes

L. 7. On the basis of the period of activity of Šamaš-udammiq the document has to be dated to the first year of Nebuchadnezzar IV. A dating to Nebuchadnezzar III is excluded because there is no place for mu.sag.nam.lugal.la.

Translation

3 kur.ra-garments ... which from the rent of houses was brought to Šamaš-udammiq and was given for the gardeners [...].

[Month x, nth day, first] year of [Nebuchadnezzar], king of Babylon.

82. Nbn 717 = BM 75625 (82-9-18, 975) Collated; 2.VII.Nbn 13

Obv. 1. 2 *ma-na* 5 gín kù.babbar [(x x)]
2. *ina* kù.babbar ⸢*i*⸣-[*di*] é.[meš]
3. *šá ina* igi-*šú*{⸢x x x⸣}
Presumably line erased
4. ^{md}ag-mu-mu a-*šú šá*
5. ^{md}utu-a-pap *a-na*
6. *é-babbar-ra it-ta-din*
7. *ina lìb-bi* 5 gín kù.babbar

Edge erased

Rev. 8. *a-na* ⸢^{d}utu??⸣ *a-na*
9. ^{md}ḫar-dù *u* ^{lú}erín.meš
10. sum^{in}
11. iti.du$_6$ u$_4$.2.kam mu.13.kam
12. ^{m*d}ag-i lugal e^{ki}

Transaltion

2 minas 5 shekels of silver from silver of the rent of houses which was at his disposal, Nabû-šum-iddin, son of Šamaš-aplu-uṣur has given to the Ebabbar temple, in it 5 shekels of silver for [Šamaš$^{??}$] to Bunene-ibni and his workers was given.

Month Tašrītu, second day, 13th year of Nabonidus, king of Babylon.

83. CT 57, 71 = BM 56505 (82-7-14, 881) Collated; 19.VII.Nbn 13

Obv. 1. ⌜5⌝7 gín kù.babbar *šá i-di*
2. é.meš *ina* é.gur$_7$.meš
3. 5 gín kù.babbar *a-na* ^{md}ag-mu-ùru
4. a-*šú šá* ^{md}u+gur-mu sum^{na}
5. pap 1 *ma-na* 2 gín kù.babbar
6. *ina i-di* é.meš *ár-ki*
7. *e-peš* níg.ka$_9$ *it-ta-din*
Rev. 8. *e-lat* 2 *ma-na* 5 gín kù.babbar
9. igi^{ú} iti.du$_6$
10. u$_4$.20.1.lal.kam mu.13.kam
11. ^{md}ag-i lugal e^{ki}

Notes

L. 4. Instead ^{md}u+gur-mu sum^{na} maybe we might read ^{md}u+gur-mu-sum^{na}.

Translation

57 shekels of silver from the rent of houses (located) in the harbour district. 5 shekels of silver which was given to Nabû-šum-uṣur, son of Nergal-iddin, total 1 mina 2 shekels of silver from the rent of houses after$^{?}$ settlement of account (was made) he has given.

(This is) except for 2 minas 5 shekels of silver of former (issue).

Month Tašrītu, 19th day, 13th year of Nabonidus, king of Babylon.

84. Nbn 752 = BM 74773 (83-1-18, 93) Collated; 5.I.Nbn 14

Obv. 1. ⌜½⌝ *ma-na* kù.babbar *a-na* é.gur$_7$.meš
2. 10 gín *a-na a-bat-tu*$_4$
3. ^{md}ag-numun-du *u* ^{m}zálag-^{d}utu
4. 1½ gín *a-na* 2 *mar-r*[*i* an].bar
5. pap ⅔* *ma-na* ⌜1½*⌝ gín kù.babbar
6. *ina* kù.⌜babbar *i*⌝-*di* é.meš
7. *šá* ^{md}ag-mu-mu
Rev. 8. *it-ta-din*
9. iti.bár u$_4$.5.kam mu.14.kam
10. ^{d}ag-i lugal e^{ki}

Notes

L. 5. The numeral ⅔ is written on long stroke of the sign pap and probably for this reason it was copied by Strassmaier as ⅚.

Translation

½ mina of silver (delivered) to the harbour storehouse;

10 shekels for *abattu* reeds (was given to) Nabû-zēr-ukīn and Nūr-Šamaš.

1½ shekels for 2 iron spades, total 41½ shekels of silver from the silver from the rent of houses which Nabû-šum-iddin has given.

Month Nisannu, fifth day, 14th year of Nabonidus, king of Babylon.

85. BM 74332 (82-9-18, 48A); 5.6 x 4.5 cm; 9.VII.Nbn 16

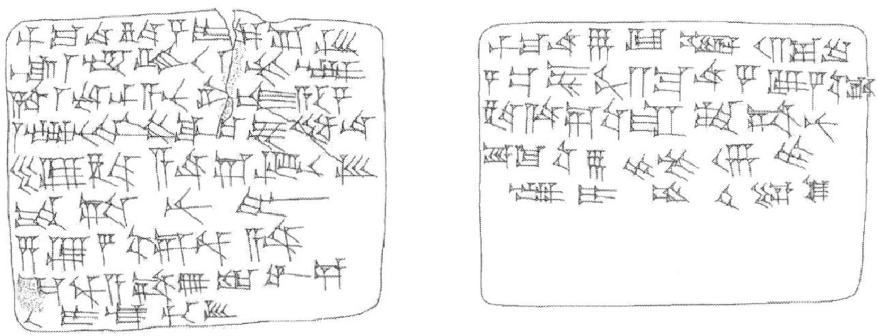

Obv. 1. ½ *ma-na* kù.babbar *šá i-di* é.meš
2. *ina* šu^{ii} ^{md}en-gi *u* ^{m}mu-^{d}ag
3. *a-na* ^{m}ìr-^{d}*a-nu-ni-tu*$_4$ a-*šú šá*
4. ^{md}ag-numun-dù ^{lú}gal giš.ban sum^{na}
5. 50 gín kù.babbar *a-na* é.gur$_7$.meš
6. *it-ta-nu-*'
7. 5 gín 4-*tú bit-qa a-na*
8. ⸢*saq*⸣-*qa-a-ta ú-ka-pi-e*
9. *u i-la-ḫu*^{meš}

Rev. 10. ½ *ma-na* 9 gín kù.babbar šám 12 udu.níta
11. *šá* giš.ban pap 2 *ma-na* 4 gín 4-*tú bit-qa*
12. kù.babbar *a-na é-babbar-ra it-tan-nu*
13. iti.du$_6$ u$_4$.9.kam mu.16.kam
14. ^{d}ag-i lugal tin.ti^{ki}

Notes

Ll. 5-7, see MacGinnis 2012, 101, who thinks that *i-la-ḫu* is the broken Plural of *ilḫu*. His translation is accepted here. For seal stamp, see Altavilla – Walker 2009, 101, no. 441.

Translation

½ mina of silver from the rent of houses was given to Arad-Anunītu, son of Nabû-zēr-ibni, the chief of bowmen by Bēl-ušallim and Iddin-Nabû;

50 shekels of silver they gave to the harbour storehouse;

5⅜ (shekels of silver) for sacks, pack-saddles (and) *ilḫu*-clothes;

39 shekels of silver, the price of 12 sheep of the bowmen(?), total 2 minas 4⅜ shekels of silver they gave to the Ebabbar temple.

Month Tašrītu, ninth day, 16th year of Nabonidus, king of Babylon.

86. BM 79611 (89-10-14, 161); 5.*0* x 4.4 cm; 28.III.Nbn 17

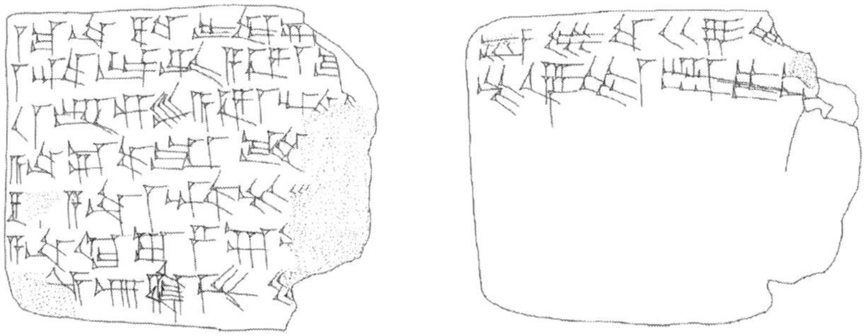

Obv. 1. 1 *ma-na* kù.babbar *i-di* é.[meš *šá*]
2. ^{md}utu-sig$_5$^{iq} a-*šú šá* ^{m}*š*[*u-zu-bu*]
3. *u* ^{md}en-gi a-*šú šá* ^{md}utu-[dù]
4. *a-na é-babbar-ra id*-[*din-nu*]
5. kù.[babba]r *a-na* ^{md}utu-mu-[(x)]
6. *a-na dul-lu šá* é ⌜x⌝ [x x]
7. [ud.ki]b.nun^{ki} {meš} s[um^{in}]

Rev. 8. iti.sig$_4$ u$_4$.28.kam
9. mu.17.kam ^{md}ag-i luga[l tin.tir^{ki}]

Notes

L. 7. ki is written over erasure; it seems that the scribe repeated the sign nun.

For the seal stamps, see Atavilla – Walker 2009, 101f., no. 442. Out of three seal stamps one, belonging to Kī-Nabû (CO2), the scribe, not mentioned in the document, was identified by the authors. The photo of unidentified seals G17 is on the attached CD.

Translation

1 mina of silver, the rent of houses which Šamaš-udammiq, son of Šū[zubu] and Bēl-ušallim, son of Šamaš-[ibni] ga[ve] to the Ebabbar temple. Silver was gi[ven] to Šamaš-iddin(?) for work in the house [...] of the Ebabbar temple.

Month Simānu, 28th day, 17th year of Nabonidus, kin[g of Babylon].

87. BM 61839 (82-9-18, 1308); 5.1 x 3.9 cm; 14.[x].Nbn 17

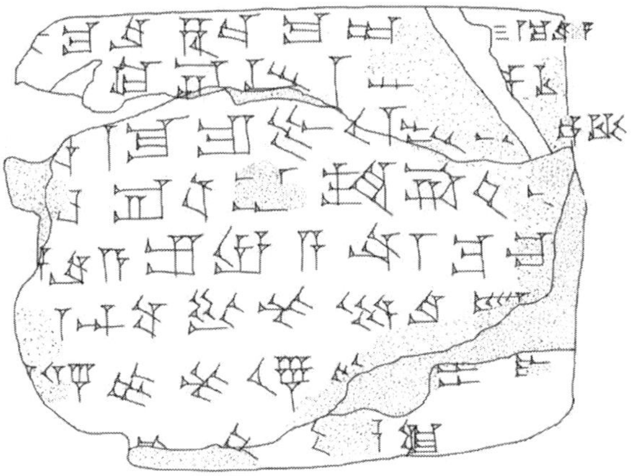

Obv. 1. ⸢1/3$^?$⸣ *ma-na* kù.babbar *ba-ab-*[*t*]*u*$_4$ 1 *ma-na šá*
2. [ta *i*]-*di* é.meš ^{md}[utu-si]g$_5$^{i}[^{q}]
3. [a]-⸢*šú šá*⸣ ^{m}*šu-zu-bu u* ^{md}⸢en⸣-^{m}[^{u}si]g$_5$^{iq}
4. [*a*]-⸢*na*⸣ *é-babbar-ra it-ta-din-*⸢*nu*⸣ [kù.babbar]
5. ⸢*a*⸣-*na a-gur-ru a-na* ^{m}*ba-la-*[*ṭu* a-*šú šá*]
6. ^{md}utu-šeš-mu sum^{na} ⸢iti⸣.[x]
7. ⸢u$_4$⸣.14.kam mu.17.kam [^{m}]^{d}⸢ag⸣-i
8. lu[gal] tin.t[i]r^{ki}

Notes

Since according to other documents the partner of Šamaš-udammiq/ Šūzubu was Bēl-ušallim/Šamaš-ibni (see above, p. 110), it seems that the scribe wrote mistakenly ^{md}en-^{mu}sig$_5$^{iq} instead of ^{md}en-gi$^{!}$

Translation

⸢20$^?$⸣ shekels of silver, the outstanding amount of 1 mina from the rent of houses, [Šamaš-udam]miq, son of Šūzubu and Bēl-ušallim! have delivered to the Ebabbar. Si[lver] was given to Balā[ṭu, son of] Šamaš-aḫ-iddin for baked bricks.

Month [x], 14th day, 17th year of Nabonidus, [king of Babylo]n.

88. Nbn 234 = BM 60095 (82-9-18, 58) Collated; (<Cyr$^?$> 6)

Obv. 1'. [x x x] ⸢x x⸣.meš-*šú a-di-i* ⸢*šá* u$_4$.2⸣.kam
2'. *šá* iti.ab mu.6.kam
3'. *am-mar* níg.ka$_9$-*šú-nu ép-šú*
4'. 5 *ma-na* ⅓ gín kù.babbar *šá a-di-i*
5'. u$_4$.1.kam *šá* iti.kin mu.6.kam

6'. *ina pa-ni* ^{m}*ina*-gissu-^{d}u+gur *ri-ḫi*
7'. kù.babbar *šá i-di* é.meš *šá* ^{lú}*ši-ra-ku*
8'. *ina ka-a-ri* ud.kib.nun^{ki}
9'. *ù* murub$_{4}$ uru *ina lìb-bi*
10'. ⸢*áš**⸣-*bu-' it-ti-šú*
Rev. 11'. ⸢*ul**⸣ *ni-ḫi-is-s*[*u** (x x)]
12'. ⸢x⸣ *maḫ-ḫir-šú-nu* ⸢x⸣[(x x)]

Translation

...till the second day of the month Ṭebētu, sixth year as much as their settlement has been made;

5 minas 20 shekels of silver which until the first day of month Ulūlu, sixth year at disposal of Ina-ṣilli-Nergal; rest of silver from the rent of houses from oblates living in the harbour of Sippar and in the middle of the city from$^{?}$ them it is not withdrawn...

89. Cyr 234 = BM 75159 (83-1-18, 485) Collated; 5.VIII.Cyr 6

Obv. 1. 11 gín kù.babbar *šá i-di* ⸢é*⸣.[meš]
2. ^{m}*ina*-gissu-^{d}u+gur *a-na* ⸢*é*$^{?}$⸣-[*babbar-ra*]
3. *it-ta-din* ud.ka.bar ⸢*a*⸣-[*na*]
4. *gan-du**-*ú šá* balag.balag ud*.⸢ka*.bar⸣
5. sum^{na} iti.⸢apin⸣ u$_{4}$.5.kam
6. mu.6.ka[m ^{m}*ku-ra*]-⸢*áš**⸣
Rev. 7. lugal e^{ki} lugal kur.kur

Notes

For the duplicate, see below BM 101435.

L. 3. Only middle vertical part of wedge ⸢*a*⸣ is preserved.

Translation

11 shekels of silver from the rent of houses, Ina-ṣilli-Nergal has given to the Ebabbar temple. Bronze for *gandû* of the bronze harp was given.

Month Araḫsamna, fifth day, sixth year of Cyrus, king of Babylon, king of Lands.

90. BM 101435 (83-1-21, 3096) a duplicate of Cyr 234; *4.4* x 3.8 cm; 5.VIII. Cyr ⸢6⸣

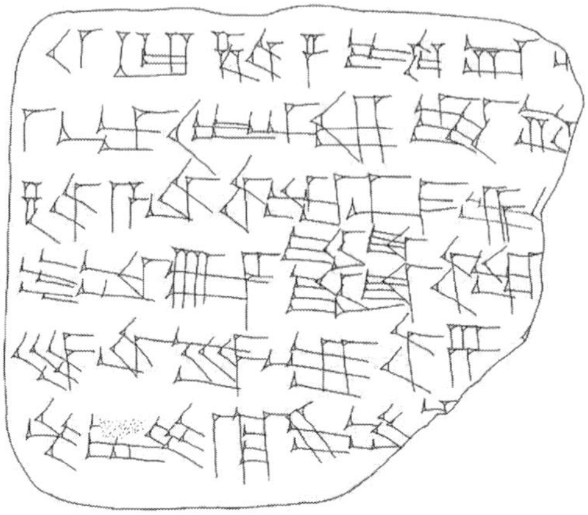

Obv. 1. 11 gín kù.babbar *šá i-di* é.m[eš]
2. ^{m}*ina*-gissu-^{d}u+gur *it-ta-*[*din*]
3. kù.babbar *a-na* ud.ka.bar *šá a-n*[*a*]
4. *gan-du-ú šá* balag.balag ud.ka.[bar]
5. sum^{na} iti.apin u$_{4}$.5.k[am]
6. mu.⸢6⸣.kam ^{m}*ku-raš* lugal ⸢e⸣[^{ki} lugal kur.kur]

Notes

L. 3. the *šá* and *a* are written over erasure.

Translation

11 shekels of silver of the rent of houses, Ina-ṣilli-Nergal has given <to the Ebabbar temple>. Silver for bronze for *gandû* of the bronze harp was given.

Month Araḫsamna, fifth day, sixth year of Cyrus, king of Babylon, king of Lands.

According to my knowledge, the *gandû* as an element of the *balaggu* occurs here for the first time. The first problem is the meaning of *balaggu,* identified in the last publication as a harp, an instrument known from the third millennium BC (Krispijn 2010, 144). Nevertheless, according to Dumbrill 2005, 402, *balaggu* might rather denote a "stringed instrument of harp family," (see 176-223), or "percussion musical instrument probably of the hour-glass-type" (see 224-226). In its latest incarnation it was probably a drum (TCL 6, 47, rev. labeled ^{d}ábxdúb; attention to this text I owe to Irving Finkel). The identification of the *balaggu* might help with an estimation of the weight of the *gandû* for which bronze was purchased for 11 shekels. Happily, there are a few texts which provide the price of bronze, imported to Babylonia from the West (Jamānu = Jonia in Asia Minor) or East (Oman), see Kleber 2017, 14-15. In two cases, bronze from Jamānu was bought in a proportion of three minas (ca. 1,5 kg) for one shekel, i.e., ca. 16,5 kg for 11 shekels of silver. A red bronze was more expensive, as only 1 mina 6 shekels (over a half of kilogram) was purchased for one shekel. In two other cases, 2 minas (ca. 1 kg) were purchased for one shekel, in another, 1 mina 46, 6 shekels (ca. 0,885 kg), and in yet another presumably 2 minas 20 shekels (ca. 1,17 kg).[520] It is impossible to say where the more expensive bronze was purchased, but we may estimate that for 11 shekels of silver an amount of ca. 11 to 16,5 kg of bronze might have been purchased, equal to the weight of a bronze *gandû*. It means that this element of *balaggu* was quite heavy, which rather excludes the possibility of a portable instrument carried on foot or kept on laps. It should be stressed that in both texts the sign is written balag on top of balag, what might suggest that two separate *balaggu*s or an instrument built of two parts (like hour-glass) is meant here. The second possibility, i.e., that it might be a quite large double drum with housing made of bronze seems more probable.

91. BM 63996 (82-9-18, 3965) = Bertin 1864 Collated; 14.VII.Camb 1 (š. B.)

Obv. 1. 5 gín 4-*tú* kù.babbar *a-na* ⸢x⸣ [x x] ⸢x⸣ *e*
2. 6 gín *a-na* ud.ka.bar [*a*]-⸢*na*⸣ ^{m}*lib-luṭ* ^{lú}simug
3. 10 gín kù.babbar *ina šam-ni šá* ^{lú}erín.meš
4. *šá* ^{lú}*qí-i-pi ina maš*-šar*-tu*$_4$ *šá* iti.bár
5. *a-na* ^{md}ag-di.kud-dù^{uš} *u* ^{m}*su-qa-a-a*
6. ^{lú}a.kin gi$_4$.meš *šá* ^{lú}*qí-i-pi* sum*^{in*}
7. pap ⅓* 1* gín 4-*tú* kù.babbar *ina* kù.babbar
8. *šá i-di* é.meš ^{md}utu-sig$_5$^{iq}
Edge 9. *a-na é-babbar-ra it-ta-din*
Rev. 10. iti.du$_6$ u$_4$.14.kam mu.1.k[am]
11. ^{m}*ka-am-bu-zi-ia* lugal e^{ki}

Notes

L. 2. For Libluṭ, the smith, see Bongenaar 1997, 377. For the seal stamp, see Altavilla – Walker 2009, 103, no. 453.

Translation

5¼ shekels of silver for ...; 6 shekels (of silver) for bronze for Libluṭ, the smith, 10 shekels of silver for oil for workers of the king's resident from the prebendary income of the month Nisannu, was given to Nabû-dīni-ēpuš

[520] Not 2 minas 30 shekels as was estimated by Kleber.

and Sūqaya, the messengers of the king's resident, total 21¼ shekels of silver from the silver from the rent of houses, Šamaš-udammiq has delivered to the Ebabbar temple.
Month Tašrītu, 14th day, first year of Cambyses, king of Babylon.

92. BM 63990 (82-9-18, 3959) = Bertin 1861 Collated; 20.IX.Camb 3

Obv. 1. 2 gín kù.babbar *ina ri-ḫi* k[ù.babbar]
2. *šá i-di* é *šá ina* šu^{ii} ^{m}*ina*-giss[u-^{d}u+gur]
3. *a-na* 10 *ma-na* síg.ḫi.a *a-na* ^{md}ḫar-dù
4. *šá* é gu$_4$ sum^{nu} 3 gín *a-na* 10 *ma-na* síg.ḫi.a
5. *a-na* ^{m}*ni-di-it šá* é anše.kur.ra sum^{nu}
6. 1½ gín kù.babbar *a-na* ^{md}ag-*it-tan-nu*
7. a ^{m}*lib-luṭ šá* é anše.kur.ra sum^{nu}
8. 1½ gín *a-na* 5 *ma-na* síg.ḫi.a
Rev. 9. *a-na* ^{md}utu-ba^{šá} a ^{md}en-*šú-nu* sum^{nu}
10. iti.gan u$_4$.20.kam mu.3.kam
11. ^{m}*kam-bu-zi-ia* lugal e^{ki} lugal kur*.kur*

Notes

For previous edition see Weszeli 2009, 441, no. 6.

Translation

2 shekels of silver from the rest [of silver] of the rent of house(s) was given to Bunene-ibni, of the cattle shed for 10 minas of wool from Ina-ṣil[li-Nergal]. 3 shekels for 10 minas of wool was given to Nidintu, of the horse stall.

1½ shekels of silver to Nabû-ittannu, son of Libluṭ, of the horse stall

1½ shekels of silver for 5 minas of wool was given to Šamaš-iqīša, son of Bēlšunu.

Month Kislīmu, 20th day, third year of Cambyses, king of Babylon, king of Lands.

93. BM 73499 (82-9-18, 13510); 5.3 x 2. 4 x cm; 28.XI.<Dar> 8

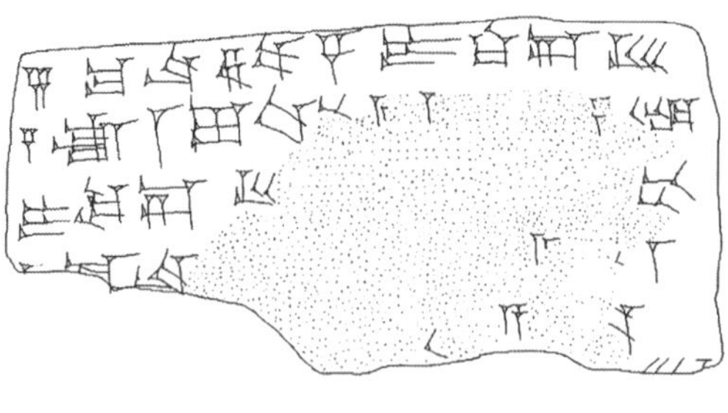

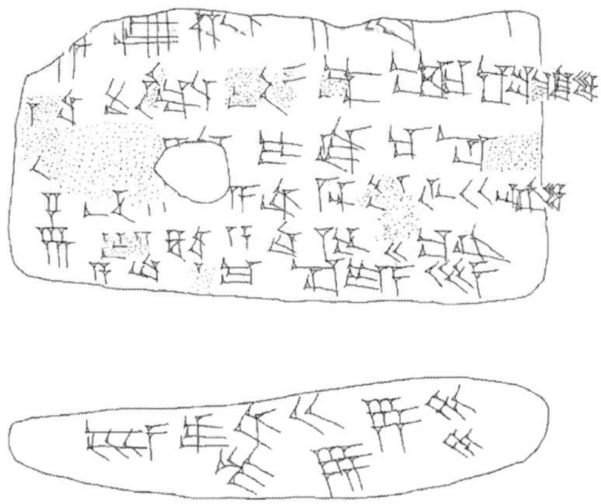

Obv.	1.	5 *ma-na* kù.babbar *šá i-di* é.meš
	2.	*šá ina* šu^{ii} ^{m}*lu*-ud.⸢du-*a*⸣-[*na*-zála]g ⸢*šá*⸣ ugu
	3.	*i-di* é.meš [x x x *ina lìb*]-⸢*bi*⸣
	4.	⸢1 *ma*⸣-*na* [x x x] ⸢*a-na*⸣
	5.	[...] ⸢x *a*-[x] ⸢*na*?⸣
	6.	[x x x x x] ⸢sum⸣
Rev.	1'.	⸢5 gín kù.babbar *a-na* x⸣
	2'.	⸢*a-na* ^{lú}⸣*dam*-[*gà*]*r*$^{?}$ dumu bàd.si.ab.⸢ba⸣^{ki} sum
	3'.	10 [gín] ⸢*a-na*⸣ *i-di* giš.má [x (x)]
	4'.	*šá ina* ⸢x⸣ [x x] *a-na* ^{md}⸢ḫar?⸣-*ši-man*^{an}-*ni* sum
	5'.	6 ⸢gín⸣ kù.babbar *a-na* 1 pi ⸢še⸣.giš.ì
	6'.	*a-na* ^{m}*ba-si-ia* sum
L.e.	7'.	iti.zíz u$_{4}$.28.kam
	8'.	mu.8.kam

Notes

L. 2. This is the second attestation of Lūṣi-ana-nūri with his title *ša muḫḫi idi bītāti*. Bongenaar 1997, 10, n. 21, recognize him in CT 55, 25: 2, which he date to "ca. Dar". If eighth year is the eighth year of Darius Lūṣi-ana-nūri was the successor of Iqīša-Marduk.

Translation

5 minas of silver, from the rent of houses, which from Lūṣi-a[na-nūri], the house rent collector [..., in] it 1 mina [...] for [...] was given.

⸢5⸣ shekels of silver for [... was given to?] the merchant, son of Borsippa.

10 [shekels] for the rent of a boat [...], which [...] was given to Bunene-šimānni.
6 shekels of silver for 1 *pānu* of sesame was given to Basia.

Month Šabātu, 28th day, eighth year.

94. BM 61555 (82-9-18, 1527); 5.8 x 7.0 cm; Cyr 2

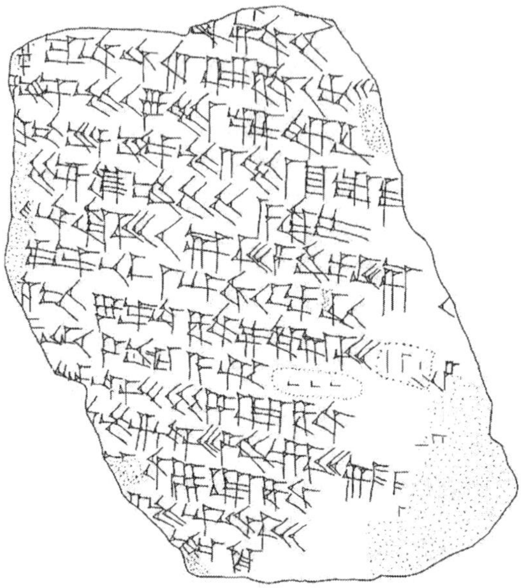

		Obv. I	Obv. II
Obv. I	1'.	[....] ⸢x x⸣	
	2'.	[...] *it-ta-din*	
	3'.	[x]+⸢7⸣ *ma-na* {na} 13 gín kù.babbar *ul-t*[*u*]	
	4'.	[it]i.ne mu.17.kam ^{md}ag-im.tuku [lugal e^{ki}]	
	5'.	[*a-di-i lì*]*b-bi* iti.ne mu.2.kam ^{m}*ku-ra-áš*	
	6'.	lugal tin].tir^{ki} lugal kur.kur *a-di-i*	
	7'.	[*muḫ*]-*ḫi na-di*^{meš} *u* é.meš *šá* ^{lú}erín.meš é	10/*u* [...]
	8'.	[*šá lìb-bi*] *áš-ba ina* igi ^{md}utu-sig$_5$^{iq}	
	9'.	[*ina lì*]*b-bi* 7 *ma-na i-di* é.meš ⸢x⸣	1⸢5?⸣ [...]
	10'.	[*na-di*]-⸢e⸣-*ti šá* ⸢*ka*⸣-*a-ri* x (ras.)	
	11'.	[... m]u.an.na.meš 55 gín kù.babbar	⸢x⸣ [....]
	12'.	[...] ⸢x⸣ mu.an!.na.meš *šá* ^{lú}un.meš é	⸢x⸣ [....]
	13'.	[..... *m*]*a-na* 9 gín kù.babbar	
	14'.	[...] ⸢2⸣ mu.an.na.meš	
	15'.	[... *a-ga*]-*dè*^{ki}	

Translation

[...] has given.

[x]+⸢7⸣ minas 13 shekels of silver from the month Abu, 17th year of Nabonidus, [king of Babylon till] the month Abu, second year of Cyrus, [king of Baby]lon, king of Lands inclusive (rent) from ruined houses and from

houses of the temple's servants who live there at disposal of Šamaš-udammiq. [... of] it 7 minas, the rent of the houses (and) ruined houses of the harbour district [...]. [...x]+2$^{?}$ years 55 shekels of silver [... [for x] years from the temple's servants [... x mi]nas 9 shekels of silver [...] ⸢2⸣ years ... A]kad [...]

95. BM 51163 (82-9-18, 2159); 5.6 x 4.9 cm

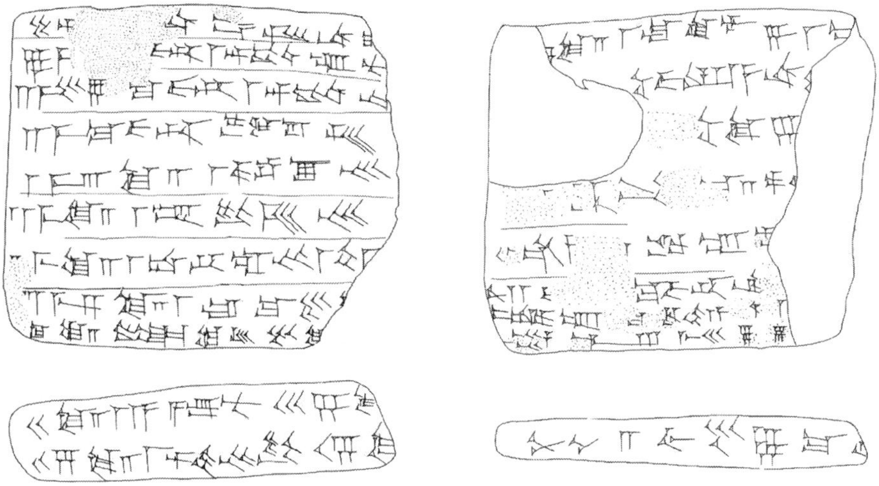

Obv. 1. še.bar [*šá i*]-*na* erín.meš *na-áš*$^{?}$-[x]
2. 7 me [x *ma*]-*ši-ḫu* ^{md}amar.utu-dub-num[un]
3. 2 me 48 *ma-ši-ḫu* ^{md}amar.utu-⸢*na*⸣-[x x]
4. 2 me *ma-ši-ḫu i-di* é.meš
5. 1 me 3 ki.min ^{m}*šul-lu-mu*
6. 2 me ki.min ^{md}en-šeš.meš-mu
7. ⸢2⸣ me ki.min ^{m}*du-ḫu-um-mu* ^{m}tin ^{m}[...]
8. ⸢3⸣ me 2 ki.min ^{m}*eri*$_{4}$*-ba* 50 k[i.min ...]
9. 60 ki.min ^{lú}*šìr-ki*^{meš} 40 ki.[min ...]

Edge 10. 20 ki.min ^{m}*a-a-šam-nu* 35 k[i.min x x]
11. 25 ki.min ^{md}šár-mu-šeš 15 ki.[min x x]

Rev. 12. [x]+⸢2⸣ ki.min ^{m}*la-qí-pi* 5 ^{m}⸢x⸣-[x x]
13. [x x x ^{m}*l*]*i-ši-ru a-na* ⸢20/x$^{?}$⸣ [x x x]
14. [x x x^{md}]utu-ki-*iá* [(x x x)]
15. [x x] ⸢*kin*-x⸣[x š]u^{ii} ⸢x x⸣[(x x)]
16. [*m*]*i-šil šá* [x] *ka-lak*-⸢*ku*⸣ [x x]
17. pap 2 li[m x x] *ma-ši-ḫu ina lì*[*b-bi*]
18. *ina*$^{!}$ *ka-lak*-⸢*ku* x x⸣.ḫi.a ⸢x⸣ [x x]

19. ⌜*ina*⌝ ká.⌜gal⌝ 3 me 38 *šá*$^{!?}$[x x]

L.e. 20. pap.pap 2 lim 46 *ma-š*[*i-ḫu šá* še.bar]

Translation

Barley, [which] has been br[ought$^{?}$b]y the workers
700 [+x]*mašīḫu*: Marduk-šāpik-zēri
248 *mašīḫu*: Marduk-nā[...]
200 *mašīḫu*: the rent of the houses
131 ditto: Šullumu
200 ditto: Bēl-aḫḫē-iddin
200 ditto: Duḫummu, Balāṭu, [PN]
302 ditto: Erība
50 d[itto ....]
60 ditto: the oblates
40 di[tto ...]
20 ditto: Aia-šamnu
35 di[tto ...]
25 ditto: Issar-nādin-aḫi
15 di[tto ...]
[x] ditto: Lāqīpi
5 [...]
[x ditto: L]īšīru for 20 ...
[...]: Šamaš-ittiya
[...] from [...]
Half ...] the silo
[....]
total 2000 [and x x] *mašīḫu*, including in the silo [...] in the gate [...]
338 [...]
grand total: 2046 *maš*[*īḫu* of barley].

96. Nbn 319 = BM 74921 (83-1-18, 242) Collated by R. Tarasewicz; (Year 8)

Obv. 1. 1⅚ *ma-na ina* kù.babbar *šá i-di* é.meš
2. ina lìb-bi ⅚ *ma-na šá* mu.7.kam
3. 1 *ma-na* kù.babbar 2-*ú* ká
4. 2 *ma-na* kù.babbar *šal-šú* ká
5. 3* *ma-na* kù.babbar 4-*ú* ká
6. pap 7 *ma-na* mu.8.kam
7. a-na ^{lú}erín.meš

Rev. 8. *šá* ^{md}en-kád sum^{in}

Translation

1 mina 50 shekels from silver from the rent of houses, in it 50 shekels from the seventh year;

1 mina of silver: second installment

2 mina of silver: third installment

3 mina of silver: fourth installment, total 7 minas (in the) eighth year for workers of Bēl-kāṣir was given.

97. Nbn 824 = BM 74979 (83-1-18, 302) Collated; 26.[x].Nbn 14

Obv. 1. *ṣi-di-tu*$_4$ *šá a-na* [...]
2. *u* ^{md}utu-ba^{šá} *šá* šuku.ḫi.a [lugal]
3. *a-na* igi dumu lugal ⌜ta$^?$ x x⌝ [x]
4. u$_4$.26.kam mu.14.kam ^{md}ag-i lugal [e^{ki}]

---

5. 7 kùr zú.lum.ma ta *šu-tùm-mu* lugal
6. šuku.ḫi.a iti.bár *a-di* iti.du$_6$ mu.14.kam
7. ^{m}*dan-nu*-^{d}u+gur sur 3 kùr zú.lum.ma
8. [(x)] ⌜*šá*⌝ iti.ne iti.kin iti.du$_6$ ^{md}utu-ba$^{⌜šá⌝}$
9. [x gín] kù.babbar *šá* 5 iti.meš *šá e-da* lú
10 [x] gín kù.babbar 2-*ta* šu$^{ii.meš}$ kù.babbar-'

Edge 11. [*a-na*] 2 ^{kuš}*nu-ṭa-nu*

Rev. 12. [2]-⌜*ta*⌝ šu$^{ii.meš}$ *šá* 2 sìla *šam-ni*
13. ⌜½⌝ gín *šá* 2 *me-e-še-e-nu*
14. 4-*tú a-na* 2-*ta* ^{túg}*kar-bal-la-a-ta*
15. *bit-qa* ta *ir-bi* šám 4 sìla *saḫ-li-e*
16. pap 10 gín *i-na ri-ḫi-tu*$_4$ kù.babbar *šá i-di* é.meš
17. *šá la*-igi ^{md}ag-mu-mu a ^{md}utu-a-ùru *na*-šá**-a
18. 1 gín kù.babbar *šá i-di bil-tu*$_4$ ^{f}*nar*-tu*$_4$
19. 1^{en} túg.kur.ra *ù* 2-*ta* ^{túg}*šìr-a-a*[*m**]
20. ta é šu^{ii} 2 gín 4-*tú* kù.babbar *ir-b*[*i*]
21. 1^{en} túg.kur.ra pap 2 túg.[kur.ra.meš]
22. 2-*ta* ^{túg}*šìr-a-am**^{meš} *a-n*[*a* PN]

L.e. 23. *u* ^{md}utu-ba^{šá}
24. *ina* gub^{zu} *šá* ^{md}en-lugal-*bul-*[*liṭ*]

L.h.e 25. ⌜pap⌝ 15 gín 4-*tú bit-qa* kù*.babbar*
26. *e-lat mu-ṣip-tu*$_4$

Translation

1-4. Travel provision which [was given to PN] and Šamaš-iqīša, in charge of [king's rations] at disposal of crown prince from the month [x], 26th day, 14th year of Nabonidus, king of Babylon.

5-7. 7 *kurru* of dates from the royal *bīt šutummu*-storehouse, provision from the month Nisannu till the month Tašrītu, 14th year, Dannu-Nergal has paid.
8. 3 *kurru* of dates for the month Abu, Ulūlu, Tašrītu (for) Šamaš-iqīša.
9. [x] (shekels) of silver for 5 months ...
10-11. [1]⅔ shekels of silver (for) two leather bags
12. ⅔ (shekel) for 2 *qû* of oil
13. ⸢½⸣ shekels for two pair of sandals
14. ¼ shekel for two *karballatu*-hats
15-17. ⅛ (shekel) from the *irbu*-income, price of 4 *qû* of cress, total 10 shekels from the rest of silver from the rent of houses, which are given from before Nabû-šum-iddin, son of Šamaš-aplu-uṣur.
18. 1 shekel of silver from the payment ...
19-20. 1 kur.ra-garment and 2 jerkins from the *bīt qāti*-rearhouse
20-23. 2¼ shekel of silver, the *irbu*-income, 1 kur.ra-garment, total 2 kur.ra-garment ... and 3 jerkins (was given to) [PN] and Šamaš-iqīša.
24-26. In the presence of of Bēl-šar-bul[liṭ], total 15⅜ shekels of silver, except for *muṣiptu*-garment.

98. BM 63552 (82-9-18, 3519); 4.7 x 7.5 cm; ⸢13⸣.V.Nbn 16

Obv. 1. ⸢9?⸣ gín [kù.babbar *i-di* é.meš níg.ga ^{d}utu]
2. *šá* <*a-na*> *a-bat-tu*$_4$ [sum^{na}...]
3. pap 1 *ma-na* 1⸢1⸣+[x gín kù.babbar]
4. ⸢½⸣ gú.un 1½ *m*[*a-na* kù.babbar]
5. *šá e-peš* níg.k[a$_9$ *šá*]
6. ^{md}utu-sig$_5$^{iq} *u* [^{md}en-gi ...]
7. 18 *ma-na* 15 gín k[ù.babbar *i-di* é.meš šub.me]
8. *šá ka-a-ri ù* mu[rub$_4$ uru ta iti.kin]
9. ⸢mu⸣.13.kam en iti.n[e mu.16.kam *šá*]
10. ^{lú}un.meš é *ina lìb-bi* [*áš-bu*]
11. 2 *ma-na* 9 gín *i-di* é.me[š ...]
12. *šá* mu.16.kam *šá it-t*[*i* ...]
13. ⸢5⸣2½ gín *i-di* é.[meš *šá ina muḫ-hi*]
14. íd ud.kib.nun^{ki} [...]
15. [x] ⸢x x⸣ [...]
Rest lost

Rev. 1'. [sum]⸢^{na}⸣ iti.ne [u]$_4$.⸢13⸣.kam m[u.16.kam]
2'. ^{d}ag-im.tuku lugal tin.tir[^{ki}]

Translation

1-6. ⌜9?⌝ shekel(s) [of silver, the rent of houses, property of Šamaš], which [was given] <for> *abattu* reed [...]. total 1 mina 11+[x shekels of silver ...] 31½ mi[nas of silver] of the settlement of account [which] Šamaš-mudammiq and [Bēl-ušallim have made….]

7-10. 18 minas 15 shekels of si[lver, the rent of houses], the ruined (located in) in the harbour district and (that) in the mid[dle of the city from month Ulūlu], 13th year to month Ab[u, 16th year] of the temple's servants who [are living] there.

11-13. 2 minas 9 shekels, the rent of houses [...] of the 16th year with [...] 52½ shekels, the rent from the houses (located) [on] the Euphrates [...].

1'-2'. Month Abu, 13th day, [16th] year of Nabonidus, king of Babylon.

99. BM 60407 (82-9-18, 375) = Str ii 348/2 Collated; Dar 10

Obv. 1. [....] ⌜x⌝ *mim-ma šá ri-ḫi*
2. [kù.babbar *šá* ^{m}*l*]*u*-ud.du-*a-na*-zálag *id**-din**-nu***
3. [mu].10.kam ^{m}*da-ri-šú* lugal ti[n.tir^{ki} *u* kur.kur]
One blank line
4. ⌜4?⌝ *ma-na* kù.babbar {⌜kù.babbar⌝} *gìn-nu ina*** šu^{ii}**
5. [x?] *ina ri-ḫi šá* ^{lú}sipa.meš
6. [*in*]*a lìb-bi* 5 *ma-na* kù.babbar *a-na* ki*.lam!* *šá*** gu$_4$**
7. *a-na* ^{m}ìr-^{d}en sum^{nu} 1 *ma-na* ⌜kù**.babbar⌝**
8. *a*-na** ki.lam uz.tur*^{mušen}* *a-na* ^{m}*la**-qip*** sum**
One blank line
9. [x]+1 *ma*-na** kù*.babbar* *šá gìn-nu ina ri-ḫi šá* ^{md}utu-kam*
10. ⌜m⌝*šá-du-nu* ^{lú}gal *bu-lu*** *ina** šu*$^{\text{ii*}}$ ^{m}*ina***-suḫ**-sur** a**^{m}mu**-*iá***
One blank line
11. 5 *ma-na* kù.babbar *šá gìn-nu* ^{m}[…]
12. *a-na* ^{m} ⌜ìr⌝-^{d}en sum[^{nu}]

Edge 13. [x *ma-na* kù.babbar] *šá gìn-nu*
14. [x x ^{m}*ri*]-*ḫi-tu*$_4$ a ^{md}en-dù
15. [x x x] ⌜x x⌝ *a-na*

Rev. 16. [^{m}]⌜ìr⌝-^{d}en sum^{nu}
One blank line
17. 2 *ma-na* kù.babbar *ina* šu^{ii} ^{m}*bul-ṭa**-a***
18. *u* ^{m}*ka**-ṣir*** *a-na i-di* giš*.má*
19. [la]m**.kur**.ru**^{ki}** *šá* šuku.ḫi.a
20. [x] ⌜giš x⌝ [x (x)] sum^{nu}
Blank space for a half line

21. [x x x] *ina* šu^{ii} ^{md}ag-⸢x x⸣
22. [x x ka]m$^{?}$ ⸢^{m}⸣bul**-ṭa**-a**it-ta-din
23. [x] ⸢x⸣ 1½ *ma-n*[*a*] kù.babbar *a-na* ki.lam$^{?}$
24. [x g]u$_{4}^{?}$ *a-n*[*a* ^{m}ìr]-^{d}en sum^{nu}
25. [x x] ⸢x x⸣ *šá* é** udu**.níta**
26. [x *ma*]-⸢*na* kù.babbar⸣ šám*35 kùr [x x]
27. [x x] ⸢x⸣ *ḫi* mu.10.kam *a-na*
28. [x x] sum**^{nu}** ^{md}ag*-mu*-du** ⸢x⸣
29. [x x] ⸢x x⸣ ½ *ma-na* kù.babbar

L.e. 30. ⸢x x x⸣ uz**.tur**^{mušen}** sum**^{nu}**

Notes

The tablet filled with earth is extremely difficult to read. It was collated by me and additionally by R. Tarasewicz. The result of our collations are marked with * (S.Z.) or with ** (R.T.)

L. 4. Taking into account l. 6 a larger sum is expected here, maybe [1]⸢4$^{?}$⸣.

Translation

1-3. […] everything of remainder [of silver which] has been giv[en] by [L]ūṣi-ana-nūri. The tenth year of Darius, king of Bab[ylon, king of Lands].

4-7. ⸢4$^{?}$⸣ minas of silver with *ginnu*-mark from […] from the remainder of the shepherds, in it 5 minas for purchase of bulls was given to Arad-Bēl.

7-8. 1 mina of sliver for purchase of ducks was given to Lāqīpu.

9-10. [x]+1 minas of silver with *ginnu*-mark from the remainder of Šamaš-ēreš (for$^{?}$) Šadûnu, the overseer of the herds, by Ina-tēšê-ēṭir, descendant of Šumaia.

11-12. 5 mina of silver with *ginnu*-mark [PN] has given to Arad-Bēl.

13-16. [x mina of silver] with *ginnu*-mark [which Rē]ḫētu, son of Bēl-ibni […] has given to Arad-Bēl.

17-20. 2 minas of silver from Bulṭā and Kāṣir for the wages for boot (to) Bāṣ (and$^{?}$) provision […] was given.

21-22. […] from Nabû-[…to?] Bulṭā has been given.

23-25. […]+$^{?}$ 1½ minas of silver for purchase$^{?}$ [… of ox]en was given t[o Arad]-Bēl.

26-28. […] of the sheep shed. [x mi]na, the price of 35 *kurru* [… …] of the tenth year was given to [PN] […] Nabû-šum-ukīn […]

29-30. […] ½ mina of silver [for ...] ducks was given.

100. Cyr 1 = BM 60744 (82-9-18, 718) Collated by Radosław Tarasewicz; [x].VII.Cyr 0

Obv. 1. 6 udu.níta *ina* šu^{ii} ^{md}en-gi a-*šu šá* ^{md}⸢utu*-pap*-a*⸣
2. *a-na* 8 gín 4-*tú* kù.babbar *i-na* kù.babbar
3. *šá i-di* é.meš* *a-na é-babbar-ra*
4. *it-ta-din* 5 udu.níta *šá* ^{m}*ka-ṣir*
5. a-*šu šá* ^{md}en-mu *a-na* 7 gín 4-*tú*
6. kù.babbar *šá muḫ-ḫi dul-lu* ^{m}mu-mu
7. *ú-šá-ḫi-zu a-na lìb-bi* sum^{na}
8. 1 udu.níta *a-na* 1 gín 4-*tú* kù.[babbar]

Rev. 9. *ina* šu^{ii} ^{md}utu-ba$^{šá!}$ [...]
10. 1 [udu.ní]ta *šá* ^{m}*du*-[...]
11. *a-n*[*a* x]+$^{?}$1 gín kù*.babbar*[...]
12. pap [x udu.níta.me]š ⸢x x⸣ [...]
13. ⸢x⸣ [.......................................]
14. iti.du$_{6}$ ⸢u$_{4}$⸣.[x.kam] mu.sag.nam.lugal.la
15. ^{m}*ku-ra-áš* lugal tin.tir^{ki} *u* kur.kur

Translation

6 sheep valued 8¼ shekels of silver from the silver from the rent of houses [...] which Bēl-ušallim, son Šamaš-nāṣir-apli, has delivered to the Ebabbar.

5 sheep which Kāṣir, son of Bēl-iddin gave for 7¼ shekels of silver, which he had owed to Šum-iddin for the work done.

1 sheep valued 1¼ shekels of sil[ver] from Šamaš-iqīša [(...)]

1 [she]ep which Du/Mukīn-[...] for [x]+1 shekel(s) of silver [...], total [x shee]p [...].

Month Tašrītu, [x] day, the accession year of Cyrus, king of Babylon and Lands.

101. BM 63967 (82-9-18, 3936) = Bertin 1328 Collated; Nbn 7

Obv. 1. [...] ⸢*i*⸣-*di* ká-íd-^{d}utu
2. [... *dul*]-*lu šá ḫar-ri na-šá-a*
3. [...] ⸢^{m}⸣^{d}utu-su ^{lú}*si-pir**
4. [...]-ba^{šá} ^{lú}uš.bar
5. [...] mu.6.kam
6. [...] ⸢x⸣
Rest lost

Rev. 1'. [...] ⸢^{m}⸣*gi-mil*-⸢*lu*⸣
2'. [...] ^{md}utu-sipa-*ú-a*
3'. [...] gín kù.babbar

4’. [... *i-di*] ⸢é⸣.meš *šá* ká-íd-^{d}utu
5’. [...] ⸢mu⸣.7.kam ^{md}ag-i
6’. [lugal tin.ti]r^{ki}

Notes

L. 3. See Bongenaar 1997, 53, s.v. Šamaš-erība.

Translation

Obv. [...] from Bāb-nār-Šamaš [... w]ork on canal [...] was brought.
[...] Šamaš-erība, the interpreter scribe
[...]-iqīša, the weaver
[...], the sixth year

Rev. [...] Gimillu
[...] Šamaš-rē’ûa
[... x] shekels of silver
[... the rent] of houses from Bāb-nār-Šamaš
[...] seventh year of Nabonidus, [king of Babyl]on.

102. BM 101573 (83-1-21, 3234) Not copied; 4. 2 x 3.0 cm; 15.[x].Nbk [x]

Obv. 1. 2 gin kù.babbar [...]
2. *a-na i-di* ⸢é⸣.[meš ...]
3. *a-na qur-ru-bu*
4. ⸢*šá a*⸣*-gur-ru a-na*
5. [^{md}]ag-du-ibila sum^{na}
Edge 6. [x x x kù]r *a-bat-tu*$_4$
Rev. 7. [x x x]-⸢*i*⸣*-ri*
8. [x x x] ⸢*me*⸣*-lu-tu*$_4$
9. [x x x]-⸢šeš⸣-mu ^{lú}šitim sum^{na}
10. [x x x] ⸢*a*$^{?}$⸣*-na* ^{md}utu-[...]
11. ⸢x x⸣ [...]
L.e. 12. u$_4$.15.k[am mu.x.kam]
13. [^{m}]⸢^{d}ag-níg⸣.[du-ùru lugal]
L.h.e. 14. tin.tir^{ki}

Notes

L. 9. The reading of the title is the result of join collation by I. Finkel and R. Tarasewicz.

Translation

2 shekels of silver [...] for the rent of houses were given to Nabû-mukīn-apli for delivery of baked bricks.
... *abattu* reeds

[… DN]-aḫ-iddin, the builder was given
[…] to Šamaš-[…]
[…]
[Month x], 15th day, [year x] of Nebucha[dnezzar, king of] Babylon.

103. BM 71880 (82-9-18, 11383); 2.65 x 2.6 cm

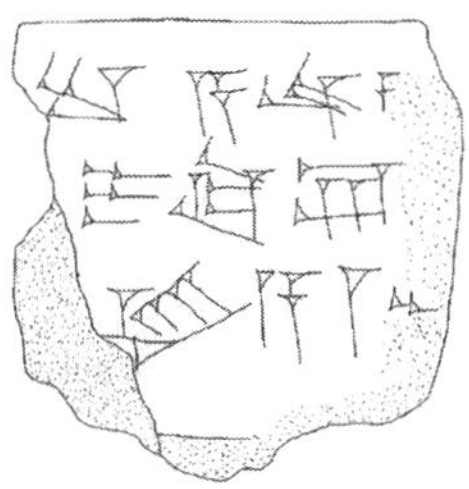

Obv. 1'. [x *ma*]-*na a-na* ⸢x⸣ […]
2'. […] *i-di* é.[meš …]
3'. […]-gi *a* m⸢d⸣ [….]
4'. [….] ⸢x⸣ […]

Translation
[x mi]na(s) for […] the rent of houses […].

104. BM 76469 (83-1-18, 1837); *4.3* x *4.8* cm

1'. […]⸢x⸣ *šá* ⸢*ina* ugu x⸣ […]
2'. […].⸢2⸣.kam *šá* iti.kin […]
3'. [….tin.t]irki en ⸢x⸣ […]
4'. […*š*]*á*? mdutu-ú-*š*[*e-zib* …]
5'. […]-*pu šá* ug[u …]
6'. […]-*ni-ip*-[...]

7’. [... x] gín kù.babbar *ri-ḫi šá* [...]
8’. [... lug]al tin.tir[$^{ki\ ...}$]
9’. [... g]ín kù.babbar *i-di* [é ...]
10’.[...] ⸢*na*⸣ *šá* é [...]

Translation

Too fragmentary to be translated.

105. BM 76536 (83-1-18,1907); 5.3 x 4.7 cm; Nrg 3

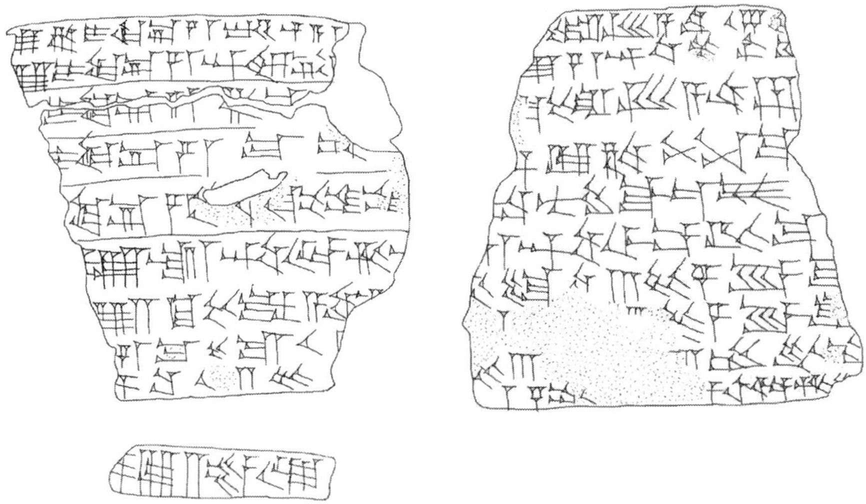

1. [x g]ín kù.babbar *i-di* é *šá* ^{md}en-sur a^{m}[...]
2. [x] ⸢gín⸣ *i-di* é *šá* ^{md}im-*ga-*[*mil* ...]
3. [x gín] *i-di* é *šá* ^{m}⸢*ḫa-ba*⸣-[*ṣi-ru* ...]
4. [x gín] ⸢*i*⸣-*di* é *šá* ^{m}*ba-*⸢*ga*$^{?}$⸣-[...]
5. [x gín *i*]-*di* é *šá* ^{f}⸢x-*di*⸣-*bi-tu*$_4$ *ép-*[*šú*$^{?}$...]
6. ⸢x⸣ gín *ina* šu^{ii} ^{md}utu-sig^{iq} ⸢x⸣ [...]
7. [x] gín 2 túg.kur.ra.<meš> *a-na* ⸢x⸣ [...]
8. [x x] ⸢*šá*⸣ ^{m}*ba-laṭ-su u* m [...]
9. [iti.bá]r$^{?}$ u$_4$.10+[x]+2.kam [...]

Edge 10. [x x] ⸢⅓⸣ gín 2 ká *ù* [...]

Rev. 11. [x túg.k]ur.ra.meš *a-na* 15 ⸢x⸣ [...]
12. [x g]ín *šá* ^{md}utu-⸢mu⸣-dù ⸢x⸣ [...]
13. [x] túg.kur.ra.meš *a-na* ⅚ [*ma-na*]
14. [x] ½$^{?}$ gín kù.babbar pap.pap 1 *ma-*[*na* kù.babbar]
15. [^{m}*šá*]-*du-nu* ^{lú}gal giš.ban
16. [*ina* šu^{i}]^{i} ^{md}utu-sig^{iq} *ma-*[*ḫir*]

17. [*u*]*l-tu* u$_4$.3.kam *šá* iti.b[ár$^?$]
18. [*a-di* u$_4$.x]+⸢3$^?$⸣.kam *šá* iti.⸢bár⸣
19. [m]u.3.[kam ^{md}u+gu]r-lugal-ùru lug[al e^{ki}]
20. ^{m}*šá-du-*⸢*nu*⸣ [*ina* šu$^{ii\ m}$]⸢^{d}⸣utu-sig^{iq} s[um$^?$]

Transaltion

1. [x] shekel(s) of silver, the rent of houses of Bēl-ēṭir, son of […]
2. [x] shekel(s), the rent of houses of Adad-ga[mil …] [x]
3. [x] shekel(s), the rent of houses of Ḫaba[ṣīru …]
4. [x] shekel(s), the rent of houses of Baga[…]
5. [x] shekel(s), the rent of houses which is m[ade$^?$ with ^{f}…]
6. ⸢x⸣ shekel(s), the rent of houses which Šamaš-udammiq […]
7. [x] shekel(s), (the price of) 2 kur.ra-garments for […]

8-9. [….] which Balāssu and [PN. Month Nisan]nu?, day 12+[x…]

10. […] ⸢20⸣ shekels, second installment and […]
11. [x] kur.ra-garments for 15 […]
12. [x she]kels which Šamaš-šum-ibni […]

13-18. [x] kur.ra-garments for 50 [shekels (and) x] + ½ shekels of silver, grand total 1 mi[na of silver] Šadûnu, the chief of bowmen has rece[ived from] Šamaš-udammiq. From the third day of month Ni[sannu$^?$ till x] + 3? day of month Nisannu, third ye[ar of Neri]glissar, king [of Babylon] Šadûnu [has received] [from] Šamaš-udammiq.

106. BM 72248 (82-9-18, 12254); 2.9 x 5.2 cm

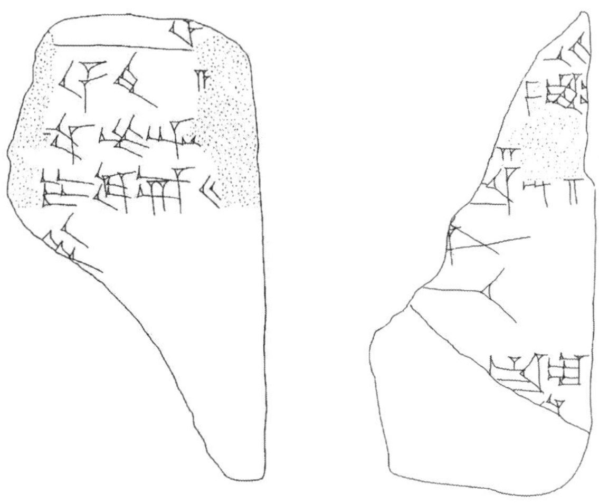

U.e. 1. [...] šuku.[ḫi.a]

Obv. 2. [...] šuku.ḫi.a

3. [...] ⸢x⸣ mu.an.n[a.meš]

4. [...] ⌜x⌝ *i-di* é. m[eš?
5. [....].⌜kam⌝

Rev. 1'. [......... *i*]*q*
2'. [...] ⌜x⌝ *it-t*[*a-din*]
3'. [.........]⌜x⌝
4'. [...] ⌜x⌝-*an-ni*
5'. [...]-dù
6'. [...] ⌜x⌝
7'. [...]-*da-ad*
8'. [...] ⌜x⌝

Notes

L. 3. The first partly preserved sign is probably *ta.*

What survives is too small to be translated.

6.6 Texts not edited

BM 60624 = Janković 2004, no. 11 (1 mina from the house rent for purchase of ducks).

BM 65024 = Zawadzki 2013, no. 641 (5 shekels from the house rent for an allowance (*pappassu*) of the weaver.

BM 74411 = Bloch 2014, no. 5. An administrative document enumerating silver taken from different sources for purchase of gold. The names of two house tenants Ana-[x x x] (who has paid 10 shekels) and Šamaš-iddin (who has paid 10 shekels) are preserved.

Nbn 439 = BM 75584 = Zawadzki 2013, no. 570 (7 shekels of silver from the house rent located inside the city (*qabal āli*).

Cyr 218: 7-8 (1/3 *ma-na* kù.babbar/ta kù.babbar *šá i-di* é.meš, "20 shekels of silver, from silver, the rent of the houses,") followed by badly preserved lines.

CT 57, 136 and 137 and 422 might be the fragments of list of tenants' payments for the rented houses, but it is not certain.

6.7 Contracts between private people

107. BM 83538 (83-1-21, 701); *4.3 x 3.3* cm; 20.˹XII$^{?}$˺.Nbk 31 Sippar

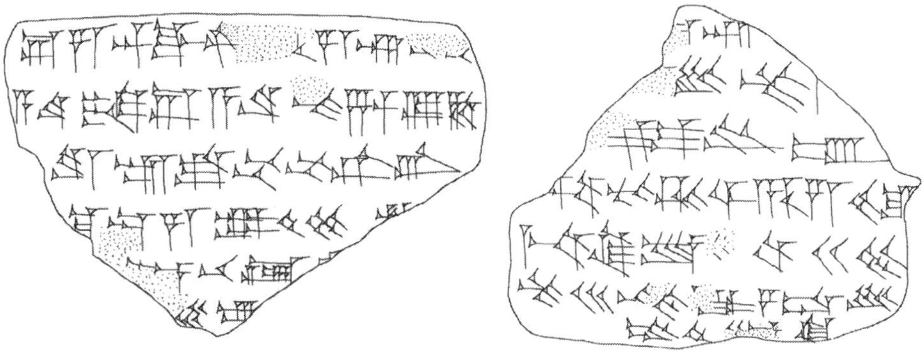

Obv. 1. é *šá* ^{m}an.gal-˹dù˺ [a]-*šú šá* ^{md}*mùš*-[*da-bi*]-[*bi-ni-ir*]
2. *a-na i-di* é *a-na* mu 5½ gín kù.babbar
3. [*a*]-*na* ^{md}mùš-*da-bi-bi-ni-ir*
4. [^{lú}]*qal-la šá* ^{md}ag-tin-kam *i*[*t-ta-din*]
5. [*bat-qa i-ṣ*]*ab*$^{!}$-*bat* ùr.m[eš ...]
6. [x x x x] ˹x *ú*˺ [...]
Rest missing

Rev. 1'. [x x x x] ˹x˺ ^{md}˹x˺ [...]
2'. [x x x x]-šeš-mu ^{m}[...]
3'. [a ^{m}*e*]*ri*$_{4}$-*ba* ^{lú}šid
4'. [^{m}]^{d}utu-numun-gál^{ši} a-*šú šá* ^{m}tin^{su}
5'. *sip-par*^{ki} iti.˹še$^{?}$˺ u$_{4}$.20.kam
6'. mu.31.kam ^{md}ag-níg.du-ùru
7'. lugal tin.tir^{ki}

Notes

L. 1 For the reading an.gal as Ištarān see Otten 1976-1980, 221. The reading ˹dù˺ I owe to I. Finkel. It cannot be excluded that one additional sign appeared in the damaged space, i.e. Ištarān-bān-[x a]-*šú šá*...

Ištar-dabībi-nīri, "O Ištar-Kill-my-Adversary". For similar nB names with Aššur and Nabû, see CAD D 9. The same person occurs as the second witness in Nbk 438 (BM 75194): 13-14 in a loan contract of barley. The debtor is Nabû-ušēzib, son of Nabû-balāṭu-ēreš, maybe the owner of Ištar-dabībi-nīri. It might explain there the presence of slave as witness which happened extremely seldom (Jursa 2005, 12, n. 55).

Rev. 4'. It is possible that Šamaš-zēr-ušabši, son of Balāssu appears also as the scribe of Nbn 205: 12-13 ^{lú}šid ^{md}utu-numun-gál^{ši}/a-*šú šá* ^{m}[tin-*s*]*u*, written 22.X.Nbn 5 (554 BC) in Āl-Šamaš. If it is really the same person, it means that he was active as a scribe at least 35 years.

Translation

The house which Ištarān-ibni(?), son of Ištar-dab[ībi-nīri] leas[ed] to Ištar-dabībi-nīri, the slave of Nabû-balāṭu-ēreš for 5½ shekels of silver yearly.

[He will c]arry out [the repairs, the beam(s)....]

[DN]-aḫ-iddin, [

[PN, son/descendant of E]rība.

The scribe Šamaš-zēr-ušabši, son of Balāssu.

Sippar, month Addaru$^{?}$, 20th day, 31th year of Nebuchadnezzar, king of Babylon.

108. BM 67913 (82-9-18, 7911); 3.7 x 3.9 cm; 10.II.Nbk [x] Sippar

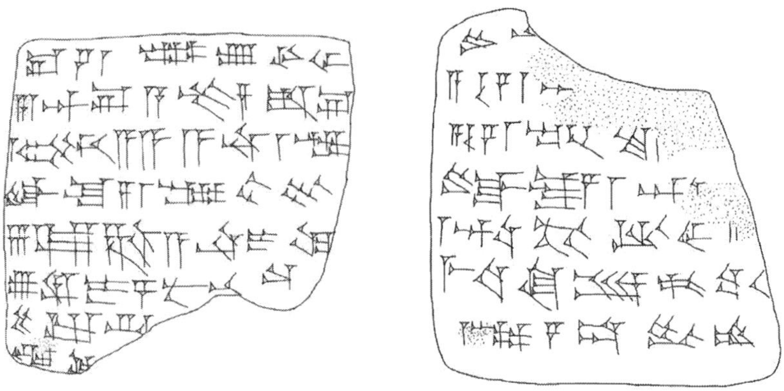

Obv. 1. é *šá* ^{md}ag-*ú-šal-lim* [...]
2. a ^{md}*é-a*-mu *šá* da é [...]
3. ^{m}*mi-ṣir-a-a a-na* ^{md}ag-[...]
4. ^{lú}*qal-la šá* ^{md}ag-tin-kam [*id-din ina* mu.an.na]
5. 6 gín kù.babbar *a-na* ⸢*i-di*⸣ [é *i-nam-din*]
6. *ú-ru i-šá-nu bat-qa* [...]
7. *še-eb-ri* [...]
8. *ù ṭi-*[*iṭ* é *gab-bi i-šak-kan*]
Rest lost

Rev. 1'. ^{lú}*m*[*u-kin-nu* ...]
2'. a-*šú šá* $^{m⸢d⸣}$[...]
3'. a-*šú šá* ^{md}en-ka[r-zi.meš ...]
4'. ^{lú}*qal-la šá* $^{md⸢}$x⸣-[...]
5'. ^{md}utu-numun-gál^{ši} ⸢a⸣-[...]

6'. *sip-par*^{ki} iti.gu$_{4}$ u$_{4}$.10.[kam mu.x.kam]
7'. ^{md}ag-níg.du-ùru lugal [...]

Notes

L. 6ff. Presumably *batqa* was followed – as usually – by [*šá a-sur-ru-ú i-ṣab-bat*]; however, it is uncertain what follows *še-eb-ri* in the next line.

L. 7 is reconstructed on the basis of no. 9 (BM 114472): 8.

Rev. 4'. The slave as witness is unusual.

Translation

A house of Nabû-ušallim, [son of ....], descendant of Ea-iddin, adjacent to the house of [......., descendant of] Miṣiraya, [rented to] Nabû-[...], the slave of Nabû-balāssu-ēreš. [He will pay] 6 shekels of silver as rent [yearly]. He will seal the roof, [repair] the damages [of wall footing ....] damages [...] and [cover whole house with cl]ay [...].

Wit[nesses:
[...], son of [...]
[...], son of Bēl-ēṭi[r-napšāte , the slave of [...]
Šamaš-zēr-ušabši, son$^{?}$ [...]
Sippar, month Ayaru, 10th, [x year of] Nebuchadnezzar, [king of Babylon].

109. VS 5, 23 (VAT 4075), NRV 113; 9.II.Nbn 4 Borsippa

Obv. 1. é *šá* ^{md}ag-du-a a-*šú šá* ^{m}tin^{su} a ^{m}en-*iá-ú*
2. *a-di ṭup-pi-šú* ^{m}*ri-mut* a-*šú šá*
3. ^{m}*e-tel-lu* a ^{md}30-*šá-du-nu* ^{m}en-*šú-nu*
4. a-*šú šá* ^{m}*bul-ṭa-a a* ^{m}lú-^{d}idim *ina lìb-bi*
5. *áš-bu-' ina* mu.an.na 10 gín kù.babbar
6. *i-di* é ^{m}*re-mu-tu u* ^{m}en-*šú-nu*
7. *a-na* ^{md}ag-du-a *i-nam-di-nu-'*
8. iti-*us-su i-di* é *i-nam-di-nu-'*
9. *i-di* é *šá la* ^{f}*qu-un-na-ba-tu*$_{4}$

Edge 10. *a-na* ^{d}ag-du-a *ul i-nam-di-nu-'*

Rev. 11. <*ba*>*-at-qu šá a-sur-ru-ú i-ṣab-ba-tu-'*
12. *ú-ru i-šá-an-nu* ½ gín kù.babbar *nu-up-tu*$_{4}$
13. *šá u*$_{4}$*-mu* ^{d}en *u ki-na-a-a-ta i-nam-di-nu-'*
14. ^{lú}*mu-kin-nu* ^{md}ag-*it-tan-nu* a-*šú šá* ^{m}tin^{su}
15. a ^{m}*é-sag-gil-man-sì* ^{md}amar.utu-su a-*šú šá* ^{md}u+gur-pap
16. a ^{m}*é-sag-gil-man-sì* ^{md}en-sur a-*šú šá*
17. ^{md}ag-du-a a ^{lú}*ma-qar-tu*$_{4}$
18. ^{m}*re-mut* a-*šú šá* ^{md}ag-en-dingir.meš a ^{lú}sanga ^{d}im
19. ^{lú}šid ^{md}utu-numun-ba^{šá} a ^{m}*si-iá-a-tú*

20. *bar-sip*^{ki} iti.gu$_4$ u$_4$.9.kam mu.4.kam
21. ^{md}ag-i lugal tin.tir^{ki} ta u$_4$.14.kam
22. *šá* iti.gu$_4$ é *ina* igi-*šú-nu*

Translation

The house of Nabû-mukīn-apli, son of Balāssu, descendant of Bēliyā'u, Rēmūt, son of Etellu, descendant of Sîn-Šadûnu (and) Bēlšunu, son of Bulṭā, descendant of Amēl-Ea live in it for one year. Rēmūt (and) Bēlšunu will pay to Nabû-mukīn-apli 10 shekels of silver yearly.

They will pay rent monthly. They do not pay the rent to Nabû-mukīn-apli without (the presence of) ^{f}Qunnabatu.

They will repair (the cracks) of the wall footing and seal the roof. They will pay half shekel of silver, for the day of Enlil and *kīnajātu*-offerings.

Witnesses:
Nabû-ittannu, son of Balāssu, descendant of Esagila-mansî
Marduk-erība, son of Nergal-nāṣir, descendant of *Esagila-mansî
Bēl-ēṭir, son of Nabû-mukīn-apli, descendant of Maqartu
Rēmūt, son of Nabû-bēl-ilāni, descendant of Šangû-Adad
The scribe, Šamaš-zēr-iqīša, descendant of Si'ātu
Borsippa, month Ayāru, eighth day, fourth year of Nabonidus, king of Babylon.
From the 14th day of the month Ayāru the house is at their disposal.

110. BM 65313 (82-9-18, 5298); 5.7 x 4.5 cm; 7.XI.Nbn 8 Babylon

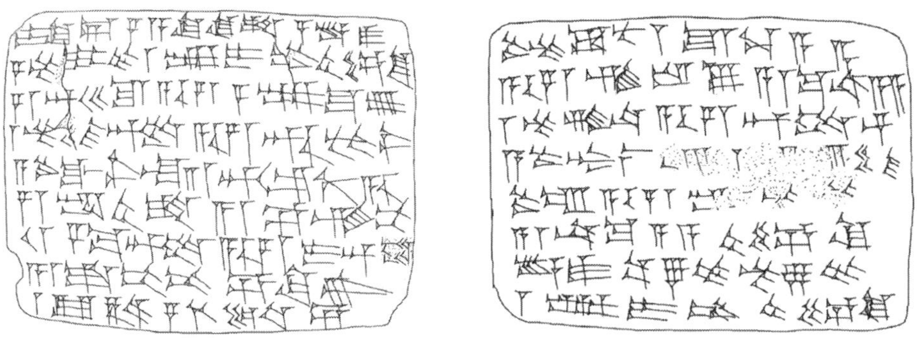

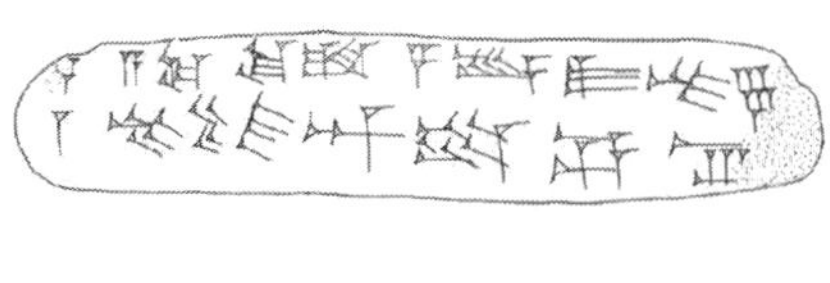

Obv. 1. *i-di* é *šá a-di qí-it šá* iti.zíz
2. *šá* mu.8.kam ^{md}ag-i lugal tin.tir^{ki}
3. *šá* ^{md}30-su a-*šú šá* ^{m}*šá*-^{d}ag-*šú-ú*
4. ^{m}*mu-še-zib*-^{d}amar.utu a-*šú šá* ^{md}šú-numun-dù
5. a ^{lú}gal.dù *ina* šu^{ii} ^{md}u+gur-pap a-*šú*
6. *šá* ^{md}en-tin^{it} a ^{m}*e-gi-bi*
7. *u* ^{m}níg.ba-^{d}amar.utu a-*šú šá* ^{md}i-amar.utu
8. a ^{m}*da-bi-bi e-ṭi-ir*
9. 1 gín kù.babbar *šá ḫaš-li-e*

Edge 10. ⸢*šá*⸣ *a-di qí-it šá* iti.zíz mu.⸢8⸣.[kam]
11. ^{m}*mu-še-zib*-^{d}amar.utu *e*-⸢*ṭir*⸣

Rev. 12. ^{lú}*mu-kin-nu* ^{m}*su-qa-a-a*
13. a-*šú šá* ^{m}*gi-mil-lu* a ^{m}*na-ba-a-na-a*
14. ^{m}mu-gi^{na} a-*šú šá* ^{md}amar.utu-sur
15. a ^{lú}gír.lá ⸢*ù* ^{md}x-*ú*⸣-*še-zib*
16. ^{lú}šid a-*šú šá* ^{md}⸢ag-mu-mu⸣
17. a ^{m}*na-ba-a-na-a* tin.tir^{ki}
18. iti.zíz u$_{4}$.7.kam mu.8.kam
19. ^{md}ag-i lugal tin.tir^{ki}

Notes

L. 9. *kaspu ḫašlu* is – according to my knowledge – not noted before. Cf. CAD Ḫ 141. s.v. *ḫašlu*, "crushed". The meaning might be distinct from *šibirtu* denoting silver in blocks or lumps. The meaning "silver scrap" may be suggested on the basis of content of hoard from Babylon (Reade 1986, 84-85).

L. 12. Presumably Gimillu, father of Sūqaya is mentioned in VS 4, 25 = NRV 298, Baker 2004, no. 1: 4 (16.IX.Nbk 35) as the owner of a house.

L. 15. Maybe ^{d}⸢en⸣, but only traces are preserved and the reading is uncertain.

Translation

The rent of the house till the end of month Šabāṭu, the eighth year of Nabonidus, king of Babylon, which is paid to Sîn-erība son of Ša-Nabû-šū (and) Mušēzib-Marduk, son Marduk-zēr-ibni, descendant of Rab-banê by Nergal-nāṣir, son of Bēl-uballiṭ, descendant of Egibi and Qišti-Marduk, son of Na'id-Marduk, descendant of Dābibī.

1 shekel of silver scrap is paid to Mušēzib-Marduk till the end of the month Šabāṭu.

Witnesses:
Sūqaya, son of Gimillu, descendant of Bānaya
Šum-ukīn, son Marduk-ēṭir, descendant of Ṭābiḫu
And [DN]-ušēzib, the scribe, son of Nabû-šum-iddin, descendant of Dābibī
Babylon, month Šabāṭu, seventh day, eighth year of Nabonidus, king of Babylon.

111. Nbn 499 (76-11-16, 182); 1.II.Nbn 11, Babylon

Obv. 1. é *a-su-up-pu* é *ka-a-ri*
2. *šá* ^{lú}mu *šá* ^{m}*šu-uš-ra-an-ni-*^{d}amar.utu
3. a-*šú šá* ^{md}amar.utu-mu-ùru a ^{md}im-mu-kam
4. ^{m}*šá-rid* ad ad *šá* ^{m}*šu-uš-ra-an-ni-*^{d}amar.utu
5. *a-na* u_4*-mu* 2 sìla *a-ka-lu*
6 *a-na i-di-šú a-na* ^{md}en-*ṣu-li-e-ši-me*
7. ^{lú}*qal-la šá* ^{md}ag-šeš.meš-mu
8. a ^{m}*e-gi-bi id-din ul-tu*
9. u_4.2.kam *šá* iti.gu_4 *ka-a-*[*ri*]
10. *ina* igi ^{md}en-*ṣu-li-e-ši-me*

Rev. 11. ^{lú}*mu-kin-nu* ^{md}ag-kam a-*šú šá*
12. ^{m}*tab-ni-e-a* a ^{m}ur-^{d}šeš.ki
13. ^{m}*la-a-ba-ši* a-*šú šá* ^{m}numun-*ia*
14. a ^{m}*na-ba-a-a* ^{lú}šid ^{m}*šá-rid*
15. a ^{md}u+gur-*na-ṣir* a ^{md}im-mu-kam
16. tin.tir^{ki} iti.gu_4 u_4.1.kam
17. mu.11.kam ^{md}ag-i lugal
18. tin.tir^{ki} *ḫu-uṣ-ṣu šá it-ti*
19. é *ka-a-ri di-bu-ú*

L.e. 20. *ina* igi ^{md}en-*ṣu-li-e-ši-me*

Translation

The outbuilding (of) the *kāru*-storehouse of the baker, belonging to Šušranni-Marduk, son of Marduk-šum-iddin, descendant of Adad-šum-ēreš, Šārid, the grandfather of Šušranni-Marduk rented it out to Bēl-ṣulle-šeme, the slave of Nabû-aḫḫē-iddin, descendant of Egibi for 2 *qû* of bread daily.

From the second day of Ayāru the *kāru*-storehouse is at disposal of Bēl-ṣulle-šeme.

Witnesses:
Nabû-ēreš, son of Tabnēa, descendant of Kalbi-Nergal
Lābāši, son of Zēriya, descendant of Nabaya
The scribe, Šārid, son of Nergal-nāṣir, descendant of Adad-šum-ēreš.
Babylon, month Ayāru, first day, 11th year of Nabonidus, king of Babylon.
The reed hut with *kāru*-storehouse with door-boards is at disposal of Bēl-ṣulle-šeme.

112. Nbn 500 (76-11-17, 674) = BM 30947 Collated; 2.II.Nbn 11 Babylon

Obv. 1. é *šá ina* sag.du *gi-iš-ri šá bar*-sip**^{ki*}
2. *šá* ^{m}*it-ti-*^{d}amar.utu-tin a-*šú šá* ^{md}ag-šeš.meš-mu
3. a ^{m}*e-gi-bi a-na i-di* é *a-na*

4. mu.an.na ½ *ma-na* 5 gín kù.babbar *a-na*
5. ^{m}*ki-na-a* a-*šú šá* ^{m}dingir-*dan-a-ni*-^{d}*gu-la*
6. a ^{lú}sanga ^{d}*gu-la id-din* iti-a_4
7. ⸢kù*⸣.babbar* *i-di* é *a-na* ^{m}ki-^{d}amar.utu-tin *i-nam-din*
8. *ú-ru i-šá-an-nu bat-qa šá a-sur-ru-ú*
9. [*i*]-*ṣa-ba-at dul-lu* sig_4.ḫi.a

Rev. 10. gi gušur *ma-la ina lìb-bi ip-pu-uš*

11. *a-na* ugu ^{m}ki-^{d}amar.utu-tin *i-man-an-nu*
12. *ina* mu.an.na 2 <^{gi}>*si**-*li**-*e šá* 1 sìla-a_4
13. *ta-bi-lu i-nam-din a-di**-*i ṭup-pi-šú* é *ina* igi-*šú*
14. ^{lú}*mu-kin-nu* ^{m}*na-din* a-*šú šá* ^{m}*mu-še-zib*-^{d}en
15. a ^{lú}ìr-$^{d}gir_4$.kù ^{m}*re-mut*-^{d}utu
16. a-*šú šá* ^{m}*mu-še-zib*-^{d}šú a ^{m}du^{eš}-dingir
17. ^{md}ag-*ú-ṣur-šú*** a-*šú šá* ^{m}*ba-la-ṭu* a ^{m}*mi-ṣir-a-a*
18. ^{lú}šid ^{m}*la-a-ba-ši* a-*šú šá* ^{m}numun-*ia*
19. a ^{m}*na-ba-a-a* tin.tir^{ki} iti.gu_4

L.e. 20. u_4.2.kam mu.11.<kam> ^{md}ag-i lugal tin.tir^{ki}

21. [*ul*]-*tu* u_4.2.kam *šá* iti.gu_4
22. é ** *ina*** igi**-*šú***

Notes

L. 1. The same house (é *šá* sag.du *gi-iš-ri šá bár-sipa*^{ki}) occurs later in Dar 379: 12 (Dar 14, 508 BC), inherited by Marduk-nāṣir-apli, the oldest son of Itti-Marduk-balāṭu. A house located at the head of the bridge (é *šá* sag.du *gi-iš-ri*) occurs also in Dar 64: 1 (Dar 3 – 519 BC). In this text which is written in Borsippa, the description *ša barsip* is omitted and the house is rented by Marduk-nāṣir-apli. This suggests that this house is not the same as that mentioned in Nbn 500 and Dar 378, which in 545 BC till the death of Itti-Marduk-balāṭu was in his possession. After the division of inheritance in 508 BC Marduk-nāṣir-apli owned presumably two houses located near the bridge of Borsippa.

L. 22 is missing in the copy of Strassmaier (collated by R. Tarasewicz, marked with **).

Translation

The house at the head of the bridge of Borsippa, which Itti-Marduk-balāṭu, son of Nabû-aḫḫē-iddin, descendant of Egibi rented it out to Kīnā, son of Ilu-danani-Gula, descendant of Šangû-Gula for 5 shekels of silver. He will pay silver as the house rent monthly to Itti-Marduk-balāṭu. He will seal the roof (and) repair (the cracks) of the wall footing. The work on bricks, reed(s) and beams, as much as he carries out on it, are charged against Itti-Marduk-balāṭu. Yearly he will deliver two *sellu* baskets of herbs, each of 1 *qû*. For one year the house is at his disposal.

Witnesses:
Nādin, son of Mušēzib-Bēl, descendant of Arad-Nergal
Rēmūt-Šamaš, son of Mušēzib-Marduk, descendant of Eppeš-ilī
Nabû-uṣuršu, son of Balāṭu, descendant of Miṣiraya
The scribe, Lābāši, son of Zēriya, descendant of Nabaya.
Babylon, month Ayāru, second day, 11th year of Nabonidus, king of Babylon.
[Fr]om the second day of Ayāru the house is in his disposal.

113. BM 65288 (82-9-18, 5273); 5.1 x 3.2 cm; 27.VIII.Nbn 11

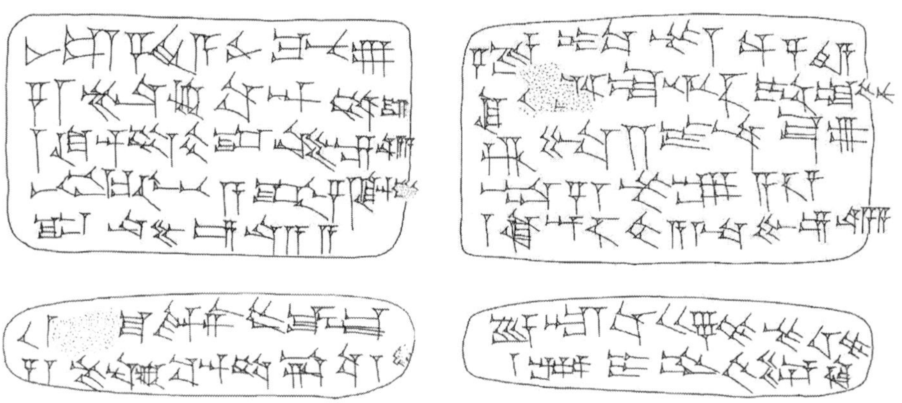

Obv. 1. 1 kùr ninda.ḫi.a *bab-ba-nu-ú*
2. *šá* ^{m}*mu-na-aḫ-ḫiš*-^{d}amar.utu dumu ⸢*šá*⸣
3. ^{m}ki-^{d}amar.utu-tin a ^{m}*na-bu-un-na-a-a*
4. *ina* ugu ^{f}be-*a* dumu.mí *šá* ^{m}ki-^{d}amar.utu-t[in]
5. dumu ^{m}*na-bu-un-na-a-a*
Edge 6. *u* ^{m}[^{d}DN]-*šu-zib-an-ni* ^{lú}*qal-la*
7. *šá* ^{m}*mu-na-aḫ-ḫiš*-^{d}amar.utu ta u$_4$.1.⸢kam⸣
Rev. 8. *šá* iti.gan *u*$_4$*-mu* 1 sìla ninda.ḫi.a
9. ki ⸢*man-da*⸣*-at-ti-šú i-na-ad-din-nu*
10. 1^{en} *pu-ut* 2^{i} *na-šu-ú*
11. *ina* gub<^{zu}> *šá* ^{m}mu-^{d}ag a-*šú šá*
12. ^{m}ki-^{d}amar.utu-tin a ^{m}*na-bu-un-na-a-a*
L.e. 13. iti.apin u$_4$.27.kam mu.11.kam
14. ^{md}ag-i lugal tin.tir^{ki}

Translation

1 *kurru* of good quality bread owed to Munaḫḫiš-Marduk, son of Itti-Marduk-balāṭu, descendant of Nabunnaya, charged against ^{f}Kabtiya, the daughter of Itti-Marduk-balāṭu, descendant of Nabunnaya and [DN]-šūzibanni, the slave of Munaḫḫiš-Marduk.

From the first day of Kislīmu they will deliver (him) 1 *qû* of bread together with a compensatory payment.

One bears responsibility for the other.

In the presence of Iddin-Nabû, son of Itti-Marduk-balāṭu, descendant of Nabunnaya.

Month Araḫsamna, 27th day, 11th year of Nabonidus, king of Babylon.

114. BM 77677 (84-2-11, 423); *4.4* x *3.1* cm; 10.VI.[Nbn] 17

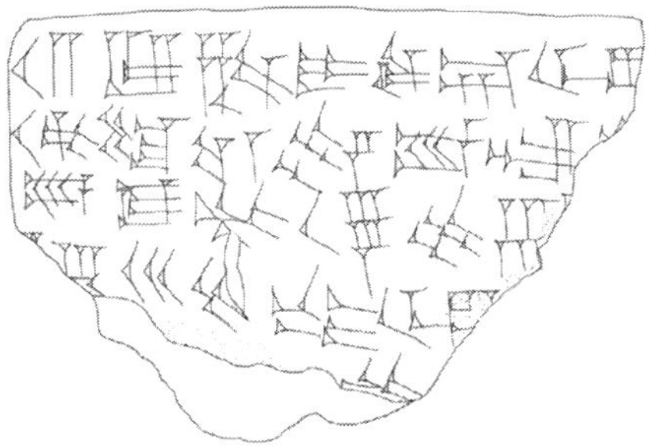

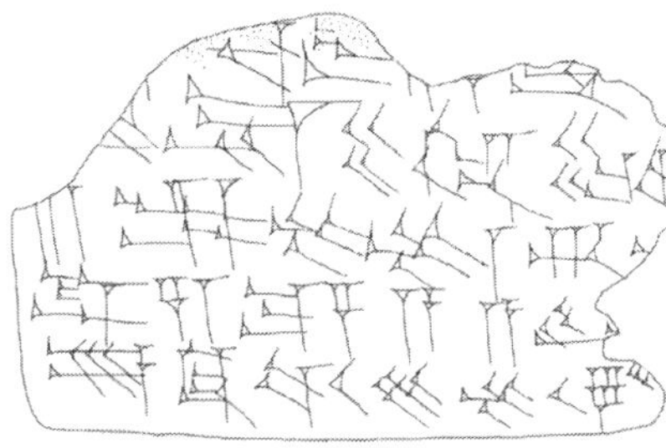

Obv. 1. 12 gín kù.babbar *i-di* é *ù* [...]
2. *ul-tu* u$_4$.1.kam *šá* iti.apin m[u.16.kam *a-di*]
3. iti.du$_6$ mu.17.kam 6 g[ín kù.babbar]
4. *šá re-eš šat-tu*$_4$ *ù* [6 gín kù.babbar]
5. [*ina mi-šil*] ⸢mu⸣.[an.na *i-nam-din*]
Rest lost

Rev. 1'. [x x ^{m}ì]r-⸢*ia*$^{?}$ x x⸣ [...]
2'. [a] ⸢^{lú}⸣šitim ^{m}*še-el-li-b*[*i* ...]
3'. ⸢a ^{m}⸣^{d}ag-mu-mu ^{m}*re-m*[*ut*$^{?}$ ...]
4'. dumu *šá* ^{m}ba^{šá}-*a* a ^{lú}⸢x⸣ [...]
5'. iti.kin u$_4$.10.kam mu.17.k[am ^{d}ag-i lugal e^{ki}]

Notes

Rev. 1'. The reading suggested by join collation by I. Finkel and R. Tarasewicz.
Rev. 4'. Maybe ^{lú}⸢ì⸣.[sur gi^{na}].

Translation

12 shekels of silver, the rent for a house and [...] from the first day of Araḫsamna, [the 16th year to] the month Tašrītu of the 17th year. [He will pay] 6 she[kels of silver] at the beginning of the year and [6 shekels of silver in the middle of the y]ear.

...

[A]rdiya, [..., descendant] of Itinnu

Šellib[i ..., descendant] of Nabû-šum-iddin

Rēmūt-[x], son of Iqīšā, descendant of [...]
[...], month Ulūlu, tenth day, 17th ye[ar of Nabonidus, king of Babylon].

115. Cam 213 = BM 31842 (76-11,17, 1569) Bertin 893. Collated by R. Tarasewicz; 15.XI.Camb 3 Babylon

Obv. 1. é *šá* ^{md}u+gur-kar a-*šú šá* ^{m}be$^{?}$-[x (x)]
2. a ^{m}*su-ḫa-a-a* é *maš-ka-nu šá* ^{m}ki-^{d}amar.utu-tin
3. a-*šú šá* ^{md}ag-šeš.meš-mu a ^{m}*e-gi-bi*
4. *a-na u$_4$-mu* 3 sìla nínda.ḫi.a *a-na*-di* é*
5. [*a-na*] ^{d}en-ad-ùru ^{lú}riq$_7$
Rest of obverse is missing

Rev. 1'. [x x] ⸢x x⸣ ^{m}*gi-mil-lu* a-⸢*šú*⸣
2' *šá* ^{md}ag-^{mu}sig$_5$ a ^{lú}šu.ḫa
3' $^{m⸢d}$en-da$^{?⸣}$ ^{lú}šid a-*šú šá* ^{m}mu-^{d}ag
4' a ^{m}*e-gi-bi* tin.tir^{ki}
5' iti.zíz u$_4$.15.kam mu.3.kam
6' ^{m}*kam-bu-zi-iá* lugal e^{ki}
7'. lugal kur.kur

Notes

L. 2. Although the reading of the name ^{m}ki-damar.utu-tin is certain both copies differ substantially. In Strassmaier's all signs except for tin are damaged, but readable, while in Bertin's copy ^{m}ki is fully damaged followed by part of amar, next a (instead of utu) and clear tin.

L. 4. Instead of *i-na* in Strassmaier's copy, Bertin copied properly *a-na*, supported by collation of R. Tarasewicz.

At the end of the line, instead of *a-na* ugu [...] in Strassmaier's copy, Bertin copied properly *a-na i-di* ⸢x⸣. According to R. Tarasewicz *i-di* is followed by clear é.

Rev. 1' is missing in Strassmaier's copy but is present in Bertin's copy, supported by R. Tarasewicz collation.

According to Petschow 1956, 106 and n. 325 Itti-Marduk-balāṭu, who possessed the house as an antichretic pledge, leased it for 3 *qû* of bread daily (described as "Alimentationsmietvertrag?").

Rev. 3'. Although the name of the scribe is preserved very badly, I recognize here Bēl-nā'id, who occurs as scribe in Cam 315: 20 (Camb 6, 524 BC) and in Dar 487: 14 (Dar 19, 503 BC). Beginning from Cam 213 (Camb 3, 527 BC) he would be active as a scribe for about a quarter of century.

Translation

The house of Nergal-ēṭir, son of ..., descendant of Sūḫaya is the pledge of Itti-Marduk-balāṭu, son of Nabû-aḫḫē-iddin, descendant of Egibi rented [to] Bēl-abu-uṣur, the oblate.

[Witnesses]:
...
Gimillu, son of Nabû-mudammiq, descendant of Bā'iru
Bēl-na'id$^?$, the scribe, son of Iddin-Nabû, descendant of Egibi
Babylon, month Šabāṭu, 15th day, third year of Cambyses, king of Babylon, king of Lands.

116. BM 82744 (94-7-17, 62); 15.X.Camb 7 Bīt-Zēriya

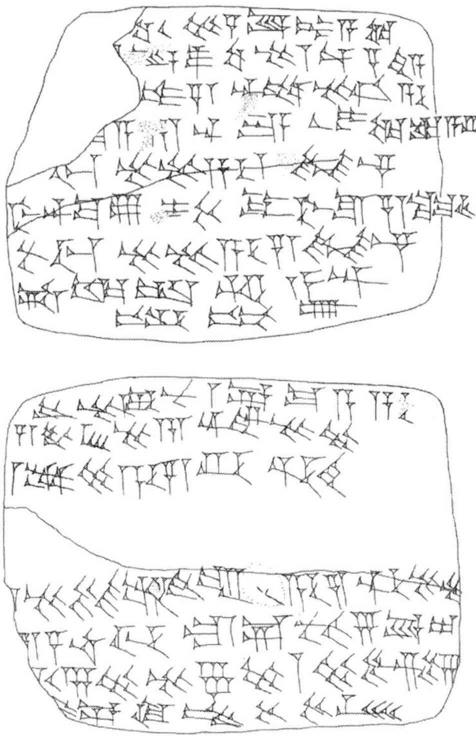

Obv. 1. [*ul-tu*$_4$] u$_4$.10.kam *šá* iti.gan *a-di*
2. [*qí-it*] ⸢*šá*⸣ iti.zíz *u*$_4$*-mu* 1* sìla ninda.ḫi.a
3. [*man-da-at*]-*tu*$_4$ *šá* ^{md}amar.utu-mu-dù a-*šú*
4. [*šá* ^{m}*šu*]-⸢*la*⸣-*a* ⸢a⸣ ^{m}dingir-*ia ina i-di ka-a-ri*
5. [*ina*] ⸢igi⸣ ^{m}mu-mu a-*šú šá* ^{m}[*ina*]-sùḫ-sur
6. ^{fd}*ba-ba*$_6$*-i-lat* dumu.mí-*su šá* ^{m}*la-ba-ši*
7. *là*-igi ^{m}mu-mu a-*šú šá* ^{m}<*ina*>-sùḫ-sur
8. *ta-ka-al* 1^{en}-*a*$_4$
9. *il-qu-ú*

Rev. 10. ^{lú}*mu-kin-nu* ^{m}*kal-ba-a a-*⸢*šú*⸣
11. *šá* ^{m}šeš.meš-mu a ^{md}im-mu-kam
12. ^{md}ag-kam a-*šú šá* ^{m}*ri-mut*
Blank space for 2 lines
13. ^{m}*mu-še-zib-*^{d}en ^{lú}šid x (ras.) a-*šú šá* ^{md}šú-mu-mu
14. ⸢a⸣ ^{m}*šá-na-ši-šú* ^{uru}é-numun-*iá* iti.ab
15. [u]$_4$.15.kam mu.7.kam ^{m}*kam-bu-zi-iá*
16. [lug]al e^{ki} lugal kur.kur.meš

Notes

The interpretation of the text is far from clear. According to Zadok, 2009, 258, no. 62 Marduk-šum-ibni was the lodger and Šum-iddin the house owner. This is doubtful for two reasons. In receipts first the owner, then the tenant is mentioned. Additionally, if we accept Zadok's suggestion to read in l. 3 [*man-dat*]-*tu*$_4$, this type of obligation was always paid to the owner, i.e. Marduk-šum-ibni would have to be the owner of the storehouse and Šum-iddin, son of Ina-tēšê-ēṭir the tenant paying rent, presumably the servant of Marduk-šum-ibni. If my interpretation is correct, it means that Šum-iddin was obligated to deliver 1 *qû* of bread daily to ^{f}Baba-ilat, daughter of Lābāši, presumably related in some way to the owner.

Translation

[Fro]m the tenth day of the month Kislīmu to [the end] of the month Šabāṭu, 1 *qû* of bread, the [compen]sation$^{?}$ for Marduk-šum-ibni, so[n of Šu]-lā, descendant of Ilīya from the rent of the harbour storehoue, [which is at di]-sposal of Šum-iddin, son of Ina-tēšê-ēṭir, ^{f}Baba-ilat, daughter of Lābāši, will consume it before Šum-iddin, son of Ina-tēšê-ēṭir.They (each) took a copy of the document.

Witnesses:
Kalbā, son of Aḫḫē-iddin, descendant of Adad-šum-ēreš
Nabû-ēreš, son of Rēmūt,
Mušēzib-Bēl, the scribe, son of Marduk-šum-iddin, descendant of Ša-nāšišu
City of Bīt-Zēriya, month Ṭebētu, 15th day, seventh year of Cambyses, king of Babylon, king of Lands.

117. BM 65336 (82-9-18, 5321); 5.5 x 4.3 cm; [Dar$^{?}$] 1 [Sippar]

Obv. 1'. [............] ⸢x⸣
2' [.........] ⸢*ma-na*⸣ kù.babbar
3' [.........*i*]-*di* é.meš níg.ga ^{d}utu
4' [...... *i-n*]*a-áš-šá-am-ma*
5' [*a-na* x x x *i-n*]*am-din pu-ut*$^{!}$ *še-e-pi*

6' [*šá* ^{m}x x]-⸢^{d}⸣u+gur ^{md}utu-kád a-*šú*⸢*šá*⸣
7'. [^{md}ag-kar-z]i.meš *na-ši*
One blank line
8'. [^{lú}*mu-k*]*in-nu* ^{m}su-^{d}amar.utu a-*šú šá*
Edge 9'. [^{md}3]0-dingir a <^{m}>^{d}en-*e-ṭè-r*[*u*]
Rev. 10'.[^{md}e]n-mu a-*šú šá* ^{md}amar.utu-mu-mu
11'.[a ^{m}ga]l-*a*$_{4}$-*šá*-^{d}maš ^{md}en-tin^{it}
12'.[a-*šú šá* ^{m}k]ar-^{d}amar.utu a ^{m}ìr-gir$_{4}$.kù
13'.[*u* ^{lú}š]id ^{md}ag-*na-din*-šeš a-*šú šá* ^{md}u+gur-*ina*-sùḫ-sur
14'.[a ^{lú}sang]a ud.kib.nun^{ki}
15'.[*sip-par*^{ki} iti.x u$_{4}$.x.kam m]u.1.kam
16'.[..........] ⸢x⸣

Notes

L. 5'. The *ut* in *pu-ut* and a in l. 12' are written over an erasure.

L. 8'. For Erība-Marduk/Sîn-ili//Bēl-eṭēru, the *ērib bīti* of Šarrat Sippar, see Bongenaar 1997, 248 (time of Darius I) and scribe (idem, 486).

L. 13'. Nabû-nādin-aḫi/Nergal-ina-tēšê-ēṭir//Šangû-Šamaš, the brother of Bēl-nādin-aḫi/Nergal-ina-tēšê-ēṭir//Šangû-Šamaš/Sippar (see Bongenaar 1997, 449, active in the period Nbk 30-Dar 8), and Nabû-ittannu, (idem, 453, active in the period Dar 17-23) and possibly Nabû-šum-uṣur (idem, 451, Dar 4). In light of these data it seems that the document was written in the first year of Darius.

Translation

[... x] mina(s) of silver [...] the rent of houses, property of Šamaš [...] he will bring [...] and give it [to PN]. Šamaš-kāṣir, [son of Nabû-ēṭir-nap]šāti assumes guaranty for [...]-Nergal.

[Witnes]ses:
Erība-Marduk, son of Sîn-ili, descendant of Bēl-eṭēru
[B]ēl-iddin, son of Marduk-šum-iddin, [descendant of Rab]â-ša-Ninurta
Bēl-uballiṭ, [son of Mu]šēzib-Marduk, descendant of Arad-Nergal,
[and the sc]ribe, Nabû-nādin-aḫi, son of Nergal-ina-tēšê-ēṭir, descendant of Šangû-Sippar.
[Sippar, month x, day x], first year of [...].

118. Dar 60 = BM 30250 Collated; 9.I.Dar 3, Babylon

Obv. 1. é *ka-a-ri šá* ^{md}amar.utu-*na-ṣir*-a
2. *u* šeš.meš-*šú* dumu-*šú šá* ^{m}ki-^{d}šú-tin
3. a ^{m}*e-gi-bi šá* da é ^{md}en-tin^{it}
4. a-*šú šá* ^{md}ag-kar-zi.meš a ^{lú}ad.kid

5. *a-na i*-di** ⸢é⸣* *a-na u*$_4$*-mu* 4 sìla *a-ka-lu*
6. ^{md}en-tin^{it} a-*šú šá* ^{md}ag-kar-zi.meš
7. a ^{lú}ad.kid *id-din*

Rev. 8. [^{lú}*m*]*u-kin-nu* ^{md}en-nigin^{ir} a-*šú šá*
9. ^{md}ag-*lu*-ud.da-*a*-{1-}*na-nu-ur*$^{!}$
10. ^{m}*ḫa-ba-ṣi-ru* a-*šú šá* ^{m}*kur-ban-ni-*^{d}amar.utu
11. ^{md}en-tin^{it} ^{lú}šid a-*šú šá* ^{md}ag-sur-zi.meš
12. a ^{lú}ad.kid tin.tir^{ki} iti.bár
13. u$_4$.9.kam mu.3.kam ^{m}*da-ri-ia-muš*
14. lugal e^{ki} *u* kur.kur

Translation

The *kāru*-storehouse belonging to Marduk-nāṣir-apli and his brothers, the son(s) of Itti-Marduk-balāṭu, descendant of Egibi, adjacent to the house of Bēl-uballiṭ, son of Nabû-ēṭir-napšāti, descendant of the Atkuppu he (Marduk-nāṣir-apli) rented it out to Bēl-uballiṭ, son of Nabû-ēṭir-napšāti, descendant of the Atkuppu for 4 *qû* of bread daily.

Witnesses:
Bēl-upaḫḫir, son of Nabû-lūṣi-ana-nūri
Ḫabaṣīru, son of Kurbanni-Marduk
Bēl-uballiṭ, the scribe, son of Nabû-ēṭir-napšāti, descendant of the Atkuppu.
Babylon, month Nisannu, ninth day, third year of Darius, king of Babylon and Lands.

119. VS 5, 67 (VAT 4094) NRV 120; *Bēliya'u*, no. 53; 7.X.Dar 5 Borsippa

Obv. 1. é *šá* ^{m}*šad-din-nu* a-*šú šá* ^{m}*ba-laṭ-su* a ^{m}en-*iá-ú*
2. *šá mu-ṣu-ú la-ṣu-ú šá* da é
3. ^{md}ag-du-a a-*šú šá* ^{m}*ba-laṭ-su* a ^{m}en-*iá-ú*
4. *a-di* 2 mu.an.na.meš *a-na i-di* é *a-na*
5. mu.an.na 13 gín kù.babbar ^{m}*ba-laṭ-su*
6. a-*šú šá* ^{m}*šu-la-a* a ^{md}idim-dù
7. *ina lìb-bi a-šib-bi ba-at-qa šá a-sur-ru-ú*
8. *i-ṣab-bat ú-ru i-šá-an-na*
9. *nu-up-tu*$_4$ *u*$_4$*-mu* ^{d}en *u ki-na-a-tú*

Edge 10. *i-nam-din* 1^{en}*-a-ta-a*$_4$
11. *il-qu-ú*

Rev. 12. ^{lú}*mu-kin-nu* ^{m}*gu-za-nu* a-*šú šá*
13. ⸢^{m}⸣[x x]-*a* a ^{m}*ši-gu-ú-a*
14. [x x x]-⸢x⸣-*lu*-^{d}ag a-*šú šá* ^{m}dub-numun
15. [a ^{m}]⸢*ki*⸣*-di-nu-*^{d}30
16. dub.sar ^{md}ag-*it-tan-nu* a-*šú šá* ^{md}ag-numun-gál^{ši}

17. a ^{m}dingir-*ia bar-sip*^{ki} iti.ab
18. u$_4$.7.kam mu.5.kam ^{m}*da-ra-'-*⌜*muš*⌝
19. lugal e^{ki} lugal kur.kur iti-*a-ta-a*$_4$
20. *i-di* é *i-nam-din*

L.h.e. 21. ta u$_4$.10.[kam]
22. é *ina* igi ^{m}*b*[*a-laṭ*]-*su*

Translation

A house of Šaddinnu, son of Balāssu, descendant of Bēliyā'u, (adjacent to) the one-way street and adjacent to the house of Nabû-mukīn-apli, son of Balāssu, descendant of Bēlijā'u for two years for the house rent of 13 shekels of silver yearly. Balāssu, son Šulā, descendant of Ea-ibni live in it. He will repair (the cracks) of the wall footing and seal the roof.

He will pay *nūptu*-payment on the day of Bēl and *kīnajātu*-offerings.

They (each) took a copy of the document.

Witnesses:

Gūzānu, son of [....]a, descendant of Šigûa

[...]lu-Nabû, son of Šāpik-zēri, descendant of Kidin-Sîn

The scribe Nabû-ittannu, son of Nabû-zēr-ušabši, descendant of Ilīya

Borsippa, month Ṭebētu, seventh day, fifth year of Darius, king of Babylon, king of Lands.

He will pay the rent monthly.

From the tenth day the house is at disposal of Ba[lās]su.

120. BM 77625+BM 77636; 5.2 x 4.6 cm; 10+[x].VIII.Dar 12 Babylon

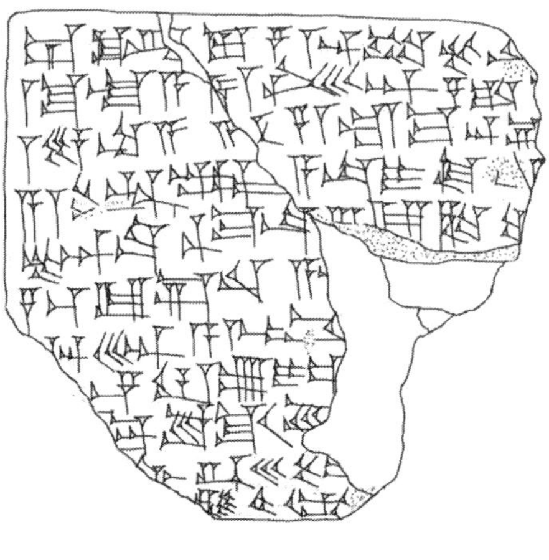

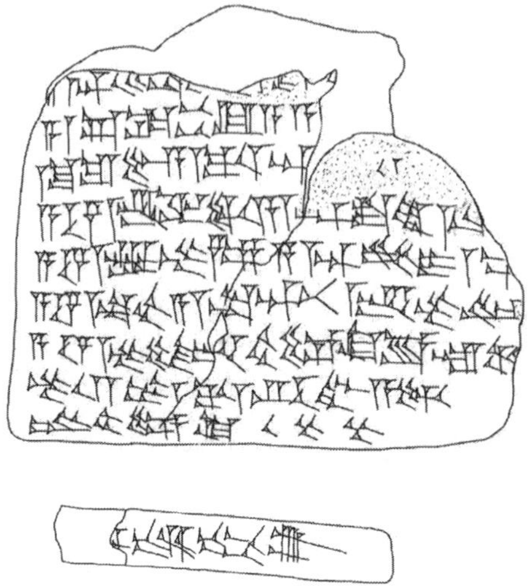

Obv. 1. é *ku-tal-lu šá* ^{md}amar.utu-mu-m[u$^?$ a-*šú šá*]
2. ^{m}*šu-la-a* a dù^{eš}-dingir *šá* da ⸢é⸣
3. ^{m}sum-*na-a* a-*šú šá* ^{m}*eri-ba*$_4$-^{d}é-[*a*]
4. a ^{lú}⸢maš⸣.maš ^{d}ag *a-na i-di* ⸢é *a*⸣-[*na*]
5. mu.an-na ⅓ *ma-na* ⸢4⸣ gín kù.babbar babbar-[*ú*]
6. *šá ina* 1 gín *bit-qa a-n*[*a* PN a-*šú*]
7. [*šá*] ^{md}30-dingir a ^{m}*ina*-giss[u$^{!?}$-DN *id-din bat-qa*]
8. [*šá a*]-*sur-ru-ú i-ṣab-*[*bat ú-ri i-šá-an-nu*]
9. [*ina* iti.b]ár iti.šu *u* it[i.gan *nu-up-tu*$_4$ *ina-an-din*]
10. [*a-ḫi* kù.babb]ar *ina re-eš šat-t*[*u*$_4$ *u a-ḫi* kù.babbar *ina*]

Edge 11. [*mi-šil šat-tu*$_4$ *i-na*]*m-din ul-*[*tu* u$_4$.x.kam]

Rev. 1'. ⸢a⸣ ^{md}30-⸢*na-din*$^?$-x x⸣ [... a]
2'. ^{m}*é-sag-gil-a-a* [PN a-*šú šá*]
3'. ^{m}*šu-zu-bu* a ^{m}da-^{d}[amar.ut]u [$^{m(d)}$...]
4'. a-*šú šá* ^{md}en-*ka-ṣir* a ^{m}⸢*an-da*⸣-*ḫar* ^{m}⸢*na*$^?$⸣-[...]
5'. a-*šú šá* ^{md}ag-mu-gar^{un} a ^{m}kaskal.kur^{i} ^{m}⸢x⸣ [...]'
6'. a-*šú šá* ^{m}*na-din* a ^{m}ìr-^{d}idim ^{md}en-mu ^{lú}ši[d ...]
7'. a-*šú šá* ^{m}*mu-še-zib*-^{d}en tin.tir^{ki} iti.apin u$_4$.1⸢1⸣.[kam]
8'. mu.12.kam ^{m}*da-ri-'-a-muš*
9'. lugal tin.tir^{ki} *u* kur.kur

L.h.e. 10'. [1^{en}-*ta-a-a*]*n il-qu-ú*

Notes

L. 4. The maš.maš seems to be written over erasure, although the signs are clear. According to my knowledge the family name Āšipu-^{d}Nabû is not attested before.

Translation

The rear house belonging to Marduk-šum-⸢iddin?⸣, [son of] Šulā, descendant of Eppēš-ilī, adjacent to the house of Iddinaya, son of Erība-E[a], the descendant of the incantation priest of Nabû, [rented it out] to [PN], son of Sîn-ili, descendant of Ina-ṣilli?-[DN] for 3⸢3⸣ shekels of white silver of one-eighth alloy in each shekel. [He will repair] (the cracks) of the wall footing and [seal the roof. In the months] Nisannu, Du'uzu and [Kislīmu he will pay the additional *nūptu*-payment. [Half of silver he] will pay in the beginning of the ye[ar and half of silver in the middle of the year]. Fr[om day x …]

… Sîn-nādin-[x, son of PN, descendant of] Esagilaya
[PN, son of] Šūzubu, descendant of Lē'i-[Mardu]k
[PN], son of Bēl-kāṣir, descendant of Andaḫar
[PN], son of Nabû-šum-iškun, descendant of Balīḫu
[PN], son of Nādin, descendant of Arad-Ea
Bēl-iddin, the scri[be], son of Mušēzib-Bēl
Babylon, month Araḫsamna, 10+[x]th day, 12th year of Darius, king of Babylon and Lands
[Each] took [on]e (copy).

121. Dar 482 = BM 31228; <x>.II. Dar 19 Babylon

Obv. 1. *i-di* é *šá* é-*ḫa-aḫ-ḫu-ru* [*šá* da é ^{md}en-*na-din*-a *šá*]
2. ^{md}en-*bul-liṭ-su ù* šeš-*šú* dumu.meš [*šá* ^{md}nà-mu]-⸢gar*⸣*un**
3. *šá* ^{md}utu-*ina*-sùḫ-sur a-*šú šá* ^{md}utu-mu! ⸢*ina*⸣ [šà] *áš-bi*
4. *šá a-di qí-it* iti.bár mu.19.kam ^{m}*da-a-ri-'-muš* lugal
5. ^{md}amar.utu-dub-numun a-*šú šá* ^{m}*mu-še-zib*-^{d}amar.utu
6. a ^{m}*sag-gil-a-a ina* šu^{ii} ^{md}utu-*ina*-sùḫ-<sur> a-*šú šá* ^{md}utu-mu
7. a ^{md}utu-*a-ba-ri ma-ḫi-ir*
8. 1^{en}-*ta-a*$_4$ *il-te-qu-ú*

Rev. 9. ^{lú}*mu-kin-nu* ^{m}mu-*a* a-*šú šá* ^{md}en-tin^{iṭ}
10. a ^{m}*ga-ḫal* ^{m}mu-^{d}en a-*šú šá* ^{md}utu-mu
11. a ^{md}utu-*ba-a-ri* ^{md}nà-*ú-tir-ri*
12. a-*šú šá* ^{m}en-*šú-nu* ^{m}*bul-ṭa-a* a-*šú šá* ^{md}utu-sum^{na}
13. ^{m}*gab-ri-ia* a-*šú šá* ^{m}*re-mut*
14. ^{lú}šid ^{md}en-dù^{uš} a-*šú šá* ^{m}*ú-bar*
15. a ^{lú}sipa anše.kur.ra
16. ^{uru}é-*ḫa-aḫ-ḫu-ru* iti.gu$_4$
17. u$_4$.<x.kam> mu.19.kam ^{m}*da-a-ri-'-muš*
18. lugal e^{ki} lugal kur.kur

Notes

L. 1. F. Joannès (http://www.achemenet.com/en/tree/?/textual-sources/texts-by-regions/babylonia/babylon) reads [*šá* da é ^{md}en-gi], presumably on the basis of Dar 485, no. 123: 1 where he reads *šá* da é ^{md}en-g[i], however, JCS 28, no. 46: 1 speaks for [*šá* da é ^{md}en-*na-din-a*] and *šá* da é ^{md}en-*n*[*a-din-a šá*] in Dar 482: 1. As was established by R. Tarasewicz, who collated the text on my request, the remaining signs copied by Strassmaier at the end of l. 1 (nothing is preserved there after *ḫa-aḫ-ḫu-ru*) are written on the edge and belong to the end of l. 2.

L. 2. Note that almost at the same time Bēl-bullissu, son of Nabû-apla-iddin, descendant of Saggilaya was active as a scribe; see VS 75, 78 = Baker 2004, no. 101: 19 (Dar 15, 507 BC); Baker 2004, no. 60: 35 (Dar 26, 495 BC) and Baker 2004, no. 61: 23 (Dar [26], 495 BC). Contrary to the opinion of Abraham 2004, 286, commentary to ll. 22-23, Bēl-bullissu was neither the son of Šamaš-ina-tēši-ēṭir, nor the brother of Nabû-mukīn-zēri.

Dar 435 (= BM 31975): 3 suggests that Bēl-bullissu did have a brother Nabû-bullissu, but this is rather unlikely since distinguishing between the similar names of two brothers by theophoric element only is unknown to me. A mistake by a copyist or ancient scribe of Bēl-bullissu is more probable. Postscript: as the collation by R. Tarasewicz confirms Strassmaier's copy, only the second possibility applies.

L. 3. Joannès reads *ina! lìb!-* ⸢*bi!*⸣ *áš-bi*, but because of the lack of space I suggest the reading ⸢*ina*⸣ [*šà*] *áš-bi.*

L. 4. Note that the second witness is the brother of a tenant.

Translation

The rent of the house in Bīt-Ḫaḫḫuru, [adjacent to the house of Bēl-nādin-apli (and) of] Bēl-bullissu and his brother, the sons [of Nabû-šum]-iškun, in which Šamaš-ina-tēši-ēṭir, son of Šamaš-iddin$^{!}$ lives, till the end of month Nisannu, 19th year of Darius, king, Marduk-šāpik-zēri, son of Mušēzib-Marduk, descendant of Saggilaya received it from Šamaš-ina-tēši-<ēṭir>, son of Šamaš-iddin, descendant of Šamaš-(a)bāri.

Witnesses:
Iddinaya, son of Bēl-uballiṭ, descendant of Gaḫal
Iddin-Bēl, son of Šamaš-iddin, descendant of Šamaš-(a)bāri
Nabû-utirri, son of Bēlšunu
Bulṭā, son of Šamaš-iddin,
Gabriya, son of Rēmūt
the scribe Bēl-ēpuš, son of Ubāru, descendant of Rē'i-sīsê.
Bīt-Ḫaḫḫuru, month Ayaru, <x> day, 19th year of Darius, king of Babylon, king of Lands.

122. JCS 28, no. 46 (FLP 1421); 22.VIa.Dar 19*

Obv. 1. dub *šá* é ^{m}*šá-aḫ-ḫu-ru šá* da é ^{md}en-*na-din*-a
2. *šá* ^{md}en-*bul-liṭ-su u* ^{m}*ni-din*-tu$_4$ dumu.meš *šá* ^{md}ag-mu-gar^{un}

3. dumu ^{m}sag-*gil*-a-a* ^{m}sum^{na}-a dumu *šá* ^{m}kar-^{d}amar.utu
4. dumu ^{m}sag-*gil*-a-a a-na i-di* é *a-na* mu.an.na
5. ⅓ *ma-na* 4 gín kù.babbar *šá gìn-nu a-na* ^{m}*ši-ir-ki*
6. dumu *šá* ^{m}sum^{na}-a dumu ^{m}*e-gì-bi id-din*
7. *a-ḫi* kù.babbar *ina re-eš* mu *u re-iḫ-it* kù.babbar
8. *ina mi-šil* mu *ina-ad-din* iti.bár iti.šu *u* iti.gan
9. *nu-up-tu*$_4$ *i-na-pi bat-qa i-ṣab-bat ú-ru-ú*
10. *i-šá-an-ni dul-lu* sig$_4$.ḫi.a gi *u* giš.ùr
11. *ma-la ina lìb-bi ip-pu-šú ul-tu* ugu 2 gín kù.babbar

Edge 12. [*a*]-*na* ugu ^{m}sum^{na}-*a i-man-nu i-di* é$^{!}$ [*šá ta*]
13. u$_4$.1.kam *šá* iti.gu$_4$ mu.19*.kam ^{m}*da-ri-a-muš*
14. lugal* e^{ki} *u* kur.kur *a-di* u$_4$.1.kam *šá* iti.du$_6$ m[u.1]⸢9⸣.<kam>

Rev. 15. *šá* ^{md}en-*bul-liṭ-su šá ina pa-ni* ^{md}utu-*ina*-sùḫ-sur kar*^{ir*}
16. ^{m}*ši-ir-ki i-na-áš-šá-am-ma a-na* ^{m}mu^{a} *ina-ad-din*
17. ^{lú}*mu-kin-nu* ^{md}ag-tin^{it} dumu *šá* ^{m}gi-^{d}amar.utu
18. dumu ^{md}30-*šá-du-nu* ^{md}en-*ú-še-zib* dumu *šá* ^{m}*sag-gi-il*
19. dumu ^{m}*sag-gil*-a-a* ^{m}*la-ba-a-ši* dumu <*šá*> ^{m}ìr-^{d}en
20. dumu ^{md}idim-dù^{eš}-dingir ^{m}ki-^{d}ag-tin dumu *šá* ^{m}*iq-bi*-^{d}en
21. dumu ^{m}*bu-ú-ṣu* ^{md}en-tin^{it} dumu *šá du*-⸢*um**⸣-*mu-qu*
22. dumu ^{m}*e-gì-bi* dub.sar ^{md}amar.utu-dub-numun
23. dumu ^{lú}gal-dù tin.tir^{ki} iti.kin u$_4$.1.kam
24. u$_4$.22.kam mu.19*.kam ^{m}*da-ri-a-muš* <lugal> e^{ki}

L.e. 25. *u* kur.kur

Notes

Lines 2, 14-15 and 21 were kindly collated by Grant Frame. Other new readings are based on excellent photo of the tablet (https://cdli.ucla.edu/dl/photo/P459930.jpg).

L. 2. Stigers copied the first sign as an a, but on the photograph (https://cdli.ucla.edu/dl/photo/P459930.jpg) I see *šá* (confirmed by a collation by Grant Frame). However, the relation between Bēl-nādin-apli, Bēl-bullissu, and his brother Nidintu is unclear, as there is no basis to think that they all were brothers and sons of Nabû-šum-iškun.

Translation

The document concerning the house in <Bīt>-Šaḫḫuru, adjacent to the house of Bēl-nādin-apli (and) of Bēl-bullissu and Nidintu, the sons of Nabû-šum-iškun, descendant of Saggilaya, Iddinaya, son of Mušēzib-Marduk, descendant of Saggilaya rented it to Širku, son of Iddinaya, descendant of Egibi for 24 shekels of *ginnu* silver yearly.

He will pay half of the silver at the beginning of the year (and) the remainder of the silver in the middle of the year.

In the months Nisannu, Du'ūzu and Kislīmu she will pay a *nuptu*-payment. He will repair the damages and seal the roof. For works in bricks, reeds and beams he does over two shekels of silver he shall reckon on account of Iddinaya.

The house rent for the period [from] the first day of Du'ūzu, 19th year of Darius, king of Babylon and Lands, till the first day of Tašrītu of the 19th year (adjacent to the house) of Bēl-bullissu, in which Šamaš-ina-tēši-ēṭir (lives), Širku will bring and gives it (the rent) to Iddinaya.

Witnesses:
Nabû-uballiṭ, son of Mušallim-Marduk, descendant of Sîn-šadûnu
Bēl-ušēzib, son of Saggil, descendant of Saggilaya
Lābāši, son of Arad-Bēl, descendant of Ea-eppēš-ili
Itti-Nabû-balāṭu, son of Iqbi-Bēl, descendant of Būṣu
Bēl-uballiṭ, son of Dummuqu, descendant of Egibi
scribe, Marduk-šāpik-zēri, descendant of Rab-banê

Babylon, first month of Ulūlu, 22nd day, 19th year of Darius, <king> of Babylon and Lands.

123. Dar 485 = BM 31274; [22].VI[a].Dar 19

Obv. 1. [dub] *šá* é-^{m}*ḫa-aḫ-ḫu-ru šá* da é ^{Id}en-*n*[*a-din*-a]
2. ⸢*šá*?⸣ ^{md}en-*bul-liṭ-su u* ^{m}*ni-din-tu*$_4$ dumu.meš *šá* ^{md}nà-mu-gar^{un}
3. dumu ^{m}*sag-gil-a-a* ^{m}sum^{na}-*a* dumu *šá* ^{m}ki-^{d}am[ar.utu-tin]
4. dumu ^{m}*sag-gil-a-a a-na i-di* é *a-na*
5. mu.an.na ⅓ *ma-na* 4 gín kù-babbar *šá gìn-nu*
6. *a-na* ^{m}*ši-ir-ki* dumu *šá* ^{m}sum^{na}-*a*
7. dumu ^{m}*e-gì-bi id-din a-ḫi* kù.babbar *ina re-eš* mu.an.na
8. *u re-ḫi-it* kù.babbar *ina mi-šil* mu.an.na [*i-nam-din*]

Edge 9. iti bár iti šu *u* iti gan *nu-up-tu*$_4$
10. [*i*]*-na-pi bat-qa i-ṣab-bat ú-ru-*[*ú*]
11. *i-šá-an-ni dul-lu* sig$_4$.ḫi.a gi ⸢*u*⸣ [giš.ùr.meš]

Rev. 12. *ma-la ina lìb-bi ip-pu-šú ul-tu* ⸢ugu⸣
13. 2 gín kù.babbar *a-na* ugu ^{m}sum^{na}-*a*
14. *i-man-nu* ^{lú}*mu-kin-nu* ^{md}⸢ag!⸣-tin^{iṭ} dumu ⸢*šá*⸣
15. ^{m}gi-amar.utu [dumu ^{md}30-*šá-d*]*u*-nu* ^{md}en-*ú-še-zib*
16. dumu ^{m}*sag-gil-l*[*a-a-a* dumu] ^{m}*sag-gil-a-a*
17. ^{m}*la-ba-a-ši* ⸢dumu⸣ [*šá* ^{m}ìr-^{d}]⸢en*⸣ dumu ^{md}idim-dù]^{eš}-dingir
18. ^{m}ki-^{d}ag-tin dumu *šá* ^{m}*iq*-b*[*i**-^{d}en dumu ^{m}*bu-ú-ṣu*]
19. ^{md}en-tin^{iṭ} dumu *šá* ^{m}*d*[*u-um-mu-qu* dumu ^{m}*e-gì-bi*]
20. dub.sar ^{md}amar.utu-[dub-numun dumu ^{lú}gal-dù]
21. tin.tir^{ki} iti.kin u$_4$.[1.kam u$_4$.22.kam]

L.e. 22. mu.19.kam ^{m}*da-ri-a-muš* lugal [e^{ki} lugal kur.kur]

23. ⌜é$^{?}$⌝-*su šá ina pa-ni* ^{md}utu-*ina**-sùḫ-s[ur]
24. [kar$^{!r}$ ^{m}*ši-ir-ki i-na-áš-šá-am-m*]*a a*-⌜*na*⌝ ^{m}mu$^{!-u}$

L.h.e. 25. *i-di* é *šá ul-tu* u$_4$.1.kam *šá* iti.[gu$_4$]
26. *a-di* u$_4$.1.kam *šá* ⌜iti⌝.du$_6$ ⌜mu.10⌝+[9.kam *ina-ad-din*]

Notes

L. 1. Joannès reads [é] at the beginning of the line, but in a parallel text, JCS 28, no. 46, there is dub.

L. 2. The sign is evidently written over an erasure and the rest of *šá* and *u* is visible. The reading *šá* is based on parallel in JCS 28, no. 46: 2.

L. 3. Contrary to the copy of Strassmaier, only part of the name of Itti-Marduk-balāṭu is preserved (collated by R. Tarasewicz). All other new readings are made on basis of excellent photograph taken by him.

L. 14. The reading ^{md}⌜ag!⌝ is based on the parallel in JCS 28, no 46: 17, although what survives is more similar to en.

Ll. 14-20, Note that the same witnesses occur in JCS 28, no. 46.

L. 16. The *gil* at the beginning of the line is followed by tiny horizontal line, presumably part of *l*[*a*. Because between this and ^{m}*sag* there is a long gap I decided to fill it with *l*[*a-a-a* dumu]. Cf. the same witness in JCS 28, no. 46: 18-19.

Ll. 23-26 are evidently parallel to JCS 28, no. 46, no. 122: 12-16.

Note that l. 24 is not damaged (as suggested by Strassmaier's copy) but because the tablet was too dry on the edge the signs are badly impressed and practically unreadable. It seems to me that the subject of *bīt-su* at the beginning of l. 23 is Širku as new tenant of the house.

Translation

[The docume]nt concerning the house in Bīt-Ḫaḫḫuru, adjacent to the house of Bēl-nā[din-apli (and)] of Bēl-bullissu and Nidintu, the sons of Nabû-šum-iškun, descendant of Saggilaya, Iddinaya, son of Itti-Marduk-balāṭu, descendant of Saggilaya rented it to Širku, son of Iddinaya, descendant of Egibi for 24 shekels of *ginnu* silver yearly.

He [will pay] half of the silver at the beginning of the year (and) the remainder of silver in the middle of the year.
In the months Nisannu, Du'ūzu and Kislīmu she will pay *nūptu*-payment.

He will repair the damages and seal the roof. For works in bricks, reeds [and beams] he does he shall reckon over two shekels of silver on account of Iddinaya.

Witnesses:
Nabû$^{!}$-uballiṭ, son of Mušallim-Marduk, [descendant of Sîn-šad]ûnu
Bēl-ušēzib, son of Saggil[aya, descendant of] Saggilaya
Lābāši, son of Arad-Bēl, descendant of Ea-eppēš-ili
Itti-Nabû-balāṭu, son of Iqb[i-Bēl, descendant of Būṣu]

Bēl-uballiṭ, son of Du[mmuqu, descendant of Egibi]
scribe, Marduk-[šāpik-zēri, descendant of Rab-banê]
Babylon, month Ulūlu, [22nd] day, 19th year of Darius, king [of Babylon, king of Lands]
The rent of his house which is at the disposal of Šamaš-ina-tēši-ēṭir for the period [from] the first day of Du'uzu, 19th year of Darius, king of Babylon and Lands, till the first day of Tašrītu of the 19th year, Širku will bring and [give it] to Iddinaya.

124. Dar 554 (BM 30814); 5.45 x 4.2 cm; 14.X.Dar <26>$^{?}$ Babylon

Obv. 1. *i-di* é-*šú šá ul*$^{\text{(over ras.)}}$-*tu* iti.kin
2. mu.22.kam ^{m}*da-ri-ia-muš* lugal
3. *a-di qí-it* iti.ab mu.26.kam
4. ^{f}*in-ṣab-tu*$_4$ dumu.mí *šá* ^{md}ag-mu-giš
5. a ^{m}*ba-la-ṭu ina* šu^{ii} ^{m}*ú-bar*
6. a-*šú šá* ^{md}en-mu a ^{md}idim-*pat-tan-nu*
7. *e-ṭi-ri* {*it ul-tu*}
8. *ul-tu* iti.zíz é *ina* igi ^{f}*in-ṣab-tu*$_4$
9. 1^{en}-*ta-a*$_4$ *šá-ṭa-ri*

Edge 10. ti^{ú}

Rev. 11. ^{lú}*mu-kin-nu* ^{m}*še-el-li-bi*
12. a-*šú šá* ^{m}gi-^{d}amar.utu a ^{m}*qaq-qa-da-ni-tu*$_4$
13. ^{md}amar.utu-mu-dù a-*šú šá* ^{m}*nar-gi-iá*
14. ^{md}en-šeš.meš-mu a-*šú šá* ^{md}en-*iq-bi*-^{d}en
15. a ^{md}en-*e-ṭè-ru* ^{m}*mu-ra-nu*
16. ^{lú}šid dumu *šá* ^{m}ìr-^{d}amar.utu a ^{lú}sanga ^{d}idim
17. tin.tir^{ki} iti.ab u$_4$.14.kam ^{m}*da-ri-ia-muš*
18. lugal e^{ki} lugal kur.kur

Notes

For Mūrānu/Arad-Marduk//Šangû-Ea, see Abraham 2004, no. 29 and duplicate no. 55.

Translation

The rent of his house for the period from the month Ulūlu, 22nd year of Darius, king, to the end of month Ṭebētu, 26th year, is paid to ^{f}Inṣabtu, the daughter of Nabû-šum-līšir, descendant of Balāṭu by Ubāru, son of Bēl-iddin, descendant of Ea-pattanu.

(Beginning) from the month Šabāṭu, the house (will be) at disposal of ^{f}Inṣabtu.
They (each) took a copy of the document.

Witnesses:
Šellibi, son of Mušallim-Marduk, descendant of Qaqqadanītu

Marduk-šum-ibni, son of Nargiya
Bēl-aḫḫē-iddin, son of Bēl-iqbi-Bēl, descendant of Bēl-ēṭir
Mūrānu, the scribe, son of Arad-Marduk, descendant of Šangû-Ea.
Babylon, month Ṭebētu, 14th day, year <26th> of Darius, king of Babylon, king of Lands.

125. BM 77421 (84-2-11, 160); 5.55 x 4.6 cm; 4.VII.Dar 2⌜9⌝ Babylon

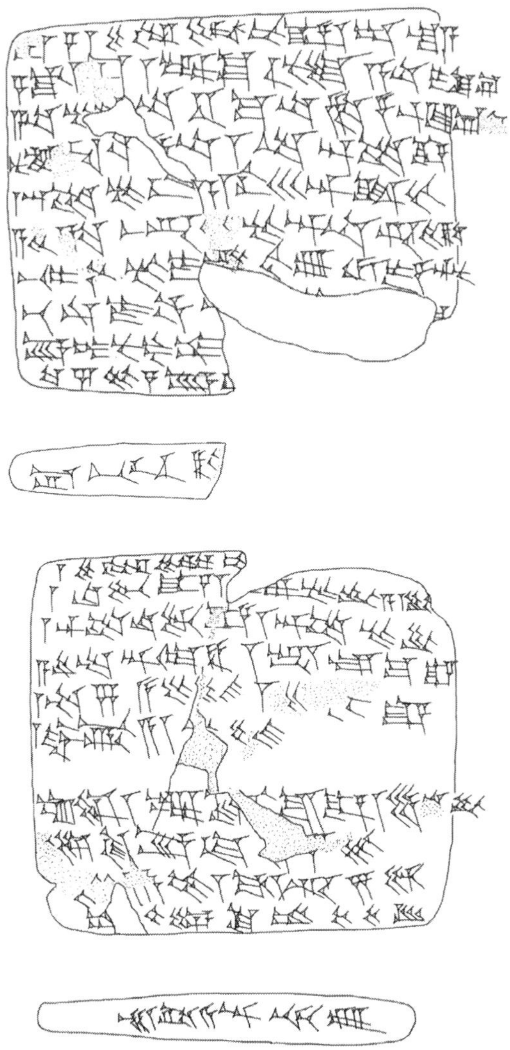

Obv. 1. ⸢é⸣ *šá* ^{m}*še-el-li-bi* dumu *šá* ^{m}*ap-la-a*
2. *šá* da ⸢é⸣ ^{md}ag-šu-*šú-nu*{*-tu*} *a-na i-di* é
3. *a-na* mu.⸢an⸣.na ⅓ *ma-na* kù.babbar *šá ina* 1 gín *bit-*⸢*qa*⸣
4. *nu-uḫ-*[*ḫ*]*u-tú* ⸢*a*⸣*-na* ^{m}ìr-^{d}amar.utu dumu *šá*
5. ^{md}amar.utu-mu-dù a ^{m}dù^{eš}-dingir *id-din*
6. *a-ḫi* kù.babbar *ina ri-*⸢*eš*⸣ mu.an.na *ri-ḫi* kù.babbar
7. *ina mi-šil* mu *i-*⸢*nam*⸣*-din ú-ru i-šá-an-nu*
8. *bat-qa i-ṣab-b*[*at ina* iti.bár iti.š]u
9. iti.gan *nu-up-tu*$_4$ [*i-nam-din ul-tu*]
10. u$_4$.4.kam *šá* iti.d[u$_6$]

Edge 11. é *ina* igi-*šú* kù.babb[ar x gín *šá mi-šil* mu]

Rev. 12. ^{m}*še-el-li-bi* [*e-ṭir* ^{lú}*mu-kin-nu*]
13. ^{m}*na-ṣir* dumu *šá* ^{m}[^{d}]ag-mu-ùru a ^{m}šeš-[...]
14. ^{md}amar.utu-*na-ṣir* dumu *šá* ^{md}amar.utu-mu-ùru
15. a $^{m!(T:lú)}$ìr-^{d}gir$_4$.kù ^{md}en-*eri*$_4$*-ba* dumu *šá*
16. ^{m}ìr-*iá* a $^{<m>}$*mu-*⸢še⸣*-zib* ^{m}⸢*šad-din-nu*⸣ dumu *šá*
17. ^{m}*lib-luṭ a* ^{m}⸢*mu*⸣*-še-zib*
one blank line
18. dub.sar ^{md}ag-*bul-*⸢*liṭ*⸣*-su* dumu *šá* ^{m}sum$^{⸢na⸣}$-šeš
19. [ti]n.tir^{ki} iti.du$_6$ ⸢u$_4$.4⸣.kam
20. ⸢mu.29⸣.kam ^{m}*da-ri-iá-muš*
21. lug[al] tin.tir^{ki} lugal kur.kur.meš

L.e. 22. 1^{en}*-ta-a*$_4$ ti^{ú}

Transaltion

A house of Šellibi, son of Aplā, adjacent to house of *Nabû-gāmil-šunu* (!), rented it out to Arad-Marduk, son of Marduk-šum-ibni, descendant of Eppēš-ilī for 20 shekels of silver per year, which in each shekel have ⅛ of alloy of *nuḫḫutu* quality.

Half of silver he will pay in the beginning of the year and half of silver in the middle of the year.

He will seal the roof and repair the damages

[In the months Nisannu, Du'ū]zu (and) Kislīmu [he will pay *nūptu* payment. From] the fourth day of the month Tašr[ītu] the house is in his (tenant) disposal. [x shekels] of silv[er for the half of (rental) year] are paid to Šellibi.

[Witnesses]:

Nāṣir, son of Nabû-šum-uṣur, descendant of Aḫu-[...]

Marduk-nāṣir, son of Marduk-šum-uṣur, descendant of Arad-Nergal

Bēl-erība, son of Ardiya, descendant of Mušēzib

Šaddinnu, son of Libluṭ, descendant of Mušēzib

one blank line

The scribe, Nabû-bullissu, son of Nādin-aḫi
Babylon, month Tašrītu, fourth day, 2⸢9⸣th year of Darius, king of Babylon, king of Lands.
They (each) took one copy (of the document).

126. BM 31824 = Bertin 2555; Šaḫrīnu 26.[III].Dar 35 (487 BC)

Obv. 1. é im.kur.ra *ù e-li-tu*$_4$
2. *šá ina muḫ-ḫi-šú šá* é ^{uru}*šaḫ-ri-nu*
3. *šá* ⸢*ina*⸣ [x x] ⸢*šá*$^?$ ^{d}en$^?$ *šá* [^{m}zalág]-⸢*e-a*⸣
4. [dumu-*šú šá* ^{m}]*kal-ba-a* dumu ^{m}*ga-ḫal* ^{m}zálag-*e-a*
5. [*a*]-*na i-di* é *a-na* mu.an.na
6. 4 gín kù.babbar babbar-*ú a-na*
7. ^{m}*ni-din-ti*-^{d}en dumu-*šú šá* ^{md}amar.utu-pap-a
8. dumu ^{m}*e-gì-bi id-din*
Edge 9. 1^{en}-*ta-a*$_4$ ti^{ú}
10. *ul-tu* u$_4$.1.kam *šá* iti.šu
Rev. 11. é *ina* igi ^{m}*ni-din-ti*-^{d}en
12. ^{lú}*mu-kin-nu* ^{md}en-tin^{iṭ} dumu *šá*
13. ^{m}*lu*-ud.du-*ana*-zálag a ^{m}*an-da-ḫar*
14. ^{md}u+gur-tin^{iṭ} dumu *šá* ^{md}ag-du-⸢x⸣
15. dumu ^{m}*ka-nik*-ká ^{m}*ni-din-ti*
16. [du]mu *šá* ^{m}⸢ki⸣-[x x ^{m}x-^{d}]⸢amar.utu$^?$⸣ dumu ^{m}da-⸢x⸣-[x]
17. ^{md}en-gi dumu *šá* ^{m}*kal*-⸢*ba-a*⸣
18. [x x (x)]-*šú* dumu ^{m}ki-^{md}ag-[tin]
19. [^{lú}šid] ^{md}en-a-mu a-*šú šá* [x x x]
20. [^{uru}]⸢*šaḫ*⸣-*ri-nu* iti.[sig$_4$]
21. ⸢u$_4$⸣.26.kam mu.35.kam
22. ^{m}*da-a-ri-muš* lugal tin.tir^{ki}
23. *u* kur.kur
L.h.e. 24. *bat-qa šá* ⸢*a*⸣-[*sur-ru*]-*ú i-ṣab-bat*
25. ⸢*ú*⸣-*ru* [*i-šá-a*]*n-nu*

Notes

Note that the clause concerning division of payment of rent in two installments is missing in this document.

Translation

The house (looking) east and the upper store, which is on the top of the house in Šaḫrinu, in […] of Bēl, [Nūr]êa, [son of] Kalbā, descendant of Gaḫal, {Nūrêa} rented it out to Nidinti-Bēl, son of Marduk-nāṣir-apli, descendant of Egibi for 4 shekels of silver yearly.

They (each) took a copy of the document.

From the first day of the month Du'ūzu the house is in disposal of Nidinti-Bēl.
Witnesses:
Bēl-uballiṭ, son of Lūṣi-ana-nūri, descendant of Andaḫar
Nergal-uballiṭ, son of Nabû-mukīn-[x], descendant of Kānik-bābi
Nidintu, son of Itti-[...] [...]-Marduk, son of Lē'i-[...]
Bēl-ušallim, son of Kalbā
[...]šu, son of Itti-Nabû-[balāṭu]
[the scribe], Bēl-aplu-iddin, son of [...].
Šaḫrinu, month [Simānu], 26th day, 35th year of Darius, king of Babylon and Lands.
He will repair (the cracks) of the wa[ll footing] (and) se[al] the roof.

127. BM 77826 = Bertin 2591 Collated; 27.III.Dar 3⸢6⸣ Sippar

Obv. 1. é im.mar.tu da é ^{md}u+gur-tin^{it}
2. ⸢a⸣-*šú šá* ^{m}dùg.ga-*iá a-na i-di* ⸢*šá*$^{?}$⸣ mu.an.na
3. 3 gín kù.babbar babbar-*ú ù* pap iti x ud [*ina*]
4. *na-áš-par-tu*$_4$ ^{md}u+gur-tin^{it} *a-na*
5. ^{f}*a-si-tu*$_4$ *u* ^{md}en-*eri*$_4$*-ba* dumu-*šú*
6. ⸢*id*⸣*-din a-ḫi* kù.babbar *ina re-eš* mu.an.na
7. *ù ri-ḫi* kù.babbar *ina mi-šil*$^{!}$ mu.an.na
Edge 8. *i-nam-din-' ú-ru-ú i-šá*-nu*
9. *bat-qa šá a-sur-ru-ú*
Rev. 10. ⸢*i*⸣*-ṣab-ba-tu-'* iti.bár
11. iti.šu *u* iti.gan *nu-up-tu*$_4$ *i-nam-din-nu*
12. 1^{en}*-ta-a*$_4$ ti-*ú ul-tu* iti.šu$^{!}$
13. é *ina* igi-*šú-nu* ^{lú}*mu-kin-nu* ^{md}en-mu a-*šú šá*
14. ^{m*d*}idim*-*lu*-mur** ^{m*d*}en*-sur* a*-*šú* šá** ^{m*d*}ṣur*-dù*
15. ^{md}utu-mu a-*šú šá* ^{m}*a-ḫi-li-ia*
16. ^{lú}šid ^{md}u+gur-tin^{it} a-*šú šá* ^{m}dùg.ga-*iá*
17. *sip-par*^{ki} iti.sig$_4$ u$_4$.27.kam
L.e. 18. mu.3⸢6⸣.kam ^{m}*da-ri-ia-muš*
19. lugal e^{ki} *u* kur.kur

Notes

My suspicion that in the copy one line is missing was confirmed by collation of R. Tarasewicz, included here.

L. 3. The signs *ù* pap iti x ud [*ina*] are clear but the sense not.

L. 5. dumu-*šú* stand evidently for dumu-*šá* as it is highly improbable that the father would lend the house to the wife of his son thereby placing her in first position. Nergal-uballiṭ (the owner of the house and the scribe of the document) had two houses adjacent to each other.

L. 12. The name of the month ends in two vertical wedges, and the only candidate is Araḫsamna. However, the long interval between the day of drafting the document and the day when the tenant took possession (usually from a few days to two weeks or little more) suggests that an emendation to Du'ūzu is needed.

L. 18. According to R. Tarasewicz trace of the second row in number 6 is visible, i.e. the text had to be dated to the last year of Darius I.

Translation

The west (looking) house, adjacent to the house of Nergal-uballiṭ, son of Ṭābiya rented it out to lady [f]Asītu and Bēl-erība, her son, for 3 shekels of silver yearly at the order of Nergal-uballiṭ.

They will pay half of the silver at the beginning of the year and the remainder in the middle of the year.

They will seal the roof and repair (the cracks) of the wall footing.

In the months Nisannu, Du'ūzu and Kislīmu he will pay *nūptu*-payment.

They (each) took a copy of the document.

From the month Du'ūzu[!] the house is at their disposal.

Witnesses:
Bēl-iddin, son of Bēl-lūmur
Bēl-ēṭir, son of Būr-ibni
Šamaš-iddin, son of Aḫiliya,
the scribe, Nergal-uballiṭ, son of Ṭābiya
Sippar, month Simānu, 27th day, 3⌜6⌝[th] year of Darius, king of Babylon and Lands.

128. BM 42393 (81-7-1, 153) Copied by R. Tarasewicz; 6.35 x 4.9 cm; 15.IV. Dar 36 (486 BC) Babylon

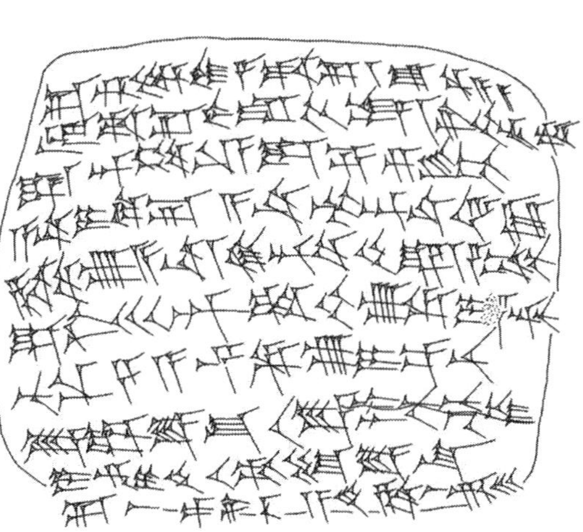

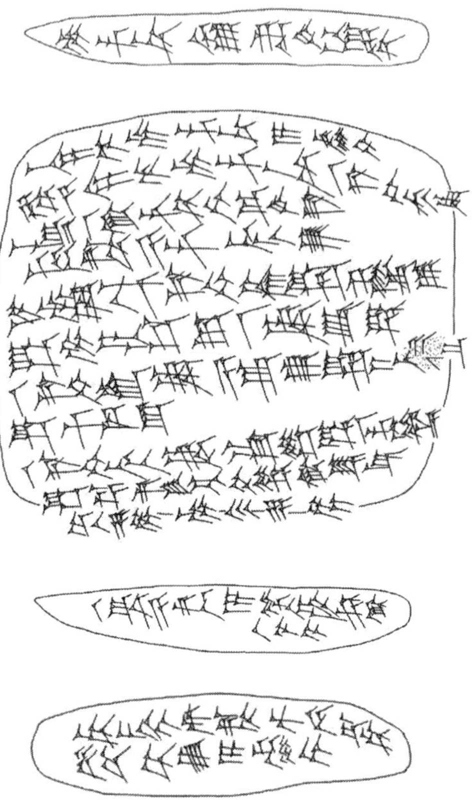

Obv. 1. é *ḫu-uṣ-ṣu šá* da é ^{m}*su-qa-a-a*

2. *ù* da é ^{f}*ra-šat-tu*$_4$ *šá* ^{m}*ni-din-ti-*^{d}en

3. dumu *šá* ^{md}amar.utu-pap-a dumu ^{m}*e-gi-bi*

4. *a-na i-di* é *a-na* mu.an.na 14 gín

5. kù.babbar babbar-*ú a-na* ^{m}ki-^{d}utu-tin dumu *šá* ^{m}*šá-du-nu*

6. dumu ^{m}dù^{eš}-dingir *id-din ú-ru i-šá-an-nu*

7. *bat-qa šá a-sur-ru-ú i-ṣab-bat*

8. iti.bár iti.šu *ù* iti.gan *nu-up-tu*$_4$

9. *i-nam-din ul-tu* iti.šu

10. é *ina pa-ni-šú a-ḫi* kù.babbar *ina re-eš*

Edge 11. mu.an.na *ù ri-ḫi-tu*$_4$ kù.babbar

Rev. 12. *ina mi-šil* mu.an.na *i-nam-din*

13. kù.babbar *šá mi-šil* mu.an.na ^{m}*ni-din-ti-*^{d}en

14. *ina* šu^{ii} ^{m}ki-^{d}utu-tin *ma-ḫi-ir*

15. 1^{en}*-ta-a*$_4$ ti-*ú*

16. ^{lú}*mu-kin-nu* ^{m}*ni-din-tu*$_4$ dumu ^{m}*gi-mil-lu*

17. dumu ^{m}*mu-tak-kil-lu* ^{md}en-su dumu *šá*

18. ^{m}*ni-din-tu*$_{4}$ ^{md}en-*a-su-ú* dumu *šá* ^{m}*ṭab*-⸢^{d}en-x⸣
19. dumu ^{m}*par-sik-ku*
20. ^{m}*ni-din-ti*-^{d}en dub.sar dumu *šá* ^{md}amar.utu-pap-a
21. dumu ^{m}*e-gi-bi* tin.tir^{ki} iti.šu
22. u$_{4}$.15.kam mu.36.kam

L.e. 23. ^{m}*da-a-ri-i-muš* lugal e^{ki}
24. *u* kur.kur

L.h.e. 25. *na-bal-kát-ta-nu* ⅓ *ma-na*
26. kù.babbar babbar-*ú i-nam-din*

Notes

Ll. 9, 21. The sign for the month name drafted in the same way in both lines, is read iti.kin by Cornelia Wunsch, AfO 50, 239 which, in my opinion, cannot be accepted. Comparison with l. 8 makes certain that the correct reading is iti. šu, i.e. Du'ūzu. This means that the contract was signed two weeks after the tenant entered the house.

Translation

A reed hut adjacent to the house of Sūqaya and adjacent to the house of ^{f}Rašattu, which Nidintu-Bēl, son of Marduk-nāṣir-apli, descendant of Egibi rented it out to Itti-Šamaš-balāṭu, son of Šadûnu, descendant of Eppēš-ilī for 14 shekels of white silver.

He (the tenant) will seal the roof and the repair (the cracks) of the wall footing.

In the months Nisannu, Du'ūzu and Kislīmu he will pay *nūptu*-payment.

From the month Du'ūzu the house is at his disposal.

He will pay half of the silver at the beginning of the year and the remainder of silver in the middle of the year.

Nidintu received the silver for half of the year from Itti-Šamaš-balāṭu.

They (each) took a copy of the document.

Witnesses:

Nidintu, son of Gimillu, descendant of Muttakilu

Bēl-erība, son of Nidintu

Bēl-asû, son of Ṭab-Bēl-[x], descendant of Parsikku

Nidintu-Bēl, the scribe, son of Marduk-nāṣir-apli, descendant of Egibi. Babylon.

Month Du'ūzu, 15th day, 36th year of Darius, king of Babylon and Lands.

The contravener who transgresses (the agreement) will pay ⅓ mina of white silver.

129. BM 33966 (Sp.62) = Bertin 2748 New copy by R. Tarasewicz; 7.2 x 5.2 cm; Babylon 5.V.Dar 36 (486 BC)

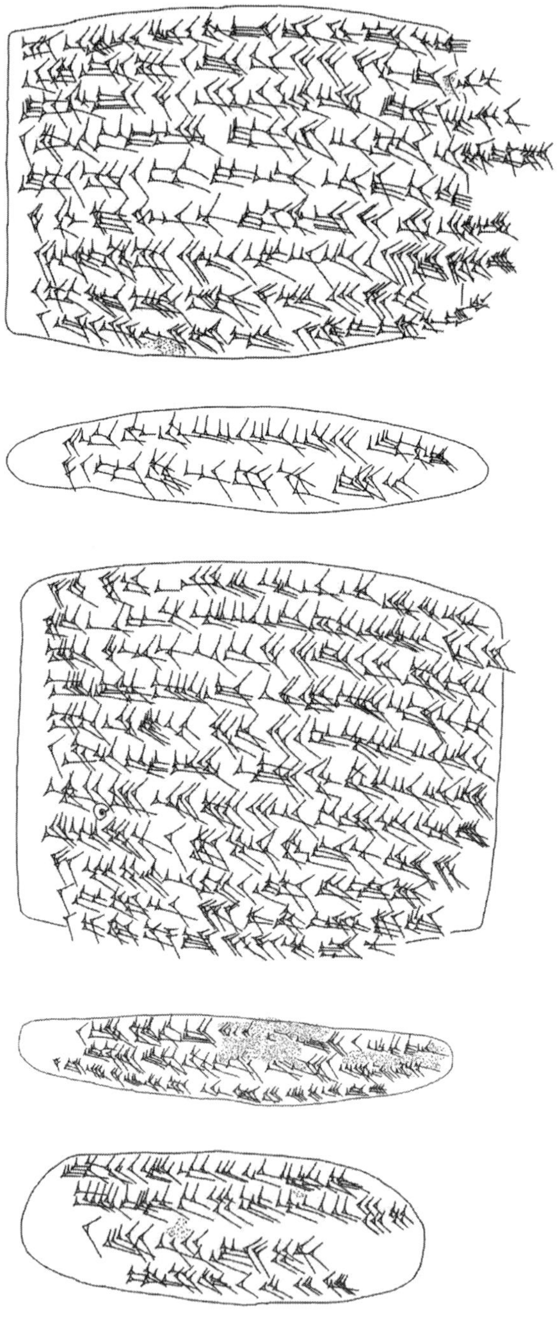

Obv. 1. é ^{gi}ḫu-us-ṣu šá da ^{f}ra-šat-tu$_4$
2. ù da é ^{m}su-qa-a-a šá ^{f}šu-⌈šá⌉-an-nu
3. dumu.mí-su šá ^{m}re-mut-^{d}en dumu ana mu-ti-šú
4. ^{m}ni-din-tu$_4$-^{d}en dumu-šú šá ^{md}amar.utu-na-ṣir-ibila
5. dumu ^{m}e-gì-bi i-na na-áš-par-tu$_4$
6. šá ^{f}šu*-šá-an-nu dumu.mí-su šá ^{m}re-mut-^{d}en
7. a-na i*-di* é* a-na mu.an.na 13 gín kù.babbar babbar-ú
8. ul-tu iti.ne šá mu.36.kam
9. ^{m}da-ri-⌈ia⌉-muš lugal a-di-i ṭup-pi ṭup-pi

Edge 10. a-na ^{f}géme-^{d}na-na-a dumu.mí-su
11. šá ^{m}ab-di**-^{d}e-si id-din

Rev. 12. a-ḫi* kù.babbar ina re-eš* mu.an.na ri-ḫi*-ti
13. kù.babbar ina mi-šil mu.an.na ta-nam-din ur-ru
14. ta-šá-an-nu bat-qa šá* a-sur*-ru ta-ṣab-bat
15. iti*.bár iti.šu ù iti.gan! (T: apin) nu-up-< tu$_4$>
16. ta-nam-din kù.babbar a-<na> mi-šil mu.an.na-šú
17. ^{m}ni-din-tu$_4$-^{d}en ina šu^{ii} ^{f}géme-^{d}na-na-a
18. maḫ-ru 1^{en}-ta-a$_4$ il-te-qu-ú
19. ^{lú}mu-kin-nu ^{m}lu-uṣ-ṣu-ana-nu-ur a-šú
20. šá ^{m}mu-še-zib-^{d}amar.utu dumu ^{mlú}ad.kid
21. ^{m}i-di**-dingir a-šú šá ^{m}pa-ni-^{d}ag-lu-mur
22. ^{m}pa-di-e-su a-šú šá ^{m}mu-ra-nu

L.e. 23. ^{md}en-bul-liṭ-su* ⌈a-šú šá⌉ [^{m}] ⌈šu**-la⌉-a ^{m}mu- še-zib-^{d}[en$^{?}$]
24. dumu**-šú** šá** ^{m**}ra**-šil**-ia** ^{lú**}šid ^{md}en-it-tan-nu
25. šá**-ṭa**-ri šá$^{!}$**-’**-ṭi**-ir** ù** ^{lú}mu**-kin**-na** šu-ú**-ú**

L.h.e. 26. dumu-šú šá ^{m}sum^{na}-a tin.tir^{ki}
27. iti.ne u$_4$.5.kam mu.36.kam
28. ^{m}da-ri-ia-muš
29. lugal e^{ki} u kur.kur.meš

Notes

The text was collated by myself, marked with one asterisk (*) and by R. Tarasewicz, marked with double asterisk (**).

Since the house was rented for one year and ^{f}Amti-Nanāya has paid rent for half a year, the clause obliging her to pay half at the beginning of the (rental) year and half in the middle of the year makes no sense.

Translation

A reed hut adjacent to the house of ^{f}Rašattu and adjacent to the house of Sūqaya, which ^{f}Šušannu, the daughter of Rēmūt-Bēl (gave) to her husband Nidinti-Bēl, son of Marduk-nāṣir-apli, descendant of Egibi. Rēmūt-Bēl rented it out at the order ^{f}Šušannu, the daughter of Rēmūt-Bēl to ^{f}Amti-

Nanāya, daughter of Abdi-Esi for 13 shekels of white silver yearly for one year (beginning) from the month Abu of the 36th year of Darius, the king.

She will pay half of the silver at the beginning of the year (and) the remainder of silver in the middle of the year.

She will seal the roof and repair (cracks) of the wall footing.

In the months Nisannu, Du'ūzu and Kislīmu$^{!}$ she will pay *nūptu*-payment. Nidinti-Bēl received the silver for half of the year from ^{f}Amti-Nanāya. They (each) took a copy of the document.

Witnesses:
Lūṣi-ana-nūri, son of Mušēzib-Marduk, descendant of Atkuppu
Idi-ili, son of Pān-Nabû-lūmur
Padi-esi, son of Mūrānu
Bēl-bullissu, son of Šulā,
Mušēzib-Bēl, son of Rašilia (and)
the scribe Bēl-ittannu, who wrote the document and was (also) witness, son of Iddinaya.
Babylon, month Abu, fifth day, 36th year of Darius, king of Babylon and the Lands.

130. CT 51, 54 (BM 34544, Sp. II 16); 5.9 x 4.3 cm; 7.V.Dar 36 Babylon

Obv. 1. é *šá* ^{m}*ni-din-ti-*^{d}en dumu ^{m}*ši-rik*
2. *šá* da é ^{m}sila-*a-a*
3. ^{m}*ni-din-tu*$_{4}$ dumu ^{m}*ši-rik* a ^{m}*e-gì-bi*
4. *a-na i-di* é *a-na* mu.an.na
5. 14 gín kù.babbar babbar-*ú a-na* ^{m}ki-^{d}utu-tin
6. dumu *šá* ^{m}*šá-du-nu* a ^{m}dù^{eš}-dingir *i-din-nu*
7. *ù* 7 gín kù.babbar babbar-*ú šá mi-šil* mu.an.na
8. ^{m}*ni-din-tu*$_{4}$ *ina* šu^{ii} ^{m}ki-^{d}utu-tin
9. *maḫ-ra* kù.babbar ^{m}*ni-din-tu*$_{4}$ *ki-i*
10. *ú-te-er-ri a-na* ^{m}ki-^{d}utu-tin ⸢*it-ta-din*⸣

Rev. 11. é ^{m}ki-^{d}utu-tin *ina* igi ^{m}*ni-din-tu*$_{4}$ *un-taš-šìr*
12. ^{lú}*mu-kin-nu* ^{md}amar.utu-ba^{šá}-*an-ni*
13. dumu *šá* ^{m}*gi-mil-lu* a ^{m}*mu-na-bit-tu*$_{4}$
14. ^{m}ìr-^{d}edin-*ú-a* dumu ^{m}*gi-mil-lu*
15. a ^{md}30-*na-din*-mu ^{md}ag-mu-gar^{un}
16. dumu *šá* ^{m}*ta-qiš-*^{d}me.me ^{m}*bul-ṭa-a* dumu *šá*
17. {dumu *šá*} ^{m}*e-tel-lu* a ^{md}30-dingir
18. ^{m}*lib-luṭ* ^{lú}šid dumu ^{m}*šá-du-nu*
19. a ^{m}lú-^{d}idim tin.tir^{ki} iti.ne u$_{4}$.7.kam
20. mu.36.kam ^{m}*da-ri-a-muš*

Translation

The house of Nidintu-<Bēl>, son of Širik, adjacent to the house of Sūqaya, Nidintu-<Bēl>, son of Širik, descendant of Egibi rented it out to Itti-Šamaš-balāṭu, son of Šadûnu, descendant of Eppēš-ilī for 14 shekels of white silver. 7 shekels of silver was received by Nidintu-<Bēl> from the hands of Itti-Šamaš-balāṭu for half a year.

If Nidinti-<Bēl> will return the silver to Itti-Šamaš-balāṭu, Itti-Šamaš-balāṭu release the house to Nidinti-<Bēl>.

Witnesses:
Marduk-iqišānni, son of Gimillu, descendant of Munnabitu
Arad-Šerua, son of Gimillu, descendant of Sîn-nādin-šumi
Nabû-šum-iškun, son of Taqiš-Gula
Bulṭā, son of Etellu, descendant of Sîn-ili
Libluṭ, the scribe, son of Šadûnu, descendant of Amēl-Ea
Babylon, month Abu, seventh day, 36th year of Darius.

131. BM 74476 (82-9-18A, 198) Not copied; 6.0 x 4.7 cm; 17.II.Xer 1 Sippar

Obv. 1. ⅓ 5 gín kù.babbar babbar-*ú i-di* é-*šú*
2. *šá ul-tu* iti.sig$_5$ mu.1.kam *a-di* iti.gu$_4$ [m]u.2.kam
3. ^{m}*áḫ-ši-ia-ar-šú* lugal e^{ki} *u* kur.kur.meš
4. ^{m}*ḫa-an-da-uk*$^{?}$*-ku* a-*šú šá* ^{m}*zi-ma-ga-'*
5. *u* ^{m}šeš-šú-nu ^{lú}kin *šá* ^{m}*ḫa-an-da-*⌈*uk-ku*⌉
6. *ina* šu^{ii} ^{f}*ú-bar-tu*$_4$ dumu.mí-*su* ⌈*šá*⌉
7. ^{m}*id-di-ia-ma-ri-iḫ e-ṭir-'*
8. 1^{en}*-a-ta-na-' i-*<*il*>*-qu-ú*

Rev. 9. ^{lú}*mu-kin-nu* ^{m}ìr-^{d}*gu-la* a-*šú šá*
10. ^{m}*i-ba-a* ^{m}*ri-mut-*[x$^{?}$] a-*šú šá*
11. ^{m}*ar-ra-bi* ^{md}en-*it-tan-nu*
12. a-*šú šá* ^{md}en-mu ^{m}*šu-lum*-e^{ki} a-*šú šá*
13. ^{m}*lu*-ud.du-zálag *sip-par*^{ki} iti.gu$_4$
14. u$_4$.17.kam mu.1.kam ^{m}*aḫ-ši-as*$^{?}$*-su*
15. lugal e^{ki} *u* kur.kur.meš

Notes

The translation of the text was published by Pinches 1886, 120-121, no. 104.

L. 10. There is quite large gap between *mut* and a-*šú šá* and it is uncertain whether it was a sign there or not.

For Handaukku and Zimaga', see Stolper 1994, 623. Cf. Tavernier 2007, 66, 221 and Zadok 2009a, 206, no. 279.

The shape of sign *as* in the king's name is strange; I accepted here the proposal of M. Stolper, cited in Tavernier 2007, 66.

Translation

25 shekels of white silver, the rent of his (sic!) house from month Simānu, the first year till the <end of> the month Ayāru, the second year of Xerxes, king of Babylon and Lands, Handaukku, son of Zimaga' and Aḫušunu, the messenger of Handaukku have received from Ubartu, the daughter of Iddiya-mariḫ. Each took one (copy).

Witnesses:
Arad-Gula, son of Ibā
Rēmūt-[x$^{?}$], son of Arrabi
Bēl-ittannu, son of Bēl-iddin
Šulum-Bābili, son of Lūṣi-<ana>-nūri
Sippar, month Ayāru, 17th day, first year of Xerxes, king of Babylon, king of Lands.

132. BM 120099 (1928-2-11, 79); 7.5 x 5.7 cm; 10.[IV].Xer 1 [Babylon]

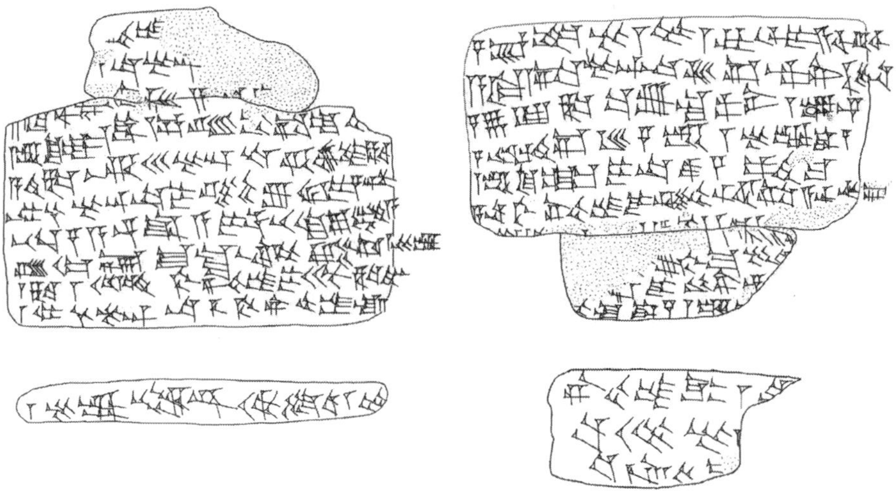

Obv. 1. [é … *šá* ^{f}*n*]*i-din-tu*$_4$ [dumu.mí-*su šá* …]
2. [… *a-na i-di* é] ⌈*a*⌉-*na* mu.an.[na x gín kù.babbar …]
3. ⌈*a-di* ½$^{?}$ x x⌉^{meš} *a*-[*na*] ⌈^{m}⌉[mu-^{d}ag dumu *šá*]
4. ^{md}en-*ki-šìr* dumu ^{m}*e-gi*-⌈*bi*⌉ *ta-ad-din*
5. *a-ḫi* kù.babbar *ina re-eš* mu.an.na *ri-iḫ-tu*$_4$ kù.babbar
6. *ina mi-šil* mu.an.na *i-nam-din ú-ru i-šá-an-nu*
7. *bat-qa šá a-sur-ra-a i-ṣab-bat dul-lu* sig$_4$.ḫi.a
8. gi *u* giš.ùr *ma-la ina lìb-bi ip-pu-uš* ^{m}mu-^{d}ag
9. *ana* kù.babbar *ana muḫ-ḫi* ^{f}*ni-din-tu*$_4$ *i-man-nu* kù.babbar-'
10. *ana mi-šil* mu.an.na-*šú* ^{f}*ni-din-tu*$_4$ *ina* šu^{ii}

Edge 11. ^{m}mu-^{d}ag *maḫ-rat ul-tu* u$_4$.1.kam

Rev. 12. *šá* iti.ne mu.1.kam ^{m}*ak-ši-ia-ar-ši*

13. *a-di* 2-*ta* mu.an.na.meš é *ina pa-ni-šú pu-ut*

14. *šá* 9 gín kù.babbar babbar-*ú la-pa-ni* ^{md}ag-sur

15. *šá ina muḫ-ḫi* é.meš *šá* ^{d}en ^{m}mu-^{d}ag dumu *šá*

16. ^{md}en-*ki-šir i-na-áš-šá-am-ma*

17. *a-na* ^{f}*ni-din-tu*$_4$ *i-nam-din* 1^{en}-*ta-a*$_4$ ti^{ú}

18. [^{lú}]⸢*mu-kin-nu*⸣ [^{m}x x] ⸢x dumu⸣ *šá* ^{md}en-⸢x⸣ [x]

19. [dumu ^{m}*bu*]-⸢*ú-ṣu* ^{m}*mu-n*[*a*$^{?}$ ....]

20. [...]⸢x⸣ dumu $^{lú!}$ì.sur [....]

21. [... -^{d}*g*]*u-la* dumu *šá* ^{md}en-⸢x⸣[....]

L.e. 22. [...^{m}]*ni-din-tu*$_4$ dumu ^{m}⸢*na*⸣-[..... e^{ki}]

23. [iti.šu] u$_4$.10.kam mu.⸢1⸣.[kam ^{m}*ak-ši-ar-ši*]

24. [lugal ^{kur}]*par-sa* ^{kur}⸢*ma*⸣-[*da-a-a* lugal e^{ki} lugal kur.kur]

Notes

The fragment *dul-lu* sig$_4$.ḫi.a gi *u* giš.ùr *ma-la ina lìb-bi ip-pu-uš* ^{m}mu-^{d}ag *ana* kù.babbar *ana muḫ-ḫi* ^{f}*ni-din-tu*$_4$ *i-man-nu* have parallel in VS 5, 64 = Baker 2004, no 99: 9-12: *dul-lu* sig$_4$.ḫi.a gi *u* giš.ùr *ma-la ina lìb-bi ip-pu-uš ul-tu* ugu 1 gín kù.babbar *a-na* ugu ^{m}mu-^{d}ag *i-man-na*; cf. VS 5, 82 = Baker 2004, no 102: 11-13 and VS 5, 84+151 = Baker 2004, no 103: 10-12.

Ll. 10-11 *ana mi-šil* mu.an.na-šú ^{f}*ni-din-tu*$_4$ *ina* šu⸢^{ii}⸣ mu-^{d}ag *maḫ-rat* has parallel in VS 5, 84+151 = Baker 2004, no 103: 13-15 *šá mi-šil/šat-ti-šú* ^{m}mu-^{d}ag *ina* šu^{ii} ^{md}*ag-šul-lim-an-ni/e-ṭir*.

Translation

[House... of ^{f}N]idintu, [daughter of ...] rented it [for x shekels of silver...] yearly to [Iddin-Nabû, son of] Bēl-kēšir, descendant of Egibi. He will pay half of silver at the beginning of the year (and) the remainder of silver in the middle of the year. He will seal the roof (and) repair (the cracks) of the wall footing. Any work in bricks, reeds and beams, that Iddin-Nabû does he shall reckon in silver on account of ^{f}Nidintu. ^{f}Nidintu has received the silver from Iddin-Nabû for half a year.

From the first day of Abu, first year of Xerxes for two years the house is at his disposal.

Iddin-Nabû, son of Bēl-kēšir assumes guaranty for 9 shekels of white silver which are from before Nabû-ēṭir, the rent house collector of Bēl and give it to ^{f}Nidintu.

Each took one copy.

Witnesses:

[PN, son of] Bēl-x x, descendant of B]ūṣu

Mun[a-x x x, son of PN], descendant of the oil-presser

[x-G]ula, son of Bēl-[...]
Nidintu, son of Na$^{?}$-[...]
[Babylon, month Du'ūzu], tenth day, first year [of Xerxes, king of] Persia, Me[dia, Babylon and Lands].

133. BM 33980 = Bertin 2851 Collated; 13.IV.Xer 1 (485 BC) Babylon

Obv. 1. é ^{m}*ni-din-tu*$_4$-^{d}en dumu *šá* ^{md}amar.utu-*na-ṣir*-a
2. a ^{m}*e-gì-bi šá* da é ^{m}*šá*-^{d}ag-*šu-ú*
3. *ù* da sila *mu***-ta-aq-qu* ^{d}u+gur *šá ḫa-di-e*
4. ^{m}*ni-din-tu*$_4$- ^{d}en *a-na i-di* é *a-di 2-ta*
5. mu.an.na^{meš} *a-na* mu.an.na 10 kùr še.bar
6. *a-na* ^{md}en-sur dumu ^{m}*mu-še-zib id-di-in*
7. *ur-ri i-šá-an-na bat-qa šá a-sur-ru-ú*
8. *i-ṣab-bat* iti.bár iti.šu *u* iti.gan
9. *nu-up-tu*$_4$ *i-na-an-din*
10. [*na*]-*bal-ká*[*t-t*]*a-nu* ½ *ma-na* kù.babbar babbar-*ú*
11. [*ina* mu.an.na 10 kù]r$^{?}$-*a*$_4$ še.bar *i-di* é *i-nam-din*
12. [*pu-ut e-ṭe-ru šá* še.bar]-*a*$_4$ *i-di* é *šá* 2*-*ta** mu.an.na^{meš}
13. [^{md}]en-*a*-na-mi-ri-*[*iḫ*]-*tu*$_4$ dumu-*šú* ^{m}*ni*-qu*-du na-ši*

Edge 14. 1^{en}-*ta*-⌜*a*$_4$⌝ [*il-te-q*]*u-ú*
15. *ul-tu* u$_4$.1.kam *šá* iti.ne$^{!}$ é *ina* igi-*šú*

Rev. 16. ^{lú}*mu-kin-nu* ^{m}*lib-luṭ* dumu *šá* ^{md}en-su
17. [dumu] ^{m}*dan-ni-e-a* ^{md}idim-mu dumu *šá*
18. ^{md}ag-tin-*su-iq-bi* a ^{m}*tar-ba-ṣu-é-sag-gìl*
19. ^{m}*pir-šu-ú* dumu *šá* ^{md}amar.utu-sur
20. a ^{lú}sipa anše.kur.ra ^{m}*bul-lu-ṭa-a*
21. dumu *šá* ^{m}*še-el-li-bi* a dù^{eš}-dingir {dingir} ^{md}en-a-mu
22. dumu *šá* ^{md}ag-*ú-šal-lim* a ^{m}*sag-gi-ia*
23. ^{md}en-tin^{iṭ} ^{lú}šid dumu *šá* ^{md}ag-*bul-liṭ-su*
24. a ^{m}ìr-^{d}idim tin.tir^{ki} iti.šu u$_4$.13.kam
25. mu.1.kam ^{m}*ḫi-ši-ia-ar-ši* lugal ^{kur}*par-su*
26. *ù* ^{kur}*ma-da-a-a* lugal tin.tir^{ki}
27. *u* kur.kur

Translation

The house of Nidinti-Bēl, son of Marduk-nāṣir-apli, descendant of Egibi, adjacent to the house of Ša-Nabû-šū and adjacent to the street, passageway of Nergal-ša-ḫadê. Nidinti-Bēl rented it out for two years to Bēl-ēṭir, son of Mušēzib for 10 *kurru* of barley yearly.

He will seal the roof and repair (the cracks) of the wall footing.

In the months Nisannu, Du'ūzu and Kislīmu he will pay *nūptu*-payment.

He who transgresses (the agreement) will pay ½ mina of white silver.

[Yearly?] that [10 *kurr*]*u* of barley he will pay.

Bēl-ana-mēreḫtu, son of Niqūdu bears responsibility for payment of that barley as rent for two years.

They (each) took a copy of the document.

From the first day of Abu! the house is at his disposal.

Witnesses:
Liblut̩, son of Bēl-erība, [descendant] of Dannêa
Ea-iddin, son of Nabû-balāssu-iqbi, descendant of Tarbāṣ-Esagil
Piršû, son of Marduk-ēṭir, descendant of Rē'i-sīsê
Bulluṭa, son of Šellibi, descendant of Eppēš-ilī
Bēl-aplu-iddin, son of Nabû-ušallim, descendant of Saggiya
Bēl-uballiṭ, the scribe, son of Nabû-bullissu, descendant of Arad-Ea.
Babylon, month Du'uzu, 13th day, first year of Xerxes, king of Persia and Media, king of Babylon and Lands.

134. BM 33979 (Sp. 75); 7.35 x 5.5 cm; 21.IV.Xer 2* (484 BC) Babylon

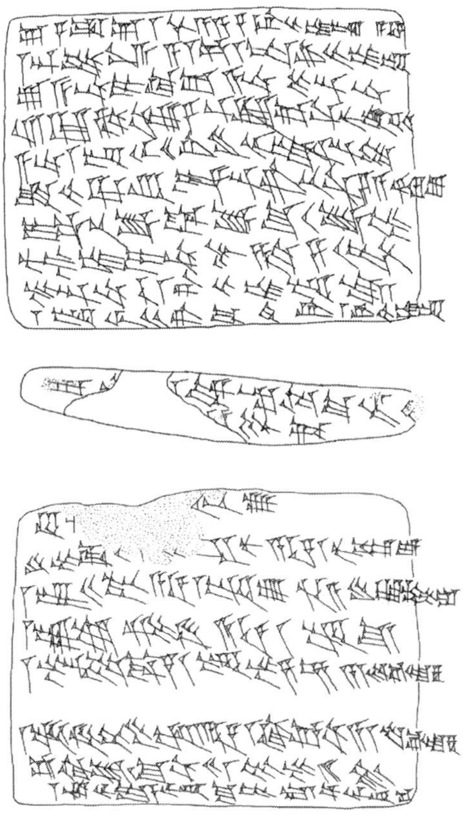

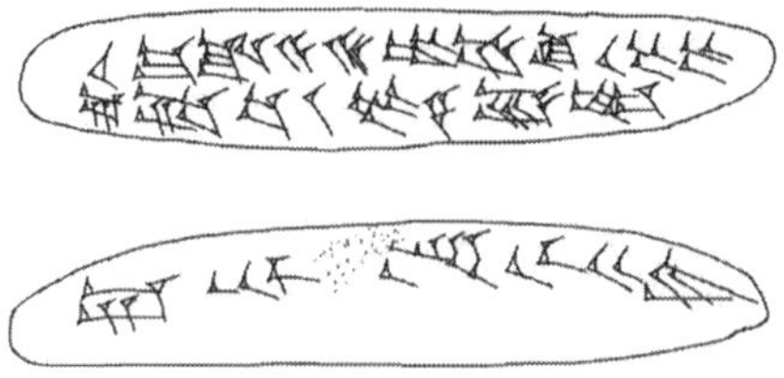

Obv. 1. é *šá* da é ^{m}sila-*a-a šá* ^{m}*ni-din-tu*$_{4}$-^{d}en a-*šú šá*

2. ^{md}amar.utu-pap-a a ^{m}*e-gì-bi* ^{m}*ni-din-tu*$_{4}$-^{d}en

3. é *a-na i-di* é *a-na* mu.an.na

4. 13 gín kù.babbar babbar-*ú šá ina* 1 gín *bit-qa nu-uḫ-ḫu-tú*

5. *a-na* ^{md}en-*ši-man-ni* ^{lú}*ši-rik* ^{d}amar.utu

6. *id-din ur-ri i-šá-an-ni bat-qa šá a-sur-ru-ú*

7. *i-ṣab-bat* iti.bár iti.šu *ù* iti.gan

8. *nu-up-tu*$_{4}$ *i-na-pu* kù.babbar *šá mi-šil*

9. mu.an.na-*šú* ^{m}*ni-din-tu*$_{4}$-^{d}en *ina* šu^{ii}

10. ^{md}en-*ši-man-ni ma-ḫi-ir* ^{m}*ni-din-tu*$_{4}$-^{d}en

Edge 11. [^{m}]⸢^{d}ag$^{?}$-x⸣ [.....] ⸢x⸣ im.si.sá *ma-aḫ*-⸢x⸣

12. [..........*i*]*p-pu-uš*

13. 1^{en}-[*ta-a*$_{4}$] ⸢ti⸣^{ú}

Rev. 14. ^{lú}*mu-kin*-⸢*nu* ^{m}*mu*⸣-[*r*]*a-nu* a-*šú šá* ^{m}*nu-úr-ia*

15. ^{md}ag-man-kam a-*šú šá* ^{m}<ana>-^{d}en-ú-paq a ^{lú}sipa anše.kur.ra

16. ^{md}ag-kar-zi.me a-*šú šá* ^{md}en-su

17. ^{m}mu-^{d}amar.utu dumu *šá* ^{md}en-mu-gar^{un} a ^{m}ìr-é(sic!)gir$_{4}$.kù

One blank line

18. ^{md}en-*ik-ṣur* ^{lú}šid a-*šú šá* ^{m}*ki-rib-tu* a ^{m}ìr- é(sic!)gir$_{4}$.kù

19. e^{ki} iti.šu u$_{4}$.21.kam mu.2*.kam

20. ^{m}*aḫ-ši-ia-ar-šu* lugal ^{uru}*pa-ar-si*

L.e. 21. *u ma-d-a-a* lugal e^{ki} *u* kur.kur

22. é ta u$_{4}$.1.kam *šá* iti.ne

L.h.e. 23. *ina* igi [^{m}]^{d}en-*ši-man-ni*

Notes

Not Xer 1 as suggested by Wunsch 2003/2004, 239 and Wunsch 2004, n. 56.

L. 15. The same person occurs in ZA 3, no. 16, no. 135: 5-6.

L. 17-18. It seems that in both cases in the family name the scribe wrote mistakenly é instead of dingir.

Translation

The house, which is adjacent to the house of Sūqaya, belonging to Nidinti-Bēl, son of Marduk-nāṣir-apli, descendant of Egibi. Nidinti-Bēl rented (this) house to Bēl-šimānni, the oblate of Marduk for 13 shekels yearly of white silver

of one-eighth alloy in each shekel.
He will seal the roof and repair (the cracks) of the wall footing.
In the months Nisannu, Du'ūzu and Kislīmu she will pay *nūptu*-payment.
Nidinti-Bēl received silver for half year from Bēl-šimānni.
Nabû-[x x] will build the east$^{?}$ wing ...
[They (each) to]ok (a copy of the document)

Witnesses:
Mūrānu, son of Nūrêa
Nabû-šar-ēreš, son of <Ana>-Bēl-upāqu
Nabû-ēṭir-napšāti, son of Bēl-erība
Iddin-Marduk, son of Bēl-šum-iškun, descendant of Arad-Nergal
Bēl-ikṣur, the scribe, son of Kiribtu, descendant of Arad-Nergal
Babylon, month Du'ūzu, 21st day, second year of Xerxes, king of Persia and Media, king of Babylon and Lands.
From the first day of Abu the house is at disposal of Bēl-šimānni.

135. ZA 3, no. 16 (BM 34547 = Bertin 1013) Collated; 22.VII.Š-e 0 (484 BC) Babylon

Obv. 1. é ^{gi}*ḫu-uṣ-ṣu šá* da ^{m}sila*-*a-a*
2. *ù* da é $^{<\text{f}>}$*ra-šat-tu*$_4$ *šá* ^{m}*ni-din-ti-*^{d}en
3. dumu *šá* ^{md}amar.utu-pap-a dumu ^{m}*e-gi-bi*
4. ^{m}*ni-din-ti-*^{d}en *a-na i-di* é *a-na*
5. *u*$_4$*-mu* 3 sìla še.bar *a-na* ^{md}ag-<man>-apin^{eš}
6. dumu *šá* ^{m}*a-na-*^{d}en-*ú-pa-qu* dumu ^{lú}sipa <anše.kur.ra>
7. *id-din* iti.bár iti.šu *u* iti.gan
8. *nu-up-tu*$_4$ *i-nam-din ul-tu* u$_4$.1.kam
9. *šá* iti.apin é *ina pa-ni* ^{md}ag-apin^{eš}

Edge 10. *baṭ-lu šá* še.bar *i-di* é ^{md}ag-apin^{eš}
11. *ul i-šak-kan*

Rev. 12. ^{ú}*mu-kin-nu* ^{md}en-*iq-bi* dumu *šá* ^{m}*ni-qu-du*
13. a $^{\text{mlú*}}$gal.dù ^{md}en-*ik-ṣur* dumu *šá* ^{md}amar.utu-pap
14. a ^{m}*da-bi-bi* ^{md}en-sur dumu *šá* ^{m}*mu-še-zib* a ^{lú}ašgab
15. ^{m}mu-^{d}amar.utu dumu *šá* ^{md}ag-gi a ^{md}30-*na-din*-mu
16. ^{lú}šid ^{md}en-*it-tan-nu* dumu *šá* ^{m}*ni-qu-du*
17. a ^{m}šeš-*ba*-ni*
18. tin.tir^{ki} iti.du$_6$ u$_4$.22.kam
19. mu.sag.nam.lugal.la ^{md}utu-su
20. lugal tin.tir^{ki} *u* kur.kur

Translation

The reed hut adjacent to the house of Sūqaya and adjacent to the house of ^{f}Rašattu, which Nidinti-Bēl, son of Marduk-nāṣir-apli, descendant of Egibi rented it out to Nabû-<šar>-ēreš, son of Ana-Bēl-upāqu, descendant of Rē'i-<sīsê> for 3 *qû* of barley daily.

In the months Nisannu, Du'ūzu and Kislīmu he will pay *nūptu*-payment.
From the first day of Araḫsamna the house is at disposal of Nabû-<šar>-ēreš.
Any interruption in payment of the house rent in barley will not occur.

Witnesses:
Bēl-iqbi, son Niqūdu, descendant of the Rab-banê
Bēl-ikṣur, son of Marduk-nāṣir, descendant of Dābibī
Bēl-ēṭir, son of Mušēzib, descendant of Aškāpu
Iddin-Marduk, son of Nabû-ušallim, descendant of Sîn-nādin-šumi, (and) the scribe, Bēl-ittannu, son of Niqūdu, descendant of Aḫu-bāni
Babylon, month Tašrītu, 22nd day, the accession year of Šamaš-erība, king of Babylon and Lands.

136. BM 109876 (1914-04-06, 779); 5.3 x 4.0 cm; 15.XII.Dar 18 Borsippa

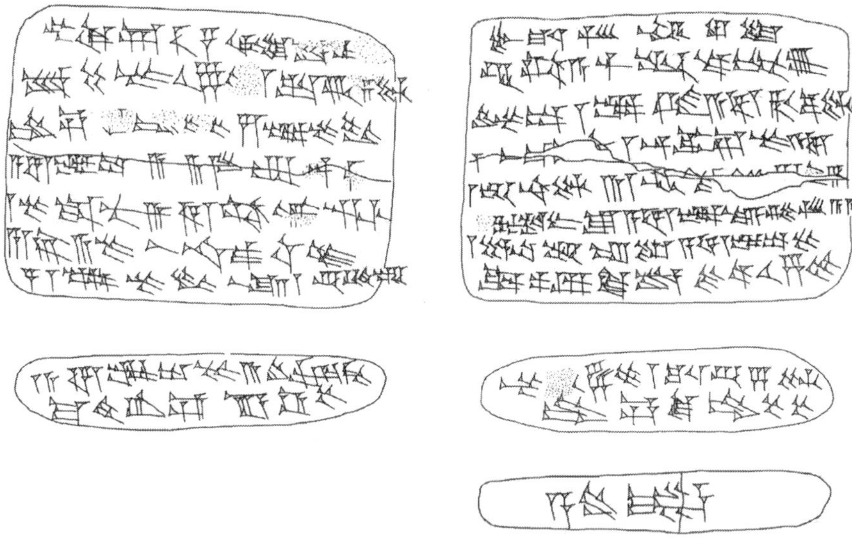

Obv. 1. *i-di* é-*šú šá ul-tu* iti.⌜ab⌝ [*a-di*]
2. iti.še mu.18.k[am] $^{⌜m⌝}$*da-ri-iá-muš*
3. lugal e$^{⌜ki}$ lugal kur⌝.kur *šá* ^{md}ag-mu-ùru
4. a-*šú šá* ^{md}ag-du-a a ^{lú}sanga $^{d⌜}$maš⌝
5. ^{m}*mu-ra-nu* a-*šú šá* ^{m}*ta-qiš*-^{d}me.me

6. a ^{m}*sa-a-mu ina na-áš-par-tu*$_{4}$
7. *šá* ^{md}ag-mu-ùru *i-na* šu^{ii} ^{m}*re-mut-*^{d}en

Edge 8. a-*šú šá* ^{md}ag-du-numun a ^{lú}sipa gu$_{4}$
9. *ma-ḫi-ir e-ṭir e-lat*

Rev. 10. gíd.da.meš *maḫ-ru-tu*
11. 1^{en}*-ta-a*$_{4}$ *il-te-qu-ú*
12. ^{lú}*mu-kin*$_{7}$ ^{md}ag-gi a-*šú šá* ^{m}*ḫa-ba-ṣir-ri*
13. a ^{m}*ina*-gi[ssu$^{?}$-$^{d?}$]⌜utu$^{?}$⌝ ^{md}dumu-é-mu a-*šú šá*
14. ^{md}en-*na-ṣir* a ^{md}en-⌜kar$^{?}$.x x⌝-*ri*?
15. ^{md}ag-*bul-liṭ-su* a-*šú šá* ^{md}ag-kar-zi.meš a ^{m}dingir-*ia*
16. ^{m}sum^{na}-^{d}en dub.sar a-*šú šá* ^{md}ag-du-numun
17. *bár-sip*^{ki} iti.še u$_{4}$.15.kam

L.e. 18. mu.18.kam ^{m}*da-ri-iá-muš*
19. lugal e^{ki} lugal kur.kur

L.h.e. 20. a ^{lú}simug

Notes

L.1. Note the atypical shape of the sign *i*.

L.h.e. The scribe added this line when on realizing that he had omitted the family name of one of the person mentioned earlier. As only the family name of the scribe is missing, in translation I replace the line in the appropriate place.

Translation

Nabû-šum-uṣur, son of Nabû-mukīn-apli, descendant of Šangû-Ninurta received (from) Mūrānu, son of Taqiš-Gula, descendant of Sāmu by the hand of Rēmūt-Bēl, son of Nabû-mukīn-zēri, descendant of Rē'i-alpê, at the order of Nabû-šum-uṣur the rent of his house from the month Ṭebētu$^{?}$ [to] the month Addaru, 18th year of Darius, king of Babylon, king of Lands. He is paid. Except for the previous documents. They (each) took a copy (of the document).

Witnesses:

Nabû-ušallim, son of Ḫabaṣīru, descendant of Ina-ṣi[lli]-Šamaš

Mār-bīti-iddin, son of Bēl-nāṣir, descendant of Bēl- [...]

Nabû-bulliṭsu, son of Nabû-ēṭir-napšāti, descendant of Ilīya

Iddin-Bēl, the scribe, son of Nabû-mukīn-zēri.

Borsippa, month Addaru, 15th day, 18th year of Darius, king of Babylon, king of Lands.

137. BM 68440 (82-9-18, 8438); *5.0* x *2.8* cm

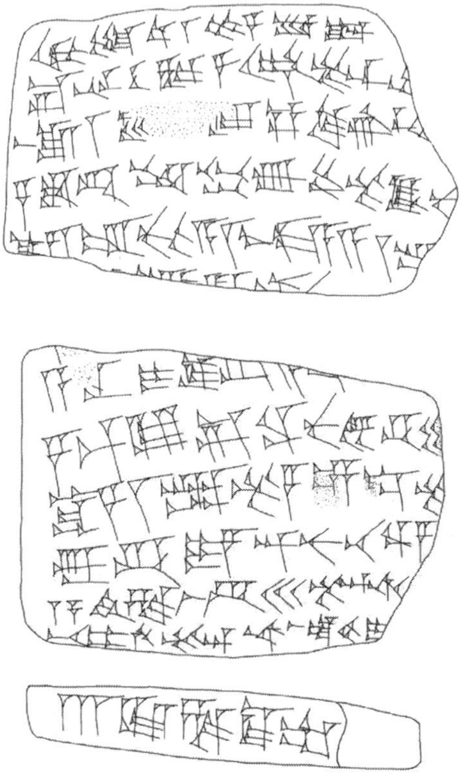

Obv. 1'. ⌜x⌝ […]
2'. *a*-⌜*na*⌝ *i-di* é ⌜*a-na*⌝ [...]
3'. *šá ina* 1 gín *bit-qa nu-uḫ-ḫu-t*[*u a-na* ^{m}*bul-lu-ṭu*]
4'. dumu *šá* ^{md}ag-mu-gar^{un} dumu ^{m}mu/*mu*-[...]
5'. *u-ri i-šá-an-nu bit-qa šá* [*a-sur-ri i-ṣab-bat*]
6'. *a-ḫi* kù.babbar *ina ri-eš* mu.an.na *u* [*a-ḫi* kù.babbar]
7'. *ina mi-šil* mu.an.na *ina-ad-din i*-[…]

Edge 8'. 3 gín kù.babbar *ku-um* […]

Rev. 9'. *ul-tu* u$_4$.1.kam *šá* iti.bár [(…)]
10'.é *ina* igi-*šú* kù.babbar *šá mi-šil* mu.an.n[a …
11'.*ina* šu^{ii} ^{m}⌜*bul*⌝-[*lu*]-⌜*ṭu*⌝ *e-ṭi-ir* 1e[^{n}-*ta-a*$_4$]
12'.*šá-ṭa-ri il-qu-ú* ^{lú}*mu-kin-nu* […]
13'.dumu *šá* ^{m}dub-numun a ^{m}*pap-pa-a-a* ^{md}e[n$^{?}$-…]
14'.[….]-⌜ag a ^{m}*na*⌝-[…]
Rest lost

Translation

...for [x shekels of sliver] of one-eighth alloy in each shekel was rented [to Bulluṭu], son of Nabû-šum-iškun, descendant of Mu/Šum-[...].

He will renew the roof and repair [(the cracks of) wall footing]. He will pay a half of the silver at the beginning of the year and [half of the silver] in the middle of the year.

[...] 3 shekels of silver instead of [...]

From the first day of the month Nisannu [...] the house is at his disposal.

The silver for half of the year is paid by Bulluṭu to [PN]

Each took one copy of the written document.

Witnesses:

[PN], son of Šāpik-zēri, descendant of Pappaya

B[ēl ...]

[x]-Nabû, descendant of Na-[...]

138. BM 40043; 5.7 x 4.3 cm; [x].⸢XI$^{?}$⸣.Da[r] 4 or 5

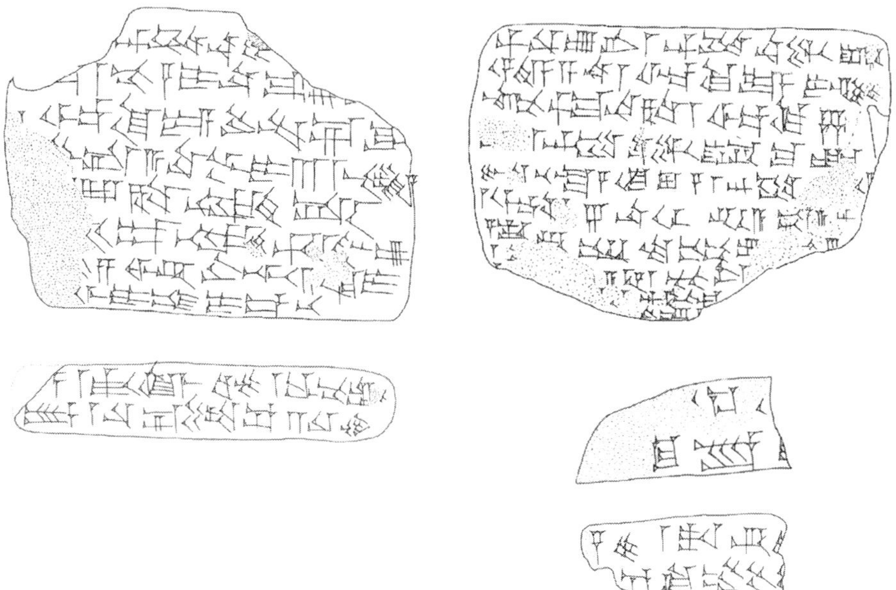

Obv. 1. [é *šá*] ^{md}amar.utu-*na-ṣir*-[ibila]

2. [a ^{m}]⸢é⸣-*gì-bi šá ina su-*⸢*ú*⸣*-q*[*u*]

3. [*šá*] ^{m}sig$_{5}$-*qí-ia* ^{lú}ìr é.gal

4. [*ip-p*]*u-uš a-na pi-i* 3 me sig$_{4}$.ḫi.a

5. [*a-na* x g]ín kù.babbar *ina muḫ-ḫi uš-šú*

6. [*i-sa-ḫ*]*a-ap ina* 1^{en}-*a'* kùš
7. [x x] ⸢x⸣-*za-ar áp/lit-ti* ⸢*a-di*⸣-*i*
8. [x] igi-*i-tu*$_4$ *i-ṣab-bat*

Edge 9. [*šá* it]i 1 (pi) 4 bán *qé-me u*$_4$*-mu* 1 pi kaš ⸢sag$^?$ x⸣
10. iti 1 sìla *saḫ-li-e* 2 sìla mun

Rev. 11. ½ sìla *šam-ni* ^{md}amar.utu-*na-ṣir*-⸢ibila⸣
12. šuku.ḫi.a *a-na* ^{m}sig$_5$-*qí-ia i-nam*-⸢*din*⸣
13. *ina lìb-bi* ½ *ma-na* kù.babbar ^{m}sig$_5$-*qí-iá*
14. *in*[*a* šu^{ii}] ^{md}amar.utu-*na-ṣir*-ibila *ma-ḫir*
15. *pu-ut baṭ-la šá dul-lu šá* ^{md}amar.utu-[*na-ṣir*]-⸢a⸣
16. ^{m}sig$_5$-*qí-iá na-ši* 1^{en}-*a-ta-a*$_4$
17. *šá-ṭa-ri il-te-qu-ú* [^{lú}*m*]*u*-⸢*kin*⸣-[*nu*]
18. ⸢^{m}⸣[x x x] a-*šú šá* ^{m}numun-dù ^{m}[...]
19. [....]-^{d}*gu-la* [...]
20. [...] ^{lú}šid ^{m}[....]

L.e. 21. [...] ⸢x⸣ [...]
22. [tin.tir]⸢^{ki}⸣ iti.z[íz$^?$ u$_4$.x.kam]

L.h.e. 23. [mu.x]+3.kam]^{m}*da-ri*-⸢'⸣-[*muš*]
24. [lugal] e^{ki} lugal kur.k[ur]

Translation

[A house of] Marduk-nāṣir-apli, descendant of Egibi, which is (adjacent) to the street, which Damqia, the master-builder will build; in proportion to 300 bricks that he will lay on the foundation [x] shekels of silver. In each cubit ... according to previous [x] he will make.

Marduk-nāṣir-apli will give to Damqia monthly 1 *pānu* 4 *sūtu* (= ca. 40 litres) of flour, and daily 1 *pānu* of good beer and monthly 1 *sūtu* of cress (and) 2 *sūtu* of salt. In it half mina of silver, which Damqia has received from Marduk-nāṣir-apli.

Damqia will bear responsibility for (any) interruption of work of Marduk-nāṣir-apli.

Each party has taken one copy of a document.

Witnesses:

[PN], son of Zēr-ibni

[...]-Gula

[...], scribe ....

[Babylon], month Šabāṭu .... 3+x year of Darius, [king of] Babylon, king of Land[s]

The text is important because the documents known to me almost never give information about the builder and the cost of building, although the title *arad ekalli*, "builder" is well known. According to the text Damqia, the builder, should receive monthly as his remuneration (*kurummatu*) 1 (pi) 4 *sūtu* = 60 *qû* or liters of flour, 1 *qû* of *saḫlu*, 2 *sūtu* of salt? monthly and 1 *pānu* (36 liters) of beer,[521] 1 *sūtu* of oil daily. Additionally Marduk-nāṣir-apli of the Egibi, who commissioned the building of a house, was obliged to pay Damqia [x] shekels of silver for each 300 bricks laid on the foundation. Damqia received also 30 shekels, presumably for the costs of materials used during the process of building. The idea is supported by Bard 36 (see Bongenaar 2001, 11), according to which the Ebabbar temple should deliver reeds, beams and bricks, i.e. all the most important building materials.

[521] This suggests that the beer was destined not only for the builder but also for the workers of his team, who are not mentioned at all.

7. Indexes

7.1 Index of Texts

Number in brackets refers to the edition in this book; fat number means that the copy is published; n. refers to footnote.

7.2 Index of Personal Names

7.3 Family Names

Saggilaya
Bēl-bullissu/Nabû-šum-iškun Dar 482, no. 121: 2; Dar 485, no. 123: 2; JCS 28, no. 46, no. 122: 2, 15
Bēl-ušēzib/Saggil(aya) Dar 485, no. 123: 15; JCS 28,no. 46, no. 122: 18
Iddinaya/Itti-Marduk-balāṭu Dar 485, no. 123: 3, 13; JCS 28, no. 46, no. 122: 3, 12
Iddinaya/Mušēzib-Marduk JCS 28, no. 46, no. 122: 3
Marduk-šāpik-zēri/Mušēzib-Marduk Dar 482, no. 121: 5;
Nidintu/ Nabû-šum-iškun Dar 485, no. 123: 2; JCS 28, no. 46, no. 122: 2, 15
Sîn-nādin-[x/PN]//Esaggilaya BM 77625+, no. 120, rev. 1'

Saggiya (Or: Saggi<la>ya
Bēl-aplu-iddin/Nabû-ušallim BM 33980, no. 133: 21

Si'atu
Šamaš-zēr-iqīša, scribe VS 5, 23, no. 109: 19

Sîn-ili
Bulṭa/Etellu CT 51, 5,. no. 130: 16
Erība-Marduk/Sîn-ili BM 65336, no. 117: 8'

Sîn-nādin-šumi
Arad-Šerua/Gimillu CT 51, 54, no. 130: 14
Iddin-Marduk/ Nabû-ušallim ZA 3, no. 16, no. 135: 15

Sîn-šadûnu
Nabû-uballiṭ/Mušallim-Marduk Dar 485, no. 123: 14; JCS 28, no. 46, no. 122: 17
Rēmūt/Etellu VS 5, 23, no. 109: 2, 6

Suḫaya
Nergal-ēṭir[/[PN] Cam 213, no. 115: 1

Ṣāḫit-sattuki
Tabnēa/[PN] BM 99901, no. 4: 7'

Šamaš-(a)bāri
Šamaš-ina-tēši-ēṭir/Šamaš-iddin Dar 482, no. 121: 3, 6; Dar 485, no. 123: 23; JCS 28, no. 46, no. 122: 15
Iddin-Bēl/ Šamaš-iddin Dar 482, no. 121: 10
Iddin-Bēl/ Šamaš-iddin Dar 482, no. 121: 3, 6

Ša-nāšišu
Mušēzib-Bēl/Marduk-šum-iddin BM 82744, no. 116: 13
Nabû-šum-iškun/Lūṣi-ana-nūri, scribe Nbn 48, no. 1: 22

Šangû-Adad
Rēmūt/Nabû-bēl-ilāni VS 5, 23, no. 109: 18

Šangû-Ištar-Bābili
Marduk-šum-ibni/Mušēzib-Marduk JEOL 40, no. 1, no. 16: 13
Nabû-šum-līšir/Balāssu BM 67707, no. 2: 19

Šangû-Nabû
Iddinaya/Erība-Ea BM 77626: 3

Šangû-Sippar
Nabû-nādin-aḫi/Nergal-ina-tēši-ēṭir, scribe BM 65336, no. 117: 13'

Šangû-Šamaš
Iqīša-Marduk/Etel-pī-Šamaš BM 61244, no. 15: 2, 7, 15, 19; CT 57, 82, no. 53: 2 (*ša muḫḫi bītāti*); JEOL 40, no. 1, no. 16: 1
Šamaš-[x x/PN], scribe BM 60707: 20
Šamaš-nāṣir/Mušallim-Marduk JEOL 40, no. 1, no. 16: 16
Šamaš-udammiq/Šuzubu BM 61839, no. 87: 2; BM 79611, no. 86: 2; BM 83110, no. 14: 4
Šulā BM 50539+, no. 6: 6

Šigûa
Guzānu/[..] VS 5, 67, no. 119: 12
Marduk-nāṣir/Madānu-aḫḫē-iddin, scribe BM 114472, no. 9: 13
Šamaš-mukīn-apli/Madānu-aḫḫē-iddin BM 114551, no. 8: 8

Ṭābiḫu
Šum-ukīn/Marduk-ēṭir BM 65313, no. 110: 14

Tarbaṣ-Esagil
Ea-iddin/Nabû-balassu-iqbi BM 33980, no. 133: 17

7.4 Geographical Names

7.5 Index of Titles, Professions and Social Groups

7.6 Selected Akkadian Words

7.7 Ideograms

Bibliography

Abraham, K.

2004 *Business and Politics under the Persian Empire. The Financial Dealings of Marduk-nāṣir-apli of the House of Egibi (521-487 B.C.E.)*, Bethesda.

Altavilla, S. – Walker, C. B. F.

2009 *Late Babylonian Seal Impressions on Tablets in the British Museum*, Part 1: *Sippar*, NISABA 20, Messina.

Baker, H. D.

2001 "Degree of Freedom: Slavery in mid-first Millennium BC Babylonia," World Archeology 33, 18-26.

2002 "The layout of the ziggurat temple at Babylon," NABU 2008/27.

2004 *The Archive of the Nappāḫu Family* (AfO Beiheft 30), Wien.

2005 "The Property Portfolio of a Family of Builders from Hellenistic Uruk," in: H. Baker – M. Jursa (eds.), *Approaching the Babylonian Economy. Proceedings of the START Projects Symposium Held in Vienna (1-3 July 2004)*, Münster, 7-43.

2010 "The meaning of *ṭuppi*," RA 104, 131-162.

2010a "Babylonian Shops," NABU 2014/88.

2014 "House Size and Household Structure: Quantitative Data in the Study of Babylonian Urban Living Conditions, in: H. D. Baker – M. Jursa (eds.), *Documentary Sources in Ancient Near East and Greco-Roman Economic History. Methodology and Practice*, Oxford – Philadelphia, 7-23.

Baker, H. D. – Jursa M. (eds.)

2005 *Approaching the Babylonian Economy. Proceedings of the START Project Symposium Held in Vienna, 1-3 July 2004*, Vienna – Münster.

Beaulieu, P.-A.

1989 *The Reign of Nabonidus King of Babylon 556-539 B.C.*, New Haven – London.

1990 "Texts and Fragments. Four Neo- and Late Babylonian Texts from a Private Collection," JCS 42, 98-104.

1991 "Neo-Babylonian Larsa: A Preliminary Study," *Orientalia* NS 60, 58-81.

2003 *The Pantheon of Uruk during the Neo-Babylonian Period* (CM 23), Leiden – Boston.

2014 "An Episode in the Reign of the Babylonian Pretender Nebuchadnezzar IV," in: M. Kozuh – W. F. M. Henkelman – Ch. E. Jones – Ch. Woods (eds.), *Extraction & Control. Studies in Honor of Matthew w. Stolper*, Chicago, 17-25.

Black, J. A. *et al.*

1987 "Ḫabl-aṣ-Ṣaḫr 1983-1986: Nebuchadnezzat II's Cross Country Wall North of Sippar," NAPR 1, 3-46.

Bloch, Y.

2014 "Judeans in Sippar and Susa during the First Century of the Babylonian Exile: Assimilation and Perseverance under Neo-Babylonian and Achaemenid Rule," JANEH 1, 119-172.

Bongenaar, A. C. V. M.

1997 *The Neo-Babylonian Ebabbar Temple at Sippar: Its Administration and its Prosopography* (PIHANS 80), Leiden.

1999 "Money in the Neo-Babylonian Institutions," in: J. G. Dercksen (ed.), *Trade and Finance in Ancient Mesopotamia* (MOS Studies 1), Proceedings of the First MOS Symposium (Leiden 1997), Leiden, 159-174.

2001 "House as Institutional Property of the Neo-Babylonina Temples," in: W. H. van Soldt *et al.* (eds.), *Veenhof Anniversary Volume. Studies Presented to Klaas R. Veenhof on the Occasion of his Sixty-Fifth Birthday*, Leiden, 9-12.

Briant, P.

2002 *From Cyrus to Alexander. A History of the Persian Empire*, Winona Lake IN.

Dandamayev, M. A.

1984 *Slavery in Babylonia. From Nabopolassar to Alexander the Great (626-331 BC)*, DeKalb.

Da Riva, R.

2002 *Der Ebabbar-Tempel von Sippar in frühneubabylonischer Zeit (640-580 v. Chr.)*, Münster.

Dougherty, R. P.

1933 *The Shirkûtu of Babylonian Deities*, New Haven.

Dumbrill, R. J.

2005 *The Archeomusicology of the Ancient Near East*, London.

Geller, M. J.

1995 "An Eanna Tablet from Uruk in Cleveland," in: Z. Zevit – S. Gitin – M. Sokoloff (eds.), *Solving Riddles and Untying Knots. Biblical, Epigraphic, and Semitic Studies in Honor of Jonas C. Greenfield*, Winona Lake, 531-542.

George, A.

1996 "Studies in Cultic Topography and Ideology," BiOr 53, 363-395.

1997 *Babylonian Topographical Texts* (OLA 40), Leuven.

2015 "On Babylonian Lavatories and Sewers," Iraq 77, 75-106.

Janković, B.

2004 *Vogelzucht und Vogelfang in Sippar im 1. Jahrtausend v. Chr.*, Münster.

2013 *Aspects of Urukean Agriculture in the First Millennium BC*, Ph.D. dissertation, University of Vienna.

Joannès, F.

1980 "Textes néo-babyloniens de Strasbourg," RA 74, 145-169.

1989 *Archives de Borsippa. La famille Ea-ilûta-bâni. Étude d'un lot d'archives familiales en Babylonie du VIII*[e] *au V*[e] *siècle av. J.-C.* (Hautes Études Orientales 25), Genève.

1992 "Les temples de Sippar et leurs trésors à l'époque néo-babylonienne," RA 86, 159-184.

2005 "Les relations entre Babylonie at Iran au début de la période achéménide: quelques remarques," in: H. Baker – M. Jursa (eds.), *Approaching the Babylonian Economy. Proceedings of the START Project Symposium Held in Vienna (1-3 July 2004)*, Münster, 183-196.

2016 "Le (*bīt*) *ḫuṣṣu* et les contrats de construction néo-babyloniens," in: P. Corò – E. Devecchi – N. De Zorzi – M. Maiocchi with the collaboration of S. Ermidoro and E. Scarpa (eds.), *Libiamo ne' lieti calici Ancient Near Eastern Studies Presented to Lucio Milano on the Occasion of his 65th Birthday by Pupils, Colleagues and Friends* (AOAT 436), Münster, 287-305.

Jursa, M.

1995 *Die Landwirtschaft in Sippar in neubabylonischer Zeit* (AfO Beiheft 25), Wien.

1995/96 Review of Wunsch 1993, AfO42/43, 255-262.

1997 "Neu- und spätbabylonische Texte aus den Sammlungen der Birmingham Museums and Art Gallery," Iraq 59, 97-174.

1998 *Der Tempelzehnt in Babylonien vom siebenten bis zum dritten Jahrhundert v. Chr.* (AOAT 254), Münster.

1999 *Das Archiv des Bēl-rēmanni* (PIHANS 86), Leiden.

2004 "Neubabylonische Texte," in: B. Janowski – G. Wilhelm (eds.), *Texte aus der Umwelt des Alten Testament, Neue Folge*, Band 1, Gütersloh, 89-110.

2004a "Auftragsmord, Veruntreuung und Falschaussagen: Neues von Gimillu," WZKM 94, 109-132.

2005 *Neo-Babylonian Legal and Administrative Documents. Typology, Contents and Archives* (GMTR 1), Münster.

2007 "The Transition of Babylonia from the Neo-Babylonian Empire to Achaemenid Rule," in: H. Crawford (ed.), *Regime Change in the Ancient Near East and Egypt. From Sargon of Agade to Saddam Hussein*, (Proceedings of the British Academy 136), Oxford, 73-94.

2008 "The Remuneration of Institutional Labourers in an Urban Context in Babylonia in the First Millennium BC, in: P. Briant *et al.* (eds.), *L'archive des Fortifications de Persépolis. État des questions et perspectives de recherches*," Paris, 383-427.

2010 *Aspects of the Economic History of Babylonia in the First Millennium BC. Economic Geography, Economic Mentalities, Agriculture, the Use of Money and the Problem of Economic Growth* (Veröffentlichungen zur Wirtschaftsgeschichte Babyloniens im 1. Jahrtausend v. Chr., Bd. 4), AOAT 377, Münster.

2010a "Der neubabylonischen Hof," in: B. Jacobs – R. Rollinger (eds.), *Der Achämenidenhof / The Achaemenid Court*, Wiesbaden, 67-106.

2015 "Families, Officialdom, and Families of Royal Officials in Chaldean and Achaemenid Babylonia," in: A. Archi (ed.), *Tradition and Innovation in the Ancient Near East. Proceedings of the 57th Rencontre Assyriologique Internationale at Rome 4-8 July 2011*, Winona Lake, 597-606.

Jursa, M. – Morena Garcia, J. C.

2015 "The Ancient Near East and Egypt," in: A. Monson – W. Scheidel (eds.), *Fiscal Regimes and the Political Economy of Premodern States, Cambridge,* 115-165.

Kennedy, D. A.

1986 "Documentary Evidence for the Economic Base of Early Neo-Babylonian Society," JCS 38, 172-244.

Kessler, K.

2002 "Harinê – Zu einer problematischen Passage in: der NABONID-Chronik," in: W. Arnold – H. Bobzin (eds.), *Sprich doch mit deinen Knechten aramäisch, wir verstehen es!, 60 Beiträge zur Semitistik. Festschrift für Otto Jastrow zum 60. Geburtstag*, Wiesbaden, 389-393.

Kleber, K.
2004 "Die Fischerei in der spätbabylonischen Zeit," WZKM 94, 133-165.
2008 *Tempel und Palast. Die Beziehungen zwischen dem König und dem Eanna-Tempel im spätbabylonischen Uruk*, Münster.
2012 "Famine in Babylonia. A Microhistorical Approach to an Agricultural Crisis in 528-526 BC," ZA 102, 212-244.
2017 *Spätbabylonische Texte zum lokalen und regionalen Handel sowie zum Fernhandel aus dem Eanna-Archiv*, Dresden.

Kozuh, M.
2014 *The Sacrificial Economy. Assessors, Contractors, and Thieves in the Management of Sacrificial Sheep at the Eanna Tempple of Uruk (ca. 625-620 B.C.)*, Winona Lake IN.

Krispijn, T.
2010 "Musical Ensembles in Ancient Mesopotamia," in: J. Dumbrill - I. L. Finkel (eds.), ICONEA 2008: Proceedings of the International Conference of Near Eastern Archeomusicology: held at the British Museum, December 4, 5, and 6, 2008, London, 125-150.

Kümmel, H. M.
1979 *Familie, Beruf und Amt im spätbabylonischen Uruk. Prospographische Untersuchungen zu Berufsgruppen des 6. Jahrhunderts v. Chr. in Uruk*, Berlin.

Linssen, M. J. H.
2004 *The Cults of Uruk and Babylon: The Temple Ritual Texts as Evidence for Hellenistic Cult Practices* (CM 25), Leiden - Boston.

Lorenz, J.
2008 *Nebuchadnezzar III/IV. Die politischen Wirren nach dem Tod des Kambyses im Spiegel der Keilschrifttexte*, Dresden.

McEwan, G. J. P.
1982 "A Babylonian *leitourgia*?," WdO 13, 25-30.

MacGinnis, J.
2000 "Some Comments on the Ebabbara in the Neo-Babylonian Period," JAOS 120, 63-67.
2003 "A Corvée Gang from the Time of Cyrus," ZA 93, 88-115.
2004 "Servants of the Sun God: numbering the dependents of the Neo-Babylonian Ebabbara," BaM 35, 27-38.
2007 "Fields of Endeavour - Leasing and Releasing the Land of Šamaš," JEOL 40, 91-101.
2012 *The Arrows of the Sun. Armed Forces in Sippar in the First Millennium BC*, Dresden.

Malatacca, L.
2017 "Ordinary People's Garments in Neo - and Late-Babylonian Sources, in: S. Gaspa - C. Michel - M.-L. Nosch (eds.), *Textile Terminologies from the Orient to the Mediterranean and Europe, 1000 BC to1000 AD*, Nebraska, 107-121.

Mayer, W.
1983 "Sargons Feldzug gegen Urartu - 714 v. Chr. Text und Übersetzung," MDOG 115, 65-113.

Meissner, B. - Tallqvist K. L.
1890 "Neubabylonische Wohnungs-Miethsverhältnisse," WZKM 4, 114-130.

Oppenheim, A. L.
1936 *Untersuchungen zum babylonischen Mietrecht,* (Beträge zur Wiener Zeitschrift für die Kunde des Morgenlandes, 2. Heft), Wien.
1955 "'Siege Documents' from Nippur," Iraq 17, 69-89.
Otten, H.
1976-1980 "Ištarān ([d]KA.DI)," RLA 5, 221.
Pinches, T. G.
1886 *Guide to the Nimroud Central Saloon* (Brtish Museum, Assyrian Antiquities), London.
Ragen, A.
2006 *The Neo-Babylonian* širku: *A Social History.* PhD disseratation, Cambridge MA.
Reade, J.
1986 "A Hoard of Silver Currency from Achaemenid Babylon," Iran 24, 79-87.
Ries, G.
1993 "Miete. B. II. Neubabylonisch, RLA 8, 1./2. Lief., 174-178.
Sack, R. H.
1976 "Some Remarks on Sin-Iddina and Zērija, qīpu and šatammu of Eanna in Erech ... 562-56 B.C.," ZA 66, 180-291.
1994 *Neriglissar – King of Babylon* (AOAT 236), Kevelaer – Neukirchen-Vlyun.
Sandowicz, M.
2015 "More on the End of the Neo-Babylonian Empire," JNES 74, 197-210.
2012 *Oaths and Curses. A Study in Neo- and Late Babylonian Legal Formulary* (AOAT 398), Münster.
San Nicolò, M.
1933 "Parerga Babylonica IX: Der Monsterprozess des Gimillus, eines širkus von Eanna," AnOr 5, 61-77.
1934 "Parerga Babylonica XII. Einiges über Tempelpfründen (*isqu*) und ἡμέραι λειτυργικαί in Eanna," AnOr 6, 179-202.
Schwemer, D.
2001 *Die Wettergottgestalten Mesopotamiens und Nordsyriens im Zeitalter der Keilschriftkulturen. Materialien und Studien nach schriftlichen Quellen*, Wiesbaden.
Still, B. J.
2016 *The Social World of Babylonuian Priest*, PhD. dissertation, Leiden.
Stolper, M. W.
1985 *Entrepreneurs and Empire. The Murašû Archive, the Murašû Firm, and Persian Rule over Babylonia* (PIHANS 94), Istanbul.
1990 "Tobits in Reverse. More Babylonian in Ecbatana," AMI 23, 161-176.
1994 "Iranians in Babylonia," JAOS 114, 617-624.
2000 "Buildings on Bow Land and Encumbrances on Buildings," in: R. Dittmann – B. Hrouda – U. Low – P. Matthiae (eds.), *Variatio Delectat. Iran und der Westen. Gedenkschrift für Peter Calmeyer*, Münster, 667-680.
Strassmaier, J. N.
1888 "Arsaciden-Inschriften," ZA 3, 129-158.
Tarasewicz, R.
2009 "Bird breeding in Neo-Babylonian Sippar," KASKAL 6, 1-64.
2016 "More about the Crisis in Uruk," in: O. Drewnowska – M. Sandowicz (eds.),

Fortune and Misfortune in the Ancient Near East. Proceedings of the 60th Rencontre Assyriologique Internationale at Warsaw 21–25 July 2014, Winona Lake IN, 347-355.

Tavernier, J.

2007 *Iranica in the Achaemenid Period (ca. 550-330 B.C.). Lexicon of Old Iranian Proper Names and Loanwords, Attested in Non-Iranian Texts*, Leuven – Paris – Dudley.

Thureau-Dangin, F.

1922 *Tablettes d'Uruk à l'usage des prêtres du temple d'Anu aux temps des Séleucides*, TCL 6, Paris.

Tolini, G.

2011 *La Babylonie at l'Iran. Les relations d'une province avec coeur de l'Empire achéménide (539-331 avant notre ère)*, PhD dissertation, Paris.

Walker, C. B. F.

1978 "Texts and Fragments," JCS 30, 234-249.

Waerzeggers, C.

2000-01 *Het archief van Marduk-rēmanni I. Studie van familie Ṣaḫit-ginê in Nieuwbabylonisch Sippar (548-484 v. Chr.)*, PhD dissertation, Gent.

2003-04 "The Babylonian Revolts against Xerxes and the 'End of Archives'", AfO 50, 150-173.

2005 "Neo-Babylonian Tablets in the Royal Museum of Art and History in Brussels," Akkadica 126, 133-158.

2010 *The Ezida Temple of Borsippa Priesthood, Cult, Archives* (Achaemenid History XV), Leiden.

2010a "Babylonians in Susa. The Travels of Babylonian Businessmen to Susa Reconsidered," in: B. Jacobs – R. Rollinger (eds.), *Der Achämenidenhof / The Achaemenid Court, Wiesbaden*, 777-813.

2014 *Marduk-rēmanni. Local Networks and Imperial Politics in Achaemenid Babylonia*, Leuven-Paris-Walpole, MA.

2015 "Babylonian Kingship in the Persian Period: Performance and Reception," in: J. Stöckl – C. Waerzeggers (eds.), *Exile and Return: The Babylonian Context*, Berlin, 181-222.

Weszeli, M.

2009 "Die Stallungen des Ebabbar von Sippar in der neubabylonischen Zeit," in: W. Arnold – M. Jursa – W. M. Müller – S. Prochaska (eds.), *Philologisches und Historisches zwischen Anatolien I und Sokotra. Analecta Semitica in Memoriam Alexander Sima*, Wiesbaden, 411-444.

Wojciechowska, J. (née Paszkowiak)

2005 *Archiwum Šaddinnu. Działalność nowobabilońskiego przedsiębiorcy w świetle tekstów z Borsippy* [*The Šaddinnu Archive. The activity of Neo-Babylonian entrepreneur in the light of the Documents from Borsippa*], PhD dissertation, Poznań.

Wunsch, C.

1993 *Die Urkunden des neubabylonischen Geschäftsmannes Iddin-Marduk. Zum Handel mit Naturalien im 6. Jahrtausend v. Chr.* (CM 3), Groningen.

2000 *Das Egibi-Archiv, I. Die Felder und Gärten* (CM 20), Groningen.

2003/2004 "Findelkinder und Adoption nach neubabylonischen Quellen," AfO 50, 174-244.

2005 "The Šangû-Ninurta archive," in: Baker – Jursa 2005, 365-379.

Zadok, R.

1985 *Geographical Names According to New- and Late-Babylonian Texts*, RGTC VIII, Wiesbaden.

2005-2006 "The Text Group of Nabû-ēṭer," AfO 51, 147-197.

2008 "The Quarters of Borsippa," in: S. Bar (ed.), *In the Hill-Country, and in the Shephelah, and in the Arabah (Joshua 12, 8): Studies and Researches Presented to Adam Zertal in the Thirtieth Anniversary of the Manasseh Hill-Country Survey*, Jerusalem, 75*-98*.

2009 *Catalogue of Documents from Borsippa or Related to Borsippa in the British Museum* I, Messina.

2009a *Iranisches Personennamenbuch*, Bd. VII: *Iranische Namen in Semitischen Nebenüberlieferungen*, Faszikel 1B: *Iranische Personennamen in der neu- und spätbabaylonischen Nebenüberlieferung*, Wien.

Zawadzki, S.

1994 "The First Persian Journey of Itti-Marduk-balāṭu," AMI 27, 123-126.

1994a "Bardiya, Darius and Babylonian Usurpers in the Light of the Bisitun Inscription and Babylonian Sources," AMI 27, 127-145.

1995 "Chronology of the Reign of Nebuchadnezzar III and Nebuchadnezzar IV," NABU 1995/55.

1955a "BM 63282 - the Earliest Babylonian Text dated to the Reign of Nebuchadnezzar IV," NABU 1995/56.

1995b "Is there a Document dated to the Reign of Bardiya II (Vahyazdata)?," NABU 1995/54.

1996 "Cyrus-Cambyses Coregency," RA 90, 171-184.

1997 Rev. of Sack 1994 in: *Orientalia* NS 66, 111-116.

2006 *Garments of the Gods. Studies on the Textile Industry and the Pantheon of Sippar according to the Texts from the Ebabbar Archive* (OBO 218), Fribourg – Göttingen.

2013 *Garments of the Gods*, vol. 2: *Texts* (OBO 260), Fribourg – Göttingen.

2014 "If you have a sheep, you have all you need". Sheep Husbandry and Wool in the Economy of the Neo-Babylonian Ebabbar Temple at Sippar," in: C. Breniquet – C. Michel (eds.), *Wool Economy in the Ancient Near East and the Aegean: From the Beginnings of Sheep Husbandry to Institutional Textile Industry* (Ancient Textile Series, vol. 17), 418-442.

2018 "The organisation of building works in Neo-Babylonian Sippar," in: A. Garcia-Ventura (ed.), *What's in a Name? Terminology related to the Work Force and Job Categories in the Ancient Near East* (AOAT 440), Münster, 417-440:

forthcoming "Contribution to the Persian nobility in Babylonia"